THE QUEST FOR
CELTIC CHRISTIANITY

Donald E. Meek

THE HANDSEL PRESS LTD
Edinburgh

Published in 2000 by
The Handsel Press
now at 35 Dunbar Rd, Haddington EH41 3PJ

British Library Cataloguing in Publication Data:
A catalogue record for this publication
is available from the British Library
ISBN 978 1 871828 51 1

Typeset in 11 pt. Garamond

Portaits will be found between pages 122 and 123 of:
James Macpherson
Ernest Renan
Matthew Arnold
Kuno Meyer
Douglas Hyde
Alexander Carmichael

Printed in Great Britain by CPI Antony Rowe Ltd.

CONTENTS

In Memory
of
Peter Hunter Blair and Kathleen Wilson Hughes

two wonderful teachers
who brought the past to life
and who would have enjoyed this debate

ACKNOWLEDGEMENTS

It is my pleasure to thank those people who have been my encouragers while I was writing this book. First and foremost come my wife and family; without their support and tolerance I could not have produced it at all. My wife, Rachel, read the entire book line by line in all sorts of drafts, correcting errors and providing far-reaching suggestions for improving its structure, content and clarity. Her scholarly knowledge of Anglo-Saxon England has been of particular relevance to the venture, and her editorial and diplomatic skills (in all senses of the word 'diplomatic') have been invaluable. My teenage daughters, Rhoda and Anna, have assisted too, not least by giving their many important insights into contemporary life and culture, especially when we watched 'Celtic' services on television and listened to 'Celtic' radio productions.

Beyond my family, I am grateful to a considerable number of individuals who have shown interest in the subject and in my assessments of current trends. Papers to academic conferences and talks to churches have been a fruitful source of action and reflection. Among the churches, I am particularly grateful to Deeside Christian Fellowship, Aberdeen, St Paul's and St George's Episcopal Church, Edinburgh, and Charlotte Baptist Chapel, Edinburgh, for inviting me to address them on the subject of 'Celtic Christianity'. My thanks are due to those who listened patiently, raised issues, and, on hearing that I was 'labouring' on this volume, encouraged me to believe that 'this book is badly needed'.

Encouragers of various kinds kept me on course when, in the midst of endless calls on my time, the project almost defeated me. I would specially wish to thank Alex and Joyce Watt, Edinburgh, and others like them, who exhorted me with kind words at low points. The Revd Jock Stein, editor of the publications of the Handsel Press, had his own way of spurring on the greatly overburdened author, and I am grateful for his patience, which has been tested beyond endurance.

Among my academic encouragers of long standing, I would specially wish to thank, first and foremost, Professor David F.

Wright, New College, Edinburgh, for providing my earliest opportunities to assess the phenomenon of 'Celtic Christianity' through the *Scottish Bulletin of Evangelical Theology*. Professor Wright has read this book at its various stages, and has eliminated no small number of errors and infelicities. His warm friendship and wry humour have been just as important as his weighty patristic scholarship. Without him, this book would have been far harder to write.

In Aberdeen, I have had the privilege of working with excellent colleagues in my own department, notably Professor Colm Ó Baoill, whose warm-hearted, humorous comments and sharp observations have cheered me on my way more than he will ever realise. Dr Ian Bradley, author of *The Celtic Way*, was my colleague in the Department of Divinity with Religious Studies from 1993 to 1998. As the reader may conclude, we have differed to no small degree over 'Celtic Christianity', but our friendship has been strengthened by bouts of mutual provocation and debate, in word and print. In addition to the support of colleagues, I owe an immense debt to my students at Aberdeen University, especially those who have taken my course on 'Celts and Celticism', and have 'taught the teacher' in several areas.

I am no less indebted to colleagues in other universities and colleges who have supplied me with useful writings of various kinds. Marion Bowman, Bath Spa University, provided copies of several of her important articles on this subject. Professor Jonathan Stephens, Aberdeen, kept a weather eye open for contemporary writings on Cornish saints, and discussed aspects of 'Celtic Christianity' with me while this book was on the loom. Father Gilbert Márkus, OP, a Research Fellow at the Department of Celtic, University of Glasgow, generously gave me copies of his own articles. Over the years, he has provided a stimulating commentary on contemporary manifestations of 'Celtic Christianity'. Professor A. M. Allchin, University of Wales, Bangor, and Professor James Kirk, Department of History, University of Glasgow, provided copies of helpful books and documents. Across the ocean, in the United States, Dr Pamela Morgan, Department of Linguistics, University of California at Berkeley, sent me books of great value in understanding the Native Americans and their response to modern reinventions of their beliefs; and Professors Frank and Margaret Szasz, University of New Mexico, shared their insights and supplied copies of articles.

My best thanks are due to those readers who, beyond my more personal range of contacts, acted as the benevolent custodians of 'quality assurance', and have responded generously to my concern about the contents of the volume. A group of readers at Aberdeen read the initial draft with an eye to its tone and structure. Another group, representing Scotland, Ireland and Wales, read the second draft with a view to ensuring its accuracy and fairness in relation to patterns in their own countries. In particular, I wish to thank Professor Máire Herbert, Department of Early and Medieval Irish, University College Cork, who read the whole text with immense care, saved me from a considerable number of errors, and suggested numerous improvements in style and content. Dr Thomas Owen Clancy, Department of Celtic, University of Glasgow, likewise scrutinised the whole text closely, corrected mistakes and misconceptions, and made a number of important suggestions for further reflection. I am immensely grateful to both readers. Dr D. Densil Morgan, University of Wales, Bangor, and his colleagues at the School of Divinity and Religious Studies were also most helpful. Professor James Kirk, University of Glasgow, read and supplemented a draft of Chapter 6, and also vetted Chapter 12.

While I gladly acknowledge the contributions of all my readers, and have taken their comments into account wherever possible, I alone must accept full responsibility for the views expressed in this book. I hope that my revisions and 'third thoughts' will go some way towards meeting their expectations. Inevitably, some errors and a fair number of personal biases will remain, the latter being particularly resistant to all recommended remedies. A book such as this, which explores a controversial topic and ranges boldly across the centuries and the historical divisions of Christianity, is unlikely to satisfy everybody, but I trust that, despite its manifest limitations, the effort to grapple with the subject will not have been entirely in vain.

In conclusion, I wish to thank the following for permission to re-use material originally published elsewhere: the editor of *Celticism* and its publishers, Editions Rodopi B.V., Amsterdam - Atlanta, GA; and the editors of *Spes Scotorum* and its publishers, T.& T. Clark, Edinburgh. I am grateful to the Hulton Getty Picture Collection for four of the six portraits, and to Professor Rolf Baumgarten, Dublin Institute for Advanced Studies, for providing a portait of Kuno Meyer.

Donald E. Meek
Old Aberdeen
March 2000

...those who appeal to bygone ages for the way, the truth and the life, are often those who know least about them. The past thus seems up for grabs, a chest of props and togs ready-to-wear in almost any costume drama, available to fulfil all manner of fantasies; and it is no accident that a crop of books has been appearing with titles like *The Invention of Tradition*....- explorations of what Raphael Samuel and Paul Thompson have elsewhere dubbed *The Myths We Live By*.

The authors of such volumes have aimed to peel away the mythic patinas gilding such institutions as the monarchy or the City, and to expose 'tradition' as an invention often designed to confer spurious sanctity and cover multitudes of sins. And, in so doing, they have reflected on the processes whereby our 'sense of the past' comes to be not just a datum, an innocent snapshot, but the product of cultural negotiation, expressive of present needs.

R. Porter (ed.), *Myths of the English*, pp.1-2

To grow up on an island is to grow up in a special world. Many of the books that I have read on the Hebrides, however, make this world appear Edenic and unreal; others suggest that the islander is a child who appears lost in the 'real world', and even invent for him a language that was never spoken by anyone. It is easy to assign the islander to this misty, rather beautiful world, and leave him there if one first succeeds in making that world unreal, and its inhabitants unreal, off the edge of things, a noble savage with his stories and his unmaterialistic concerns. After all, is he not a Celt and are the Celts not meant to be rather vague, impractical, poetical, not at all like 'us', who succeed in both admiring and patronising the natives, simultaneously accepting that it would be nice to be poetic (and after all the islanders are nice) and also believing that such niceness is not after all suitable to the world in which we live.

Iain Crichton Smith, *Towards the Human*, p.14

INTRODUCTION

This book has been written in response to popular demand. Popular demand has been influential at two levels. First, the work has been stimulated by the wave of intense popular enthusiasm for matters 'Celtic' which began to emerge in the British Isles in the late 1970s. By the mid-1980s it was clear that many people were devotees of what was termed 'Celtic Christianity'. As the 1990s have progressed, the 'revival' of 'Celtic Christianity' has shown no sign of abating. The shelves of bookshops continue to groan (like the present writer) under the weight of books exploring this previously 'forgotten' form of devotion. The second level of popular demand to which this book responds is the perceived need for a volume which analyses the phenomenon of 'Celtic Christianity' and also describes the context of the Christian faith in the British Isles across the centuries.

The book is also the result of deep personal interest in the subject in all its manifestations. As an academic who has been trained in the history of the Christian faith in the British Isles in the early Middle Ages, and as a participant observer of Christian expression in the late twentieth century, I was spurred into critical evaluation, and tried to offer my first critiques of the subject, in the late 1980s. The book has grown out of my own wide-ranging reflections on the morphology of the Christian faith in the British Isles, from the so-called Dark Ages to the present. I have a particular interest in how culture and Christianity inter-relate and influence one another, but I have an equally strong interest in the interpretation of history, in the light of changing approaches to knowledge and perception. This dimension has special relevance to 'Celtic Christianity', since the subject appears to have been influenced and shaped by dogmatism, romanticism, modernism, and, at the end of the twentieth century, by what is called (for better or worse) postmodernism.

The most recent wave of 'Celtic Christianity' takes many forms, and is complex in the variety of its manifestations. It has its academic wing. The approaches of certain writers are (at least superficially) close to, and ostensibly governed by, academic practices. The subject is therefore gaining academic respectability within the wider curriculum. Courses in 'Celtic Christianity', run by specialists, are to be found in several universities and colleges. Postgraduate degrees validate its academic potential and affirm its arrival as a discipline. However, it must be noted that academics who would not subscribe to the presuppositions of 'Celtic Christianity', but who are equally concerned to illumine our understanding of Christianity in the early British Isles, also operate within universities.

The subject has a wide popular following, far beyond the universities. At the heart of 'Celtic Christianity', as popularly construed, lies a highly creative approach to the reconstruction of the past, and particularly the religious history of Britain and Ireland before the Norman Conquest. Yet the movement is more than the reconstruction of the past. It is viewed by many as a pattern for the present, and some would argue that it is a way of 'doing Christianity' which is still detectable in the writings and even the lifestyles of certain people today. Others suggest too that it is not only something for the past and present, but also something for the future, which could yet be a tool for the revitalisation of moribund Christian faith and its institutions. Christian leaders are therefore 'buying in' to 'Celtic Christianity', apparently in the hope that it will fan the dying sparks of postmodern faith.

The time has come for the production of a volume which offers the discerning reader a critical overview of the movement, and allows contemporary clerics, academics, students and enthusiasts of various kinds to think through the various issues which are raised by it. It is, however, equally important that a volume which exposes the warps and weaknesses of modern interpretations should point to more reliable ways of perceiving and assessing the real achievements and qualities of the Christian faith in the British Isles in the early Middle Ages. This book attempts to do both.

The book is therefore constructed in two parts. The first part (Chapters 1-6) deals with, and offers a critique of, 'Celtic Christianity' in its modern form. The second part (Chapters 7-12) tackles (in an accessible and, I trust, readable manner) questions relating to the historical records and representations of the Christian faith in these islands from the early period to the present day. The concluding section (Chapters 13-14) raises issues which need to be considered by those who subscribe to current popular interpretations of 'Celtic Christianity'. The twin-track approach is intended to offer guidance to the reader in a difficult field, in which imagination may all too easily outstrip reality.

The reader who already knows the arguments against 'Celtic Christianity' and wishes to look from the chronological end of the telescope, so to speak, may begin at Chapter 7. I have resisted the temptation to arrange the book chronologically because of the danger of giving the impression that 'Celtic Christianity' is a continuum, progressing happily through the centuries. The fundamental premise of this book is that 'Celtic Christianity', as popularly conceived today, is largely a post-1800 'view' which must not be confused with the historical record of 'Christianity in the Celtic areas of the British Isles'.

My intention, therefore, is not to spin the yarn of 'Celtic Christianity' yet again; rather, it is to disentangle the threads, old and new, that have gone into the creation of this fashionable, contemporary cloth which seems so neatly tailor-made to fit the profile of our time. Rather than provide a blow-by-blow account of the arrival and expansion of the Christian faith in the Celtic areas of the British Isles, I try to offer perspectives within which to evaluate the modern movement and also to observe the wider course of Christian history in these parts. The besetting sin of much that calls itself 'Celtic Christianity' nowadays is that its promoters all too often reach conclusions which do not take these wider perspectives into account and are founded on the flimsiest of evidence. Ultimately, this is a book about the perception of the 'Other' in terms of faith and culture, and the consequent creation of romantic spirituality.

This has not been an easy book to write. The nature of the subject has demanded knowledge of a very wide range of themes, historical, cultural and philosophical, both medieval and modern. I have found myself stretched beyond my academic limits as I have tried to pull the various strands together into a coherent pattern, and I have no doubt that the book will reflect some of these stresses. To its more scholarly readers, and especially to those at the cutting edge of current research, the historical material will be old hat, and perhaps even out of date. To others who are new to the subject, or have not yet discovered a volume to give them basic information, it may seem remarkably fresh. The book represents some sections of Celtic culture better than others; I am very much aware that the chapters vary in their depth of treatment, and that almost all could become books in their own right. I have tried to bear the wider Celtic areas in mind throughout, but, as a Gaelic-speaking Scot from the Inner Hebrides, I have (inevitably) drawn much of my specific exemplification from Scotland. Writers from Wales or Ireland would probably place their thematic emphases in their respective areas, and I hope that they will produce their own complementary studies in due course.

The fact that I have had to pass judgement on a contemporary movement and specifically on some living writers and exponents has added to my pains. I am also aware that I will have broken my own image irreparably in the eyes of many. When lecturing on the theme, particularly to groups who expect an evangelically minded Professor of Celtic to champion his field and to provide deeper insights into the spirituality of the 'Celts', I have often felt like a traitor to my own culture when unmasking the more deceptive side of 'Celtic Christianity'.

The popularity of the subject has created an expectation which anticipates a glowing portrait of the 'Celts' and their spirituality. Listeners assume that the academic 'insider' will reinforce the perception of the 'external' majority. Audiences invariably want to know 'what we can learn from the Celts'. However, neither my knowledge of the history of the Christian faith nor my loyalty to the proper discipline of Celtic Studies will allow me to offer misleading and comforting tales of a spiritual Shangri La somewhere back in the mists of time which is overflowing with wisdom for our postmodern age.

The volume is based, to some extent, on lectures that I have given to various groups, including university students at Edinburgh and Aberdeen, over the last decade. It also draws on two articles that I have written and published elsewhere, but it is substantially a new work. The format of the book has permitted me to furnish much more information than the usual half-hour or forty-five minute 'talk slot'. The reader can now reflect on the arguments, and, where necessary, take tea-breaks between the paragraphs, before reaching her or his own conclusions. The academic apparatus is light, and references (within the text) are kept to an essential minimum. A substantial bibliography is provided for the person who may wish to study the subject at deeper, wider or more specialised levels.

The book is thus intended for a variety of readers, from the casual quester after 'Celtic Christianity' to the more serious seeker who wishes to know how modern 'Celtic Christianity' squares with the historical antecedent. It will also be of interest to the enquirer who has an interest in the perennial process of myth-making, especially the making of those myths which pertain to perceptions of the Christian faith, to say nothing of the 'Celts' across the centuries. The crafting of the book should allow easy 'dipping in' for readers who have specific interests, whether ancient or modern, in the subject. The book is designed to be of special relevance to readers who are encountering 'Celtic Christianity' in the context of Christian life and experience.

CHAPTER 1
THE COME-BACK OF THE CELTS:
A PROFILE OF THE MODERN MOVEMENT

Books galore

If you go into any of the large bookshops in our towns and cities, and look in the sections designated 'Religion' or 'Mythology' or even 'New Age', there is a good chance that you will encounter books which promote 'Celtic' themes of one kind or another. Prominent among the selection are books on different aspects of 'Celtic' religion, including 'Celtic Christianity'. Even in smaller bookshops which may be concerned mainly with Christian literature, it is likely that titles presenting 'Celtic Christianity' will be found on the shelves, commonly in a special section.

Books on this subject are appearing in remarkable profusion, and extend from the popular to the more solidly academic. The bibliographical flow has been maintained consistently since the mid-1980s, and shows no sign of abating as we enter the new millennium. If anything, the approach and arrival of the third millennium appear to have stimulated the flow. The revival of things Celtic, at the level of popular interest and publication, seems to be taking place as new philosophies, religious, secular and sometimes totally pagan (or incorporating mixtures of these brands) also gain prominence in the run-in to what many people hope will be a fresh start for humanity.

'Celtic Christianity' can also be encountered beyond the bookshops. It is actively fostered by certain types of religious communities, and it is finding its way into the worship forms of particular churches. Liturgies which claim to be 'Celtic' are being produced to meet the needs of those who may wish to incorporate 'Celtic' prayers and other items into their worship, and 'study guides' are available for those who may wish to explore 'Celtic Christianity' in group discussion. Manifestations of 'Celtic Christianity' may also be seen in the overtly secular context of heritage centres, in which a certain prominence is sometimes afforded to local saints who may become the subject of video displays or other visual types of presentation. In short, 'Celtic Christianity' is a major growth industry, which appears to be thriving at many levels.

Understanding the label

The label 'Celtic Christianity' is not new. In English it can be traced
at least as far back as 1896, when it was used by William G. Hutchison
in his translation of Ernest Renan's essay on 'The Poetry of the Celtic
Races', originally written in French and first published in Paris in
1854. The relevant sentence states: 'It remains to be said that, even in
our own days, the powerful originality of Celtic Christianity is far
from being effaced' (Renan, transl. Hutchison, p.48). Renan's words
could be applied directly to the late twentieth century, since both the
concept and the phrase have gripped the popular imagination afresh
on the threshold of the new millennium.

The notion of 'Celtic Christianity' was one of the enduring
spiritual sub-streams of the twentieth century, but it appears to have
begun its climb to present-day prominence, without any obviously
direct debt to Renan, in an academic context in the 1970s, when it was
employed by scholars such as Nora Chadwick in her Penguin volume
on *The Celts* (1971) and John T. McNeill in his book on *The Celtic
Churches* (1974). Both Chadwick and McNeill used 'Celtic Christianity'
as a convenient short-hand for 'Christianity in the Celtic lands', that
is, primarily the regions of the British Isles in which Celtic languages
(Gaelic, Irish, Manx; Welsh, Cornish and Breton) have been spoken
at different stages in history. When used in this way, the term gives a
degree of precedence to the Christian dimension, while accepting that
the faith has been contextualised within language-based cultures
which could be broadly described as 'Celtic'. The danger inherent in
the term - so neatly alliterative and attractive - is that it can give the
impression that there is consistency and, indeed, uniformity in the
ways in which the Christian faith was represented in all the 'Celtic'
areas of the British Isles. This may not have been the case, though it
is quite evident that the originator of the term, Ernest Renan, believed
it to be so (see Chapter 3).

Since the mid-1980s, the 'Celtic Christianity' label has, in fact,
been used, not merely to specify a cultural context for Christianity,
but primarily to designate a form of Christianity which is believed to
be distinctive of the Celtic areas of the British Isles and Brittany. The
emphasis in such a definition is placed on the 'Celtic' *quality* of the
faith, rather than on its cultural context. When used in this way, with
the emphasis on the adjective 'Celtic' as a qualitative designation, the
term tends to encourage the view that 'Celtic Christianity' is indeed
an entity which is different from 'conventional Christianity'. Even as
used by Nora Chadwick and John McNeill, the term contains the
danger of becoming a self-fulfilling concept. Having been invented, it
is impossible to de-invent, and, when given a 'spin' in the direction of

distinctiveness, it tends to carry a strong presuppositional load. It encourages the hope, often (and not surprisingly) realised, that 'Celtic Christianity' is not only something which was common to all the Celtic countries, but also a viable, self-sustaining, differentiated form of the faith 'once for all delivered to the saints'.

It is evident that those who would argue that 'Celtic Christianity' is distinctive would define that distinctiveness in different ways. Some of its more scholarly advocates tend to see the distinctiveness of 'Celtic Christianity' more as a question of emphasis within a wider 'tradition'. While rejecting any romantic, airy-fairy interpretations of 'Celtic Christianity', some modern Welsh writers (for example) draw attention to particular themes or approaches which, they claim, are given greater prominence in the expression of the 'Celtic' varieties of Christianity than in other forms. Among these is a concern with, and delight in, God's creation. 'Celtic Christianity', by this argument, is not necessarily at serious theological variance with the main tenets of Christianity as practised in the West or East across the centuries; what is different is the theological profile rather than the theology itself. This interpretation of 'Celtic Christianity' is espoused and promoted by certain academics who are familiar with cultural and theological contexts, and are capable of deploying a wider body of (seemingly) supporting evidence. They are therefore much more nuanced and plausible in their approach to their material. Arguments of this kind are less amenable to critical analysis because they are based on a subjective approach to surviving literature.

The popular brand of 'Celtic Christianity' which is most commonly found on the bookshelves goes much further in its claims by providing a much more tendentious framework for the interpretation of 'Celtic' material, old and new. This is mainly because the writers are not at all familiar with what is normally classed (by scholarly analysis) as Celtic on the basis of language or culture. They are not usually conversant with any of the Celtic languages, and bring to their interpretation a whole range of external presuppositions based on the context in which they themselves are located, usually English-based metropolitan culture. Reacting negatively to social, political and ecclesiastical stringencies of various kinds in contemporary society, they attribute certain contrastingly positive positions to 'Celtic Christianity'.

That word 'Celtic'

A major reason for the acceptability of 'Celtic Christianity' is that the term 'Celtic' has become one of our contemporary buzz-words. It has spread far beyond its origins. It is rooted in the name *Celtoi*, used by the classical (Roman and Greek) writers to identify the barbarian

peoples lying to the north of Italy and Greece, and once occupying a
substantial proportion of Europe and Asia Minor in the first millennium
before Christ. It was sometimes used by these same writers to
designate the languages of these peoples. From the early seventeenth
century, but more consistently from the nineteenth century, it was
applied as a scholarly description of the distinctive 'Celtic' family of
languages, formerly spoken by the Continental Celts and later
associated chiefly with the British Isles and Brittany. Bodies of
linguistic and archaeological evidence (the latter from the Bronze and
Iron Ages) have been brought together (sometimes uncomfortably) to
provide the rationale for the so-called Celtic cultures of continental
Europe.

The difficulties inherent in finding a firm anchor for the term
'Celtic' are well recognised by scholars, and, from time to time, there
is considerable debate about the validity of the 'Celts' as an ethnic or
cultural concept. Such debate, which often expresses a sceptical view
of earlier interpretations of 'Celts' in the light of more recent
evidence, is usually initiated either by archaeologists (such as Simon
James) or social anthropologists (such as Malcolm Chapman) who are
not themselves speakers, far less scholars, of Celtic languages. It is
increasingly common for such specialists to raise doubts about the
very existence of 'Celts' as a 'real' entity, rather than as the 'other'
group perceived by an 'external' body. 'Celtoscepticism' is further
fuelled by the romantic ethnic reconstruction of which 'Celtic
Christianity' forms a part, since commentators like Chapman and
James are able to 'rumble' the trend. They read their scepticism
backwards into the past, and even outwards to contemporary Celtic
scholars, and pronounce an unfavourable verdict on most Celtic
pursuits, whether scholarly or unscholarly. Celtic scholars who
know the languages at first hand, but are also conversant with
contemporary trends, are much less prone to identity crises of this
kind, since they stand on a firm linguistic bedrock, and are capable of
discerning the various levels at which the term 'Celtic' is being applied
or (more frequently) misapplied. The conclusion that the term can be
applied fairly to a particular family of languages is borne out by a
substantial body of philological evidence. The linguistic anchor is
undoubtedly the most secure mooring which can be provided for the
term. The modern representatives of the Celtic language family are:
Irish (in Ireland); Scottish Gaelic (in Scotland); Manx (now being
revitalised in Man); Welsh (in Wales); Cornish (now being revived in
Cornwall); and Breton (in Brittany).

Nowadays, while the term 'Celtic' is still used by scholars in its
linguistic and cultural sense, it is widely employed as a form of
shorthand to denote more or less anything which is believed to be

associated with the non-English aspects of the cultures of Scotland, Ireland, Man, Wales, Cornwall and Brittany. This expansion of the term is occurring in the context of an enthusiasm for 'Celtic' matters which can be detected at various levels. Increasing numbers of people are trying to learn one or other of the Celtic languages; 'Celtic heritage' is being marketed assiduously by enterprise bodies within the Celtic areas, promoting an image of a healthy, alternative society; and arts and crafts of various kinds, offering a huge variety of 'Celtic' wares, are prominently advertised. You can go for a 'Celtic' holiday or sit in a 'Celtic' chair. It is not surprising that many people appear to dream 'Celtic' dreams. Some enthusiasts are reliving their 'Celtic' childhoods, which (curiously) had remained undiscovered until they had reached years of considerable maturity. The word 'Celtic' has thus become infinitely expandable, and has left its linguistic moorings far behind. To be 'Celtic' is to be trendy, cool, 'other' and even marketable. The word moves easily from the market to the monastery, and back again, as secularisation takes its toll of even the most hallowed spiritual icons. The name of a 'Celtic' saint like Columba, when wedded to a worthy, but largely secular, cause, can work wonders for the promoters, including that most valued of all modern miracles - the acquisition of finance to support ventures relating to culture and heritage. To reassign an old (non-Celtic) saying, 'there's gold in them there Columbas'. In the secular world, the word 'Celtic' has thus become a symbol - a symbol of alternative lifestyles, romantic hopes and struggling local economies, but a symbol too of unrealised potential with a remarkable amount of energy at its heart. The 'Celtic Tiger' of prosperous, modern Ireland lies down with the lamb-like, reconstructed 'Celtic saint' of the early Middle Ages.

Symbols and sunsets

In the contemporary religious sphere also, 'Celtic' is a word imbued with symbolism. Few people who use the word will actually think in linguistic terms. Rather, they will think visually, seeing beautiful stone crosses in 'Celtic' locations (Iona in the Hebrides, Monasterboice in Ireland); splendidly executed manuscripts (like the Book of Kells, housed at Trinity College, Dublin); remote islands, far from the noise of modern living (Iona, Lindisfarne); special individuals called saints (Columba, Ninian, David) with the aura of colourful stained glass, radiating light to a darkened room. People not only 'see' Celtic things; they 'feel' them: peace and tranquillity in distant islands and 'peripheral' rural areas; purity of environment; an indefinable loveliness in wind and sea and sky; dazzling sunrises and soothing sunsets.

Such thinking contains within it features of what may lead to an 'alternative spiritual lifestyle'. The bits and pieces form a jigsaw which is constructed into a kind of mental map, configured to the requirements of the user. This map acts as a counterbalance to the grid-plan of mundane existence. The various highways on the map - artistic, contemplative, charismatic - provide slip-roads for the mind. The spiritual tourist can travel 'the Celtic way' by a variety of routes, some more superficial, others more obviously leading to encounters with deeper experiences, and sometimes even with occasional facts. Collisions with uncomfortable facts can be avoided by taking one of the many bypasses on the way (see Chapter 7).

The influence of 'symbolic thinking' about 'Celtic Christianity' is clearly demonstrated in the format of the general run of popular publications. Many are beautifully, if beguilingly, illustrated by line drawings in 'Celtic' style; impressions of stone crosses, knotwork, interlace, foliage, whorls, and much more. Artwork of this kind serves two functions; it makes an immediate link with major visual symbols, thus reinforcing the idea that the work is somehow genuinely 'Celtic', and it provides a degree of cohesion between the contents of the book and the presentation of the material, demonstrating a creative 'wholeness' which appears to be of the essence of being 'Celtic'. Text and context seem to be in agreement; if the book looks 'Celtic', and if the presentation somehow feels 'Celtic', it must be 'Celtic'. Most consumers of 'Celtic Christianity' simply do not have the knowledge of Celtic languages and cultures which enables them to discern the modern mirage which lies at the heart of this kind of presentation.

The influence of 'symbolic thinking' is also apparent in the presuppositions that writers make about the 'Celts' and especially 'Celtic Christianity'. Because most writers (and readers, too) are unable to gain access to the sources in the original languages, they are largely unaware that the early exponents of Christianity in the British Isles studied the Scriptures in Latin, produced commentaries, and engaged their minds in the debates and discussions of their own times. They applied their minds to other less lovely matters also, including the compilation of some of the grimmest penitentials (containing graded punishments for particular sins) which exist in Europe. Yet, while the wide range of poems and prose texts composed or transcribed by 'Celtic' monks is largely inaccessible to the popular writers, they can see and appreciate the surviving artistic products of the monasteries and their workshops, such as the stone crosses and illustrated gospel books. Consequently, it is popularly argued that the 'Celts', in contrast to the bureaucratic 'Romans', loved symbols, and were more concerned with expressing themselves through image and picture than through the written word. This is partly responsible for the enthusiasm for 'Celtic Christianity' which exists today. 'Celtic

Christianity' is seen to be 'holistic', putting its emphasis on feelings as expressed in art and in a small proportion of the poetry of the time, whereas 'Roman' and institutional Christianity is held responsible for the treatises and catechisms and works of exegesis which present such a challenge to the tired brains of modern people. Institutional Christianity is seen to be too cerebral, whereas 'Celtic Christianity' is believed to be a beautifully artistic revelation. Imagination, rather than mental effort, is required to understand it, and, for that reason, works on 'Celtic Christianity' are highly creative - creative with form and sometimes also with fact. The obsession of some writers with explicating the significance of the famous 'Celtic knot' (the one and only knot out of several hundred different types!) underlines the point. 'Knots and crosses' thus play a very large part in the popular interpretation of 'Celtic Christianity'.

The sign of the cross

The use of the word 'Celtic' and the symbol of the 'Celtic' cross to give meaning and cohesion to a very un-Celtic book is nowhere more graphically illustrated than in the case of the volume *Celtic Daily Prayer: A Northumbrian Office*, compiled by Andy Raine and John T. Skinner (1994). Its green cover carries a golden representation of a 'Celtic' cross-head. This book, however, is a concoction of excerpts from a wide variety of writers and compilers, few of whom have any 'Celtic' connections; Horatius Bonar, C.S. Lewis, Brother Lawrence, John Bunyan, and some twentieth-century moderns like Roy Searle (a contemporary Baptist minister) and David Adam (a major contributor to the current vogue for 'Celtic Christianity'), rub shoulders with Bede, Adomnán and Columba. The book bears as close a relationship to genuine Celtic tradition (as defined in terms of language and culture) as sand does to moon-dust; the use of the word 'Celtic' here seems to denote no more than a haggis of citations which defy definition by any other designation. Yet, in some quarters, it is nevertheless acceptable - and evidently profitable - to slap the term 'Celtic' on hybrid compilations of this kind, and to present them to the unknowing public. In this way the term 'Celtic' is further emptied of meaning, and, rather than being strengthened, genuine Celtic culture is being undermined by covering it with layers of highly dubious interpretation. This is a particularly obvious example of the manner in which the more insensitive wing of the 'Celtic Christianity' movement, operating within a majority mass culture and under the cloak of religious acceptability, adopts certain characteristics of a minority culture and exploits them shamelessly for its own commercial ends.

It is relatively easy to identify books which employ the term 'Celtic' merely as a convenient selling point. It is much more difficult for the majority of readers (who are not specialists in Celtic matters) to identify those dimensions of 'Celtic Christianity' which, while claiming to be 'Celtic', are very recent creations. Within the last fifteen years, the new movement has produced a range of writers who have established themselves as authority figures, and are immediately associated with 'Celtic Christianity'. Their works are read by many as if they were genuinely 'Celtic', and they are frequently regarded as 'experts' by critics and reviewers within the popular Christian press.

Pre-eminent among these writers is David Adam, Vicar of Holy Isle (Lindisfarne). Adam is an accomplished, unassuming and very enjoyable author who is concerned to use the 'Celtic' past as a means of conveying Christian teaching to readers who are losing their appetites for traditional ecclesiastical 'means'. He is transparently open and honest about his aims and methods, but his works are often assimilated to wider 'ancient Celtic Christian tradition' by their blurbs and rearwords. His prayers, most of which have been produced since 1980, are now accepted as a standard part of the canon of 'Celtic Christianity'. Adam's writings embrace both prose and verse, but it is probably true to say that his verse is more successfully accepted as 'Celtic' because he uses metrical forms which imitate those of the English translations of the celebrated collection of Gaelic prayers, *Carmina Gadelica*. The act of translation removes the source material from its immediate Gaelic context, but this presents no obstacle to those who wish to claim the translation and the subsequent imitation as 'Celtic'.

Prose is, of course, much more difficult to fashion as 'Celtic' in stylistic terms. The blurb on one book of English prose by David Adam claims that he is 'writing in the Celtic tradition'. The style of the book is in no way 'Celtic', and it would be much fairer to claim that, on this occasion, the writer is constructing an alternative 'Celtic tradition'. The word 'tradition' is as seriously misleading as the term 'Celtic', since the use of neither word in this context has any connection with a Celtic language or with a particular pattern or form of writing in such a language.

Such, however, is the status afforded to the poetry of David Adam that it is sometimes allowed to stand alongside occasional gleanings from the more properly Celtic period before 1100. Neither literary discernment nor historical awareness is evident in the principles applied by the compilers of 'Celtic' anthologies. This is demonstrated clearly in Chris King's book, *Our Celtic Heritage: Looking at our own Faith in the Light of Celtic Christianity* (1997), intended as 'A Study Guide for Christian Groups'. The cover of the book carries the silhouette of a Celtic cross, caught in a golden sunset. A large proportion of its prayers is derived from David Adam's books, supplemented by specimens from Alexander Carmichael's post-1860 collection of charms and prayers from the Hebrides, *Carmina Gadelica* (see Chapter 4). Neither Adam's prayers nor Carmichael's *Carmina* are safe guides for any seeker who wishes to discover true 'Celtic Christianity'. They simply do not belong to the period of the faith associated with the supposed 'Celtic Church', whose upper limit we can set at approximately 1100. The possibility that 'Celtic Christianity' is not an historically validated entity, but a construct manufactured to meet contemporary needs, does not seem to cross the minds of anthologisers and study-guide writers. As we shall see in Chapters 5 and 6, the supposed existence of 'Celtic Christianity' and the 'Celtic Church', especially that made in the image of its modern creators, is one of the great illusions of our time.

Presentation

In addition to anthologies and study guides, 'Celtic Christianity' is regularly presented in various packages. The following represent the main types of presentation, broadly in the order in which they have emerged, particularly since the mid-1980s:

(1) The prayer package: The earliest type consists of a fairly unadorned presentation of selections of the translated texts of Alexander Carmichael's *Carmina Gadelica*. Collections of these texts have been produced fairly regularly since the early 1960s, in the anthologies of Adam Bittleston and G.R.D. MacLean (see Chapter 4). This process reached its consummation with the publication of all the *Carmina* translations in a single volume by Floris Books, Edinburgh, in 1992.

The format of these anthologies has been followed by David Adam in his selections of his own compositions, imitating the style of the *Carmina*, as in *The Edge of Glory: Prayers in the Celtic Tradition* (1985).

Collections of translations of prose and verse texts from other sources, many dating from the late nineteenth century, are also increasingly represented, as in Robert Van de Weyer's *Celtic Fire* (1990). De Weyer tries to show the relevance of the literature, as he would see it, to the problems of the age.

(2) The hymn and sermon package: The second type of presentation consists of exposition of early Irish hymns, based on the translations of Kuno Meyer, Eleanor Hull, and Mrs C. F. Alexander.

The master of such exposition is David Adam, who has published two volumes, entitled *The Cry of the Deer: Meditations on the Hymn of St Patrick* (1987) and *The Eye of the Eagle: Meditations on the Hymn 'Be Thou my vision'* (1990). Written in a well crafted and readable homiletic form and illustrated beautifully with striking line drawings in 'Celtic' style, these books have become best-sellers. They often discuss the problems of modern living (e.g. stress, the fragility of human existence, the challenges of illness and death) in a sympathetic and pastorally warm and caring manner.

(3) The history package: This is represented in books which mingle history and homily in an effort to place the 'Celtic' tradition, as perceived by the writer, in the wider context of ecclesiastical and spiritual development. They therefore draw comparisons and (more commonly) contrasts with Christianity in other cultural contexts in the British Isles and beyond. Examples include Esther de Waal's book, *A World Made Whole: The Rediscovery of the Celtic Tradition* (1991), now reprinted as *Celtic Light*, and Ian Bradley's highly influential *The Celtic Way* (1993). Bradley's book has been translated into several European languages, though not (so far) into a Celtic language.

(4) The lesson package: The material produced by writers in category (3) contains a considerable amount of 'lessons' which, the writers believe, are exemplified by the 'Celts', and ought to be considered by present-day churches and Christians. The books by Bradley and de Waal have been particularly potent in stimulating a further wave of mainly didactic writing which seeks to teach further 'Celtic' lessons, and has become the predominant product of the movement in the later 1990s.

This more recent category of exposition contains relatively little historical analysis; it tends to take snap-shots from the material in category (3). It offers a large number of lessons which are thought to derive from the 'Celts' and are considered to be relevant to contemporary church life. It is all too evident that, for writers of this sort of book, the 'Celts' are little more than posts to which they can tether their own hobby-horses, ranging from charismatic renewal to the accommodation of secular culture and the church's contemporary agenda, particularly along the lines of 'the church as we think it ought to be'.

Some recent writers are not averse to using the 'Celts' to present their own views on modern political developments, usually to bolster the case for maintaining the United Kingdom at a time when Scotland has been given its own Parliament, and Wales has established its own devolved assembly. As we shall see in Chapters 2 and 3, the 'Celts' are seen as a substrate which belongs to the whole of the British Isles, including England, and, so the argument goes, the 'Celtic' heritage betokens an underlying unity which should be preserved. An example of this somewhat anachronistic and politically nuanced message is found in the concluding chapter of Roger Ellis and Chris Seaton, *New Celts: Following Jesus into Millennium 3* (1998).

New Angles on Old Celts

Much of the modern reconstruction of 'Celtic Christianity' takes place far beyond the regions in which Celtic languages are still spoken. In fact, the most vigorous activists of the new movement are to be found in England. Publishers based in London (such as SPCK, Darton, Longman and Todd, and Hodder and Stoughton) have been at the forefront of productivity. Some publication in Scotland, Wales and Ireland is attested, but it tends to be (on the whole) of a more scholarly kind. As a general rule, it is probably fair to say that the closer the writers are to the properly Celtic heartlands and to genuine Celtic culture, the more robust the material tends to be - but this does not always hold true.

It is evident that there are at least two waves of writing in contemporary (post-1960) 'Celtic Christianity'. The majority of writers within the first wave are Anglicans. Stimulated by the earlier works of G. R.D. MacLean (one of the first to initiate the modern recycling of *Carmina Gadelica*), the representatives of the first wave include Robert Van de Weyer, of the community of Little Gidding; David Adam; Esther de Waal, and John Finney, Bishop of Pontefract. Although *Carmina Gadelica* has exerted a potent infuence on this group of writers (as indeeed on most others), there are variations in their presentations: de Waal and Van de Weyer, for example, attempt a more 'historical' approach to 'Celtic Christianity', and delve more deeply into earlier patterns. Esther de Waal, who is an academically trained historian of considerable distinction in her own field, is a persuasive and thoughtful author with a deep delight in 'Celtic' matters and a broad knowledge of historical sources which is off-set by a tendency to return invariably to the *Carmina* as the primary source for 'Celtic Christianity'.

This approach also characterises the work of Dr Ian Bradley, a former Anglican who is now an ordained Church of Scotland minister, and has given wide currency to 'Celtic Christianity', particularly through his book, *The Celtic Way*. As a teacher in two of Scotland's universities (Aberdeen and now St Andrews), Bradley has helped to establish 'Celtic Christianity' not only as a viable Christian stream, but also as a university subject. His ability to appeal to both popular and academic levels of interest, through his warm-hearted style of writing and lecturing, has been of considerable importance to the burgeoning of the movement. In his latest works, however, Bradley has assumed a much more critical approach to the subject, and has disavowed several of the perspectives which informed his earlier writings, notably *The Celtic Way*. His most recent volume, *Celtic Christianity: Making Myths and Chasing Dreams* (1999), argues that

'Celtic Christianity' through the ages has been produced by a series of Celtic revivals, one of which is reflected in current enthusiasm for the theme. It remains to be seen whether this book will become sufficiently widely known within the 'popular' field of 'Celtic Christianity' to counteract the pervasive influence of *The Celtic Way*.

A more recent wave of writers consists of Anglicans who have been touched by charismatic renewal during the last twenty-five years or so. They are usually less formal and/or more traditionally evangelical in their approach to 'Celtic Christianity'. Such writers are frequently to be found in communities and retreat-centres which combine charismatic experience with only a light veneer of denominational identity. Their ranks include Ray Simpson of the Community of St Aidan and St Hilda, Lindisfarne, and Michael Mitton, formerly Director of Anglican Renewal Ministries and currently Deputy Director of the Acorn Christian Healing Trust. The model for such centres, and for the concept of 'Celtic' retreat, is the Iona Community in Scotland, established in 1938 by the Revd George MacLeod, initially as a means of providing work and a sense of Christian vocation for unemployed men from the Scottish Lowlands, who were employed in the reconstruction of the medieval abbey. As the amount of rebuilding has decreased, the role of the Iona Community has changed gradually. Since the restoration of the old Benedictine abbey, the Community and its premises have functioned as an ecumenical focus for pilgrimage and renewal. The Community's influence remains potent, as both centre and symbol, in the world of 'Celtic Christianity'.

In the last couple of years, a desire to cultivate 'Celtic Christianity' has emerged in the independent charismatic networks which have arisen in the British Isles since 1970. Again, the main exponents of 'Charismatic Celtic Christianity' are in England; curiously, and somewhat in contrast to the provenance of Anglican authors, who (for the most part) are associated with the northern archdiocese of York (which includes Lindisfarne), its most ardent charismatic devotees are to be found in the very south of the country. At least one branch of the charismatic movement, the Pioneer network led by Gerald Coates, has shown a particular interest in 'Celtic Christianity'. A restorationist body within the Pioneer network, namely Revelation Church, which functions in 'cells' in Chichester, Bognor Regis, Portsmouth and Selsey, has identified itself strongly with what it calls the 'New Celt' motif. Its leaders, Roger Ellis (who founded Revelation Church in 1983) and Chris Seaton, are the authors of *New Celts: Following Jesus into Millennium 3* (see category (4) above). Ellis and Seaton are very evidently in the business of reconstructing 'Celtic Christianity' in a form which will appeal to charismatic Christians who are adopting aspects of modern mass culture (rather than genuinely Celtic culture). In keeping with a characteristic charismatic emphasis, a key element in their interpretation of 'Celtic Christianity' is 'prophecy'; 'words of prophecy', relating to the re-opening of old wells, provide inspiration for a rediscovery of the forgotten Celtic spiritual heritage of the British Isles. Clearly, there is a market for such works, and it seems likely that charismatic Christianity will supply a considerable proportion of the demand in the years ahead.

'Celts' across the water

'Celtic Christianity' tends to flourish in proportion to its distance from the real Celtic sources. It is not therefore surprising that a significant body of interest in the subject exists in the United States of America. One reason for its transatlantic popularity is the substantial number of people of Irish descent in the population. Writers of Irish descent are prominent exponents of the theme. Thomas Cahill, author of the flamboyant and swashbuckling book, *How the Irish Saved Civilisation* (1995), is of Irish extraction, as is Timothy Joyce, a Benedictine monk and author of *Celtic Christianity: A Sacred Tradition, A Vision of Hope* (1998). Joyce's book offers a romantic overview of 'Celtic' and especially Irish religious history, but it is more firmly earthed than the corresponding British volumes by de Waal and Bradley. Joyce informs us that his interest in Celtic culture was stimulated by the glittering exhibition of 'Treasures of Early Irish Art' which visited Boston in 1978: 'Tears came to my eyes as I wondered what happened to this marvelous civilization and why I had not known anything about it... Something stirred within me, connecting me to a reality I had not previously recognized' (p.viii). In much the same way, Edward C. Sellner, in his book *Wisdom of the Celtic Saints* (1993), tells us that he has Irish ancestors from Co. Mayo, and that 'Celtic Christianity' 'probably lived deep within [him] at an unconscious level' before he became interested in the subject (p.27).

For people like Cahill, Joyce, Sellner and their readers, 'Celtic Christianity' supplies a sense of 'roots'. The consoling possibility that these roots lie even farther back than the era of Irish emigration to the United States is occasionally entertained; Cahill, for instance, makes (in passing) the astonishing observation that the Iberian Celts may have reached as far as New Hampshire in the period of the major Celtic migrations, several centuries before Christ. We may suppose that wishful thinking of this kind provides, when necessary, a potential 'origin legend' with primitive associations which can compete with the ancient culture of the Native Americans (see Chapter 2). The claim to 'original' status is one of the most important - and most vigorously contested - shibboleths in contemporary cultural rivalries.

While it is evident that 'Celtic Christianity' is attractive in the USA for many of the same reasons as in Britain, its profile reflects not only the dominant patterns of immigration, but also the ecclesiastical leanings of the immigrants. Roman Catholic and Orthodox versions of 'Celtic Christianity' are much more prominent in the United States than in Britain. They are also much more ambitious in their forms. A particularly interesting feature of the North American brand of 'Celtic Christianity' is the emergence, since the mid-1990s, of fully fledged 'Celtic' churches, with sophisticated structures, episcopal leadership and impressive websites. These include Anamchara Celtic Church, the Church of the Culdees, and the Celtic Christian Church, which, in earlier forms, all belonged to the Celtic Christian Communion until it was dissolved in 1997 because of disagreements. These churches appear to have substantial followings. The website account of Anamchara Celtic Church claims that 'from a monthly fellowship in Willis Point, Texas, in 1995 the Anamchara Celtic Church has grown to 18 congregations in 9 states and 5 countries and includes two religious orders'. One of its associated congregations is St David's Celtic Catholic Church of Canada, located in Victoria, BC, and its missionary interests extend to Scotland, New Zealand and Russia.

In Protestant and specifically charismatic circles in the United States, 'Celtic Christianity' appears to be flourishing in much the same way as in Britain, but, as is evident with the Catholic and Orthodox versions, it has considerably greater organisational power. The strength of American enthusiasm is such that a Celtic Christianity Conference is held annually in North Carolina, with evangelical ministers and evangelists among the speakers. In Britain and Ireland, 'Celtic Christianity' does not yet have its own annual festivals, though it is sometimes given space at evangelical jamborees such as Spring Harvest. Churches which claim to be 'Celtic' are also much less prominent in Britain and Ireland, though they are gradually making an appearance, especially among devotees of Orthodox persuasion (see Chapter 6).

It would seem that 'Celtic Christianity' in the USA has a thematic profile similar to that in Britain and Ireland. There are, however, different emphases. Since the early 1990s, the American brand of 'Celtic Christianity' has tended to give a special place to the theme of 'soul-friendship', based on a particular understanding of the *anamchara* (originally 'confessor') as a form of spiritual mentor (see Chapter 5). This theme has recently begun to appear in British and Irish interpretations of 'Celtic Christianity'.

'Celts' at home

The evidence suggests that 'Celts' are currently on a 'roll' which has grabbed the popular imagination in certain parts of the United States and the British Isles, and probably in other parts of Europe. Obviously, the 'Celts' are meeting a need in the modern mindset, but it is palpably evident that, in the process of meeting that need, the 'Celts' are being refashioned by external forces to a considerable degree. This, perhaps, explains why, in the 'home countries' of the insular Celts, namely Ireland, Wales, and Gaelic Scotland, the modern 'Celtic' bandwagon is moving relatively slowly compared with its pace in England and the United States; the countries where real Celtic culture (including an active knowledge of the languages) is still maintained are able to discriminate between Celts and pseudo-Celts, and are less willing to accept the reconstructed 'Anglo-Celts' of popular imagination.

In Ireland, however, the publications of John O'Donohue, notably his book *Anam Chara*, have become best-sellers since 1996. *Anam Chara* can be found on airport bookstalls, which suggests that it makes some appeal to contemporary jet-setters. O'Donohue, who is primarily a poet and philosopher, offers an alluring literary concoction of 'Celtic' chemicals which counteracts the hangovers of postmodernity; its ingredients include primordial imagery (stone, water; light, darkness etc.) drawn from rural Ireland, philosophical reflection reinforced by citations from recent continental writers, and extracts from *Carmina Gadelica*. Although his work claims to represent 'Spiritual Wisdom from the Celtic World', it contains comparatively little material that is genuinely Celtic. In keeping with the approach of much popular writing on 'Celtic Christianity', vast generalisations, seemingly backed up by occasional references to Celtic sources, are its hallmark. There is obviously no lack of consumers. Popular courses on 'Celtic spirituality' are offered in Ireland, as in Britain, by people with no academic knowledge of the original sources.

As the example of Ireland shows, none of the Celtic countries is immune from the influence of cultural reconstructionism at various levels, and indeed some of the processes which have produced the modern reaction lie at their front door. Recent language-related revivalism is at least partly responsible for the emergence of 'Celtic Christianity' and other allegedly 'Celtic' delectations. Admirers 'over the border' acquire a romantic notion of cultural revival, feel 'left out', and try to claim a slice of the action for themselves. Where there is a hankering for 'Celtic' identity in a country with relatively little linguistic residue, 'Celtic' arts and crafts, and various spiritualities, provide a substitute 'Celtic' culture. Thus, when sustained interest in 'Celtic Christianity' emerges in the Celtic countries, it tends to be

most vigorous in those regions which have largely lost their distinctive
Celtic languages, such as Cornwall. Perhaps a sense of language loss
influences certain parts of Ireland and Scotland too. Responsiveness
to 'Celtic Christianity', however, is conditioned by a range of factors
beyond language loss. An important consideration is perception of
the nature or history of regions in which people find themselves.
Through modern migration by 'incomers' from English-speaking
regions, 'Celtic Christianity' may gain a foothold in areas where a
Celtic language is still spoken. In the island of Skye, for example, the
glossy journal, *SkyeViews*, represents the interests of incoming groups
with a marked predilection for 'Celtic' themes, including New Age
and 'Celtic Christianity', which is regularly featured. Here the
incoming groups form a network which seems to want to 'go Celtic'
in its own ways - noticeably through arts, crafts and spiritualities - in
what it perceives to be a 'Celtic' environment. Migrations of various
kinds, with inevitable uprooting and relocation in Celtic or potentially
'Celtic' areas, appear to be significant catalysts in spreading the word
of 'Celtic Christianity'.

It is noticeable that expatriate Irish writers, some of them Irish
speakers, contribute more to modern 'Celtic Christianity' than do
Scottish Gaels or the Welsh, and sometimes help to promulgate it in
Wales and Scotland. The predominant pattern of 'Celtic Christianity'
in these countries is, however, that of absorption from England, or
promulgation by non-natives, as is demonstrated by the writings of
Arthur MacDonald ['Donald'] Allchin in Wales and Ian Bradley in
Scotland, neither of whom is native to the countries concerned.
Native enthusiasts of 'Celtic Christianity' who actively promote the
subject are in short supply in both Wales and Scotland, but 'Celtic
Christianity' does have its very occasional - and crucially influential
- devotees within genuine Celtic tradition. Usually these supporters
are impressed by the manner in which the external majority culture
assigns positive qualities of a certain kind to the internal minority
culture. Accommodation or 'brokering' of this sort, by members of
minority cultures who are anxious to distribute the values assigned to
the 'inferior' internal culture by the 'superior' external culture, has a
long history in the Celtic lands. Genuine Celts, on occasion, have thus
participated in the myth-making process, usually when myths are
seen to be a way of presenting a better image of the 'barbarous'
minority culture to the outside world. Alexander Carmichael, collector
of the immensely influential *Carmina Gadelica*, was in part motivated
by precisely this consideration when he presented the first two
volumes of his labours to the public in 1900. The virtues, rather than
the vices, of Highlanders needed to be emphasised, and the spirituality
of the *Carmina* helped to redress the balance (see Chapters 4, 5 and

12). On the other hand, the case for 'Celtic Christianity' can be used as a way of defining, and even defending, a minority culture against the all-embracing generalisations of a majority culture.

Despite such variations in use and purpose, some distinctive national trends in the presentation of 'Celtic Christianity' can be discerned. Overall, advocates in Wales and Scotland tend to approach the theme of 'Celtic Christianity' in a more scholarly manner, and with a greater awareness of historical perspective, than one encounters elsewhere. The Irish popular brand appears to encourage a higher degree of sentimentality, as O'Donohue's work suggests. In contrast to O'Donohue's vague romanticism, the more scholarly Welsh approach is based on close reading of a selection of texts. The works of Professor Donald Allchin, for instance, are founded on a well-informed interaction with Welsh literature. This reflects Allchin's knowledge of the Welsh language, which he (unlike most devotees of 'Celtic Christianity') has taken the trouble to learn. Allchin's works, such as *God's Presence Makes the World: The Celtic Vision Through the Centuries in Wales* (1997), are beautifully written critiques of relevant literature. They are characterised by an inherent mysticism and a wistful desire to discover distinctive themes and emphases in 'Celtic' theological compositions (including secular material, chiefly poetry) across the centuries. The perceived distinctiveness is then ascribed to 'Celtic Christianity' or to the maintenance of 'the Celtic vision'. The existence of 'Celtic Christianity' appears to be taken for granted, and no compelling argument for its validity is offered. The flaw, of course, is that, while such emphases may be apparent in a small sample of writers, chosen across a millennium and a half, it is harder to believe that they represent a sustained 'Celtic' continuum, typical of all the Celtic countries and their cultures over so vast a period of time. They may be Welsh, but are they also Gaelic and Irish? Dr Oliver Davies, based at Lampeter, argues for parallels with Ireland in his book, *Celtic Christianity in Early Medieval Wales: The Origins of the Welsh Spiritual Tradition* (1996). There is a fairly obvious element of collaboration between himself and Donald Allchin, and his work, like Allchin's, presupposes the valid existence of 'Celtic Christianity'.

A more popular and reactive form of writing, seeking to defend Wales from English misconceptions, is offered by Patrick Thomas in *Candle in the Darkness: Celtic Spirituality from Wales* (1993). Thomas attempts to show that, despite Canterbury's claims for itself, 'there were Christians in Britain long before Augustine's mission' and that 'the spirituality of this earlier, Celtic expression of Christianity' survived and developed in Wales. Thomas's book, however, fails to produce a convincing argument for the preferred interpretation, and relies (as such volumes tend to do) on the accumulation of evidence

from across the centuries. Even if it is not possible to accept the special
agenda at the heart of this book and others like it, it is nevertheless true
that their writers are closely familiar with Welsh literature and quote
it extensively. In terms of its relationship to genuine sources, the
Welsh form of 'Celtic Christianity' is by far the most satisfying, and
it can yield scholarly insights in ways which its promoters may not
always anticipate.

The type of 'Celtic Christianity' found in Scotland is very much
a mixed bag, but, through the work of Professor James Mackey and
Dr Mary Low, it too has a relatively high academic content, and it can
justly be said that their approaches have opened up some serious and
important lines of enquiry, particularly in the area of contextualisation.
Although 'Celtic Christianity', in Scotland as elsewhere, is in grave
danger of becoming a slippery, hold-all term, filled with hankerings
of various kinds, academic volumes which appear to pander to taste
and trend by including the phrase in their titles are not to be dismissed
out of hand simply because of the 'spin' implied by the catch-phrase.
The volume of essays edited by James Mackey, *An Introduction to
Celtic Christianity* (1989), illustrates this point very well. It contains
several fine, though now dated, pieces of writing by leading scholars
in Wales, Scotland and Ireland, as well as a clutch of less satisfactory
offerings, mainly on modern and literary topics. The scholarly pieces
counter some of the misconceptions with which the present volume
is concerned. Nevertheless, it is very much open to doubt whether
there is sufficient common ground in all the essays to produce an
argument for 'Celtic Christianity' as an overarching concept. As is the
case with the Welsh academic volumes, the general *a priori* assumption
is not always confirmed by the *a posteriori* deductions.

As a result of its espousal by academics, courses on 'Celtic
Christianity' are to be found in theological colleges and departments:
at Aberdeen (until recently), Edinburgh (until recently), Bangor
(North Wales) and Lampeter. Within the departments of Celtic, Irish
and Welsh in the universities, however, emphasis is placed on the
scholarly exploration of literary and historical sources, and modern
'Celtic Christianity' is treated with a considerable degree of reservation
and caution, as the authorship of the present book will doubtless
testify. Even so, no amount of warning can prevent people from
believing what they wish to believe, especially since 'Celtic Christianity'
seems to be in tune with the moods of the age. The twentieth century
has provided very favourable circumstances for the cultivation of
'Celtic Christianity' beyond the academic cloisters.

CHAPTER 2
CELTS, CULTS AND CULTURE:
THE CONTEXT OF THE CONTEMPORARY
QUEST

Why is it that people are currently so interested in rediscovering and re-creating 'Celtic Christianity'? In the previous chapter we considered several of the superficial attractions which apparently belong to the 'Celts', including their highly visual, image-based profile, and their location within a remote and attractive landscape. Physical points of reference undoubtedly feed the process of reconstruction, but they are not in themselves sufficient to account for the current surge of enthusiasm for the Celts and their 'spirituality'. We must also take the wider contemporary mind-set into consideration. The moods of the age are surely among the most potent factors which have nurtured the recent rise of popular interest in 'Celtic Christianity'.

There are some general, contemporary perspectives in which we must view 'Celtic Christianity'. These broader frames relate to the processes of thinking and understanding which have emerged in the last quarter of the twentieth century. First, we need to note that a strong popular mood of *fin de siécle* retrospection and nostalgia was evident in many parts of the northern hemisphere as the century and the millennium drew to a close. The 'sentimentalisation of modern society' was apparent at several levels. Simultaneously, the prospect of a new century and the start of a new millennium served to heighten expectations. This helped to foster cults of various kinds, of both prospective and retrospective types, the one looking forward to a new era, and the other looking back nostalgically to a past which was believed to have contained many virtues which are lacking in the present. It was, and is, believed that rediscovery of these virtues could aid the revitalisation of society. Pre-millennial tension undoubtedly played its part in bringing 'Celtic Christianity' to the fore.

Second, the period since 1970 has witnessed the emergence of what is now generally termed 'postmodernism', a loose label used to define the fragmented package of perceptions and beliefs commonly found among people today. Although challenges to orthodoxy and to dogmatism can be found across the centuries, as well as the challenge to meaning at the heart of modern existentialism, 'postmodernism' is said to be characterised primarily by its loss of most of the certainties and absolutes of an earlier age, and particularly those characteristic of

pre-1970 scientific 'modernism'. The earlier pre-eminence of reason
and intellect has been displaced in favour of a greater emphasis on
personal feeling and perception; absolute truth is ruled out by
relativism; 'metanarrative', the 'big story' that explains the meaning
of life, is lost in favour of local narratives; and images and stories
(predominantly in film) are given a central place in people's thought
patterns. Postmodernism also contains a strongly romantic component,
and is perhaps most readily identified by the innocent romanticism
through which it tends to repossess and reformulate the past.

Postmodernism has influenced the churches, including their
evangelical wings. Christians within several evangelical traditions are
now less likely to accept what is sometimes termed 'propositional
truth'. The acquisition of spiritual knowledge, for those who still
maintain the validity of the concept, is more likely to be perceived as
less of a 'crisis' and more of a journey or a quest which allows them
to explore different approaches to understanding within different
'traditions'. Knowledge of any kind, as assent to a categorical body of
absolute truth, is given a less prominent place in conceptual thinking.
This affects doctrine, to the extent that confessionalism, with an
accompanying loyalty to particular denominations, is displaced by
what is generally labelled 'spirituality'. Religion is no longer to be
found in the local church alone; it can be acquired from a whole range
of sources. Society itself seems to function as a kind of spiritual DIY
store, from which all sorts of beliefs and rituals can be purchased, at
little cost, and put together in a manner which pleases the consumer.

As it has emerged in the last twenty-five years or so, the popular
brand of 'Celtic Christianity' is to some extent a response to, and a
reflection of, postmodernism. Among its postmodern characteristics
are: its low factual base and lack of historical rationale; its tendency
to rely on a motley collection of snapshots and images of the past,
which are assembled to meet the needs of the collector, and made to
bear a very large element of subjective interpretation; and the localised
focus of much of the material, which stresses Britain and Ireland as its
matrix.

Within the wider frame of contemporary society, however, a
general hankering for 'Celtic Christianity' has been created by a large
number of political, social, religious and ecclesiastical problems, for
which it is seen to offer a solution.

Politics

In the last quarter of the twentieth century, many became weary of
existing trends in politics and national life, having suffered burn-out
in the fiercely competitive world of the 1980s and 1990s. The current

'Celtic Christianity' bandwagon began to roll vigorously in England in the mid-1980s. By then the young middle class, encouraged by Mrs Thatcher to aspire to self-centred, materialistic excellence, began to feel the debilitating effects of negative equity. Disillusionment was found not only in cardboard city, but also in the fashionable domains of suburbia, especially in the English 'Home Counties'. Children of the new economy who were tired of the modern treadmill, and had their fingers burnt up to the elbows in massive mortgages, were on the lookout for something different - something that was more benign than the structures of monetarist economic policies and more sympathetic than the religious perspectives of contemporary Christian society.

The modern wave of 'Celtic Christianity' emerged as churches, particularly in England, confronted the social implications of Thatcherite monetarism. The Anglican Church succeeded in rousing the ire of right-wing Conservative ministers by having the audacity to question some of their policies. It may, or may not, be sheer coincidence that the volume of literature on 'Celtic Christianity' reached almost epidemic proportions as the appeal of New Labour became more evident. Since the General Election of May 1997, the flow of books has subsided somewhat. The emergence of the notion of 'New Celts' from the southern, charismatic depths of Tony Blair's 'Middle England' may be suggestive of an ongoing symbiosis between popular politics and religious expression. The sanitising of old political parties may have its counterpart in the revamping of historical concepts like 'spiritual Celts' in order to appeal to Christians who are disillusioned with conventional orthodoxy.

Environment

During the 1980s, a number of important concerns began to surface in the British Isles (and elsewhere). These had to do with issues of ecology. The environment was a primary concern. As cities grew, the ozone layer began to deplete. Questions of land utilisation and care for the natural world became significant. The Green Party began to attract a substantial following, and strove to make its voice heard in the corridors of power. Greenpeace took a stand on several major issues, including (in the 1990s) the dumping of the infamous Brent Spar oil platform. As urban sprawl continued to abuse what remained of the countryside, the 'Celtic Fringe' began to be viewed afresh as a region where life could be lived as God and nature intended.

A decade earlier, the 1970s had witnessed the rise of alternative lifestyles which often took their adherents to the 'Celtic Fringe', as drop-outs from the rat-race and choked underground trains of Glasgow and London. Protest also appeared within the cities, as people voted with their feet, sometimes on marches through the streets, challenging the nuclear deterrent and global mass cultures, or supporting campaigns on behalf of the environment, animal rights, questions of gender and a host of other issues which needed to be brought before the public. For some, commitment to such matters began to be a religion in itself, creating a new orthodoxy of political and environmental correctness. Out of the earth, to give leadership to the emerging New Age, came the neo-pagan goddess Gaia, representing (among other things) the forgotten rural roots of 'cool Britannia' and offering a more accessible and caring face than the God who seemed increasingly remote as new religions filled the gaps left by the old.

Neo-paganism thus appeared alongside neo-Celticism, and it left its mark on certain brands of 'Celtic Christianity', particularly in the notion that 'Celtic Christianity' was once, and ought now to be, pagan-friendly. Certain writers, such as Michael Howard, who espouse this view in relation to the 'Celtic Church', argue for a closer rapprochement between Christianity and neo-paganism as a possible way forward for the church. Howard comments (*Angels and Goddesses: Celtic Christianity and Paganism in Ancient Britain*, p.141):

> At first glance interest today in the Celtic Church seems to be confined to a few university academics and historians studying the rotting bones of historical fact. However this study is not confined to the halls of academe...and it is actively being pursued as a living tradition by an eclectic collection of minority interest groups. They include folklorists, Earth Mysteries researchers, New Agers, modern druids, neo-pagan revivalists and even a growing number of liberal-minded clerics and Christians. This interest in Celtic spirituality, pagan and Christian, is growing steadily as more and more people become disillusioned with the modern Church and seek viable alternatives to orthodox, established religion.

Howard sees close parallels between the environmental beliefs of 'Celtic Christians' and the Creation Spirituality of Matthew Fox, a former Dominican who was expelled from the Order, and who is sympathetic to 'Celtic spirituality'. Howard defines Fox's spirituality as representing 'a distinctly "pagan" and pantheistic world view which sees God in all things and all things in God. Humanity is firmly placed within the natural world and cosmos, the beauty of the natural world is recognised as is the sacredness of sexuality. Female as well as male images are equally accepted as representations of the divine.' The accommodation between neo-paganism and 'Celtic Christianity' envisaged by Howard (doubtless following Fox's predilections) is

made possible by laying stress on the 'Celtic' components of the new
mixture and by equating what remains of 'Christianity' with
'spirituality', a term wide enough to embrace any form of belief or
'spiritual' system.

As Michael Howard was writing his book, the type of postmodern
eclecticism which he advocated was already being introduced to the
ecclesiastical context in Britain, notably in the Nine O'Clock Service
(NOS) in Sheffield. This well-meaning Anglican experiment in modern
'alternative Christianity' with some 'Celtic' dimensions, including
participants who resembled druids, was aimed specifically at youth
culture, and outwardly it seemed a success story. Fox's 'creation
spirituality' was championed by Chris Brain, the leader of NOS, and
became a significant ingredient of the new approach to worship.This
included a 'Planetary Mass' which impressed Fox deeply when he
visited the service in 1993. Largely because of its increasingly cultic
dimensions, however, NOS ended in disaster in 1995. Many of those
within the church were badly scarred emotionally by the experience,
and serious charges of misconduct were laid against its leader (Roland
Howard, *The Rise and Fall of the Nine O'Clock Service*). This does not
mean that all 'alternative services' are doomed to scandalous failure,
nor does it damn 'Celtic spirituality' in and of itself, since the reasons
for the failure of NOS were much more cultic than Celtic, but it does
suggest that 'creation spirituality', if combined with Celtic spirituality
and mixed with a 'creative' form of Christianity, could be less than
beneficial for worship patterns in the British Isles.

Pluralism

As people in the West internalised their worries about economy and
environment, they began to study the religious systems of the East.
This was due partly to the 'culture transfer' which came in the wake
of immigration into the British Isles in the 1960s and 1970s. Multi-
culturalism (found in the British Isles long before the late twentieth
century, but scarcely noticed because it was associated with the
previously despised 'Celtic Fringe') was matched to multi-faithism.
Immigrants introduced a variety of major and minor faiths other than
Christianity. Growth in global communication and increasing ease of
transport allowed the East to 'evangelise' the West in new ways. Cults
and alternative spiritualities of various kinds emerged, one of the most
influential of the earlier wave being the Unification Church, which
was established in Korea in 1954 by the Revd Sun Myung Moon, and
whose members are consequently popularly known as the 'Moonies'.
Dr Eileen Barker (*New Religious Movements: An Introduction*, p.165)
estimated in 1989 that there were '500 or so groups or movements in
Britain'. Those who were disillusioned with contemporary forms of

Christianity could now choose from a very large menu of alternative religious movements. The various items on the menu could also be mixed on a single dish, because religion was becoming a matter of personal taste rather than ecclesiastical imposition. As a result, the new religious fads were often syncretic, gathering bits and pieces of ideas from here and there, and mixing them together. The New Age movement, a pastiche of cults and -isms, ancient and modern, Eastern and Western, exemplifies the religious *smorgasbord* of our time.

Pluralism brought new quests to the seekers, and offered new ways of seeing the world. 'Celtic' sites and symbols began to be viewed through the lens of Eastern religions and mysticism. A coincidental but highly significant transaction occurred in 1992, when a Buddhist community bought Holy Isle, off Lamlash in Arran, formerly the site of a group of 'Celtic' monastic cells. The history of 'Celtic Christianity', as perceived by certain 'Easternised' writers, had characteristics which they were pleased to equate with Buddhism and particularly with Zen.

Church decline

While the secular world began to experiment with its versions of religion as an antidote to the pains of postmodernity, the churches themselves, Catholic and Protestant, evangelical and liberal, old and new, faced major challenges. In the older denominations in both Scotland and England, serious contentions emerged, and, in certain instances, stopped only marginally short of splitting traditional alignments. Rows of an increasingly acrimonious kind between 'conservatives' and 'modernisers', between heresy-hunters and anti-heresy-hunters, between supporters and opponents of confessionalism, or the ordination of women, were often conducted in full public view, with acres of dirty linen hung out to dry. Disillusionment with traditional alignments inevitably followed. Membership dropped in the older church bodies, as it continues to do, but it began to increase in those which were prepared to go down more innovative, and seemingly less contentious, tracks.

Charismatic churches and house-churches gained much ground from the 1970s, placing a strong emphasis on corporate leadership (as distinct from one-person leadership), the gifts of the Spirit (rather than the sermons of the minister), and caring for the 'church family'. Twenty-five years down the line, a sense of burn-out, restlessness, and even weariness pervades many of those bodies which had once ridden on the crest of the charismatic wave. In the 1980s and 1990s, the 'Signs and Wonders' movement, of which the 'Toronto Blessing' was but the latest manifestation, has failed to provide lasting satisfaction. People are hungry for new approaches to the faith. A fresh conversion to 'Celtic Christianity' has apparently had a revitalising effect on some groups. What is true of the group is also true of the individual; it is the enthusiasm of the convert to the 'Celtic' cause that motivates many of the authors on the theme, and provides their works with much of their emotional power and undoubted appeal.

Liberalising the faith

The poor public image of the traditional churches has contributed to an increasingly unsympathetic secular perception of religion. This, together with the churches' quest for new experiences, has encouraged, and formed part of, what many would see as a paradigm shift in the way that people view religion of any kind. In particular, the pendulum has tended to swing away from a rational approach to faith, which stresses the place of the intellect and structured worship, to one which lays greater emphasis on the emotions, informality, and individual preference. 'Spirituality' fills the gap that was once filled by the Christian faith.

The trend affects the churches. Churches which are not bound by credal confessions have been particularly liable to move to the less constricted approach. In many evangelical churches, people are less attracted than they used to be by the deeper study of the Scriptures and by the older styles of worship, and are in a mood for experiments of various kinds. 'Celtic Christianity' thus meshes with the ups and downs of the ecclesiastical roller-coaster. Having gone through the happy-clappy, 'feel God' phases of charismatic experience, a considerable number of evangelicals are currently searching for something more contemplative. 'Celtic Christianity' is sufficently flexible to be seen by some as the product of 'charismatic Celts', but it can also be associated with 'contemplative Celts'. Consequently, it is being introduced in certain, mainly charismatic, churches as an aid to prayer and worship (see Chapter 13).

On the more liberal wing of the traditional churches, which generally eschews the supernaturalism of the evangelical camp, many (including some leading scholars) are discovering their spiritual bankruptcy as the acids of modernity eat what remains of their souls. They have few signs to enjoy, and even fewer wonders, but they do not want to go along the evangelical road. To them, it seems, the Celtic saints and 'Celtic Christianity' offer a reassuring half-way house, a form of evangelicalism by proxy. They are more inclined to accept the word of the 'Celts' than the word of the New Testament. The more liberal camp finds remarkably close parallels between the writings of modern philosophers and the sentiments which they attach to 'Celtic Christianity' (see Chapter 5). 'Celtic Christianity' is therefore in the curious (and, some might say, dubious) position of being able to unite both the liberal and evangelical wings of the faith, at least at a relatively superficial level.

Native roots

In the midst of such rootlessness in church and society, it is not surprising that many people are suffering a loss of secular and spiritual identity; labels are less attractive now, and individualism asserts itself. 'Believing without belonging' is one of the keynotes of the age. Nevertheless, however powerful the cult of the individual may be, there is apparently still a need for a point of reference, and for roots both new and old. Paradoxically, our ultra-modern seekers for a new age often 'go retro' by looking back to the past. Simultaneously they look outwards from their congested city cages to 'peripheral' societies that may preserve something better than they have. They admit that they are in a mess, and reach the conclusion that things could not have been so bad in the past. They presume that things were simpler then, and purer. It is a romantic, postmodern concept of the past, which compensates for a pessimistic view of the future. The 'roots industry' can be usefully combined with both the 'Celtic industry' and the 'identity industry' to offer attractive courses on 'Rediscovering Our Celtic Roots'. It is for this reason that romantic 'Celtic' package tours beckon the many weary travellers who feel that somewhere, somehow they will find the missing part of their identity.

How our ultra-modern seekers approach the search for spiritual identity is thus conditioned by their present circumstances across a whole range of issues - philosophical, spiritual, politicial, economic - and it may even be influenced by their geographical locations. While many in Britain today are attracted to Eastern philosophies, there are others (obviously plentiful) who look for alternative or more accommodating religions in their own primordial backyards. The trend to look at the religious expressions of earlier societies is summarised incisively by Dr John Drane (*Faith in a Changing Culture*, pp.14-15):

> For some, [the desire to rediscover spirituality] takes the form of studying major non-western thought-systems such as the great religions of the Orient. For others, it means a concern to rediscover and preserve the native cultures that were displaced when white people first invaded the Americas, Australasia, or Africa. Yet others see the solution in a kind of reversal of history, by jumping backwards over the last 1000 years or more into the dim and distant pre-Christian past of Europe itself, to embrace and affirm the long-lost values and worldviews of our pagan ancestors. As a result,

a dazzling and bewildering array of different spiritualities compete for attention, each of them claiming to be able to offer something that will help us find our souls again, and chart a safe course for the future. The goods on offer in this religious marketplace range from messages from spirit guides and extra-terrestrials, to neo-paganism, celtic mythology and aboriginal spirituality - not to mention renewed interest in astrology and a vast range of psychological therapies offering the prospect of a renewed, holistic humanity.

Finding the 'aboriginals'

Elsewhere in the same book, Dr Drane identifies perspectives which lead modern seekers to embrace earlier religious forms closer to their own locations:

> Others question whether we need to look so far away [as Eastern religions such as Taoism and Buddhism]. In places like North and South America, Australia and Aotearoa New Zealand, other ancient nations flourished long before white Westerners arrived in those lands. Insofar as anyone can tell, their worldviews and lifestyles were spiritually-oriented and environmentally friendly - but they were brutally suppressed and devalued by the imposition of Western culture.
>
> With the benefit of hindsight, it can now be seen that native Americans and other aboriginal peoples had much spiritual wisdom. Could it be that by reaffirming them, Western people might not only expiate some of the guilt of their own past, but also find new ways forward into the future?

Such reflections go to the heart of the current interest in 'Celtic Christianity'. The 'Celts' are a prime example of people who can be seen, within the British Isles, as 'aboriginal' and endowed with 'much spiritual wisdom'. Indeed, the desire to find 'aborignal' faith is very evident in Ellis' and Seaton's volume, *New Celts*. The authors are desperate to prove their case that 'the ancient roots of Christianity in these islands are essentially non-Roman' (pp.37-8). They proclaim (p.85) that:

> One of the greatest strengths of the Celtic Christian movement is that it was indigenous. Pioneers like Columba and Aidan were not just the original Christian apostles to these islands, they were truly *our aboriginal apostles* [italics added]. Their expressions of orthodox spirituality struck a

chord with the people in that they led them into the light of
the gospel in a way that enhanced their roots and identity as
a Celtic people.

It would be hard to find a quotation which so obviously succeeds in
using, in a single short paragraph, all the buzz-words of the
contemporary postmodern social and spiritual quest for a distinctive
identity. The modern quest is read back into the early Middle Ages,
as is immediately evident in the anachronistic final sentence; 'roots
and identity as a Celtic people' would not have been of any significance
to those who listened to Columba and Aidan. Most interesting,
however, is the manner in which the term 'aboriginal' is used. Here
it is complimentary, and contains qualities which we are meant to
admire and seek for ourselves. In the early nineteenth century, by
contrast, the term was one of abuse and disparagement, applied alike
to Scottish Highlanders and Native Americans by justly notorious
exponents of social engineering such as Patrick Sellar, who arranged
the Strathnaver Clearances in Sutherland in 1814. 'Our aboriginal
apostles' is also a concept which meshes with the restorationist ethos
of charismatic Christianity, since it appeals to the example of the past
and implies that it can be recovered in much the same way as the
practices of the New Testament church, including charismatic 'gifts',
can be 'restored' in the present time.

In such a discourse, 'aboriginals' are represented as superior (and
not inferior) beings, thus superficially redressing the negative
perspectives which have prevailed across the centuries, often in those
very areas which are now embracing 'native spiritualities'. Like
'aboriginals' elsewhere in the world, the Celts have also been 'suppressed
and devalued' by a majority culture, and the so-called 'Celtic Fringe'
has been created in large measure by that process. As Dr Drane
suggests, 'expiation of guilt' may indeed be one of the reasons that the
Celts are attracting attention. Yet the quest for 'Celtic Christianity'
involves the reconstruction of the past as much as any desire to put
right past wrongs. In fact, it could be claimed that, far from righting
the wrong, it continues the same process of suppression, by imposing
still another level of obfuscation and Anglocentric misinterpretation
on what remains of the supposed 'Celts'.

Celtic Christianity and other 'native' spiritualities

Whatever the motive, the Celts are by no means the only ethnic or
regional group which has been, and continues to be, subjected to
reinterpretation of this kind. The romantic repossession of regions
and cultures which have been abused by imperialism seems to be one
of the ways by which the well-heeled, modern descendants of the

conquerors come to terms with their own and their forefathers' misdeeds. Romanticism of this kind glamorises the past, sanitises the present, assuages guilt, and compensates for loss; but some would argue more cynically that it is largely an aromatic salve which allows its partakers to enjoy and 'preserve' (in their own terms) a certain part of a minority culture, while doing little to support what remains of the living reality. One can 'go native' without *becoming* a 'native' or having to endure the lot of the 'natives'. One can even tell the 'natives' how they ought to behave, according to the prevailing paradigm.

The practice of investing cultures which were 'other', and previously disparaged, with particularly appealing qualities has a long history. In the second half of the nineteenth century, for example, the cause of Africa was championed by apologists like Edward Wilmot Blyden, a West Indian born citizen of Liberia, who made a case for the 'African Personality' which, he claimed, was characterised by 'cheerfulness, a sense of harmony with nature, a religiousness and openness to the spiritual dimension of existence, as well as a capacity to suffer and to serve' (Kwame Bediako, *Christianity in Africa*, p.12). Such qualities are very similar to those which devotees of 'Celtic Christianity' usually claim to discern in spiritually-minded Celts, and it is very evident that postcolonial rehabilitation of native African traditions has influenced the creators of contemporary 'Celtic Christianity' (see Chapter 4).

'Celtic Christianity' finds its closest parallels, however, in the contemporary appropriation of the religions of the Native Americans by Euro-Americans. Like the so-called 'Celtic Fringe', the domains and cultures of the Native Americans have been progressively annexed and reduced by the cultural imperialism of a greater power. Over the last twenty years or so, as campaigns have been mounted for the preservation of the last vestiges of Native American languages on the brink of extinction, Native American culture has been subjected to a thorough-going process of reinterpretation which mirrors much of the current fad for 'Celtic Christianity'. The modern revamp is sometimes known as 'American Indian Spiritualism'. Armin W. Geertz writes (in Hinnells (ed.), *A New Handbook of Living Religions*, p.543):

> Many Euro-Americans have more or less adopted a conceived 'Native American' ideology as their own, enacting, as it were, their own fantasies about the Native Americans. They are jokingly called 'Wannabes' by Native Americans because they 'wannabe' Indians. The various types of Euro-American Wannabe styles are explicit identification, symbolization, creative syncretism, activism and tourism/hobbyism. The

term wannabe is now also being applied to young Native
Americans searching for their roots.

Native Americans have been core symbols in New Age
thought and activities. This position is clearly based on
Euro-American primitivism.

Geertz further points out that the links between Native American
religion and New Age have been forged by young intellectuals who
have 'gone native' and, in some cases, have established centres such as
Michael Harner's Centre for Shamanic Studies in Connecticut. A
parallel with British academics and clerics who take up the cause of
'Celtic Christianity', and become its leaders in the context of retreat
centres of various kinds, springs readily to mind. What is being
created in both cases is a kind of 'spiritual reservation' where what is
seen as a (supposedly) 'native spirituality', but is in reality a relatively
new product, is promoted under the pretext of rediscovery or
preservation.

Contemporary interpretations of Native American spirituality
make very much the same points as 'Celtic Christianity'. A special
place is given to the close relationship between the Native Americans
and the natural world, which (it is suggested) can be recovered with
revitalising effect by contemporary practitioners far from the original
cultural heartlands. 'All Native American rituals serve as opportunities
to bring the participants into harmony with themselves, with their
tribe and with all of life. The Pipe Ceremonies, the Sun Dance,
Smudging, the Sweat Lodge, and so on, all "purify" the participants
by reaffirming for them their interconnectedness with each other and
with their world...The result of the lies of the White Man is the
disharmony we see all around us today' (Renault and Freke, *Native
American Spirituality*, pp.68-9).

Unfortunately, 'the lies of the White Man' still create disharmony,
especially among the Native Americans. The White Man's new
interpretations of their religions have provoked a sharp response
from indigenous scholars and writers who are deeply concerned about
the distortion and misrepresentation of genuine Native American
culture. In a chapter entitled 'Spiritual Hucksterism: The Rise of the
Plastic Medicine Man' (*Fantasies of the Master Race,* pp.215-6), Ward
Churchill, himself a Native American, is scathing about non-Native
American authors who, 'writing bad distortions and outright lies
about indigenous spirituality for consumption in the mass market...
grew rich peddling their trash while real Indians starved to death, out
of sight and mind of America.' He quotes Oren Lyons, a traditional
chief of the Onondaga Nation, who comments:

> Non-Indians have become so used to all this hype on the part
> of imposters and liars that when a real Indian spiritual leader
> tries to offer them useful advice, he is rejected. He isn't
> 'Indian' enough for all these non-Indian experts on Indian
> religion. Now, this is not only degrading to Indian people,
> it's downright delusional behavior on the part of the instant
> experts who think they've got all the answers before they
> even hear the questions.

In reacting against the misuse of their indigenous spirituality, some
Native Americans have gone as far as to declare war on their perceived
New Age exploiters. In June 1993, the Lakota, Canadian Lakota,
Dakota and Nakota nations passed a 'Declaration of War Against
Exploiters of Lakota Spirituality', in which they protested against
'having our most precious Lakota ceremonies and spiritual practices
desecrated by non-Indian "wannabes", hucksters, cultists, commercial
profiteers and self-styled "New Age shamans" and their followers'
(Riebsame, *Atlas of the New West*, p.115).

The manner in which Native Americans and their spirituality
have been remade to meet the needs of contemporary society beyond
the reservations has drawn quieter, but no less trenchant, comments
from recent historians. For instance, James Wilson writes (*The Earth
Shall Weep: A History of Native America*, pp.14-15):

> If you accept [the idea] of a kind of pre-ordained pattern of
> development measured by an evolutionary time clock, then
> peoples like the American Indians are, in a sense, living in
> our past. Our response to them is profoundly ambivalent;
> we pity (and perhaps despise) them for their backwardness,
> while at the same time seeing them wistfully, even longingly,
> as vestiges of our own lost innocence. We study them for
> clues to our own history; we debate whether their
> primitiveness is the result of circumstances or innate
> inferiority; we try to help them fulfil their destiny by
> making them more like us; we pilfer their cultures for
> fragments of the ancestral wisdom which we forfeited
> through Original Sin or the rise of capitalism or the
> development of Patriarchy. What we cannot do is accept
> that they live with us in a contemporary reality.

There is much in Wilson's observation that can be applied to the
current interest in 'Celts', who are very evidently perceived to be part
of the British past (see Chapter 3). The process whereby authors and
publishers 'pilfer' that past, and create a market which they then feed
by endlessly recycling their innovative product, is apparently not
peculiarly 'Celtic'. It is also evident that, while the problems being

faced by the Native Americans are particularly serious examples of culture-abuse allegedly perpetrated by utterly roguish confidence-tricksters who have roused the ire of Oren Lyons, the remaking of their 'spirituality' may bear broad comparison with what happens to a Celtic culture when it falls into the hands of outsiders with a vested interest in giving an 'ancient tradition' a modern make-over. Indeed, the difficulties confronting the 'real Indian spiritual leader' are not unlike those faced by well-informed authorities on Celtic cultures who attempt to undo the damage inflicted by pseudo-Celtic writers. The writer of this book has experienced precisely that attitude on the part of pseudo-Celticisers with whom he has engaged in debate. Those who attempt to defend genuine Native American culture - or Celtic culture, for that matter - can all too easily be branded as 'extremist' or 'polemicist' or 'non-native' or even 'revisionist', especially by those who have themselves little knowledge of the internal realities of the culture concerned.

Parables of the past

Such parallels could suggest that 'Celtic Christianity' is basically no more than part of a trendy global fad, and that it is liable to run in cyclical patterns. It may well fade as we go into the new century, and as the public tires of its current idols, in politics, pluralism and postmodernism. It is clear that the rise of 'Celtic Christianity' has come about partly because its popular promoters have been able to find publishers who (like themselves) are largely unaware of the scholarly application of the word 'Celtic' and are prepared to invest in the current mania for things 'Celtic'; but, supremely, it is gaining ground because, at many levels in church and society, it is popularly perceived to be a potent antidote to the ills of the age. The beguiling simplicity of 'Celtic Christianity' rises from the rubble of the broken icons of modernity, and it enlists its most willing supporters within, but also beyond, the churches. It is thus a Christian 'new age' movement; but it also appeals beguilingly to 'old age' and to history. In order to provide its enthusiasts with 'roots', it seeks its original home in a pliable 'structure' which appears to have historical validation and will appeal to all and sundry - a function amply fulfilled by the old, yet ever new, outlines of the 'Celtic Church' (see Chapter 6).

'Celtic Christianity' is not, however, the only historically-based myth which engages the attention of postmodern people; parables of the past, containing moral, spiritual or political messages, are much in vogue. Interest extends from 'lost' continents and civilisations to lost ocean liners. In the same period as the current wave of 'Celtic Christianity' has emerged, the story of the *Titanic* - the huge, Belfast-built, White Star liner which collided spectacularly with an iceberg on its maiden voyage in 1912 with the loss of 1500 people - has assumed cult-like proportions, and has been accompanied by a torrent of books and videos, a blockbuster film, and (for the super-rich) even tours to see the wreck, strewn across the ocean floor. The tale of the *Titanic* carries the opposite message to 'Celtic Christianity', since it serves as an eternally grim warning against hubris, technological sophistication, megalomania and competitive expansionism. It gains additional relevance at the dawn of a new century, and derives power too from residual admiration for heroic self-sacrifice and consequent undying fame in the midst of tragedy. 'Celtic Christianity', on the other hand, asserts the virtues of humility, primitivism, simplicity and an egalitarian concern for communal life. It holds out the possibility of a happy return to the past, while the tale of the *Titanic* mercilessly teases the minds of people who suspect that the past may well be a premonition of the future, and that they may not be able to escape the consequences of their own achievements. Yet, despite their differences, the *Titanic* and 'Celtic Christianity' are complementary myths. Fear of the present and the future drives both.

It is also clear that 'Celtic Christianity' is not solely the product of late twentieth-century worries. As we shall see in the next two chapters, the second half of the nineteenth century and the early twentieth century witnessed outbreaks of 'Celtomania' and 'Celtic Christianity', but, although these were of foundational significance, they were generally restricted to romantic intellectuals, and the malady was thus relatively easily contained. The position is quite different at the end of the twentieth century and the beginning of the twenty-first; 'Celtic Christianity' has become massively pervasive. Borne along by a ceaseless flow of books and booklets, pouring out of red-hot word-processors and patronised by publishers who are gasping for all things 'Celtic', 'Celtic Christianity' has now achieved a very wide following. The academic sector is merely a small, though influential, element of the overall picture. The quest has become a postmodern national obsession - but its theoretical roots lie much farther back in history. In fact, the contemporary construction appears to be largely a reinvention, or rediscovery, of patterns which came to the fore in the eighteenth and (pre-eminently) the nineteenth century.

CHAPTER 3

MISTS AND MYSTICISM: THE ROOTS OF 'CELTIC CHRISTIANITY'

Parallels to 'Celtic Christianity' are readily apparent in the modern reconstruction of 'indigenous' religions elsewhere in the globe, thus demonstrating that the current 'Celtic' movement forms part of a wider postmodern attempt to discover and apply a 'native' spirituality. Yet, while the movement is very much a child of its time, the contemporary quest for 'Celtic Christianity' has a surprisingly long history. It is, to a large extent, the continuation of an earlier quest. The idea of a 'Celtic' philosophy with a spiritual dimension which is different from that of metropolitan mass culture can be traced back at least to the middle of the nineteenth century. Influential writers in French and English, notably Ernest Renan and Matthew Arnold respectively, were then inclined to explore various aspects of 'the Celtic character', and to identify particular attributes which, in their opinion, were different from those of the city-dwelling, Germanic philistines. Wittingly or unwittingly, 'Celtic Christianity' has inherited or revived a number of nineteenth-century preconceptions of 'the Celtic character'.

Ossianism

The nineteenth-century forms of the quest for a distinctively Celtic set of characteristics were themselves rooted in, and much indebted to, eighteenth-century reconstructions of the manners and traditions of the 'Celtic' peoples. A particularly potent and well-managed literary exercise appeared in the mid-eighteenth century. To cut a very long story very short, James Macpherson (1736-96), a native of Invertromie, near Ruthven in Badenoch, published two highly controversial 'translations' of supposedly epic poems which he had discovered in the Highlands. These were respectively *Fingal* (1761) and *Temora* (1763), which were said to be the works of an ancient Gaelic bard called Ossian. A sharp and long-lasting controversy followed with regard to the authenticity or otherwise of the works. Their authenticity was supported by men like the Revd Hugh Blair, but disbelieved by others like Dr Samuel Johnson. Scholarly examination of Macpherson's texts in the present century has shown conclusively that he did use genuine Gaelic material, particularly

Gaelic heroic ballads, as the basis of his 'translations', but that he made creative use of these texts, and encased their narratives in a frame which was largely of his own making.

Regardless of the controversy, Macpherson's 'Ossian' imparted a new view of the Highlands to the gullible and expectant public. In the early centuries A.D., according to Macpherson's scheme, the region was the home of warriors who had many noble qualities which had not been acknowledged by those who saw the area as barbaric, especially in the aftermath of the ' Forty-five rebellion. After the rebellion there was a need to show the 'opposite' side of the Highlander from that commonly perceived by external forces. In addition to the followers of the brave and generous Fingal, who is the principal hero of Macpherson's works, we are presented with a ghostly atmosphere, spectres and larger-than-life images of heroes. These have played their part in fixing a certain view of Highlanders which outlives the circumstances for which it was designed. The Highland landscape was presented in terms of mist and mystical gloom, and its inhabitants shared these features. Romantic supernaturalism in a non-Christian form was a by-product of 'Ossianism'.

James Macpherson influenced, for both good and ill, the way in which people, including native Gaels, viewed Gaelic culture. The possibility that epic poetry existed in the Highlands was enough to stimulate rational, academic enquiry into the nature of Gaelic oral and literary tradition. This led to the collection of material relating to the history and culture of the Highlands. The second half of the eighteenth century is distinguished for the amount of collecting activity which becomes apparent, particularly in the field of Gaelic heroic ballads. Field-workers, several of them ministers, made extensive collections of the ballads which had provided the starting-point for Macpherson's translations. This helped to move Highland creativity closer to the printed record. Preservation in print, rather than transmission within an oral context, became one of the goals of both collectors and composers. The desire to publish Gaelic poetry had emerged before the time of the Ossianic controversy, but there can be little doubt that the controversy sowed the seeds of literary revival. By the end of the century, major collections of Gaelic poetry were appearing in print, such as the 'Eigg Collection' of 1776, made by Ranald MacDonald, son of the great Jacobite poet, Alexander MacDonald; and also the splendid 'Gillies Collection', compiled by John Gillies of Perth, and published in 1786. These collections contain much bona fide Gaelic poetry, but it is significant that they also contain a considerable amount of spurious Gaelic verse, following the model of Macpherson's 'Ossian'. The fakes are generally easily detectable amid the genuine articles.

There was therefore a good side and a bad to Macpherson's achievement. On the one hand, it created a genuine desire to rescue real Gaelic poetry from oblivion, but, on the other, it set an unfortunate example, since it encouraged people to follow Macpherson's style, and to produce, in Gaelic, verse of the kind that Macpherson had produced in English. The Ossianic model also tended to contaminate certain aspects of the real tradition. Even some of the ballad collectors were given to tinkering with the evidence, and to interpolating bogus verses into their work. In this respect, Macpherson's work resembled a radioactive explosion which released a great deal of energy, stimulated opposition and protest, and raised the profile of the Highlands in a flurry of ill-informed debate.

Nevertheless, we can discern, through the Ossianic mists, the beginning of an awareness which benefited Gaelic culture in the longer term. The first half of the nineteenth century in both Ireland and Scotland witnessed the foundation of properly academic scholarship.The Highland Society of Scotland's Enquiry into Macpherson's 'Ossian', which published its report in 1805, was indicative of a new approach to the culture and traditions of the Highlands. The collecting of folktales in the Highlands, on scholarly principles, was initiated, and publications of major significance were appearing by the middle of the century. In Ireland, scholarly activity similarly began in the first half of the nineteeth century, with the compilation of massive editions of historical source material, tales and poetry by such scholars as Eugene O' Curry (1796-1862) and John O' Donovan (1806-61). This helped to lay a foundation for the future academic discipline of Celtic Studies. From an early stage, therefore, Celtic scholarship was aided by romantic interest in the Celtic areas.

Romanticism

Macpherson's 'Ossian', as his work is popularly called, was arguably the most influential piece of literature ever to have been concerned with the Highlands and Islands of Scotland. It radically influenced not only the course of scholarship, but also people's perceptions of the Highlands from that point onwards. How people saw the Highland landscape, interpreted the mountains, the people, their actions, their literature - all of this was seen through the window of Macpherson's 'Ossian'. Macpherson's 'Ossian' provided a kind of observation coach in which tourists and travellers, and special pleaders of various sorts, could view the Highlands. Cultural tourism - which is no new phenomenon - got under way, as poets such as William Wordsworth came to visit the Highlands. Their quest was to find that special commodity which was so close to Enlightenment thought, namely 'the sublime'. 'The sublime' was believed to exist not only in the literature of primitive peoples, but also in the landscape. Patrick Graham, minister of Aberfoyle, who wrote on the authenticity of Macpherson's 'Ossian', claimed that 'the prospect which perpetually engages the eye of the Highlander, of barren heath, lofty mountains, rugged precipices, and wide stretched lakes, has a natural tendency to call forth sentiments of sublimity, which are unfavourable to frivolousness of thought.' Robert Burns, the celebrated Scottish poet, was among the number who caught this enthusiasm for the Ossianic Highlands. He visited Highland Perthshire in September 1786, and was enchanted by what he saw. He wrote to his brother, Gilbert,

> Warm as I was from Ossian's country, where I had seen his very grave, what cared I for fisher-towns and fertile carses?

The Highland landscape was seen as misty, windy, and wild, but it harboured great virtues and people who reflected them. It was assumed that, if these virtues had been in existence in Ossian's time, they were still to be found there, protected by a timeless countryside. Consequently, the Highlands went through a paradigm shift. The vices which existed before the 'Forty-five rebellion became virtues which were to be admired, cherished and even imitated. The figure of Ossian, the blind bard, recalling past days, became the epitome of the great qualities which all should emulate. In the Gaelic Highlands themselves, the authenticity of 'Ossian' was accepted widely, mainly because Gaelic speakers related Macpherson's 'Ossian' directly to their own knowledge of genuine Gaelic ballads. 'Ossian' interacted with society at many levels, including the spiritual. One major Presbyterian evangelist, the Revd John MacDonald of Ferintosh (1779-1849), was so deeply affected by 'Ossian' that he embarked on a literary tour to collect Gaelic ballads. Even in the late nineteenth century, divinity students in Edinburgh, soon to serve in the Free Church and the Free Presbyterian Church, entered into the spirit of Ossian, and at least one went so far as to advise his friend in 1891:

> Edinburgh has its attractions but I'm very sorry that you did not stay in Lochaber, for the sake of the Gaelic. Perhaps, however, after the bustle of the Assembly you may retire to some Highland glen where you can drink in the language of Ossian (MacLeod, 'Highland-Lowland Divide', pp.410-11).

If it was not always possible to 'drink in the language of Ossian', it was possible to 'drink in' his spirit, and 'Ossian' contributed massively to the rise of romanticism. Ossian-driven romanticism was still swirling like mist in the glens when the evangelical movement (see Chapter 12) began to take its strongest grip of many parts of the Highlands and Islands.

This perspective was taken far beyond the Highlands. The way in which the region was presented by James Macpherson influenced how people saw the Celts, and led to the discovery of the Celts as an antidote to Germanic philistinism. People began to see certain qualities and characteristics in the Celts which they admired and longed to have for themselves. It was possible to define these characteristics and to isolate them in such a way that a multi-faceted Celt was constructed and reconstructed, so to speak, according to the needs of the moment. Macpherson's work also interacted with, and stimulated, cultural reconstructionism with a 'Celtic' tinge. It fed into a broader British series of movements - 'creative antiquarianism' - which aimed to recapture the 'Celtic' past. In England, an Anglican clergyman, William Stukeley (1687-1765), was studying the stone monuments of Stonehenge and Avebury, and met Macpherson towards the end of his life. He linked the megaliths and henges to his interpretation of the druids - the priestly caste whose mysterious ways had fascinated the Classical commentators of ancient Greece and Rome. In a mixture which is strikingly similar to some present-day concoctions, Stukeley tried to integrate the druids' supposed teachings with those of Moses, Plato and the Anglican Church. Fascination with druids and druidism was also evident in Wales and Ireland. In Wales, druids of a certain kind were rehabilitated by the ingenious labours of the long-lived and highly original 'scholar', Edward Williams (1747-1826), better known as *Iolo Morganwg*. Through Williams' forgeries, druids in much more recent guise became part of the ceremonial of the Welsh Eisteddfod. In Ireland, the key thinker in accommodating the druids within a deist framework was John Toland (1670-1722), whose works have remained influential to the present day. Since the eighteenth century, druids and druidism, in a highly reconstructed form, have become iconic figures in the popular perception of 'Celtic spirituality'.

Macpherson's 'Ossian' reached the world beyond the British Isles, and succeeded in permeating the minds of contemporary men of letters across the northern hemisphere. The notion that the primitive hero was to be seen in the Scottish Highlands in his pristine environment influenced the French philosopher Jean-Jacques Rousseau (1712-78), who developed the concept of the Noble Savage. 'Ossian' attracted the attention of Thomas Jefferson in America, and provided perspectives by which writers such as James Fenimore Cooper, America's first major novelist, could embrace the Native Americans as figures from an innocent, primitive past (deGategno, *James Macpherson*, pp.129-34). By means of translations into several major European languages, including German and Italian, Macpherson moulded literary styles and cultural aspirations on the continent. In its German version by Goethe, Macpherson's work reached Rudolf

Steiner, whose theories about the relationship of matter and spirit subsequently helped to shape the popular interpretation of 'Celtic Christianity' in the later twentieth century (see Chapter 4). In an address given in Berlin in 1911, Steiner reflected on 'how it was that James Macpherson's revival of these ancient songs in the eighteenth century made such a mighty impression upon Europe' (Allen and Allen, *Fingal's Cave*, p.188). He continued:

> Nothing can be compared with this impression. Goethe, Herder, Napoleon, harkened to it, and all of them believed they discerned in its rhythms and sounds something of the magic of primeval days. Here we must understand that a spiritual world as it had existed during Fingal's time, arose within their hearts, and they felt themselves drawn to what sounded out of these songs!

In Steiner's opinion, Macpherson's 'translations' had put people in touch with an ancient, primeval spirituality, and Fingal, the hero of Macpherson's narrative, was in Steiner's terms 'the clairvoyant hero' who was 'active in the defense of the ancient spiritual beings against those who wished to endanger them' (Allen and Allen, p.191). The spiritualising of the Ossianic heroes might have surprised Macpherson, since they were set in pre-Christian times, but there can be little doubt that the atmosphere which he created had a ghostly, surreal dimension, readily capable of sustaining the notion that a pure and primitive 'spirituality' was to be found among Noble Savages. It was easy to assume that those who were pure in their habitats were also pure in their hearts. Macpherson thus laid the foundation for the emergence, in due time, of a 'Celtic spirituality' which could make connections with 'primitive' peoples across the globe. Much of what is popularly considered to be 'Celtic' today derives from the tidal wave of romanticism unleashed by the literary earthquake of Macpherson's 'Ossian'.

Orientalism

'Ossianism' was a child of the eighteenth century, and so too was 'Orientalism' - the study of the Orient, by which was meant not so much a geographical region, as a concept which was amenable to, and sustained by, the desires and theories of pioneering scholars who were concerned to elucidate the relationship between the various language families of the world. Growing awareness that languages descended from a common root which had produced a tree with various branches led to close study of the historical development of languages and their related groups. This was the basis of the linguistic science known as philology.

The Orient and the Occident were connected by linguistic theory. This connection was strengthened when a German philologist concluded in 1838 that the Celtic languages belonged to a wider family of languages, Indo-European, which also included Sanskrit, the language of the earliest literary and religious texts of India. It was an expatriate Welshman of Angelsey stock, Sir William ('Oriental') Jones (1746-94), an Oriental scholar and judge at the High Court in Calcutta, who first gave prominence to the concept of the Celtic family of languages and suggested its relationship with Sanskrit. In his celebrated lecture to the Royal Asiatic Society in 1786, Jones enthroned Sanskrit as the queen of all languages:

> The Sanscrit language, whatever may be its antiquity, is of a wonderful structure; more perfect than the Greek, more copious than the Latin, and more exquisitely refined than either, yet bearing to both of them a stronger affinity, both in the roots of verbs and in the forms of grammar, than could possibly have been produced by accident... (Franklin, *Sir William Jones*, p.90).

Jones thought that there were grounds 'for supposing that both the Gothick and the Celtick, though blended with a very different idiom, had the same origin with the Sanscrit...' 'Oriental' Jones thus initiated a fascination with, and quest for, the Oriental roots of languages which was to hold the attention of scholars, and particularly Celtic scholars, until our own time.

There was, however, another dimension to the Orient. Although philologists were concerned with the detailed scholarly elucidation of linguistic roots and relationships, some were capable of considerable flights of fancy. They were not averse to constructing a conceptual otherworld of romantic make-believe. The Orient thus created was, in many respects, the opposite sort of world to that of the Occident, the progressive, modern, materialist, western world to which the scholars themselves belonged. In putting some stress on creative thinking, as well as on translating (somewhat freely at times) key specimens of literature, Orientalism shared a frontier with Ossianism. The Orient, indeed, was no mere academic Eden; it exercised a fascination at the popular level, too, ebbing and flowing through the decades, encouraging visitors and writers to visit and chronicle its delights.

The creation of the 'myth' of the Orient, with its ancient writings, potent men and alluring women, its perfumes and pagodas, has been examined incisively by Professor Edward Said in his seminal volume, *Orientalism*. Said draws attention to the contribution of still another scholar who had a close link with a Celtic country, namely Ernest Renan (1823-92), a native of Brittany. Renan was a painstaking philologist and major Hebrew scholar whose linguistic researches in Oriental languages were of fundamental significance in their own time, and are widely acknowledged as important in fashioning the concept of Orientalism. Renan also made an immense contribution to creating a particular image of the Celts which has a direct bearing on the development of 'Celtic Christianity'.

Celticism

Although Renan was primarily a philologist, concerned with the *minutiae* of languages, he devoted himself much to the study of theology and philosophy. He was particularly fascinated by the spiritual dimensions of human existence. His theological training, undertaken with a view to service in the Roman Catholic Church, involved exposure to higher criticism. This led him to question the infallibility of the Bible and that of the church, and by 1845 he had lost his orthodox Roman Catholic faith. Yet, although he abandoned orthodox Catholic doctrine and was no stranger to religious controversy in later life - his account of the life of Christ, *Vie de Jésus* (1863), resulted in his removal from his professorship at the Collège de France - Renan did not discard religion. It is said of him that he combined 'serious scholarship with a romantic vision of a new "religion of humanity", prob[ably] inspired by George Sand's Joachimist novel *Spiridion* (1839)' (*Oxford Dictionary of the Christian Church*, p.1383). He appears to have drawn much of his romantic vision from his boyhood experiences. His homeland in Brittany, portrayed in terms derived from Macpherson's 'Ossian', evidently functioned for him as a 'land of lost content', since it was on the western edge of Europe, and supremely in Brittany, that he saw the type of ethnic spirituality which he himself admired. As a native Breton filled with retrospective longing for the lost innocence of his homeland, Renan viewed the Celts in typical post-Macpherson style as a pure race dwelling on the remote periphery, and he thus created an alternative to the romantic Orient - in effect, a Celtic Occident. The Celts derived their purity from their isolation (Hutchison, pp.4-5):

> Never has a human family lived more apart from the world, and been purer from all alien admixture. Confined by conquest within forgotten islands and peninsulas, it has reared an impassable barrier against external influences; it has drawn all from itself; it has lived solely on its own capital... Roman civilisation scarcely reached them, and left among them but few traces.

Dr Rachel Bromwich (*Matthew Arnold and Celtic Literature*, p.6) aptly summarises Renan's view of the Celts as follows:

> Renan's Celts are a shy, sensitive and imaginative race, pushed back to the outermost fringes of Europe, where, lost to the world, they cling tenaciously to their unique institutions, language and traditions, asking only to be left alone. Their society is bound together by the bond of kinship, and they have no gift for organised political institutions. They have always been thrust back upon themselves, and they are given to defending lost causes. Fatalistic and resigned, their obsession with the past is seen in their cult of the dead, and in the sadness of their poetry and music. Yet in the Middle Ages it was this race, he asserts, whose literature altered the course of the European imagination by its gifts to Europe of the chivalrous ideals and of the fables embodied in the Arthurian legend.

Renan elaborated the concept of the Celts as spiritual beings and visionary dreamers - a notion which lies right at the heart of modern 'Celtic Christianity' of the more romantic kind. In his highly influential essay, *La Poesie des races celtiques* ('The Poetry of the Celtic Races'), Renan wrote that 'the Celtic race'

> ...has worn itself out in taking dreams for realities, and in pursuing its splendid visions. The essential element in the Celt's poetic life is the *adventure* - that is to say, the pursuit of the unknown, an endless quest after an object ever flying from desire. It was of this that St. Brandan dreamed, that Peredur sought with his mystic chivalry, that Knight Owen asked of his subterranean journeyings. This race desires the infinite, it thirsts for it, and pursues it at all costs, beyond hell itself. The characteristic failing of the Breton [i.e. insular Celtic] peoples, the tendency to drunkenness - a failing which, according to the traditions of the sixth century, was the cause of their disasters - is due to this need of illusion. Do not say that it is an appetite for gross enjoyment; never has there been a people more sober and more alien to all sensuality (Hutchison, p.9).

Christianity had come to these visionary, peripheral people in a pure form, unsullied by any Roman intermediary:

> ...the Celts were, even in the third century, perfect Christians. To the Teutons Christianity was for long nothing but a Roman institution, imposed from without. They entered the Church only to trouble it; and it was not without very great difficulty that they succeeded in forming a national clergy. To the Celts, on the contrary, Christianity did not

come from Rome; they had their native clergy, their own
peculiar usages, their faith at first hand. It cannot, in fact, be
doubted that in apostolic times Christianity was preached in
Brittany; and several historians, not without justification,
have considered that it was borne there by Judaistic
Christians, or by disciples of the school of St John.
Everywhere else Christianity found, as a first substratum,
Greek or Roman civilisation. Here it found virgin soil of a
nature analogous to its own, and naturally prepared to
receive it (Hutchison, p.46).

Renan not only infused the Celts with a peripheral existence, a
propensity to dreams, and a pure faith, he also credited them with an
enlightened approach to the integration of paganism and Christianity.
'No race,' he claimed,

took over Christianity with so much originality...The
Church did not feel herself bound to be hard on the caprices
of religious imagination, but gave fair scope to the instincts
of the people, and from this liberty there resulted a cult
perhaps the most mythological and the most analogous to
the mysteries of antiquity to be found in the annals of
Christianity (cited by Gougaud, *Christianity in the Celtic
Lands*, p.46).

This vision of a 'Celtic Church', unfettered by creeds and extending
the hand of friendship equally to pagan practice and Christian ritual,
is one of the cherished dreams of much modern 'Celtic Christianity'
(see Chapters 6 and 8). Such too is Renan's portrait of the 'pure' Celtic
Church. He wrote:

Few forms of Christianity have offered an ideal of Christian
perfection so pure as the Celtic Church of the sixth, seventh
and eighth centuries. Nowhere, perhaps, has God been
better worshipped in spirit than in those great monastic
communities of Hy or Iona, of Bangor, of Clonard, or of
Lindisfarne (Hutchison, p.46; quoted by Magnus MacLean,
The Literature of the Celts p.289).

Renan also admired the saints of the 'Celtic Church', who were
likewise ethnically pure, maintaining 'natural' links with their own
cultural contexts:

No hagiology has remained more exclusively natural than
that of the Celtic peoples; until the twelfth century those
peoples admitted very few alien saints into their martyrology.
None too shows so many naturalistic elements. Celtic
Paganism offered so little resistance to the new religion, that
the Church did not hold itself constrained to put in force

against it the rigour with which elsewhere it pursued the slightest traces of mythology (Hutchison, p.48).

The opposition to the Christianity of the Celts did not come from paganism, in Renan's paradigm; it came ultimately from Rome. Speaking primarily of the Bretons, but extending the term to embrace the Celtic peoples of the British Isles, he wrote (*ibid.*, p.47):

> Strong in their moral superiority, persuaded that they possessed the veritable canon of faith and religion, having received their Christianity from an apostolic and wholly primitive preaching, they experienced no need of feeling themselves in communion with Christian societies less noble than their own. Thence arose that long struggle of the Breton churches against Roman pretensions, which is so admirably narrated by M. Augustin Thierry, thence those inflexible characters of Columba and the monks of Iona, defending their usages and institutions against the whole Church, thence finally the false position of the Celtic peoples in Catholicism, when that mighty force, grown more and more aggressive, had drawn them together from all quarters, and compelled their absorption in itself. Having no Catholic past, they found themselves unclassed on their entrance into the great family, and were never able to establish for themselves an Archbishopric. All their efforts and all their innocent deceits to attribute the title to the Churches of Dol and St. Davids were wrecked on the overwhelming divergence of their past; their bishops had to resign themselves to being obscure suffragans of Tours and Canterbury.

In Renan's essay, the main features of, and approaches to, what is known today as 'Celtic Christianity' were clearly sketched. At its centre lay a wistful, personalised vision of a spiritual Arcadia, replacing a lost orthodoxy. Renan's techniques for recovering that vision, like those of modern writers and enthusiasts, included a generalised, romantic approach, lacking detailed interaction with primary sources. Most noticeable in the last quotation is the repressive role ascribed to Rome, and it is difficult not to see something of Renan's personal struggle, and sense of isolation, in these words. This struggle, in various forms, is found in contemporary 'Celtic Christianity' (see Chapter 5).

Renan well merits the title of 'Father of Celtic Christianity', but his ideas would not have become so pervasive without the help of a scholarly Englishman. Shortly after they were first articulated, they were taken up enthusiastically by his friend, the enormously influential literary critic,

Matthew Arnold (1822-88), who had likewise been influenced by Macpherson's 'Ossian'. In his lectures on *The Study of Celtic Literature*, delivered at Oxford in 1865-66, Arnold affirmed Renan's views, and argued that 'sentiment' was 'the word which marks where the Celtic races really touch and are one'. He believed that the 'Celtic nature' was 'an organisation quick to feel impressions, and feeling them very strongly; a lively personality therefore, keenly sensitive to joy and to sorrow' (p.84).

In his foundational writings, Renan had placed his Celts on the western edge of the European stage, but it was Arnold who made them accessible to England - and this was a step of the utmost significance for the future development of 'Celtic Christianity'. Although contemporary twentieth-century writers on 'Celtic Christianity' tend (like Renan) to regard it as a faith which was created on the 'Celtic Fringe', they believe passionately that its values can be accessed even by the English in the present day, and that, somehow, by digging back into their own past, they can re-establish a meaningful link with this pure form of the faith. The notion of a link between the 'Celts' and the English is one of the most enduring aspects of Arnold's legacy. In his lectures, Arnold argued that the English had within them a submerged 'Celtic' element, and he suggested that it was this that made them different from other Germanic races. He wrote (p.104):

> The English hold a middle place between the Germans and the Welsh; their religion has the exterior forms and apparatus of a rationalism, so far their Germanic nature carries them; but long before they get to science, their feeling, their Celtic element[,] catches them, and turns their religion all towards piety and unction.

Thus, if we believe Arnold, the faith of the English had been moulded by the 'Celtic' component in their racial character. The modern implications of this theory are clear: the faith of the 'Celts', potentially, lies deep within those English visionaries who look outwards to the 'Celtic Fringe' to find their personal version of 'Celtic Christianity'. 'Celtic Christianity' is a shared inheritance, and is by no means to be restricted to a particular race. Therein lies the key to much of present-day thinking.

Ernest Renan and Matthew Arnold have undoubtedly been very potent figures in the romanticising of 'the Celt' and in establishing some of the constructs which come within the image-building programmes now known collectively as Celticism. 'The Celt', according to this paradigm, was the opposite type to the hard-headed rationalist: she (as the prevailing notion was of femininity) was a being whose chief responses were emotional, visionary, and non-rational. This concept of 'the Celt', constructed as a foil to the philistinism and materialism of the Germanic world, became a perennially warm ember which could be fanned readily into flame by the romantic movements of the late nineteenth and early twentieth centuries.

Although most present-day popular writers on 'Celtic Christianity' subscribe to this paradigm of 'the Celt' (see Chapter 5), they do not acknowledge any direct debts to Renan or Arnold, and may well know relatively little about them. They appear to derive their impressions independently from the general effusion of romanticism which flowed outwards from these texts and moulded non-Celtic, and predominantly English-language, notions of the Celts. More specifically, they have probably been influenced by scholars and collectors who applied, to varying degrees, the paradigms enunciated by Renan and Arnold. Some major collectors, such as Alexander Carmichael, who were, in Renan's phrase, gathering 'the divine tones thus expiring before the growing tumult of uniform civilisation' (Hutchison, pp.2-3), were among their number (see Chapter 4).

Peripheralism

The concept of 'the Celt', pure in form but pre-eminently pure in faith, dwelling apart from the wider world and constantly under threat, while preserving many of the ancient customs lost elsewhere, became a prominent theme in the work of foundationally important Celtic scholars. It appears, for instance, in the writings of pioneering academics who wished to exalt the cultural achievement of the insular Celts as a phenomenon which flourished beyond the boundaries of the Roman Empire. One of its greatest exponents was Kuno Meyer.

Professor Kuno Meyer (1858-1919), a native of Hamburg who trained as a philologist at Leipzig, lectured at Liverpool and later at Berlin. A figure of the utmost importance to the development of Celtic Studies at the end of the nineteenth century and the beginning of the twentieth, Meyer was also a passionate supporter of Gaelic revivalism in Ireland and (to a lesser extent) in Scotland. He advocated the creation of a School of Irish Learning which was established in 1903, and became the forerunner of the School of Celtic Studies of the Dublin Institute for Advanced Studies; and he was close to influential leaders of Gaelic revivalism. As revivalism gained momentum, Meyer's scholarship was sometimes produced in response to critics who, in his view, belittled the value of early Irish literature in comparison with that of continental Europe. His views on early Irish nature poetry (see Chapter 5) were first articulated in 1901 to counteract the opinions of Professor Robert Atkinson, editor of the Yellow Book of Lecan, who had remarked (in Meyer's words) 'on the paucity and monotony of Irish literature when compared with other vernacular literatures of the Middle Ages' (*King and Hermit*, p.6).

Meyer was a meticulous editor who produced magisterial editions of early Irish texts, but he also appealed to a constituency beyond the academic cloisters. Alongside his more profoundly scholarly writings, Meyer sought to introduce a wider readership to the special qualities of early Irish literature, and published some works consisting mainly of English translations, chief among them his *Selections from Ancient Irish Poetry* (1911). Second only to *Carmina Gadelica* as a quarry for texts supportive of 'Celtic Christianity', this has been a key volume in the provision of readily accessible material of early Irish provenance. It is used by John Taylor for the translation of 'The Deer's Cry' in *The Primal Vision* (see Chapter 4), and also by Ian Bradley and Esther de Waal and a number of other writers. Meyer's immensely skilful English style and his quietly romantic touch in translation invested his work with a distinctive sparkle which retains its attraction to the present day.

Meyer used his popular works to argue the cause of Gaelic Ireland, and, more broadly, of the Celts. In his brilliantly concise but politically nuanced introduction to *Selections from Ancient Irish Poetry* (p.vii), he took up (without acknowledgement) some of Renan's chief themes. He was eager to point out that 'the fact is becoming recognised in wider circles that the vernacular literature of ancient Ireland is the most primitive and original among the literatures of Western Europe...Whatever may be its intrinsic merit, its importance as the earliest voice from the dawn of West European civilisation cannot be denied.' Meyer's view of the Celtic world of the insular West was constructed with obvious admiration for 'the nations of Western and Northern Europe' which 'have had to struggle hard for the preservation of their national life against a powerful denationalising influence proceeding from Rome'. Continental nations had suffered loss of identity. His claims for the 'outskirts' were far-reaching (p.viii):

> It was only on the outskirts of the Continental world, and beyond the sway and influence of the Roman Empire, that some vigorous nations preserved their institutions intact, and among them there are only three whom letters reached early enough to leave some record of their pagan civilisation in a vernacular literature. These were the Irish, the Anglo-Saxons, and comparative latecomers, the Icelanders.

Meyer draws particular attention to the achievement of Ireland:

> In Ireland, on the other hand, which had received her Christianity not direct from Rome but from Britain and Gaul, and where the Church, far removed from the centre of Roman influence and cut off from the rest of Christendom, was developing on national lines, vernacular literature received a fresh impulse from the new faith. A flourishing primitive Christian literature arose...Ireland had become the heiress of the classical and

theological learning of the Western Empire of the third and
fourth centuries, and a period of humanism was thus ushered in
which reached its culmination during the sixth and following
centuries, the Golden Age of Irish civilisation. The charge that is
so often levelled against Irish history, that it has been, as it were,
in a backwater, where only the fainter wash of the larger currents
reaches, cannot apply to this period.

Peripherality, with the essential female orientation of Renan's 'Celt' at its
core, here embraces a vision of an independent Ireland, and the slur of
backwardness is roundly dismissed. In Meyer's heady brew, geographical
relativism dictates a literary theory which rules out even the 'influence' of
Rome. Isolation is a virtue, not a vice, since it holds back the relentless force
of progress, and allows ancient qualities to survive undisturbed.

The ability of Ireland to preserve the earliest, and even the unborn,
literature of Europe may have been as much consolation as special
pleading on Meyer's part. Yet it is beyond question that he helped to turn
scholarly attention away from a narrow classicism to a healthy interaction
with early Gaelic literature. The preservation in Ireland of a significant
amount of such literature was, and is, worthy of scholarly recognition. No
Celticist can quarrel with Meyer for redressing the balance against the
reductionists. The danger was - and remains - that such recognition, if
unqualified, could lead to an excessive emphasis on 'archaism' and to
claims of 'uniqueness' which are not wholly supported by closer inspection
of the evidence. Present-day constructors of 'Celtic Christianity', with holes
in their cultural hearts and wonder in their eyes as they read Meyer's
translations, are unable to decode the political signals, since they have little
knowledge of the course of Celtic scholarship.

Romantic primitivism underpinned the perspectives which
surrounded Meyer's work. It offers now, as it did then, inspiration in
the face of harsh challenges, but it has even greater powers; it fills
cultural gaps, builds nations, creates identities, and reinforces ideologies.
The central vision of a neglected 'Celtic Fringe' which was allegedly
a cornucopia of ancient literature, preserved and protected by a robust
resistance to external pressures, was good news for those who wished to
champion a Gaelic revival, with nationalistic overtones, in Ireland. In
putting some emphasis on the unprogressive nature of the Celtic areas, as
Renan's foundational vision had done, it continues to be potentially a
double-edged weapon. Yet readers of Meyer's work in the present day
continue to enjoy his warm-hearted, confident, pro-Celtic assertions, and
incorporate them happily into their own reimagined versions of the 'Celtic
Fringe'. As enthusiasts of primitivism now tend to look west rather than
east, a form of Occidentalism based on a Celtic foundation replaces
Orientalism, and it does so very largely because the labours of scholars like

Meyer have made a proportion of the riches of the Gaelic west easily accessible and irresistably attractive to non-Gaelic readers.

Twilightism

In constructing his views of the 'Celts' of the west, Meyer was typical of his time in being carried along by the undertow of 'Celticism' in the forms elaborated by Ernest Renan. But he was also affected by, and formed part of, still another movement which owed much to Renan and Arnold, but also had its ultimate roots in Macpherson's 'Ossian'. Centred on the interpretation of rural Ireland, this movement was named the 'Celtic Twilight' from the title of a book published in 1893 by the immensely influential Anglo-Irish poet, W.B. Yeats (1865-1939), who was central to its development. Professor Joep Leerssen has summarised succinctly Yeats' view of rural Ireland as follows (*Remembrance*, p.191):

> With Yeats, the commonplace of an Irish folk community, preserved in a time-warp outside history, obtains its most powerful literary treatment...There is, to begin with, the fact that Yeats, as a would-be mystic, sees the Irish west as a congenial ambiance. The congeniality is nothing less than overdetermined; Yeats was born there, had invested the place with pre-lapsarian childhood memories (much as Bretagne connoted, to the older agnostic Renan, the days of his Catholic, pious youth), and its reputation as an otherworldly place matched his occult, symbolist interests and quests for an extramaterial, platonic, higher reality. For Yeats, the Irish peasantry is the repository of an ahistorical, pre-Christian faith and wisdom, which may redeem readers from the banality of contemporary values.

One of the marks of the Twilightists was their desire to find 'Celtic' traits in other writers who did not necessarily use a Celtic language. Kuno Meyer was ready to perceive 'Celtic' features in the work of Robert Burns:

> There was one Scottish poet on whom the genius of the Celtic muse had descended in all its characteristic beauty - Robert Burns. Burns was wholly un-English, wholly Celtic. There was in him that Celtic fire and power of the imagination, that humour - now delicate and light, now grotesque; but, above all, that wonderful eye for nature which was so peculiar to the Celtic mind' ('Genius of Celtic Poetry', cited by MacDonald, 'Celticism', p.238).

Meyer, the rigorous scholar of Celtic languages, was thus prepared to accommodate the standard stereotypes of his day, and to extend the use and implications of the term 'Celtic' far beyond the purely linguistic. Though he was a distinguished academic, Meyer was not embarrassed by his apparent espousal of Twilight perspectives. Nor was he alone; Douglas Hyde (1860-1949), who was an influential figure in the Gaelic League and revivalist politics of late nineteenth-century Ireland, transmitted similar messages. Hyde was the first Professor of Irish at University College, Dublin (1905-32), and in 1938 was elected the first President of Ireland. Hyde had also reacted against the views of Atkinson regarding the alleged poverty of early Irish literature. His work in collecting charms and prayers in the west of Ireland, represented in his *Religious Songs of Connacht* (1906), complemented that of Alexander Carmichael in the Hebrides. Hyde, like Carmichael, made a very significant contribution to the concept of the 'spiritual Gael' (see Chapter 12). Eleanor Hull (1860-1935), one of Kuno Meyer's students, followed in his and Hyde's footsteps, providing her own English versifications of early Irish hymns and also a selection of translations by Meyer, Hyde and others in *The Poem-Book of the Gael* (1912) (see Chapter 5).

The flowering of 'Celtic' romanticism in the late nineteenth and early twentieth century was very marked, and, like 'Ossianism' in the eighteenth century, it had its good and bad sides. Taken out of context, it could lead to exaggeration and misrepresentation. Yet it was also an essential, usefully emotive part of the package which led to the creation of Celtic Studies as a modern university discipline within the British Isles. The establishment of Chairs of Celtic at Oxford (1877) and Edinburgh (1882) belongs to this period; the Chair at Oxford was founded as a direct consequence of Arnold's *Lectures*, while that at Edinburgh was set up in the midst of a strong movement for land rights for Highland crofters and greater recognition of Gaelic in education, in schools and universities. At the heart of the Scottish campaign was Professor John Stuart Blackie (1809-95), an archetypal romantic who generated both popular enthusiasm and finance to establish the Edinburgh Chair. The first occupants of both Chairs, Sir John Rhys at Oxford, and Professor Donald MacKinnon at Edinburgh, were able to channel romantic notions about 'Celts' into much more sober scholarship which was of foundational significance for the emergence of the scholarly discipline of Celtic Studies in the British Isles.

Primitivism and pilgrimage

'Celtic' romanticism continued to exert a potent influence in the first half of this century. It affected popular perceptions and presentations of the Highlands and Islands. Among its most successful promoters was the Revd Kenneth MacLeod (1871-1955), a native of Eigg, who produced a well-known book, *The Road to the Isles*, which was first published in 1927, although parts of it had appeared earlier in the century in such respected journals as *The Celtic Review*. *The Road to the Isles* is a remarkable mixture of genuine fragments of folklore, drawing on MacLeod's boyhood recollections of Eigg, laced with an exaggerated romanticism which employs a distinctive form of English in an attempt to convey the idioms of the Gaelic language. Its cloying style and the larger-than-life canvas of its brand of 'Celtic mysticism' can be sampled in the following paragraph (pp.77-8):

> Eigg was in those days, and until recently, a nest of antique Celticism. Every inch of it was alive with legends and other-world beings. Mysterious tales made the caves and the kirkyard a terror by night; the sealwoman crooned on the reefs; the mermaid bathed in the creeeks; the fairies sang and piped in the knolls; the water-sprite washed in a certain burn, the shrouds of the dying; the kelpie hatched plots in the tarns, against beautiful maidens; the spirits of murdered baby-heirs sobbed in gloomy nooks; mystic boats, 'with a woman in the prow ever weeping, and a woman in the stern ever shrieking,' glided into the bays at twilight; and on the first Monday of each quarter, a fire-ship passed the island at midnight, with 'a long lean black creature on board, a fiddle in his hand, and he ever playing, and dancing, and laughing,' while 'tween-decks lost souls clanked their chains, and shrieked and cursed. Such was the Eigg night under the stars.

The Road to the Isles carried an introduction by Marjory Kennedy-Fraser who, assisted generously by MacLeod, produced *Songs of the Hebrides*, a set of volumes which filled the drawing-rooms of the 1920s and 1930s with the sounds of seals and mermaids, and the elegiac cries of forlorn Hebrideans on lone shielings and misty islands. This phase of romanticism portrayed Scottish Gaels as rather fey individuals, given to music and wistfulness, and able to communicate with the supernatural world. The image formed the staple output of early Gaelic broadcasting in Scotland from 1923 to 1939. The labours of MacLeod and Kennedy-Fraser helped to assuage the sorrows and bitterness of the Great War by providing a happy shieling-land of song and music. They also affirmed the Hebrides as the last outpost of Highland mysticism, and encouraged other writers to produce similar works on a smaller scale, such as Alistair MacLean's rather surreal *Hebridean Altars: The Spirit of an Island Race*, first published in 1937 and reprinted in 1999, with a Foreword by David Adam. Adam's enthusiastic endorsement of MacLean's book - 'a book that has enriched my life and extended my vision of the world and its Creator' - forms a tangible link between the romanticism of the inter-war years and modern 'Celtic Christianity'. MacLean, the father of the famous novelist of the same name, was minister in the Church of Scotland charge of Daviot, Inverness-shire.

Romantic primitivism reveals itself in the present day in the desire of 'Celtic Christians' to make contact with the original locations of the faith in the British Isles, and especially in the Hebrides. As part of the wider tide of modern primitivists, seeking to 'get away from it all', they are aided in their quest by the heritage and tourism industries. Such industries derive at least some of their power from the creation and maintenance of centres of pilgrimage and visitation which become very attractive to the popular mind as the 'power points' at which Christianity entered the country. These 'power points' are unconsciously 'wired in' to the ideologies of the nineteenth century which imparted a potent image to the Celtic west. This image set it forever apart from the eastern and southern Germanic regions of the British Isles, and goes some way to explaining why the Anglo-Saxon spiritual heritage of England (and Scotland too) has failed to kindle the same glow as 'Celtic Christianity'. Even Caledonian MacBrayne, whose ultra-modern car-ferries maintain the contemporary 'road to the isles', draws some warmth - and no doubt some revenue - from the embers of pre-1940 Hebridean romanticism by attributing a 'magical, mystical' quality to the islands on the front pages of their brochures.

The link between tourism and pilgrimage can be seen particularly clearly in the case of Iona. The flame of romanticism in the later nineteenth-century Highlands contributed to the development of tourism, which gained strength from the interest which was taken in Iona, the 'cradle of Scottish Christianity', as it is sometimes (wrongly) known. The 'sacred ruins', described with pathos by Dr Samuel Johnson in 1773, became a *leitmotif* in the writings of successive tourists. Here was a link which, with a bit of imagination, could be made to connect with Columba, more or less directly. This, in broad terms, was what happened; William Sharp (1855-1905), perhaps Scotland's foremost Twilightist who frequently wrote under the female pseudonym, Fiona MacLeod, made much of Iona in his/her stories and descriptive writings.

The initiation of the reconstruction of the old abbey by the 8th Duke of Argyll, half a century before the Iona Community was even imagined, was the first stage in a process destined to provide a focal point for pilgrims and travellers in search of 'Celtic' spiritual roots. The later foundation of the Iona Community in 1938, for purposes quite distinct from cultural tourism, fixed Iona eternally in the emotional geography of spiritual experience, and created yet another set of myths about the rebuilding and revitalisation of the old abbey.

The location of Iona, as an island once isolated on the western edge of Scotland, was, and remains, a primitivist's dream. There can be little doubt that it played a significant part in helping the waiting world to perceive the Highlanders, and especially Islanders, as the possessors of a great catholic spirituality which belonged to the pure and primitive periphery.

The sound of silence

The common factor linking 'Celtic Christianity' with 'Ossianism', 'Celticism' and 'Orientalism' and a host of other romantic -*isms*, is the belief that the 'Celts' are a 'primitive' people who preserve aspects of culture and society which have been long lost, discarded or destroyed elsewhere. They are thought to have remained uninfluenced by modernity. Kuno Meyer's comments on early Irish literature laid no small emphasis on its 'primitive' attributes, and he has been followed by many subsequent writers, including devotees of contemporary 'Celtic Christianity'.

Commenting on primitivism in art, Daniel Miller (cited by Stafford, 'Primitivism', p.81) has noted that there is a definition of the movement 'which employs as a reference point other contemporary societies, where spatial distance has been conflated with temporal distance so that they appear to us as present visages of our own pasts'. One of the apparent aims of 'Celtic Christians' is precisely to make the Celtic world a present visage of their own past, and to render its indigenous form of Christianity even more readily accessible to contemporary seekers who are outside the Celtic areas. This is done through the British majority language - English. Thus a considerable proportion of the output of the movement consists of translations of texts which are regarded as 'Celtic' and 'Christian' in their ethos. The Celtic areas assume the role of what Dr Fiona Stafford has termed 'silent object', furnishing materials and concepts but not participating in the debate. This, as Stafford defines it ('Primitivism', p.82), is consistent with the essence of 'primitivism':

> For while 'primitivist' generally implies admiration for the 'primitive', the praise is inevitably expressed in the language of the 'non-primitive'observer. In place of a dialogue with the ostensible subject, the primitivist is forced into a panegyric addressed to other primitivists, while the occasion for the discussion recedes as silent object. What appears to be about primitive society very often turns out to be more concerned with the observer, who defines himself or his culture against

a silent alternative. Whether it be the primitivism of Thomas
Blackwell, enthusing over Homeric Greece, or of
Wordsworth, listening uncomprehendingly to the Solitary Reaper,
the form depends on an image of those who have no right of
reply.

Edward Said has similarly commented on the silence of the Orient in the
Orientalist context.

These perspectives are very evident today. 'Celtic' primitivism
has taken on a life of its own, with an agenda which, unlike the earlier
concerns of Renan, Meyer, Hyde and Hull, is not so much a reflection
of the needs of the Celtic areas themselves. Rather, the discourse is
now largely external to the Celtic areas, and reflects a desire on the
part of others to identify with the romantic qualities (in this case pre-
eminently the spirituality) of their inhabitants. Contemporary
advocates of 'Celtic Christianity' probably do not expect the 'natives'
to reply to their writings, since they are not the target readership;
indeed a tendency to overlook the 'natives' seems to be a feature of the
modern movement. Celtic 'natives' have a long history of suffering in
silence while an external view of themselves and their culture is
promulgated by the 'superior' power. 'Interpreting the natives'
probably has a longer history in the Celtic context than in any other.
In the case of 'Celtic Christianity', the discourse is so strongly positive
(in contrast to the negative reporting of past centuries) that the native
spokesperson, if such can be found, would be expected to accommodate
the arguments gladly and make an irenic response. A response which
questions the assumptions and constructs within 'Celtic Christianity'
(as the present book does) will seem churlish to some, given the praise
lavished on the 'Celts'.

All popular writers on 'Celtic Christianity' take an affirmative
and broadly romantic view of the complexion of the Christian faith
in the Celtic lands. They tend to look back to the 'Celtic' period as a
cultural and ecclesiastical Golden Age. Most emphasise the beauty of
landscape as presented in Celtic literature, the splendour of Celtic art,
the Celts' love of, and concern for, the natural world, the purity and
simplicity of their ecclesiastical structures, the healing power of Celtic
poetry, and other palliatives (see Chapter 5).

The qualities and priorities of 'Celtic Christianity' are thus seen
to be superior to modern values, and are frequently advocated as
models for today. 'Real' Celts (if they are even considered by the
writers) would not be expected to disagree. Yet thoughtful Celts, or
at least those people (even non-Celts!) with a properly informed
knowledge of the historical and contemporary circumstances of
Celtic languages and cultures, may well feel uncomfortable with what
is happening, and may justly reach the conclusion that 'Celtic

Christianity' is part of a second Celtic Twilight movement, occurring a century after the first. They may also recognise that many of the characteristics of earlier infatuations with 'Celts' are repeating themselves; bogus 'Celtic' literature, delusions about 'fringe-dwellers', and myths about the 'purity of the periphery' are among the most prominent symptoms of the latest bout of Celtophilia. The left luggage from the nineteenth century is constantly being reclaimed and uplifted by new sets of travellers on 'the Celtic way', who, though largely unconscious of their cultural kleptomania, transfer packages from the old, hard portmanteaux into modern, soft-sided, infinitely expandable suitcases. Many other 'Celtic' enthusiasts, of course, owe little or nothing to these theories, and are seemingly happy to employ the term 'Celtic' as a label for a wide-ranging, eclectic spirituality which incorporates at random both Christian and non-Christian elements.

Yet, while 'Celtic Christianity', as it has developed in the twentieth century, may be viewed as an external frame of reference, or as a metanarrative, for observing and interpreting the spirituality of the 'Celtic Fringe', it needs to be remembered that some of its deepest roots are to be found in the Celtic west itself. In fact, the current version owes much of its contemporary appeal to the post-1960 rediscovery of *Carmina Gadelica*, a major treasury of Gaelic prayers and charms which Alexander Carmichael, a Gaelic-speaking islander, presented to the public with consummate success in 1900. It was Carmichael who, above all others, transplanted continental and English theories about 'Celtic Christianity' to the unusually fertile soil of the Hebrides, where they were cross-bred with indigenous species.

CHAPTER 4

FROM HINDUSTAN TO THE HEBRIDES: THE CREATION OF CONTEMPORARY 'CELTIC CHRISTIANITY'

The most important components, indeed the foundational units, in the making of modern 'Celtic Christianity', were the prayers, charms and incantations gathered by Alexander Carmichael (1832-1912) in the Gaelic-speaking Western Isles of Scotland, and especially the Uists, in the second half of the nineteenth century, between 1855 and 1899. Carmichael was a native of the island of Lismore (near Oban), and was posted as an exciseman to the Hebrides, where he served in Islay, Skye and Uist. He was evidently reared in a richly Gaelic environment, and this doubtless influenced his subsequent direction as a collector of folklore. His greatest contribution to Gaelic culture lay less in controlling illicit distilling in the Isles, than in the collection of a remarkable range of orally transmitted Gaelic lore, including charms and prayers, much of which was subsequently published from 1900 in six sumptuous volumes best known by their Latin title, *Carmina Gadelica*. The first two volumes, edited and introduced by Carmichael himself, have been of particular significance.

Carmichael lived at a time when the collection and study of Gaelic folklore were being actively fostered. From c. 1850, a great deal of material was rescued from oblivion by a number of collectors who operated in the Highlands and Islands, chief among them John Francis Campbell of Islay (1822-85), who became famous for his splendid collection of *Popular Tales of the West Highlands*, published between 1860 and 1862. Campbell of Islay, who was influenced by the work of Jakob and Wilhelm Grimm, encouraged others to join him in his labours, and to send him regular assignments. Besides charms and prayers, Carmichael also recorded traditional tales and proverbs. He sent specimens of the former to Campbell, while many of the latter were incorporated in Alexander Nicolson's major proverb collection, published in 1881. The collecting movement of the time both contributed to, and derived energy from, a broader social and political effort to enhance the profile of Scottish Gaels. Carmichael was very much alive to the potential value of his own forthcoming collections in improving contemporary perceptions of Highlanders, a decade after Highland crofters had achieved a significant degree of political recognition in the Crofters' Holdings (Scotland) Act, passed during Gladstone's Third Ministry in 1886. As he wrote to the Revd Father Allan MacDonald, the parish priest of Eriskay, in 1898 (two years before the publication of his first two volumes), Carmichael was only too painfully aware of the need to present his specimens in the best possible light:

> I had another secret hope in my soul - that by making the book up in as good a form as I could in matter and material, it might perhaps be the means of conciliating some future politician in favour of our dear Highland people. For example, had the book been in the hands of Mr. Gladstone some twenty years ago, who knows but it might have interested him still more in our dear lovable people. These aspirations come in upon me and waylay me to my sore detriment (Campbell, 'Notes on Robertson's Studies', p.1).

Thanks to the labours of Alexander Carmichael, the pagan Highlander of Scotland moved from the barbarian backside of the wilderness, so to speak, and was ultimately to be given a central place in the modern, multi-cultural, visitor-friendly theme-park of so-called 'Celtic spirituality'. A perusal of recent books and writings on 'Celtic Christianity' leaves us in no doubt at all about the importance of the Scottish Gael in this context; indeed, Carmichael's reinterpretation of the Highland Gael as a quintessentially spiritual being created an image of great power, which, in turn, helped to transform the perceptions of other regions which we now call 'Celtic'.

The themes and forms of the *Carmina*

Carmichael's *Carmina* consist of a variety of functional poems, sayings and formulae for many occasions. Professor Derick Thomson (*Companion to Gaelic Scotland*, p.36), has categorised the most important types as:

> invocations (e.g., prayers for protection, justice, before sleep, house blessing, baptism and death blessings); seasonal hymns or prayers; addresses to saints (especially Bride and Michael); blessings for common or everyday tasks (e.g. smooring or banking up the fire, reaping, grinding with the quern, milking, weaving, herding, hunting); incantations or charms (e.g. for the skin condition known as 'rose', toothache, jaundice, sprain, evil eye, stye, indigestion), many of these using herbal specifics such as yarrow, St John's Wort, catkin wool; prayers for baptism, morning prayers, prayers for protection, supplication of the saints, invocation of the Graces, journey prayers, prayers to moon and sun; rhymes

about animals and birds; blessings on cattle and stock; milking songs; waulking songs; fairy songs; auguries; miscellaneous songs including songs of love and praise songs.

The remarkable range of material in the *Carmina* will be evident from Thomson's summary. Its immense richness was rendered accessible to non-Gaelic readers by means of translations, made by Carmichael himself (in the first two volumes) and by subsequent editors, who included his daughter, Ella (wife of Professor William J. Watson, who held the Chair of Celtic at Edinburgh), and his grandson, Professor James Carmichael Watson. The English translations gradually assumed a life of their own, and formed the means by which the *Carmina* became known far beyond the Hebrides. The latest bumper edition of the *Carmina*, produced by Floris Books (1992), dispenses with the Gaelic texts entirely, which implies that the *Carmina* are now regarded as part and parcel of an English cultural environment.

The original Gaelic texts were sometimes recorded in several different versions. On other occasions, only a single version could be obtained, or even less. Carmichael operated in what must have been very difficult conditions, writing down his material from informants who sometimes could reproduce no more than a fragment of the item concerned. As an editor who was conscious of the expectations of the time for well-wrought, drawing-room presentations of 'primitive' texts, Carmichael had to smooth out the inconsistencies of his raw drafts. Occasionally he appears to have functioned in a manner not unlike that of the archaeologist who rebuilds a pot from a few shards which have been collected during an excavation. Indeed, this was the image which Carmichael himself used of some of what he was able to rescue (*Carmina Gadelica*, Vol. 1, p.xxxii):

> The reciters of religious lore were more rare and more reticent than the reciters of secular lore. Men and women whom I knew had hymns and incantations, but I did not know of this in time. The fragments recalled by their families, like the fragments of Greek or Etruscan vases, indicated the originals.

Not only had Carmichael to deal with uneven structures; he had also to provide meanings for certain words and phrases which had dropped below the level of ready comprehensibility. He wrestled with obscurities and archaisms, but eventually managed to produce texts of no small stylistic polish, which secured his reputation as a major 'rescuer' of traditions on the point of extinction. Undoubtedly, this is a just assessment. By any standards, the production of the first couple of volumes of the *Carmina* alone was an outstanding achievement, and the assembling of the entire body of material was a stupendous feat. Nevertheless, Camichael's editorial methods (and those of his later editors) have aroused considerable controversy. The extent to which he appears to have reworked his material has caused at least one researcher, Hamish Robertson, to raise doubts about the authenticity of some of the items. Yet this seems to do less than justice to Carmichael; he was candid about the difficulties that he faced as a collector, and his methods of reconstruction can be deduced without too much difficulty from his introduction.

Contextualising the *Carmina*

Carmichael's introduction to his great 'lost lexicon of piety' (as Dr John MacInnes splendidly calls it) is a fascinating document in its own right. Not only does it give a picture of Carmichael's methodology in, and between, its lines, but it also demonstrates his desire to accommodate islanders and their spirituality within the ideologies and constructs about Celts and 'the old Celtic Church' which informed the perspectives of his day.

The special spirituality of the Highlander was elaborated first and foremost (*Carmina Gadelica*, Vol. 1, p.xxxiii):

> The people were sympathetic and synthetic, unable to see and careless to know where the secular began and the religious ended - an admirable union of elements in life for those who have lived it so truly and intensely as the Celtic races everywhere have done, and none more truly or more intensely than the ill-understood and so-called illiterate Highlanders of Scotland.

In the last phrase of the quotation - 'the ill-understood and so-called illiterate Highlanders of Scotland' - Carmichael was dismissing the prejudice of the three centuries since 1600. Illiteracy could not be equated with ignorance. Education existed in the community beyond the classroom, and was not dependent on the presence of pen and ink. The charms and incantations which he had discovered in the Hebrides had been passed down, as he himself states, 'not through the lettered few, but through the unlettered many - through the crofters and cottars, the herdsmen and shepherds of the Highlands and Islands.' By implication, the living, spoken Gaelic language was the mode of transmission. The poems, which were a 'blending of the pagan and Christian religions, which to many minds will constitute their chief charm', were passed down in a great succession (*ibid.*, p.xxxiv)::

> It is the product of faraway thinking, come down on the long stream of time. Who the thinkers and whence the stream, who can tell? Some of the hymns may have been

composed within the cloistered cells of Derry and Iona, and some of the incantations among the cromlechs of Stonehenge and the standing-stones of Callarnis.

Carmichael was prepared to claim that the tunes of the hymns - 'this peculiar and beautiful music' - were 'probably the music of the old Celtic Church'. He was also very much aware of the antipathetic attitudes of evangelical Presbyterianism towards secular Gaelic culture, and, by contrast, sketched out the profile of an older, more tolerant form of faith, found among Highlanders but conforming to wider Celtic characteristics (*ibid.*, p.xxxii-xxxiii):

> Perhaps no people had a fuller ritual of song and story, of secular rite and religious ceremony, than the Highlanders. Mirth and music, song and dance, tale and poem, pervaded their lives, as electricity pervades the air. Religion, pagan or Christian, or both combined, permeated everything - blending and shading into one another like the iridescent colours of the rainbow...
>
> If this work does nothing else, it affords incontestable proof that the Northern Celts were endowed, as Renan justly claims for Celts everywhere, with 'profound feeling and adorable delicacy' in their religious instincts.

As the second paragraph of this quotation amply indicates, Carmichael was assessing his collection in accordance with the ethnic preconception of the 'spiritual Celt' which had been elaborated by Ernest Renan; his quotations come directly from Hutchison's 1896 translation (p.1) (see Chapter 3). This raises a range of interesting questions with regard to what criteria were used by Carmichael to collect, select and edit the poems and hymns which have made him famous today. To what extent was the material made to fit the message, both by discarding what was not suitable, and by selecting and presenting what was published, in accordance with what might be expected of the 'Celtic race'?

We cannot yet answer these questions, but it is clear that Carmichael was far from being a disinterested collector or editor. The Gaels needed a new, more flattering public face. Carmichael was prepared to help their cause as a 'culture broker' (see Chapter 12). That he did so successfully, to the wider advantage of all 'Celts', is admirably demonstrated by modern enthusiasm for 'Celtic Christianity'. Carmichael, who appears to have anticipated many of the concerns of twentieth-century synthetic religion, laid the foundations for a New Age for both Gaels and Celts.

Occident and Orient

Carmichael's theories about the origins of the *Carmina* placed them in both local and and international contexts. On the one hand, Carmichael regarded the Outer Hebrides as the homeland of Gaelic spirituality, and thereby helped to create the potent figure of 'the spiritual Hebridean', whose image resides at the centre of present-day 'Celtic Christianity'. In so doing, he also gave a special place to the Roman Catholic communities of the Uists and Barra, though not exclusively so. On the other hand, Carmichael was also willing to argue the case for a direct connection between the fragmented prayers and charms that he found in the Hebrides and the Columban foundations of Iona and Derry. It was at least partly in response to this perception that the broader concept of a sea-united spiritual Gael, in Ireland and Scotland, eventually emerged. The emergence of that Gael, in a splendid ecumenicity of culture and spirit, is reflected in the writings of the Irish scholar, Eleanor Hull, who was able to pull all the images together and ascribe the essential creative role to 'the Celtic mind'. To achieve this she collated some of the collections of Alexander Carmichael and Douglas Hyde, whose writings have been central to 'Celtic Christianity' ever since. Hull wrote in the introduction to her collection, *The Poem-Book of the Gael* (pp.xxxvi-xxxvii):

> The deep religious feeling of the Celtic mind, with its far-stretching hands groping towards the mysterious and the infinite, comes out in these spontaneous and simple ejaculations; I have therefore endeavoured to bring together a few others to add to the groups gathered by Dr. Hyde in the west of Ireland and by Dr. Carmichael in the Western Hebrides; but in their original Gaelic they are the fruit of others' collections, not of my own.

Yet, in order to find a cultural context for the spirituality of the *Carmina*, Carmichael was ready to expand his horizons much farther than Ireland. He was prepared to set the 'spiritual Hebridean' in an international context. When describing the old church at Rodel, Harris, Carmichael composed a remarkable paragraph which exudes more of the hot air of the Orient than the cool breezes of the Hebrides (*Carmina Gadelica*, p.xxxiii):

> There are sculptures within the church of much originality of design and of great beauty of execution, but the sculptures without are still more original and interesting. Round the sides of the square tower are the figures of birds and beasts, reptiles and fishes, and of men and women representing phallic worship. Here pagan cult joins with Christian faith, the East with the West, the past with the present. The

traveller from India to Scotland can here see, on the cold, sterile rocks of Harris, the petrified symbols of a faith left living behind him on the hot fertile plains of Hindustan. He can thus in his own person bridge over a space of eight thousand miles and a period of two thousand years.

When writers on 'Celtic Christianity' enthuse about 'Celts', they are enthusing mainly about the perceptions of Hebrideans found in the work of Carmichael. These Hebrideans function in a reconstructed context which provides an overall picture of a tolerant, pagan-friendly form of Christianity, drawing on primordial roots which can be traced back to Hindustan. In Carmichael's mind, the Hebrideans appear to form the outermost of a series of ever-widening concentric circles, representing India, Ireland, and the Hebrides. His interpretation reflects the prevailing orthodoxies of the later nineteenth century in having both Orientalist and Celticist features, but especially in subscribing to the common scholarly view that myths and tales were diffused from a primitive common core. By taking the Hebrides as his primary focus, however, Carmichael puts the Hebrideans at the centre, and develops a form of Occidentalism.

Why did Carmichael present his *Carmina* in this wide-ranging, synthetic, multicultural form? We have already noted his concern to rebuff the charges of ignorance levelled at the Gaels by outsiders, but it is also entirely fair to see Carmichael's arguments and presentation as, partly at least, a response to the strong imagery and 'narrow' parameters of the Protestant, evangelical view of spirituality (discussed further in Chapter 12) which was potent in the contemporary Highlands and Islands. Carmichael's collection demonstrated, to its creator's satisfaction at least, that Highland people had a traditional, respectable, tolerant, pre-Protestant faith of great antiquity, reaching into the mists, and indeed the myths, of time. The rocks of Harris had an intimate spiritual connection with the plains of Hindustan. The Hebrides were pereceived to be no less than the repository of the last vestiges of original, human spirituality, and this had a special attraction for those who followed the teachings of philosophers such as Rudolf Steiner.

Rudolf Steiner and the *Carmina*

Despite the questions of modern scholars, selective use of the treasure-trove contained in *Carmina Gadelica* has become the corner-stone of modern 'Celtic Christianity'. The polished and dignified style of the translations, together with the readers' lack of familiarity with the challenges faced by Carmichael, ensured that the English forms of the *Carmina* passed into general currency without any significant misgivings about the manner in which they were edited and restored. From the early 1960s, indeed, the *Carmina* began to be reprocessed by anthologisers who saw within the material important principles which, in their view, ought to be recovered for the good of contemporary spiritual life. This was the beginning of the revival which resulted in the recovery of 'Celtic Christianity' in the late twentieth century. In particular, the *Carmina* began to find their way into minds that had already been shaped by theories and ideas which had originated far beyond the Hebrides.

It could be said that this process began as soon as Carmichael transferred these hymns and prayers from their original Gaelic contexts into their English translations, and offered them to the general public. The presentation of the *Carmina* also raised the possibility of relating them to global issues. In finding a wider frame for the *Carmina*, Carmichael himself had been exposed to, and inevitably programmed by, those theories about the 'spiritual Celt' which were dominant in the second half of the nineteenth century. The *Carmina* were thus predisposed by their 'packaging' to interact further with other philosophies which had been created before 1900, and were gaining prominence in the course of the twentieth century. The shape of things to come in the closing decades of the century was demonstrated by the anthology from the *Carmina* produced by Adam Bittleston in 1960, and entitled *The Sun Dances: Prayers and Blessings from the Gaelic*. Bittleston's introduction shows that he was a follower of the anthroposophist theories of Rudolf Steiner (1861-1925).

Steiner, who had been strongly influenced by an earlier commitment to theosophy, a religious movement which embraced both Eastern and Western systems of belief, argued that humans were originally spiritual beings who possessed 'intuitive and clairvoyant modes of expression', but were progressively encased in flesh through evolution. The process of enfleshing obscured the spiritual dimension of humanity, but, at a critical juncture, Jesus Christ came to reverse the effect of material existence, and to begin a new era of 'spiritual reintegration'. Steiner and his followers looked for, and emphasised, evidence of the spiritual dimensions which attended enfleshed humanity; they stressed 'the cultivation of spiritual nature and the way to gain spiritual awareness of a higher world' by recovering the earlier spiritual modes for such purposes as meditation (Hinnells, *Dictionary of Religion*, pp.43-4; Blackburn, *Oxford Dictionary*, p.19). It was the presence of spiritual awareness in Carmichael's material, intermingling with the physical dimensions of human life, which appears to have attracted Bittleston to the *Carmina*. The acknowledgement of angels in the *Carmina*, particularly at times of sleeping, was particularly appealing to Bittleston, who suggested (p.xvii) that 'some kind of integration is necessary between the conscious self of waking life and the wider span of the Unconscious. The desire of the Highlander or Islander to prepare his mind, with the help of great words handed down to him, before he passes over into sleep, will seem, when we begin to take such things into account, as of great practical value. Students of Rudolf Steiner's work will recognise much here, once more, that is in harmony with his results.'

Strange though it may seem at first sight, the influence of Rudolf Steiner has been quietly potent throughout the current revival of 'Celtic Christianity'. In particular, Floris Books, who are known to be sympathetic to Steiner, have had a key role in publishing small anthologies, and ultimately the full (1991) volume, of the English translations of the *Carmina*. The key to this unexpected relationship lies in Steiner's interest in the spiritual experiences of the Celtic people of the western regions of the British Isles. As we have already noted in Chapter 3, he had become familiar with Macpherson's 'Ossian', probably through Goethe's German translation. In the address which he delivered in Berlin in 1911 after a performance of Mendelssohn's Hebridean Overture, Steiner accorded a spiritual dimension to Fingal and the Ossianic heroes, but he also perceived a wider mission for the Celts. Looking at 'those times that coincide with the first impulses of Christianity and the centuries that followed', he went on (Allen and Allen, *Fingal's Cave*, pp.188-9):

> What happened in the vicinity of the Hebrides, in Ireland and Scotland, in ancient Erin, on the neighboring islands between Ireland and Scotland, as well as in northern Scotland itself? It is there we must seek for the kernel of those peoples of Celtic origin, who had most of all preserved the ancient Atlantean clairvoyance in its fullest purity. The others who had wandered more to the east, having developed further, no longer kept their earlier connection with the ancient gods. In contrast the Celtic peoples preserved the capacity of experiencing the old clairvoyance, and therefore they were fully immersed in the element of individuality. These people were guided to that particular part of the earth, as if for the accomplishment of a special mission...Here those human beings were prepared who later were to receive the Christ Impulse with their full humanity, and were here to undergo something highly unique by way of preparation.

Steiner believed that the Celts had migrated from the lost world of Atlantis, which was the source of their 'clairvoyance' (as is indicated by the adjective 'Atlantean' in the foregoing quotation) and the original locus of the druids. He considered that the naturally-made geotectonic architecture of Fingal's Cave (located in Staffa, close to Iona) 'mirror[ed] their own musical inner depths', and that, as a temple created by earlier spiritual beings, it acted as a 'focus-point' in which they were made ready 'to receive the Christ Impulse'.

Followers of Steiner's theories might thus be expected to assign a special place to the Hebrides and to the *Carmina* in preserving 'the old clairvoyance' of the Celts in a Christian context, but his philosophy also had a broader interpretative significance within the wider approach to 'Celtic Christianity'. Most notably, Steiner's principles influenced the mind of George MacLeod, the founder of the Iona Community, in the 1930s and early 1940s. MacLeod was attracted by the way in which Steiner's theories gave prominence to the spiritual dimension of humanity, and sought to recover it; he also admired the Steiner community's undoubtedly fine achievements in its 'work with handicapped children, and its care for the environment'. According to Ron Ferguson, MacLeod 'felt the Christian Church exhibited little or no concern for the earth, and his insistence in the early 1940s on an ecological dimension to theology and practice was truly prophetic' (*George MacLeod*, p.191).

MacLeod's enthusiasm for Steiner's theories was prophetic in more ways than one. His perspectives were passed on to those who admired his work with the Iona Community. Esther de Waal, a major contributor to modern 'Celtic Christianity', records that she met MacLeod on one occasion in Iona (*A World Made Whole*, p.10):

> As we walked together round the cloisters, he spoke of how urgent he felt it was that people should find again the living tradition of the Celtic world. 'Everyone today keeps asking, "What is the matter?"', he said, 'and the short answer is MATTER is the matter.' It is our view of matter, the extent to which the church has spiritualized the faith and set it apart from the material world, that has brought us where we are today.

Mediated and modified by MacLeod and others, Steiner's theories helped to draw attention to the alleged antipathy between 'spirit' and 'matter' which is often regarded as a characteristically Western malaise by those who expound the virtues of 'Celtic Christianity'. In contrast to modern, Western Christianity, which is seen to operate too closely by Cartesian and Neo-platonic models, so that it differentiates sharply between spirit and matter and denigrates the latter, 'Celtic Christianity' is popularly believed to lay positive emphasis on matter as well as spirit, and to recognise spiritual dimensions in material things. 'Celtic Christianity' is also seen by some as an antidote to over-emphasis on the mind (again, a Cartesian position) at the expense of the spirit - allegedly the baneful legacy of the Enlightenment. It is therefore but a short step to portraying 'Celtic Christianity' not only as 'integrative' and 'holistic', but also as friendly to nature and to the environment, in contrast to modern environmental degradation. In the opinion of its adherents, the supreme excellence of 'Celtic Christianity' is its capacity to achieve a synthesis of spirit and matter, and especially to accommodate matter positively. The apparent blending of sacred and secular, the spiritual and the material, was perceived fundamentally within the *Carmina*, which seemingly enfolded ordinary, earthly things (and thus matter) in an envelope of spirituality.

The message of the *Carmina*, first defined by Carmichael, and later reinforced by Bittleston, became the central message of modern popular 'Celtic Christianity'. It did so not because everyone had read Rudolf Steiner or had come into contact with George MacLeod or the Iona Community (though many were influenced by the latter), but supremely because the syncretic approach of Steiner, which integrated Eastern mysticism with much else, became an increasingly pervasive way of thinking in the West in the last quarter of the twentieth century (see Chapter 2). Such thinking is a characteristic of the broad amalgam known as 'New Age'. Steiner, like Carmichael, was ahead of his time in anticipating the displacement of Cartesian models of seeing the world.

It is, however, open to doubt whether the anthroposophist approach to the reading of the *Carmina* is a justifiable interpretation of the evidence. It could be argued that the prayers and charms in the *Carmina* tell us nothing whatsoever about the way in which Highlanders viewed spirit and matter as such; rather, the *Carmina* focus on the activities and the day-to-day lives of the people, and invoke the blessing of God and the saints on all relevant human endeavour. Such invocation surely implies that the material world is a hostile environment which inspires fear and requires to be kept under control by superior and more benign forces. There is little in such a perspective to suggest that the users of the *Carmina* had a positive view of the physical world around them. In addition, the *Carmina* may represent essentially 'folk religion', blending folklore and saint-lore, pagan and Christian, in ways which ought not to be confused with the formal teaching of any 'Celtic Church' or indeed with the theories of any modern philosopher. This is popular, demotic Christianity which has come down through the centuries, with inevitable reshaping and admixture. Consequently it shows the type of syncretism which can be found readily across the globe in similar contexts (and is sometimes equated with 'primal religion'). Professor Hugh MacLeod (*Religion and the People of Western Europe*, pp.55-6) notes that:

The rural population of nineteenth-century Europe lived in a dangerous world in which droughts, hail-storms, crop blights, animal epidemics continually threatened the precarious livelihood of the population, and in which the peasant had few natural means of defending himself against such disasters. Prayers, pilgrimages, spells, rituals of all kinds were called in aid by the individual or by the community as a whole. Belief in the proximity of a world of spirits potent for good or evil, and in the significance of particular times, places, objects, animals as harbingers of good or ill fortune patterned all areas of life. Everywhere the institutions of Christianity were in some measure bound up with this magical world; but the precise nature of the relationship between magic and the church varied greatly, just as did the specific forms of this magic.

Carmina Gadelica may be distinctive in their form, but their rationale belongs to a world far broader than that of Hebrideans or even Celts. Currently we do not know when these prayers and charms were created; some may have their roots in the Middle Ages, but how deeply, and how far back in time, is by no means clear.

One may also raise questions about the premises which underly 'Celtic Christianity' itself, and are allegedly supported by *Carmina Gadelica*. In reacting against perceived 'splits' between spirit and matter, and between mind and spirit, it adheres, in its own way, to a dualistic model of perception. It is of the essence of 'Celtic Christianity' to create a rigorous and supposedly typical 'Western' rationalist, Cartesian model against which it can react along experiential lines. Western Christianity and modern Christianity more generally are thus seen as hostile to the qualities exhibited in 'Celtic Christianity', which, when reduced to a set of simple positive observations, becomes a self-validating closed system of understanding, thriving on sharp contrasts and false dichotomies (see Chapter 5).

The 'Carminising' of Celtic tradition

Notwithstanding these difficulties, the *Carmina* have been taken as representative of how Gaelic-speaking islanders, mainly in the Outer Hebrides, interpreted the material world. Not only so; this body of lore has come to be regarded as 'Celtic', and it has been used consistently as the key to understanding 'Celtic Christianity' more widely. Although modern exponents of 'Celtic Christianity' generally disbelieve Carmichael's suggestion that some of the *Carmina* may go back to the early 'Celtic Church', they nevertheless tend to see the *Carmina* as part of the milieu of that church. Indeed, the *Carmina* have become the 'bible' of Celtophiles, and appear to have assumed a normative function in the approach of some exponents of 'Celtic Christianity'. Several writers who expound 'Celtic Christianity' derive almost all their evidence from the *Carmina*. The readiness of academically trained writers to take the *Carmina* as representative of 'Celtic Christianity' is an indication of their lack of chronological methodology. It underlines the elasticity of their concept of 'Celtic Christianity', and also tends to suggest that they view the 'Celtic Fringe' as a region in which time stands still. Evidence from the nineteenth century can thus be coupled to that from the ninth or earlier. In terms of philosophy, however, it may signal that rationalist frames are being displaced by experiential models which make feeling and sense (rather than reason) the basis of knowledge.

The process by which the *Carmina* moved from the fringe of folklore to the centre of 'Celtic Christianity' began around 1960 with Bittleston's anthology. The versified forms of the *Carmina* produced by G.R.D. MacLean (*Poems of the Western Highlanders*, 1961) continued the trend. In the 1980s these had a potent influence on David Adam, and Adam's *Carmina*-style prayers (in English) took the notion of 'Celtic' prayers, imitating MacLean's models, to a mainstream English readership throughout the United Kingdom and beyond. Much more important in terms of generating a scholarly approach with a contextual basis has been the work of Esther de Waal and A.M. Allchin. Together they edited a small volume of hymns and prayers entitled *Threshold of Light: Prayers and Praises from the Celtic Tradition* (1986), later published in Welsh translation as *Ar Drothwy Goleuni* (1992). The book contained, on facing pages, poems and prose passages, the one Gaelic or Irish and the other Welsh, from widely different chronological periods which illustrated some aspect of the 'Celtic tradition'. The first item was taken from the *Carmina*; it was balanced by an eleventh-century Welsh poem on the facing page. The fourth pair of poems derived from the ninth century and the twentieth respectively. The bridging of the centuries and the expansion of the 'canon' of 'Celtic Christianity' was justified because, in the editors' estimation, there were certain 'Celtic' ways of seeing the world which transcended time and place. The editors argued in their introduction that there was a 'special quality of vision or understanding which characterizes the spirituality of the Celtic peoples'.

The centrality of the *Carmina* within that 'vision' was consolidated in 1988, when Esther de Waal published her anthology, entitled *The Celtic Vision: Prayers and Blessings from the Outer Hebrides*. The common themes in the *Carmina*, as interpreted by the editor, were set within the wider 'Celtic' context by drawing comparisons with the themes of particular poems by the twentieth-century Welsh poets, Euros Bowen,

Bobi Jones and D. Gwenallt Jones. The quest for this 'Celtic Vision', spanning the centuries and including medieval and modern specimens of text, has become the distinguishing feature of the Welsh school of 'Celtic Christianity', as is demonstrated clearly by the later writings of A.M. Allchin and Oliver Davies. Davies devotes more attention than Allchin to the literature of the Middle Ages.

The importance of the *Carmina* as a key to 'Celtic Christianity' was further reinforced by Esther de Waal in her book, *A World Made Whole: Rediscovering the Celtic Tradition* (1991). This beautifully written volume, partly reflective and devotional, but primarily concerned to provide an historical account of 'Celtic Christianity', devotes its first chapter to a sensitive analysis of the *Carmina* entitled 'God's World'. The chapter tacitly prepares the reader's mind to interpret the earlier stages of 'Celtic Christianity' through this analysis of the *Carmina*. The *Carmina* appear from time to time as supportive evidence throughout the book, though the greater amount of study is devoted to the early Middle Ages. The volume, however, acknowledges and interacts with modern religious concerns, including the traditional religions of Native Americans and Africans.

Africa and the postcolonial Celts

One of the most important stimuli in establishing the *Carmina* as the normative text of 'Celtic Christianity', and in enhancing the status of 'Celtic Christianity' itself as a subject worthy of study, appears to have come from beyond the British Isles. From the mid-1960s, the process of decolonisation helped to produce a more sympathetic view of the indigenous cultures of those countries which had been under British rule. Western culture became aware of the extent to which colonialism had suppressed the indigenous instincts - including the spiritual instincts - of those who came under its sway. Just as repressed Scottish Highlanders at the end of the nineteenth century gained some degree of political recognition and found an ambassador in Alexander Carmichael who would provide them with a new image at a critical juncture in their history, so countries which had shaken off British rule found spokespersons to champion the indigenous causes. New voices from within these cultures were heard, as self-expression, including scholarship, was liberated. British and American scholars of religion also looked to the former colonies with renewed interest, and with a fresh appreciation of their native 'spiritualities'.

A concern with 'primal religion' emerged strongly. In 1965 John V. Taylor produced an influential book entitled *The Primal Vision: Christian Presence amid African Religion*. Subsequent scholars, notably Harold Turner writing in 1977, undertook to define the key elements of primal religions, which he regarded as 'the most basic or fundamental religious forms in human experience'. The six features of primal religion identified by Turner are very close indeed to the characteristics of so-called 'Celtic Christianity'; these are (1) kinship with nature; (2) a sense of creaturehood; (3) a belief that we are not alone in the world, but live in a personalised universe; (4) a belief that we can enter into relationship with a benevolent spirit world; (5) a sense that the relationship between human beings and the gods continues beyond death, and that dead ancestors are linked with the living; and (6) 'the belief that we live in a sacramental universe where the physical acts as a vehicle for the spiritual and there is no sharp dichotomy between the two' (Low, *Celtic Christianity and Nature*, p.19). This paradigm is also similar to the presuppositions about the *Carmina* which had already been made by Alexander Carmichael, but more specifically by Adam Bittleston and the Steiner school of 'Celtic Christianity'.

The growth of interest in the *Carmina* was thus complemented in the longer term by much larger globalising forces which brought primal religion to the attention of contemporary scholars. The influence of Taylor's book, *The Primal Vision*, in linking African and 'Celtic' dimensions is suggested, in the first instance, by the recurrence of the word 'vision' in the contents and titles of books by Esther de Waal (*The Celtic Vision*) and A.M. Allchin (who subtitles one of his books *The Celtic Vision across the Centuries*). In the introduction to *A World Made Whole* (p.13), Esther de Waal affirms the 'primal vision' of 'Celtic Christianity':

> Here is a Christian understanding which is basic and universal; the primal vision which takes us into the heart of earliest Christendom, and which speaks to that primal vision within all of us. It is something which many people today are looking for but tragically are finding that that search is carrying them outside the structures of the institutional Church.

Within the next couple of pages, she acknowledges her awareness of African perspectives, and later (pp.15, 135) overtly expresses her indebtedness to the scholars of American and African primal religion, particularly John Taylor:

> There is order and harmony in the universe as the Celtic world saw it, a unitive simplicity which finds echoes in native American spirituality or in African traditional religion. Towards the end of that marvellous book *The Primal Vision. Christian Presence Amid African Religion* John V. Taylor writes: 'The primal vision is of a world of presences, face to face meeting not only with the living, but just as vividly with the dead and with the whole totality of nature.' Here is life seen in its wholeness - and it is something that most people in the West

today have forgotten, and are beginning to search for again. It is not impossible to find, though it asks for sensitivity and for time. I believe that the gift of the Celtic world is to renew that lost vision.

Given the direction of influence, it would have been much fairer if de Waal had stated that the 'unitive simplicity' of American and African traditional religion 'finds echoes' in the Celtic world. The main driving force of the current movement probably does not derive from 'Celtic Christianity' in the British Isles, but from studies of primal religion and the interaction of Christianity with primal religion in other parts of the globe. It is highly significant that (as Esther de Waal notes approvingly) John Taylor concludes *The Primal Vision* with a chapter on 'The Practice of the Presence', in which he states (p.193) that 'The God whom, all along, Africa has guessed at and dreamed of, is One who is always and wholly present for every part of his creation'. The theme of Presence is prominent among writers on 'Celtic Christianity', such as de Waal and Bradley.

Even more relevant, however, is the ending of *The Primal Vision*. Taylor rounds off the book (pp.195-7), not with an African song, but with a 'Celtic' (i.e. Early Irish) hymn - 'St Patrick's Breastplate'. His last paragraph, introducing the 'Breastplate' is as follows:

> There have been few moments in the history of the Church since the writing of the epistles to the Ephesians and the Colossians when men have built their faith upon this understanding of God. Irenaeus was one such, and the great Celtic saints followed in the same path. The eighth-century writer of the famous 'Deer's Cry', which we know as St Patrick's Breastplate, invoked in one prayer all the presences that met him with grace in the world of sense and of spirit. It sums up and contains all the spiritual awareness of the primal vision and lifts it into the fulness of Christ. Would that it were translated and sung in every tongue of Africa!

Although this *desideratum* has never been achieved, Esther de Waal and others have given readings of 'these Celtic invocations and prayers, creation credal hymns and hermit nature poems' in Africa, and have found a ready response among those who have heard them. It is also very evident that the process has worked in the opposite direction, since the African response to the *Carmina* and other items has encouraged writers like de Waal to explore 'traditional African spirituality' more closely. A notion of 'Celtic' primal religion, drawing much on African and other global perspectives, undergirds significant segments of 'Celtic Christianity'. These wider perspectives can be seen particularly in the academic form of 'Celtic Christianity', as represented in such works as Mary Low's important study *Celtic Christianity and Nature: Early Irish and Hebridean Traditions* (1996) and

Oliver Davies's *Celtic Christianity in Early Medieval Wales*. Davies affirms (p.143) that one of the themes of his volume has been 'to argue that the phenomenon of Celtic Christianity can more generally be explained by reference to the interaction between Christianity and native forms of Celtic primal religion', and he goes on to discuss the concept of 'inculturation' in the light of experiences from Angola and Peru. The interaction of primal religion and Christianity is a matter to which we shall return later in this book (see Chapter 8).

Careful work by academics properly concerned with inculturation and anxious to derive insights from the comparative study of world religions is entirely proper, and, as Dr Low's book shows, it can be very fruitful and illuminating, if only in dispelling the view that 'Celtic Christianity' is somehow unique. Yet it is open to question whether the wholesale importation of African and other perspectives to the 'Celtic Fringe' is entirely beneficial. Indeed, one may seriously consider whether the presuppositions underlying the general concept of 'Celtic Christinaity' actually liberate the region from the thrall of earlier cultural imperialism, or in reality (and paradoxically) subject it to another form of colonialism. The overall pattern, at least at the popular level, tends to suggest that the 'Celts' have become (once again) the 'dream children' of a predominantly external cadre of writers who are much less enamoured of the Orient and Africa than their predecessors used to be, and are now turning to the West rather than the East to find solace.

While the new writers are aware of Africa, and frequently refer to it, they appear not to have been able to possess it as an alternative Orient. The distinctive languages and cultures of Africa cannot be easily ignored; they are being maintained, and indeed reinvigorated, by Africans themselves. The 'Celtic Fringe' is less obviously *terra incognita* for the more romantic, western seeker, and meets the deep need of the Anglocentric West for an 'Other' country which exemplifies 'lost' virtues. It is closer to home than Africa, and less complex in terms of languages and cultures, particularly as the English language continues its relentless drive into the Celtic areas. It is also less likely to offer a dismissive or hostile response. Consequently, the 'Celtic Fringe' is more vulnerable to external repossession and reinterpetation than the vast continent of Africa.

However we explain the dynamism of the 'Celtic Christian' phenomenon, it can be said that the reclaiming of the Scottish Highlands and, by extension, the whole Celtic west by a new and expansive religious vision is no recent development. The globalising perspective was already present in the work of Alexander Carmichael, who derived it from a wider nineteenth-century trend which embraced, among other things, the riches of the Orient. Carmichael's integrative vision, aimed to rehabilitate the Highlands on the greater British stage, effortlessly spanned the distance from Hindustan to the Hebrides, and it is hardly surprising that, in the course of the twentieth century, this perspective has been recontextualised in terms which belong to other countries and cultures. The capacity to mesh with contemporary ideologies across the centuries has been one of the most enduring features of 'Celtic Christianity'.

Finding the vision

It is probably significant that the post-1960 interest in *Carmina Gadelica* and 'Celtic Christianity' begins, chronologically and thematically, where Taylor ends. It has undoubtedly come to prominence in the postcolonial period, and has been stimulated in part by the more sympathetic discourse through which the West has embraced indigenous African spirituality, and particularly African primal religion, in the last forty years. Interpretations of *Carmina Gadelica* have interacted with the African 'primal vision' and have produced the 'Celtic vision'. The presence and appeal of this vision are evident both in popular works, like those of de Waal, and in more thorough-going academic studies. The Celtic world is therefore being reassessed (as is frequently the case) through frames of reference which originate far beyond itself. Whether this is good or bad (or both good and bad) in terms of perceptions of the indigenous Celtic tradition can be debated.

The result of the progressive expansion of the concept of 'Celtic Christianity', and its interaction with other spiritualities, is to make the subject potentially as large as the entire body of Celtic - and other - literature will allow. The huge time-span and the number of samples potentially available within it offer immense opportunities for 'translation fishing' with a well baited hook in many different oceans, but it also means that 'Celtic Christianity' as a label, far from furnishing a conceptual unity, merely runs the risk of gathering together, and disguising as 'Celtic', a very wide range of differing approaches to theology and culture. The imported preconceptions and assumptions become ever more apparent as relevant Celtic religious texts are examined by scholars properly qualified to undertake the task. In practice, of course, few of the popular writers have any knowledge of the Celtic languages, and are largely dependent on translations by others. Their active source-base is thus severely restricted. The ready availability of the *Carmina* has been of some significance in giving that body of material a particularly important definitive role, out of all proportion to other sources; indeed, it can be said fairly that the discussion of 'Celtic Christianity' has been skewed almost irreparably by over-reliance on the *Carmina*.

'Celtic Christianity' nevertheless retains an attractive and beguiling, but essentially superficial, cohesion. It does this largely by keeping a close conceptual link with the 'Celtic Fringe' and by presenting the 'Fringe' as a single cultural construct, functioning according to a primitivist model in which the inhabitants are perceived to have had (and in some cases to retain) values which are now lost to the society of the observer. The values which are lost are often presented as lessons which the 'external' society needs to relearn. The recovery of the lost primal vision, together with the values contained within it, thus becomes the chief concern of many of the popular writers. The 'faith of the Fringe' is thereby created.

CHAPTER 5

THE FAITH OF THE FRINGE: PERSPECTIVES AND ISSUES IN 'CELTIC CHRISTIANITY'

Although 'Celtic Christianity' appears to be thoroughly contemporary in its profile as an 'alternative' form of Christianity, and is strongly influenced by postcolonial perceptions of primal religions elsewhere in the world, it is nevertheless grounded in a particular view of culture and history which, at first sight, appears to conflict with the progressive mindset of modernity, though it is not necessarily in conflict with the tenets of postmodernity. 'Celtic Christianity' is highly retrospective in its view of 'Celtic' tradition. Comparatively few of its promoters are themselves participants in the affairs of the contemporary 'Celtic' world, and know little of how that world functions.

In their broadly retrospective and romantic 'vision', the exponents of 'Celtic Christianity' follow an approach which can be traced through Arnold and Renan and as far back as Macpherson's Ossianic translations of the early 1760s (see Chapter 3). They also pursue outdated lines of scholarship.Alongside collections like *Carmina Gadelica* (see Chapter 4), several key writers such as Ian Bradley, Esther de Waal and David Adam are rediscovering influential scholarly studies and translations which derive from the turn of the twentieth century. As most of the modern writers are not themselves Celtic scholars, and (with some more honourable exceptions) generally not speakers of a Celtic language, they are often unaware of the extent to which earlier perspectives have been superseded by much more recent scholarly inspection. They are therefore primarily observers of a culture which is, on the one hand, remote from them, but, on the other, accessible, recoverable and even transferable, through the labours of earlier scholars who have furnished translations of key texts. Without the impediments of the distinctive Celtic languages of the British Isles, the appropriation of the 'Celtic' material is greatly facilitated, and an alternative 'Celtic' culture is created largely for the consumption of 'outsiders' and non-speakers of Celtic languages who continue to colonise the 'Celtic Fringe', either physically or spiritually.

The debt of modern writers to late nineteenth-century and early twentieth-century scholarly translators and interpreters is writ large on one of the standard themes of contemporary 'Celtic Christianity', namely the 'peripherality' of the Celtic areas of the British Isles. As appropriation of the 'periphery' takes place, a primitivist vision of the 'Celtic Fringe' also reasserts itself. This primitivist vision is, however, frequently counterbalanced by a (post)modernist vision which derives from the imagination and creativity - literary, philosophical, and theological - of the English-language world with which the writers are, of course, much more familiar. The beguilingly contemporary profile of 'Celtic Christianity' is further enhanced by its apparent relevance to, and ability to resolve, a raft of issues of common contemporary concern which were of no relevance whatsoever to the real Celts of these islands before 1100. Paradoxes of this kind are the stuff of 'Celtic Christianity'. This chapter will examine the main concerns of contemporary 'Celtic Christianity', and assess their validity in the light of contextual, historical and literary evidence earlier than the twelfth century.

Postmodern primitivism

The primitivist, peripheralist vision at the heart of 'Celtic Christianity' is articulated by its modern advocates at every possible opportunity. Thus, Ian Bradley is able to write eloquently (*The Celtic Way*, p.30):

> Celtic Christianity is a faith hammered out at the margins. The Celts lived on the margins of Britain, on the margins of Europe and on the margins of Christendom. They lived close to nature, close to the elements, close to God and close to homelessness, poverty and starvation...
>
> The great upsurge of interest in Celtic Christianity in recent years can be compared to the re-evaluation of the religious beliefs of other peoples who have lived on the margins like the Australian Aboriginees and the native Indians of North America. It reflects a realisation that what is primitive and simple can also be profound and highly original. It expresses also a deeply Christian view that it is among the voices of the most marginalised and oppressed that we may find the greatest wisdom.

Bradley's perspectives are those of a post-imperial and postcolonial society with a conscience about the exploitation of the 'natives' by earlier imperialism (see Chapter 2). They are also those of a technologically advanced society, no longer 'primitive and simple', but aware of the pains and aches of its own progress, and prepared to recognise, in a somewhat patronising way, the achievements of a 'primitive and simple' society. They also encapsulate a reaction against the squalor of contemporary urban life; a vision of 'cardboard city' appears to underlie such words as 'close to homelessness, poverty and starvation', and implies that the 'Celts' have something to say to those who endure such problems nowadays.

Such perspectives, however, are not necessarily relevant to the early Christian 'Celts'. It is unlikely that 'Celts' would have regarded themselves as being in any way 'marginalised and oppressed' when their culture was at its strongest. Such a view of the past is constructed from an eastern and southern British point of reference which sees the contemporary 'Celts' as inhabitants of a remote fringe. It is, in fact, historically inaccurate to claim that 'the Celts lived on the margins of Britain, on the margins of Europe and on the margins of Christendom.' Celtic cultures were extensive in the British Isles in the so-called Dark Ages, and the regions which archaeologists and others have identified as the homelands of the continental Celts were hardly on the 'margins' of Europe.

Misleading concepts of marginality have become pervasive in the twentieth century as the majority mass culture of the British Isles has developed an increasing interest in the 'Celtic Fringe'. They reflect an external and essentially Anglocentric standpoint. Even today, the crofting communities of the Western Isles do not necessarily see themselves as marginal. They may be perceived as such by others, and the failures of economic macro-forces to acknowlege their needs may compel them to believe that they are indeed regarded in that way by those who control the 'energy centres' of modern society; but they are central to their own existence, and Glasgow and Edinburgh, to say nothing of York or Canterbury or Rome, are (from the West Highland perspective) the periphery.

Contrary to the view of many of the proponents of 'Celtic Christianity', Christians in the so-called 'Dark Ages' were not out of touch with Rome. In fact, Christians in Ireland were regularly in contact with Rome in the seventh and eighth centuries, and at no time considered themselves to be beyond its grasp. Issues pertaining to the dating of Easter (see Chapter 7) were discussed with Rome, and important letters were exchanged. Again, the evidence of religious manuscripts and works from early Ireland shows few signs of intellectual isolation on the periphery of Christendom; the commentaries on religious texts make it quite clear that Irish monks were au fait with many of the latest European writings. They were, for example, among the very earliest users and admirers of the etymological works of Isidore of Seville (c.550-636). Furthermore, the use of the terms 'primitive' and 'simple' underestimates the skills that were regularly employed by the Insular Celts. In terms of the value-system of the areas thus described, the terms 'advanced' and 'sophisticated' might be better. Where, today, is the person who can reproduce the brilliance of the Book of Kells, or the artistry of the

Class Two Pictish stones? Yet all of that was normal to those 'primitive' and 'simple' folk who lived on the 'periphery'.

The natural world

Modern 'Celtic Christianity' places a strong emphasis on the harmonious relationship which is perceived to have existed between early 'Celtic Christians' and their environment. The early Christian Celts, according to Ian Bradley and numerous other commentators, lived 'close to nature'. In this too the paradigm is running along primitivist lines, and following the arguments elaborated by Douglas Hyde and Kuno Meyer, but it is also supplemented by some of the perceptions of more recent scholars of primal religion. It is, however, now stimulated primarily by modern ecological issues.

It needs to be made clear that living 'close to nature' was not an option for the Celts of the British Isles. Of course, their natural environment was less spoilt by human hands, and they were not faced with modern ecological issues - environmental degradation caused by cities, industries, fossil fuels, CFC gases and other alleged sources of ozone depletion. That, however, is not to say that they may not have played their own part in disfiguring the landscape. Some scholars would argue that large centres of population were unknown in Ireland before the Viking period, but others have claimed that the creation of monasteries, some developing into mini-cities, was the first step towards urbanisation. If this is the case, Celtic Christians, far from protecting the environment, laid the foundation of the urban lifestyles which are rejected by contemporary 'Celtic Christianity'. The attempt to make the Celts role-models for environmental conservation may thus be somewhat misguided. Like several of the themes discussed in this chapter, it presupposes a dichotomy which was not of any relevance in the early Middle Ages.

Literary sources, in Early Gaelic and Early Welsh, in both poetry and prose, demonstrate that the Celts did have an appreciation of the world around them, in all the variety of its forms. However, exponents of 'Celtic Christianity' argue that there is a special affinity between 'Celtic' monks and the natural world, an affinity which is said to stand in contrast to the lack of concern for nature which is typical of modern Western Christianity. Douglas Hyde, in his *Story of Early Gaelic Literature* (published in 1895), linked Columba very closely with poetry and with nature (p.148). 'Columkille', he wrote,

> like Ossian and the Pagan Irish, was enthusiastically alive to the beauty of Nature. If - apart from form - there is one distinguishing note more than another, peculiar to the literature of the ancient - and to some extent the modern - Gael, it is his fondness for Nature in its various aspects. He

seems at times to have been perfectly intoxicated with the mere pleasure of sensations derived from scenery.

Less than a decade later, Kuno Meyer (see Chapter 3), in the introduction to his anthology of translations, *Selections from Ancient Irish Poetry*, reinforced Hyde's sentiments and created what has become a virtually indissoluble connection between 'Celtic Christianity' and nature:

> Many of [these quatrains] give us a fascinating insight into the peculiar character of the early Irish Church, which differed in so many ways from the rest of the Christian world. We see the hermit in his lonely cell, the monk at his devotions or at his work copying in the scriptorium or under the open sky; or we hear the ascetic who, alone or with twelve chosen companions, has left one of the great monasteries in order to live in greater solitude among the woods or mountains, or on a lonely island. The fact that so many of these poems are fathered upon well-known saints emphasises the friendly attitude of the native clergy towards vernacular poetry.
>
> In Nature poetry the Gaelic muse may vie with that of any other nation. Indeed, these poems occupy a unique position in the literature of the world. To seek out and watch and love Nature, in its tiniest phenomena as in its grandest, was given to no people so early and so fully as to the Celt.

In this way, Meyer sets up the unique 'Gaelic' response to nature, based on his reading of early Irish poetry, and transmits it to 'the Celt'. Underlying Meyer's deductions is the notion that such poems record real experiences and are directly attributable to hermits or monks who are living the ascetic life in close communion with nature. This perception was developed even more fully by Meyer's former student, Eleanor Hull, who contrasted the world-affirming vision of the Irish hermit with the world-rejecting perspectives of the great Cistercian abbot, Bernard of Clairvaux (1090-1153), noted for his strictures on luxury and excessive embellishments (*Poem-Book of the Gael*, p.xx):

> St Bernard, walking round the Lake of Geneva, unconscious of its presence and blind to its loveliness, is a fit symbol of the tendency of the religious mind in the Middle Ages. Sin and repentance, the fall and redemption, hell and heaven, occupied the religious man's every thought; beside such weighty themes the outward life became almost negligible. If he dared to turn his mind towards it at all, it was in order to extract from it some warning of peril, or some allegory of things divine.

But the Irish monk showed no such inclination, suffered no such terrors. His joy in nature grew with his loving association with her moods. He refused to mingle the idea of evil with what God had made so good. If he sought for symbols, he found only symbols of purity and holiness. The pool beside his hut, the rill that flowed across his green, became to his watchful eye the manifestation of a divine spirit washing away sin; if the birds sang sweetly above his door, they were the choristers of God; if the wild beasts gathered to their nightly tryst, were they not the congregation of intelligent beings whom God Himself would most desire?

Thus Eleanor Hull - conveniently overlooking the very evident fact that sin and repentance and other 'weighty themes' are extremely prominent in early Irish monastic literature (see below) - shaped the idea of the nature-adoring 'Irish monk' and the 'Celtic hermit' in a manner which is repeated *ad infinitum* in present-day writings. Modern Celtic scholars, however, are uneasy with the notion that such poems, extolling the great outdoors, were produced by hermits *in situ*. They stress that there is little or nothing in the literary context of these poems to link them directly with eremitic authorship. They are aware that poets, then as now, could assume poses and pretend that they were experiencing a particular set of circumstances. In the case of so-called 'hermit poetry', the pose need not require any active participation in the 'hermit experience'. All that was needed was a scribe who, when wearied of copying a dull manuscript in a scriptorium, glimpsed the sunshine and the trees outside the monastery, and scribbled a few wistful verses in his margins. He would not have considered for a moment that his humble doodles would later assume so much significance for twentieth-century romantics panting for the hermit life.

Broader themes of exile and separation, closely associated with Columba, for instance (see Chapter 10), could be fashioned in a similar way, and ascribed to the appropriate saintly 'voice'. Such poems would express an ideal along the lines of 'this is how we feel it must have been, or how we would like it to be'. The main aim of some at least would be 'idealisation of the ideal'.

In certain poems, nature may be no more than a pretext for the expression of less exalted sentiments which are quietly tucked into the lines. In one of the best known of these early nature poems, the 'hermit' leads us to believe that he is writing in arboreal bliss. His lines are translated by Kuno Meyer as follows (*Ancient Irish Poetry*, p.99):

THE SCRIBE

A hedge of trees surrounds me,
A blackbird's lay sings to me;
Above my lined booklet
The trilling birds chant to me.
    In a grey mantle from the top of bushes
The cuckoo sings:
Verily - may the Lord shield me! -
Well do I write under the greenwood.

Professor Patrick Ford has recently suggested (in 'Blackbirds, Cuckoos and Infixed Pronouns') that this poem may be a wry, scholarly, off-the-cuff attempt to demonstrate the working of forms of the infixed pronoun found in Early Irish. Several uses of the first person singular pronoun are evident, even in the translation, and the poet may have been trying to show the richness of early Irish grammar in respect to such pronouns. The poem, in fact, occurs in the context of a copy of Priscian's Latin grammar preserved at the continental monastery of St Gall, but probably written in ninth-century Ireland. Although it is ostensibly a poem 'about nature', its immediate context may be indicative of an interest in the *minutiae* of language rather than the 'tiniest phenomena' of the natural world.

While it cannot be doubted that Celtic literature across the centuries does show a lively response to nature, it is highly unlikely that any significant link between 'happy hermits' and early Irish nature poetry can be sustained. The validity of the larger claims that 'to seek out and watch and love Nature...was given to no people so early and so fully as to the Celt' has likewise been challenged by modern scholars, who point out that there is nothing uniquely Celtic in such a response to nature. Hebrews (in the Old Testament), Greeks, Romans and Romanised Africans (like Augustine of Hippo) also responded positively and appreciatively to the natural world. The supposedly 'Celtic' response to nature has also been shaped across the centuries by external influences, as diverse as the Bible and James Thomson's eighteenth-century verse on *The Seasons* (see Chapter 12). In the minds of the modern advocates of 'Celtic Christianity', however, the perceived uniqueness of Celtic nature poetry, developing in isolation from the rest of the world, becomes the basis for its distinctiveness.

Essentially the 'happy hermit' of 'early Celtic nature poetry' is a version of the myth of the Noble Savage, which has been reshaped and given a spiritual profile. It contains an element of sharp contrast with other ecclesiastical or environmental approaches. Further overlays give it a present-day resonance. Modern writers commonly weave the body of 'hermit nature verse' into an interpretative pastiche which, while acknowledging the objectivity of such poetry, covers it with a subjective, highly romantic, eco-friendly, and frequently pagan-friendly, glow. Some spiritualise the 'Celtic' view of nature into a belief-system reminiscent of modern descriptions of African primal religion, and they also draw attention to similar themes in Native American spirituality (see Chapters 2 and 4). The great virtue of the Irish poetry - its unadorned detail - thus stands in sharp contrast to the elaborate manner of its modern presentation. The overall aim of this presentation appears to be to produce a distinctively 'Celtic' brand of 'creation spirituality', but the allusions to other 'creation spiritualities' suggest that wider agendas are at work and that the final product is by no means uniquely Celtic.

Simplicity

Given the supposedly close-to-nature lifestyle of the Celts, it is not surprising to find that, in writings on 'Celtic Christianity' generally, there is a presupposition that the Celts did not have complex structures of any kind. These writings express unease with what may be termed broadly 'metropolitan structures'; that is to say, organisations and value systems which are held at the centre by an influential body or group of bodies and exercise control of people's lives. Such metropolitan structures can be political, social or religious; they are often large-scale, as in the case of the Church of England, or the Church of Scotland, or the Roman Catholic Church, or the concept of the United Kingdom itself. Reaction against the metropolitan structures can take a variety of forms, including a flight to the 'periphery'. For those who are weary of the metropolitan lifestyle or value-system, the primitive periphery holds out the hope that a less demanding, less pressurised, less angst-ridden and ultimately more caring form of life may be preserved somewhere in the world.

Reaction against metropolitan control reveals itself in a rejection of central authority and authority figures, and also in the displacement of structured forms of worship in favour of the unstructured, the spontaneous and the individualistic. The trend is consistent with the ethos of post-Impressionist, culturally modernist Britain (and doubtless also Ireland). 'Modernism as a cultural phenomenon', writes Professor David Bebbington, 'was...the result of a shift of sensibility as major as the transition from the Enlightenment to Romanticism a century before' (*Evangelicalism*, 233). The movement was carried over into postmodernism.

Modernism began to affect religious life in the British Isles after 1970. British churches then became familiar with the charismatic movement, which emphasised spontaneity, unstructured worship and individual participation, with such other manifestations as glossolalia (speaking in tongues) and prophecy. Some would contend that certain features of this movement bordered on the anarchic, while others, in more positive vein, would stress its contribution to personal spiritual development, by allowing people to come out of the shadow of the 'one-man ministry'. The ideals of the charismatic movement, however, while modern and even postmodern in ethos, reflect a form of primitivism (and thus of romanticism): its practitioners, in abandoning hierarchical structures, believe that they are returning to the form of the early churches in the New Testament.

The Celts, perceived to have been simple and uncomplicated souls, have become role-models or at least validators for this new anti-hierarchical movement. Thus David Dewey, who reviewed Ian Bradley's book in the *Baptist Times* (21 January 1993), rams home the point:

> Celtic Christians had little time for a hierarchical ecclesiastical order. Their worship was centred in independent monastic communities led by an abbot (or abbottess [*sic*]) rather than a parish structure replete with diocesan bishop and ornate cathedral.

This statement minimises the amount of structure that most definitely existed within individual monasteries and in the wider *familiae*. Abbots like Columba had a general jurisdiction over a set of monasteries which they themselves had founded. This must have required planning and meetings and conflicts with local big-wigs and politicians. The clergy of the Gaelic west also attended synods and councils; Columba is said to have been excommunicated by one such synod. Clergy from the Gaelic world were also much involved in ecclesiastical legislation. Adomnán's *Lex innocentium* ('Law of the innocents'), promulgated at Birr in 697, was one such measure. The fact that it was supported by no less than ninety-one guarantors, consisting of forty ecclesiastics and fifty-one kings, suggests that churchmen were active political and social lobbyists, as well as formidable organisers within their own structures (see also David Dumville, *Councils and Synods of the Gaelic Early and Central Middle Ages*). A committee-free Arcadia may be very appealing to burnt-out clerics in present-day national churches, but it is unlikely to have existed in the Celtic west.

In an earlier article in the *Baptist Times* (20 February 1992), Dewey pointed up the alleged contrast between Celtic Christians and those sent to Britain as missionaries from Rome:

> When the British Isles were first evangelised, the missionaries came from two directions. From across the Channel those

sent from Rome, speaking Latin and representing the culture
of the - by then - Christianised Roman Empire. Theirs was
a formal Christianity with its hierarchical structures of
church authority.

Then there were those who came from Ireland into
Scotland and Northern England. Their Christian faith was
less formal. Following a monastic way of life with a key
centre on Holy Island, they were unencumbered by wealth
and less bothered by status and power. They demonstrated
a simplicity and lightness of touch that their Latin
counterparts often lacked; in many ways they were the
charismatics of their day.

Again, this passage demonstrates the dangers of over-simplification,
and repeats the groundless stereotyping typical of nineteenth-century
writings on the 'Celtic Church' (see Chapter 6). Celtic monks would
have been more than familiar with Latin, and, to put it mildly, Irish
monasteries had a tremendous interest in power, and in the advance
of their own cause. It is certainly true that Irish monks in their cells
could have great visions (as Columba is represented as having in the
island of *Hinba*), but similar visions are ascribed to monks within the
Anglo-Saxon world. Whether such visions are sufficient to make
them 'charismatics' in the modern sense is open to doubt.

Ecumenism

As Dewey's enthusiastic support of 'Celtic Christianity' shows, the
new movement is able to span the denominational divisions of
Christianity. Members of relatively old denominations and religious
bodies such as Baptists, historically hostile to monasticism, wary of
liturgies, and suspicious of symbols such as crosses, are prepared to
accommodate these elements into their 'Celtic' experiments. The
establishment of pilgrimages to holy places, retreats into meditative
communities and liturgies such as the Northumbrian Office, are now
acceptable to many who, twenty years ago, would have been uneasy
at any of these prospects. Here one can perceive the decay of doctrinal
and theological distinctivism, in the face of a new, syncretic 'pick and
mix' approach to religious belief. In addition, one notices the growing
trans-denominational allure of what Professor Bebbington, in the
context of his penetrating discussion of the charismatic movement,
has called 'an extraordinarily unEvangelical delight in symbol - "a love
of oil, candles, crosses etc."' (*Evangelicalism*, 244). The knots and
crosses of the Celts are easily assimilated into this medley of charismatic
catholicity, and become the keys by which the 'Celtic mind' is
supposedly unlocked. All denominations are united as they admire

their own reflections, intermingling with those of others, in the hall of mirrors which is revealed by opening the mysterious 'Celtic mind'.

The supposed ecumenicity of 'Celtic Christianity' derives from a number of modern perceptions which are projected into the past. First, there is the general idea that, as an expression of faith, 'Celtic Christianity' predates Roman Catholicism. It is thus perceived to be earlier than the major schisms and fractures of Christianity, although some would claim that its real roots lie in Eastern (Greek) Orthodoxy, rather than Roman (Latin) Catholicism (see Chapter 6). There is certainly evidence of Coptic influence on the early Christian tradition of Ireland, but Christianity in the Celtic lands was in touch with Rome, not Constantinople. To subscribe to 'Celtic Christianity', whatever its roots, is allegedly to enter a purer world, devoid of denominationalism, and to entertain the hope that 'we can get back to where we used to be before things went wrong'. Second, many believe that 'Celtic Christianity' was free from doctrinal distinctiveness of the kind that has (in their view) bedevilled the later expression of the faith, and has separated believers from one another (see the discussion of theology below). In contrast to modern denominationalism, 'Celtic Christianity' is broad enough to accommodate every shade of faith and practice.

Unfortunately, the historical evidence presents difficulties which militate against the easy acceptance of these views. The Christian faith in the Celtic lands did indeed take root at a time when there were no major denominational differences (as we would define them) within Christendom, but this surely suggests that 'Celtic Christianity' is irrelevant as a supposedly unifying force or model of practical ecumenism. The growing separation between what became Eastern and Western (Roman) Christendom reached its final breaking-point only in the eleventh century. There was thus no need for a unifying body on any significant scale before 1000.

Furthermore, the expression of the faith before that date, even in the Celtic areas, was not without its doctrinal disagreements and squabbles, caused by issues such as Pelagianism, and the dating of Easter. On the latter bone of contention, there were some 'Celts' who had no desire to compromise, and events at Whitby in 664 (see Chapter 7) may be closer to late twentieth-century ecclesiastical controversies regarding points of order and practice than we might care to admit. Some 'Celts', on the arrival of Augustine in 597, showed no great willingness to accommodate the 'Roman' mission (see Chapter 7). Ecumenism was not part of the spirit of their age. It seems, rather, that there might be innate conservatism and a spirit of competitive expansionism among some Christian communities. Expansionist strategy appears to have been embraced readily by some early Irish monasteries, and is scarcely a good model for ecumenism even in the local context.

It also needs to be recognised that contemporary 'Celtic Christianity' is a curiously double-edged weapon to use in the ecumenical cause. It is frequently employed by its supporters in all bodies to berate what they perceive to be the top-heavy bureaucracy of their own churches, and they appear to be less than kindly disposed to Canterbury, to say nothing of Rome. Rome is commonly portrayed as the oppressor, the papal-driven steamroller that crushed the gentle 'Celts'. By claiming an ecumenical agenda for itself, the vision of the 'aboriginal' Christian faith in these islands is self-contradictory; on the one hand it is seen to hold out hope for unity, but, on the other, it seems to be a tool for the creation of distinctiveness, discord and (ultimately) disunity. This is one of the most perplexing paradoxes of the new movement, particularly since, in its eyes, Rome often appears to be more of an enemy than a friend. The unity to which the movement aspires thus seems to be one which embraces the disillusioned in all camps, rather than one which reconciles these camps.

In this particular context, as in others, the historical facts are disregarded, and the 'Celts' become the ultimate primitivist symbols, capable of being refashioned according to the needs of the seeker, regardless of his or her denomination - but with the capacity (if needed) to validate or challenge trends within that denomination. Charismatic power, artistic brilliance, quiet meditation, uncontentious Christianity - all of these are symbolised in the Celts, who become all things to all men (and women, too), as the occasion demands. Now unable to answer for themselves, these pliable people represent still another modern virtue which lovingly beckons the world-weary, spiritual pilgrim who is tired of clash and clamour - tolerance.

Tolerance

Tolerance, leading to the acceptance of a variety of religious groupings, both Christian and non-Christian, is one of the keynotes of the late twentieth century. This may mean overlooking significant differences while making contact with similarly minded individuals who are likewise chafing under their own metropolitan yoke. Thus, the charismatic movement helped to foster ecumenism by bringing 'charismatics' within the Roman Catholic Church to the attention of those beyond it. In Britain today, with its multi-faith society, there is a strong emphasis on tolerance at various levels, especially in the religious context, where major distinctions may be apparent between Christianity and other world religions.

This irenic approach to beliefs has brought the Celts into favour, since they are perceived to have been tolerant of pagan customs and beliefs which predated the arrival of Christianity. The tolerance of the 'Celts' is stressed time and again by writers within the new movement. Esther de Waal, in *A World Made Whole* (p.68), writes:

> The perception of the holiness of the earth and the sacredness of matter belonged to the world familiar to them, the world in which the natural and the divine still met. Elsewhere in Europe the Christian Church was fulminating against the natural world, imposing its strictures on the landscape, cutting down sacred trees, despoiling sacred wells, and denying the natural rhythm that depended on the slow turning of the sun and moon and planets. The anti-pagan violence and admonitions of the councils in sixth-century Gaul and Spain, which were nothing less than a conflict between man and nature, had no place in the Celtic approach to God.

This passage, beautifully and movingly written, as are many of the books on 'Celtic Christianity', simplifies greatly the range of attitudes to paganism displayed by the church in early medieval Europe. To ascribe a single monolithic anti-pagan position to 'the Christian Church' while exonerating pagans from environmental degradation is broadly misleading, as Professor Ronald Hutton - not a supporter of Christianity of any kind! - makes clear in his book on *The Pagan Religions of the Ancient British Isles* (pp.252-3). He asks - and answers - the critical question:

> Did the early Christian Church encourage a more destructive attitude to the natural environment? Again, the evidence at first sight seems to support the proposition. Pagans all over Europe venerated certain groves of trees as sacred. The Romans believed that all natural things were associated with spirits which had to be respected, while the Irish Celts believed that every district was under the protection of a goddess, whose custody of the land had to be honoured. Christians, on the other hand, taught that the whole natural world had been given into the dominion of humans, and cut down the old sacred groves. But such a contrast will not stand up to further analysis. The followers of Christ may have felled the groves, but they sanctified many springs in the name of their own faith and they stopped the ritual slaughter of huge numbers of animals in the course of rituals. More important, the peoples of Europe and the Mediterranean lands have shown the same disposition to

destroy or manipulate the natural world since the Stone Age. Comments upon the damage done in the British Mesolithic, Neolithic and Bronze Age have been made...the Iron Age Celts in what became England may have had their holy stands of trees, but this did not stop them from clearing virtually all the large areas of forest spared by their predecessors, especially in the midlands. Under the pagan Roman Empire, the remaining woods were stripped from much of the North African coast, producing an ecological catastrophe when most of the ploughed-up soil was washed into the Mediterranean. It seems to have been in the same period that the lion was exterminated in Europe, the elephant and the hippopotamus in North Africa and the bear in England. Christianity was absolutely irrelevant to this process.

In early Ireland, the law tracts show that it was necessary to legislate for the protection of trees and woodland, a point which hardly suggests that the natural world in a Celtic Christian society was somehow secure from human rapacity. Fines and penalties for tree-damage were extensive and detailed. Different levels of fine existed for different types of trees. Professor Fergus Kelly (*Early Irish Farming*, pp.387-8) notes that::

> In legal material a distinction is regularly made between trees which are classed as *nemed* 'sacred, privileged', and those which are not. The penalty for damage to a sacred tree (*fidnemed*) is much higher than for an ordinary tree (*fid comaithchesa*). For example, the penalty-fine (*díre*) for an apple-tree classed as *nemed* is given as twenty *séts*, four times greater than for an ordinary apple-tree...A tree's status may make it a target for enemy attack: the *Annals of Ulster* record how the Ulstermen chopped down sacred trees (*biledha*) at the royal inauguration site of the Cenél nEóghain at Telach Óc in AD 1111.

The evidence thus indicates that sacred trees individually were highly esteemed, but this did not render them inviolate. As Kelly further points out, 'early Irish tradition lays much more stress on single trees than on trees as a group'. It is therefore difficult to claim that Christianity in the Celtic areas somehow gave the natural world greater protection than was the case elsewhere. It is unlikely that environmental protection (in our terms) was of any real significance as a general principle in early Irish society, or indeed in any of the early Celtic societies of the British Isles. Woodland was to be found in abundance, and only the particularly special specimens - special because of their religious function, and not because they were trees as such - were of great value.

The desire to turn 'Celtic Christianity' into a tolerant, nature-protecting, and ultimately pagan-affirming, faith also leads its supporters to underestimate the extent of confrontation between pagans and Christians, as exemplified in the Lives of Patrick and Columba, for example. Tolerance was not always a feature of the Celtic saints, whose capacity to curse to death any recalcitrants or opponents is well attested in the writings of their biographers (see Chapter 9). Selectivity with the evidence does, nevertheless, present a picture of accommodation and co-operation broadly in tune with the feelings of our own day.

Such accommodation results in a moderation of the traditional evangelical emphasis on 'aggressive' evangelism. This intention was especially evident during the 1990s, which had been designated the Decade of Evangelism by evangelistic Christian bodies. The reviewer of Ian Bradley's book in the *Baptist Times* wrote appreciatively:

> Celtic missionaries lacked nothing in their zeal to win people for Christ, but their evangelism knew little of the aggressive, confrontational stance adopted in some quarters today. Instead they sought to get alongside people and to build on whatever positive good they could find in the culture in which they bore witness.

What is surely most significant here is that the Celts, viewed through the prism of modern society, become the model for action, rather than the New Testament itself. 'Celtic Christianity' has become an anodine substitute for New Testament Christianity.

The theology of 'Celtic Christianity'

Although 'Celtic Christianity' in its alleged social, cultural and ecclesiastical contexts is perceived within an essentially primitivist frame by its advocates, its theology appears to be remarkably up-to-date. When it came to theology, the Celts were apparently very much in advance of their time, since they appear to have anticipated many of the thoughts and theories of the most significant modern theologians of Europe. Their theology somehow leapt centuries ahead of itself, thus defying the stasis which dominated their social setting.

Because of the restricted source-base used by most popular writers, the theological positions which are often said to be representative of popular 'Celtic Christianity' are seldom deduced from detailed analysis of sources in early Irish or Welsh. They are usually derived, in the first instance, from *Carmina Gadelica*, supplemented by observations based on a few well-known Early Irish hymns and other readily accessible material. As has been argued in Chapter 4, the *Carmina* act as a form of lens, through which the available bits and pieces of genuine evidence are viewed.

Contemporary theology too is used to unlock the 'Celtic' past. The first of the recent flow of modern Protestant writers were generally theologically liberal, and read their version of 'Celtic Christianity' not only through the lens of the *Carmina*, but also through the lenses supplied by liberal theologians. Thus they endowed the 'Celts' with the views of much more recent (and often modern) theologians and philosophers. We have already observed the influence of Rudolf Steiner (Chapter 4). The more academic exponents of 'Celtic Christianity' are fond of citing the controversial Roman Catholic philosopher Pierre Teilhard de Chardin (1881-1955) on 'the sacredness of matter', and occasionally they refer to the existentialist theologian Karl Rahner (1904-84), 'probably the most important and influential Roman Catholic theologian of the twentieth century', who argued that it was possible for salvation to be realized 'without knowledge of the historical Christian revelation and, without explicit faith in Christ, by "anonymous Christians"' (*New Dictionary of Theology*, pp.556-7). The insights of Jürgen Moltmann (1926-), a highly respected German Reformed theologian, are quoted with approval in a number of books. Another modern authority of very considerable influence is Thomas Merton (1915-68), a Trappist monk, mystic and devotional writer resident in Kentucky, whose reflections have appealed to Anglicans such as Esther de Waal. Merton's later interests included Zen Buddhism and Eastern spirituality. Quotations from these writers are often a fairly conspicuous part of volumes on 'Celtic Christianity', whereas quotations from authentically Celtic sources (especially those from the period before 1100) are sometimes remarkably few.

The logic of such quotations would suggest that whatever is being offered in such books is unlikely to be distinctively 'Celtic' since it is so readily paralleled among modern theologians who have no connection whatsoever with the Celtic lands. The frames of reference which are used to define 'Celtic Christianity' are largely external to the proper Celtic community of faith; we have already noted similar perspectives in the use of African insights and comparisons (Chapter 4). This process no doubt helps to validate 'Celtic Christianity' in a global perspective, but it also raises the suspicion that the 'Celts' are being used to further particular agendas, and even to inject subtle doses of (generally) liberal theology into the popular spiritual mainstream. The silence of the Celts as primitivist icons - more spoken about than speaking - permits writers to ascribe modern theology of this kind to their account. In this way, 'Celtic Christianity', braced by 'evidence' from the world of twentieth-century theology, has a deceptively authoritative validating power similar to that of the 'old Celtic Church' (Chapter 6).

Unfortunately, there is (so far) no comprehensive scholarly account of the theological understanding of early 'Celtic' Christians, though an expanding range of texts is gradually being made available by scholars. Exponents of 'Celtic Christianity' therefore tend to rely on one another's works, for this as for much else. The evangelical writers have usually arrived at 'Celtic Christianity' by reading the books of more liberal commentators. The latter frequently expound the 'Celtic' approach to conversion, for example, as 'process' rather than 'crisis'; 'Celtic Christians' are thus invoked in order to put a dampener on 'aggressive evangelism'. This is echoed in the writings of evangelicals too, who are currently putting a great deal of emphasis on 'lifestyle evangelism'.

Liberal writers are also more sympathetic to the accommodation of Celtic culture within a Christian perspective, and this lesson is applied to the modern church, which is believed to be much less open to secular culture. Evangelical writers (who belong, on the whole, to the charismatic wing of church life) are similarly anxious to claim 'Celtic Christianity' as a model for conservative Protestant practice. Some, like Ray Simpson, are prepared to challenge the New Age and the creation spirituality of Matthew Fox, but succeed only in producing a more benign form of 'the mixture as before', with some additional spurious ingredients such as the perspectives of Jungian psychology. Others make light of, or completely avoid, those aspects of early medieval Catholic doctrine and practice which are characteristic of real Celtic Christianity. Protestant writers who wish to claim 'Celtic Christianity' as their model make little or no mention of the mass, the practice of penance or the widespread belief in the efficacy of relics. Thus it can be said fairly that, while the exponents of 'Celtic Christianity' often assert its distinctiveness, they also use it as a means of eroding the distinctiveness of existing doctrines within Protestantism and Roman Catholicism. The 'Celtic Fringe' ultimately becomes the theologically misty Middle Ground.

Sin and penance

The modern doctrinal reformulations of 'Celtic Christianity' are well illustrated by the ways in which contemporary authors present key doctrines of the faith, particularly those relating to God and human nature. Selective use of the original material and a failure to read the sources relevant to the period result in major generalisations and ultimately in overall misrepresentation. Thus Philip Newell (*Listening for the Heartbeat of God*, p.59) can speak of 'Celtic spirituality's emphasis on our essential goodness'. In this Newell, basing his views mainly on *Carmina Gadelica*, is at variance with at least one major Irish monk from the late sixth and early seventh century, namely Columbanus, who (as Kathleen Hughes observed in *The Modern Traveller to the Early Irish Church*, p.2) was 'deeply aware of human sin'. In fact, Columbanus went so far as to justify severe asceticism on the grounds that 'it requires great violence to seek by toil and to maintain by exertion what a corrupted nature has not kept.' The fact that the flesh was perceived to be, in the words of Columbanus, 'unclean by nature' was the greatest single reason for the practice of penance by the real Celtic Christians; the urge to clean the flesh led Columbanus to compile what Hughes has described as 'the most brutal of all the Irish penitentials'.

The better-informed writers on 'Celtic Christianity' are usually aware that the curing of sinners by means of penance was of central importance in all the 'Celtic' churches of the early Middle Ages, but, on the whole, the theme is generally seriously underplayed in popular books, and direct quotations from the penitentials are either carefully filtered or conspicuous by their absence. However, the particularly heavy emphasis on penance characteristic of real Christian Celts is one of the few basic practices which unequivocally unite the churches of the Scots, the Irish and the Welsh, and its influence is evident in the contribution which they made to the development of the sacrament of penance throughout Europe. Due partly to the influence of British (Welsh) and Gaelic (including Irish) practices of private penance, involving individual confession before a confessor, known in Irish as *anamchara* ('soul friend'), the earlier practice of public penance, which was a once-in-a-lifetime event and often delayed until shortly before death, was discontinued, and private penance was adopted as the norm throughout Western Christendom by the twelfth century.

The privatisation of penance led to extensive codification, by which lists of sins were compiled and penances prescribed for each. These compilations, which acted as handbooks for the confessors, are known as 'penitentials', the most significant of which, like that of Columbanus, are ascribed to several of the founding fathers of the monastic movement, including Gildas and Finnian. The compilers strove to provide a remedy for every conceivable form of sin. The penitentials define the minutiae of sins, and prescribe penalties accordingly, to an extent that seems unhealthy and even prurient to modern readers. Charles Plummer, an outstanding scholar of medieval Irish Christian literature, and editor of many saints' Lives and other key texts, decried the genre: 'The penitential literature,' he wrote, 'is in truth a deplorable feature of the medieval Church. Evil deeds, the imagination of which may perhaps have dimly floated through our minds in our darkest moments, are here tabulated and reduced to system. It is hard to see how anyone could busy himself with such literature and not be the worse for it' (cited by O Cróinín, *Early Medieval Ireland*, p.198). More recent writers have drawn attention to the concern with sexual deviance which seems to be such a prominent feature of these texts. Professor Dáibhí Ó Cróinín (*ibid.*, p.199) has noted that:

> ...there was apparently no crime that could not be thought of: heterosexual and homosexual relations (male and female), the regulation of 'proper' methods of intercourse, aphrodisiacs and potions, physical relations, bestiality (Columbanus has two canons on the subject, one for clerics or monks, the other for laymen), wet dreams, stimulation, abortion, contraception, abstinence from sexual relations, and an endless litany of reprobate behaviour that ranged from drinking in the same house with a pregnant servant woman to keening or wailing for the dead.

Sexual sin is, however, only a part of the concern of the penitentials. True to biblical teaching, they cover the sins of the heart as well as those of the body. For example, the *Old Irish Penitential* tackles such vices as avarice and envy. With regard to the latter, it states bluntly (Bieler, p.269): 'Anyone in whom is the nature of envy and malice, there is no dwelling for God in his heart, and so there will be no dwelling for him with the God of heaven.' It goes on:

> Anyone who makes mischief against his brother through (love of) talk or drunkenness, let him spend a day in a silent fast. If it be through gossiping that he finds fault, he recites twelve psalms, or receives a hundred blows on his hands.

Whether we like it or not, the basic premise of penance and of penitentials is that humanity is, as Columbanus claimed, 'unclean by nature'. Although the *anamchara* is commonly reduced in popular writing to little more than a spiritual chum, in historical reality the confessor was regarded as the stringent physician of the soul, with a deep concern to cleanse the flesh, and to prepare it for readmission to the spiritual community here on earth, or ultimately to lessen the severity of processes of purification in the afterlife. As we have seen in the case of malicious talk, the specific sin had to be counteracted by means of its opposite; thus gluttony was cured by an appropriate period of fasting, and sexual indulgence by abstinence and bread-and-water diets. Dietary restrictions were supplemented by pilgrimages, floggings, and recitations of the penitential psalms in uncomfortable physical positions. Commutation was possible, whereby the original penalty could be commuted for a less time-consuming mode of atonement.

The compilers of the penitentials were by no means cloistered in their perspectives; their writings are filled with a wider concern for the well-being of society. 'Therefore', says the *Old Irish Penitential*, 'is envy to be shunned beyond everything, because it creates enmity between son and father, and between daughter and mother, and between king and queen, and between kinsmen so that each of them slays the other.' Malefactors guilty of serious crimes such as homicide and kin-slaying required an extensive period of rehabiliation away from normal society, and were sometimes sent to serve their sentences in isolated penitentiaries. Within the monastic *familia* (or family of monasteries) of Columba, for example, certain communities were apparently set aside for rehabilitation of this kind, notably in Tiree and *Hinba* (perhaps to be identified with Oronsay, close to Colonsay). By sending serious offenders to such institutions, monastic leaders in the early British Isles provided what were in effect spiritual, reformative prisons which complemented the punitive regimes of secular society (see Chapter 8).

Nevertheless, indigenous 'Celtic' theology, allegedly exemplified chiefly in the works of Pelagius (*floruit* c. 410) and John Scotus Eriugena (c.810-c.877), is presented by exponents of 'Celtic Christianity' as supposedly sympathetic to the foibles of human nature and the natural world. Such perspectives are commonly contrasted with the views of Augustine of Hippo (354-430). The latter is considered to be hostile to the natural world, stressing the fallenness of humanity, and is held responsible for introducing the concept of original sin, together with the split between spirit and matter allegedly characteristic of Western Christianity. Pelagius, of course, is held in high regard by enthusiasts of 'Celtic Christianity' because he does not adhere to the doctrine of original sin. The penitentials, however, are based firmly on the view that sin is indeed a part of human nature.

Given the drift of modern society, it is readily understandable that some critics will regard the penitentials as a form of voyeurism by monks who, because of monastic rules, were unable to express their natural desires except covertly and in manuscript. Again, one can understand why the prescriptive nature of the penitentials, laying down stiff penalties for 'sin' which is not regarded as such today, should be unpalatable to those who are trying to formulate a type of 'Celtic Christianity' which is compatible with the aspirations of postmodernity. The 'grubby' side of human life conflicts with the desired romantic image of a comfortable 'Celtic' spirituality, designed for people who have lost the concept of sin.

God and judgement

Just as the natural world is generally perceived within modern 'Celtic Christianity' as essentially good, and in harmony with humanity (and vice versa), God is also seen to be close to his creation. Thus it is common to find that exponents of 'Celtic Christianity' emphasise God's 'nearness', rather than his 'apartness'. He is perceived to be all around, a pervasive Presence, involved in people's daily chores, and not aloof, as he supposedly is in modern Western Christianity. The 'Celtic vision' presents a God who is immanent rather than transcendent. Here too, most writers take their cue from the standard interpretation of the prayers found in Carmichael's *Carmina Gadelica*. The evidence of hymns and nature poetry composed before 1100, on the other hand, shows that early Irish Christians invoked *Rí secht nime*, 'the King of seven heavens', and *Airdrí nime*, 'the High-king of heaven' (as in 'Be Thou my Vision', originally composed in Early Middle Irish, and popularised in Eleanor Hull's translation). They assumed no automatic availability of his grace or protection. Their experience of his creation caused them to wonder at his power and his goodness to them.

Again, 'Celtic Christianity' draws attention to God's love rather than his judgement, and downplays the latter. Early Irish believers, in contrast to modern romantic liberals, had a very strong awareness of judgement, damnation and hell, and acknowledge their need of Christ's protection and deliverance (see Murphy, *Early Irish Lyrics*, pp.23-7). These themes, along with the transcendence and power of the Creator, are frequently portrayed in early hymns, including the celebrated seventh-century *Altus Prosator*, attributed to Columba (Clancy and Márkus, *Iona*, p.49). To judge by this hymn, the faith ascribed to Columba was something very different from that of his latter-day 'Celtic' admirers. It gives a particularly graphic description of hell:

> It seems doubtful to no one that there is a hell down below
> where there are held to be darkness, worms and dreadful animals;
> where there is sulphurous fire burning with voracious flames;
> where there is the screaming of men, weeping and gnashing of teeth...

Such sentiments were not the peculiar property of the poets. They form the essence of some of the 'vision literature' which has come down to us in Latin and early Irish. The description of hell offered in *Fís Adomnáin* ('The Vision of Adomnán') is probably unsurpassed (even in Protestant evangelical preaching and writing) for the wealth of lurid detail with which it describes the fiery fate which befalls different categories of sinners. The text survives in a twelfth-century source, and is retrospectively attributed to the biographer of Columba.

One sample alone will be sufficient to give its flavour (Carey, *King of Mysteries*, p.271):

> There are others with streams of fire in the orifices of their faces, others again with nails driven through their tongues, still others with nails driven into their heads. Those who endure that torment are the folk given to grasping and refusal, lacking charity and the love of God; thieves and perjurors and traitors and slanderers and ravagers and raiders, unjust judges and troublemakers, witches and satirsts, relapsed brigands and scholars who teach heresy.

This awesome potrayal of the fate of the damned - a mere prelude to the even more excruciating torments which they will endure after the Day of Judgement - occupies the second half of the 'Vision'. The first half describes heaven, the eternal home of the saints, as 'a fruitful, radiant country'. Entry into heaven and progression through the 'seven heavens' involve testing and cleansing by fire even for the saints themselves, because the soul has previously been 'the companion and neighbour of the flesh with its slumber and luxury and comfort'.

Such, in reality, were the exacting standards of the real Christians of early Ireland, and they go far towards explaining why they were determined to 'mortify' their flesh, as Columbanus sought to do, through penance and the tough prescriptions of penitentials. The self-indulgent 'soft theology' expounded by many advocates of 'Celtic Christianity' bears little relationship to that found in the original Irish or Welsh texts, and it would be unrecognisable, except as a poor caricature, to the Celtic saints. They might well conclude that it had been manufactured by those 'scholars who teach heresy', mentioned by the composer of *Fís Adomnáin*.

Dreams and visions

The bulk of this chapter has been devoted to modern writers' perceptions of the relationship between 'Celtic Christians' and the world around them, both the natural world and that of the church. Writers on 'Celtic Christianity' do not regard the 'Celts' as deep or profound thinkers in theological matters; rather, they are seen to be 'simple' folk, possessed of mystical, dreamy characteristics which modern authors consider to be distinctive of the psyché of the 'Celts'. Racial stereotyping of this kind, deriving from nineteenth-century perspectives (see Chapter 3), is particularly evident in Ian Bradley's *Celtic Way*. 'As we begin to discard some of the excessive rationalism of Western Christianity,' he writes (p.92), 'we can perhaps begin to appreciate too that other great feature of the Celtic Christian imagination, its tendency to dream dreams and see visions, experience premonitions and feel hidden presences.' Bradley (p.93) believes that in explaining the Celts' alleged propensity towards 'sightings of angels and visions and of the world to come... perhaps the most important factor was the Celtic temperament, dreamy and other-worldly, given to possessing second sight and experiencing premonitions and omens. This marked feature of the pagan Celtic outlook was, like so much else, baptised and incorporated into Celtic Christianity. Where pagan Celts had seen fairies and felt premonitions of impending doom, their Christian descendants saw angels and had visions of the Last Judgement.'

Within contemporary 'Celtic Christianity', the supposedly visionary dimension of the Celts has a particular allure for modern charismatic Christians, who lay emphasis on dreams, visions, and 'signs and wonders'. As Andy and Jane Fitz-Gibbon amply demonstrate by their book, *Prophetic Lifestyle and the Celtic Way*, some charismatic enthusiasts believe innocently that, in giving a place to dreams, they are following the distinctive example of 'Celtic Christians'.

Even if we were to allow that the Celts had a propensity to visionary experiences, this would not make them distinctive within the early medieval world. Visions of various kinds were fairly common within a wide range of cultures; the most far-reaching vision of all was that of the Roman Emperor, Constantine, who saw a vision of the cross in the sky prior to the battle of the Milvian Bridge in 312. His subsequent victory was an important turning-point towards the eventual supremacy of the Christian faith in Europe in the following centuries. The Christian faith in Anglo-Saxon England also ascribed importance to dreams and visions, as Bede's *Historia Ecclesiastica* amply indicates.

Critical issues

Modern 'Celtic Christianity' thrives on reinventing the romantic, 'Renanesque' constructs of the 'Celts' that were produced in the nineteenth century. In the present day these are presented in contrast to the tenets of 'conventional' Christianity, usually by reducing the latter to simple negative propositions, and ascribing correspondingly positive - and simplistic - positions to 'Celtic Christianity'. Generalisations and assumptions abound, and wishful thinking reaches its zenith. Despite the denials of several writers, a second Celtic Twilight glows attractively in many of the concepts at the heart of the movement, glossing over the less appealing features of the real faith of Christians in these islands in the early Middle Ages. As a result of further make-overs and manipulations, 'Celtic Christianity' functions largely as an up-to-date 'designer spirituality' which has been constructed to meet a range of contemporary needs. Because the Celts are perceived to be so 'far out', so utterly dead in historical terms, they can be treated with impunity as a *tabula rasa* on which to inscribe consoling responses to contemporary concerns. Somewhat paradoxically, the creators of 'Celtic Christianity' have thus disguised any possible distinctiveness in the 'Celtic' expression of the Christian faith under a cover of contemporary theory and creativity. The 'primitive' context is intended merely to carry and to affirm the modernist message, which, for the most part, has nothing whatsoever to do with the historical Christianity of the Celtic areas.

The distinctiveness of 'Celtic Christianity' is a key question worthy of further study. Was 'Celtic Christianity' really different from other forms of Christianity in the period before 1066? Is it correct to draw a firm line between 'Roman Christianity' and 'Celtic Christianity'? We have already noted that Christians in the Celtic areas of the British Isles were not out of step with Rome on major doctrines. The main differences were over the timing of the celebration of Easter and the form of the tonsure. Christianity in the British Isles was contextualised in terms of Celtic societies, but that does not mean that its fundamental beliefs and doctrines were different from those of the rest of Europe.

A further critical question relates to the alleged continuity of 'Celtic Christianity' into the present century, if not down to the present day. Does 'Celtic Christianity' still exist? We shall consider these matters in the course of Chapters 7-12 which tackle the story of the Christian faith in the British Isles - its origins, structures, attitudes to culture and veneration of the saints - from an historical perspective. At the heart of the 'historical' perspective, as popularly construed, however, there lies the 'Celtic Church'. This acts as a powerful symbol of 'Celtic' spiritual cohesion and supposed continuity across the centuries, offering a bridge from the historical to the contemporary, and it now requires to be examined.

CHAPTER 6

FOUNDATION OR FABRICATION? THE CONCEPTION OF THE 'CELTIC CHURCH'

People naturally associate 'Celtic Christianity' with the 'Celtic Church'; the one presupposes the other in the popular mind. Nowadays, however, 'Celtic Christianity' is the dominant theme; the 'Celtic Church' is a secondary issue, though still a potent concept. The change of focus is prompted partly by an awareness (on the part of most, though not all, writers) that the 'Celtic Church' belongs firmly to the past, and that it is difficult to argue the case for its existence much beyond c.1100. Some writers are gradually realising that the concept of the 'Celtic Church' is not easily defended even in the period before 1100, if this is indeed a meaningful boundary (see Chapter 11).

'Celtic Christianity', on the other hand, is not so readily restricted to particular periods. Like some elusive botanical species, it is able to defy environmental degradation, and lurk undetected in many nooks and crannies until the moment when the spiritual wayfarer stumbles happily upon it. Like the botanist, the finder becomes (sometimes overnight) an expert on the new species, and presents its family tree to an ever expectant public. When rescued skilfully from oblivion on the rugged hills, moors and shores of the 'Celtic Fringe', where it has been mystically nurtured by the wind and the waves, 'Celtic Christianity' appears to offer something that transcends time, and is both old and refreshingly new, remarkably relevant to the angsts of the age. It is thus even more flexible than the multi-faceted 'Celtic Church', and readily transmutes from rural plant to artificial flower of many varieties, lending itself gladly to countless exercises in flower-arranging. It is all too easy to yield to the temptation to display these colourful reconstructions in the antique vase of the 'old Celtic Church'.

The church of our fathers?

Despite modern enthusiasm for the 'spiritual' rather than the 'structural', most people who have an interest in the subject believe that the 'Celtic Church' lies at the heart of 'Celtic Christianity'. They are also generally aware of the ancient lineage of the 'Celtic Church'. It is indeed true that, unlike 'Celtic Christianity' in its present form, the conception of the 'Celtic Church' is no recent event. This

hallowed institution, wrapped in the mists of time, has attracted the
interest of a wide range of seekers and observers, historians and
ecclesiastical defenders, across the centuries since at least the time of
the Reformation. It has influenced the ways in which later churches
and denominations have defined themselves. Usually it has emerged
as a potent concept in the context of 'successionism', when post-
Reformation churches and various other groupings have felt a need to
find a place in a respectable pre-Reformation pedigree going back to
the early days of the Christian faith in Britain and Ireland. An interest
in the 'Celtic Church' has also emerged in recent years among
evangelical, and particularly charismatic, Protestants who subscribe
to 'restorationism', and seek to 'restore' an earlier model of the
church, usually on the basis of the New Testament. The 'Celtic
Church' has thus functioned, and still does, as the ancestral mother
church of these parts, offering a sense of history to new bodies and
helping to justify conventions and practices in older churches and
religious alignments.

For postmodern questers, the 'Celtic Church' helps to assuage
disillusionment with existing ecclesiastical structures, since it allows
them to believe that the perfect church, made in their own image,
once existed. It also provides a frame in which to interpret what they
see and hear in their search for 'Celtic Christianity'. Given the early
medieval associations of Celtic crosses, seekers of 'Celtic Christianity'
readily think that what is being presented to them goes right back to
Christianity as it was to be found in Ireland, Scotland and Wales - and
also Cornwall and Brittany - before 1100. Christianity was well
represented in these lands at that time, and it is easy, indeed comforting,
to assume that what 'Celtic Christianity' is offering is a rediscovery
of a form of faith which was well known in the early medieval period
but subsequently lost. It is also equally easy to conclude that 'Celtic
Christianity' derives from the so-called 'Celtic Church'. Crosses and
decorations and patterns add up to 'church' in the minds of most
people, and so the conclusion that there was once a single, cohesive
'Celtic Church', governed by a theology comparable to that of
modern writers, thrusts itself forward, filled with romantic charm for
many who have become tired of their own denominations or have
abandoned them entirely.

The church of the saints?

As we shall see in Chapters 7 and 8, there were indeed churches and
monasteries led by powerful leaders in Britain and Ireland before
1100. Some very well known leaders from this period include two
saints, Columba and Ninian, whose names are associated with early

Christianity in Scotland and are particularly prominent in the popular consciousness, not least because of the recent celebrations associated with the commemoration of the 1400th anniversary of the death of Columba in 597. Columba is primarily associated with the Inner Hebridean island of Iona, and, as the founder of a major monastic house whose memory has been well preserved, he has a claim to distinction which few fellow saints can rival. Other significant saints, recognised throughout the Insular world, include Patrick of Ireland, and David of Wales. Besides these men, we know the names of a host of other saints - like Mo-luag, Maolruba, and Cainnech - who, according to the sources, were active in the sixth and seventh centuries, but who did not achieve the degree of national and international recognition afforded to the likes of Columba and David (see Chapters 9 and 10).

In the modern popular mind, however, the 'Celtic Church' is pre-eminently a church of great and distinguished saints, and it is often difficult to convince its modern devotees that saints were the exceptional people. For every saint there were hundreds of unknown monks and clerics, going about their rituals and routines.

A singular church?

Yet, even if saints and lesser mortals were active in the British Isles, founding monasteries and churches in the period before 1100, such activity, in and of itself, does not add up to the existence of a single, institutional 'Celtic Church' which covered early Scotland, Pictland, Ireland, Wales, Cornwall, Brittany and (through the 'outreach' from Iona) the north of England. In each of these areas, different languages and cultures were dominant, and, while (nowadays) it is convenient to call some of these cultures 'Celtic', this label would have been meaningless to those who were alive in Columba's time and even in Bede's. It is perhaps closer to reality to identify more than one church - possibly a 'Gaelic Church' which functioned in the Gaelic-speaking regions of Ireland and Scotland, a 'Welsh Church' in Wales, and the corresponding entities in Cornwall, Brittany and Northumbria, each with a different complexion depending on the prevailing local culture. Most historians who are properly conversant with the evidence would support the view that not one, but several, 'Celtic Churches' existed in the 'Celtic' lands. John T. McNeill acknowledged this point in the title of his book, *The Celtic Churches* (plural). The truth is that any term involving the noun 'church' (singular), used in the collective sense, is likely to be misleading. Monasteries founded by particular abbots would have owed their allegiance to the founder and mother-house in the first instance, and allegiances of this kind could cross territorial boundaries with comparative ease (see Chapter 8).

It could also be argued that a descriptor such as 'Celtic', 'Gaelic' or 'Welsh' is equally misleading to the modern mind. What are we defining when we use such a term? We are defining part, but only part, of the cultural context of the church concerned. That part has to do with the local context. The early churches of Britain and Ireland had at least two cultural contexts, the one local, and the other international. In the early churches the Bible was studied in Latin, not in a vernacular translation. This is an important consideration, since it is a common popular misconception that the 'Celtic Church' differed from the 'Roman Church' in providing and using vernacular texts of the Scriptures, and eschewing Latin. The facts are otherwise; the so-called 'Celtic Church' was part of the much broader world of Christendom, and could be seen as belonging to the wider Latin Church. The use of the term 'Latin', however, is much less attractive; the 'Celtic' mystique is lost, and too much is conceded to the 'Roman' camp. This is unacceptable to those who (wrongly) perceive the two churches, 'Celtic' and 'Roman', as existing in fundamental distinction, if not outright opposition, to one another.

Not only does the term 'Celtic Church' impose its own range of cultural and ecclesiastical presuppositions on the early churches of Britain and Ireland, it also tends to produce an image of a single institution frozen in time and even in belief. The period covered by the 'Celtic Churches' extends across six or seven centuries, during which there were several reform movements (which will be discussed in greater detail in later chapters). These movements tackled the relationship of the churches to secular society and also to the practices of Christendom as a whole. The long-running debate about the dating of Easter was one such movement; the debate was by no means settled at the Synod of Whitby in 664, nor did the 'Celtic Churches' cease to exist thereafter (see Chapter 7). The early churches in Ireland were deeply influenced by their own society, and the acquisition of status and wealth brought decadence and spiritual torpor to some (see Chapter 8). In the eighth century, Irish churches were urged out of their worldly compromises by reformers known as the *Céli Dé* ('Clients of God'), who took a much stricter view of devotion and service. Indeed, the fondly imagined and allegedly pure 'Celtic Church' had its failings and abuses in various places at various stages in its history, and, like modern churches, it had to be called back to basic principles of faith and practice. Though in Scotland they seem to have merged eventually with the newer (post-1100) monastic orders, such as the Augustinians (see Chapter 11), the reforming *Céli Dé* nevertheless remained alive in the popular imagination, where they were periodically rediscovered and recycled as the 'Culdees', serving as role-models for those who wished to argue that a stream of pre-Reformation Presbyterianism had flowed across the centuries, to emerge strongly after 1560.

The 'Celtic Churches' which functioned in Britain and Ireland before 1100 varied in the manner in which they practised the faith, and there was no single regulatory body to impose a common identity. Yet it is also clear that these churches did have certain common features. They were in touch with one another, as the hagiographical accounts of training (in Wales) of early Irish monastic founders indicate. Monasticism flourished widely. The early Insular churches supported coenobitic monasticism, with monks living in very large and (by the standards of the time) very wealthy communities, but they also had a place for those living a hermit existence, some of whom would set off on voyages to remote islands (see Chapter 8). Christians in the Celtic lands also shared common doctrines. They believed in the efficacy of saints' relics. They were also particularly severe in their concepts of penance. Indeed, severe penance was one of the most conspicuous contributions made by Irish monks to the emerging profile of early medieval Christendom in Europe (see Chapter 5). This stricter and (to us) grimmer side of ecclesiastical life must be acknowledged fairly alongside the more appealing artistic and literary achievements of the churches.

We must take due note also that monasticism was not the only practical expression of the life of these churches. We must guard against seeing everything in terms of monastic establishments, while forgetting the pastoral aspect of ecclesiastical existence. Pastoral care was a significant concern of some churches, and seems to have been exercised through small chapels, served by inconspicuous priests who do not figure as prominently in the records as the monastic abbots. It is equally misleading to envisage a church or churches served solely by monastic *peregrini* who spent their lives perched on pinnacles, or inhabiting small islands, or traversing continents, in their deadly serious search for God. Such men did not sustain churches. Indeed, it might be said that their departure could do damage to monastic communities. Certainly the sources suggest that not all ecclesiastics were enthusiastic about those who departed to seek God in far-away places (see Chapter 9).

Reconstructing the 'Celtic Orthodox Church'

Besides the error of viewing the 'Celtic Church' as a monolithic entity, there is the danger of assuming that this hallowed institution was 'just like our own' - 'our own' being consistent with the ecclesiastical or theological position preferred by the seeker. The 'Celtic Church' which is thus a mirror-image of the seeker's views is writ large on the pages of much of modern 'Celtic Christianity'. This perception of the 'Celtic Church' is not necessarily the result of premeditated mischief. Often it occurs simply because the reconstructionist is (for want of a better word) ignorant, and unaware of the historical evidence for the proper 'Celtic Church' (if such there was); an unconscious remoulding thus takes place, which lends convenient support to whatever orthodox or unorthodox views may be held by the seeker.

On the other hand, the reconstruction of the 'Celtic Church' may take place quite deliberately by applying present-day perspectives retrospectively to the early evidence. The reconstructionist may feel constrained to remake the past for ideological, ecclesiological, theological, or even political reasons. Refashioning is undertaken in order to provide a means of repossessing the past in a manner which suits the position of the modern reconstructionist. The past is thus harnessed to validate the present.

Of course, the past is seldom a neutral commodity. Indeed, it is a commonplace that it can become the victim of the standpoint of the researcher. The reconstruction of the 'Celtic Church' represents a striking example of biased repossession of history. The 'Celtic Church' is particularly vulnerable to refashioning because of the changing nature of the church across the centuries, the perceived superiority of 'Celtic' Christians, and the need to find precedent for new alignments which emerge because of ecclesiastical fractures; but it is also sufficiently far back in the past to allow a very considerable degree of flexibility to the reconstructionist. It is much harder to reconstruct (let us say) the Methodist movement of the eighteenth century, since the facts of history tend to get in the way, and there are people who are sufficiently knowledgeable to protest at the spin-doctors when misrepresentation of historical fact assumes the position of truth. The 'Celtic Church', however, is fair game for all - Roman Catholics and Protestants of different hues, and various groups within the Eastern Orthodox family of churches.

In North America, new versions of the 'Celtic Church' have been produced during the 1990s (see Chapter 1). Currently a case is being presented in Britain for 'the restoration of the Celtic Orthodox Church', which claims a line of descent from a 'Celtic Church' which 'had much in common with the Eastern Church and holding the Orthodox Catholic Faith'. An attempt to recover the 'ancient Celtic/ British heritage of the old Church' is said to have been made when, 'in 1866, a Bishop was consecrated by the Old Syrian (non-Chalcedonian)

Orthodox Church and he arrived in Britain assuming the title "Bishop Julius of Iona" thus affirming, at the start of his Orthodox mission, his spiritual affinity with the historic centre of Celtic Christianity, Iona, where St Columba had his monastery.' This resulted in the creation of 'a tiny British Orthodox Church', which came to be 'centred on the ancient Celtic See of Glastonbury'. The British Orthodox Church achieved linkages with other like-minded groups, including Father Tudgual's monastery in Brittany. More recently, a connection was made with the Coptic Orthodox Church, but this has proved to be controversial. The present attempt to establish the 'Celtic Orthodox Church' distances itself from Coptic connections, and claims to belong to the 'Continuing Orthodox Church of the British Isles'. Broadly, the 'Celtic Orthodox Church' intends to restore Orthodoxy in a form which is consistent with what it sees as the 'Celtic' culture of the British Isles, and to avoid 'ludicrous gestures' such as the importing of Russian Orthodox nomenclature for priests and converts. 'Orthodoxy in Britain', it states, 'must be unpackaged from its foreign wrappings and allowed to adopt a native expression with its own Celtic ethnicity' (John Ross, *The Orthodox Family*, pp.23-6). In this spirit, the British Orthodox Church attempted to make 'a selection from the Scottish Metrical Psalter' which would be sung to 'traditional psalm tunes' (Deacon Kentigern MacGregor, letter to the author, 17.5.1994).

Thus, by means of new initiatives and various modern linkages between earlier customs and later foundations, the 'Celtic Church' is reincarnated in the Orthodox tradition in the British Isles. It is evident that certain aspects of the 'Celtic Church' are being reinvented in the process, and that an element of deliberate reshaping takes place in both directions. The 'Celtic Church' is moulded towards Orthodoxy, and Orthodoxy assumes features which it believes represent 'Celtic ethnicity'. This is common practice in other traditions also, and there too the process may include some very obvious refashioning. Recognising differences but wishing to accommodate the 'Celtic Church' as a worthy ally, if not the lineal ancestor, of his/her own cause, the refashioner may indulge in selective reconstruction, finding certain aspects of the 'Celtic Church' and its saints which are particularly appealing, and emphasising these at the expense of other less attractive tendencies. As a result of these processes, several different models of the 'Celtic Church' can be encountered, each of which meets the needs of a particular set of 'seekers' with an axe (or several axes) to grind. The following models represent the main Protestant versions.

The pre-Reformation Protestant 'Celtic Church'

The making and faking of the 'Celtic Church' is a hobby which reaches back into the late Middle Ages. It has flourished pre-eminently, though not by any means solely, within Protestant circles, and arises from the belief that a pure and uncorrupted faith preceded the rise of Rome. Many Protestant apologists have represented the 'Celtic Church' as if it were the precursor of reformed Christianity. There are various reasons for this. The chief reason is that the Reformation presented Protestants with a major problem in repossessing the pre-Reformation past. The concept of 'pre-Reformation Protestantism', based on an appeal to antiquity, was therefore elaborated by the Magdeburg Centuriators, whose thinking is represented by the work of Matthias Flacius Illyricus (1520-75). The allegedly Protestant line was traced back through martyrs who had been condemned as heretics by the papacy, and included such well-known groups as the Waldensians, Wycliffites and Hussites. Purity and protest, later to be overlaid by papistical corruption, were at the heart of the case.

While it can be readily accepted that there were serious abuses in the medieval church, the argument for a pre-Reformation stream of Protestantism is open to serious doubt. The Middle Ages in the West, prior to the eleventh century and the separation of Eastern (Greek) Christianity from Western (Latin) Christianity, were broadly catholic; thereafter, distinctive western and eastern traditions emerged. In the 'Celtic' areas, a dominant catholic Christian ethos interacted with the 'Celtic' culture of each region (see Chapter 11). In Ireland, after the Reformation, Roman Catholicism was maintained as the dominant form of Christianity. In Wales and Scotland, on the other hand, the Reformation came with particular force, leading to the adoption of Protestantism and the establishment of Protestant national churches (see Chapter 12). As a result, Protestants faced major challenges when seeking a precedent for their expression of the faith. Because they were reluctant to admit that true spiritual enlightenment existed within the Roman Catholic church, they had to blank out much of the later Middle Ages. Yet God had to be shown to be active in the past. This induced Protestants in Wales, Scotland and Ireland to construct a tunnel which ran beneath the Roman Catholicism of the Middle Ages. When they arrived at the far end of the tunnel, and emerged into the bewitching moonlight of their imagined past, they found a 'Celtic Church' which showed remarkably Protestant features. This allowed them to claim 'Celtic' backing for Protestantism.

The Welsh version of this retrospective repossession of history, as packaged by Bishop Richard Davies of St Asaph in his preface to the first translation of the New Testament into Welsh in 1567, is described by Professor Glanmor Williams (*The Welsh and their Religion*, p.40):

Like Reformers elsewhere, Davies was convinced that the
Reformation was no new-fangled heresy but that it
represented a return to the purity of teaching and worship
established by Jesus Christ and his followers in the early
Church; only at later stages were corruptions introduced by
the papacy and its agents. As far as Wales was concerned he
rehearsed a number of firmly-held convictions but gave
them a strongly Protestant twist. He referred lovingly to the
belief that Britain had first been converted to Christianity
by Joseph of Arimathea, who had planted the faith in all its
gospel immaculacy. It had subsequently been maintained by
the people of Wales intact and uncontaminated in spite of
Roman persecution, the heresies of Pelagius and others,
Anglo-Saxon paganism, and - most crucial of all - in face of
that brand of Christianity tainted by papal superstition
which Augustine of Canterbury had brought to England as
an emissary of Rome. Only as a result of being forced to
accept the adulterated papism at the point of the sword had
the Welsh eventually been dragged down into the mire of
Roman superstition and idolatry. Now, after centuries of
benighted ignorance and papal corruption, Davies argued,
the people of Wales were being led back to the realm of truth
and light by virtue of what he described as the 'second
flowering of the Gospel'.

Glanmor Williams goes on to comment that 'Davies's reconstruction
of their history proved to be compellingly influential and appealing
among many of his fellow-countrymen on three counts. It bonded the
Reformation to some of the oldest and most venerable themes of the
history of the Welsh. Further, it bluntly refuted the commonly-made
suggestion that Reformation teaching was a neoteric, upstart heresy,
lacking roots in earlier faith and history, and sought to show, on the
contrary, that it was grounded in the earliest and most glorious phase
of Christianity in Britain. Finally, it met, head-on, the criticism that
the Reformation represented an alien, English creed, imposed on the
Welsh by the diktat of an unsympathetic government; in Davies's
eyes it was papist beliefs which had originally been forced on the
Welsh by their Saxon enemies. Implicit in all that he wrote was the
idea that it was the Reformation that was the great purpose for which
God had preserved the Welsh people and their language.'

Lurking behind Davies's view, and that of other reformers, was
the notion that 'the faith of the early Britons had been unshakeably
founded on scriptural authority and that a vernacular Bible had been
an essential and greatly loved possession among them. To restore such
a Welsh version of the Scriptures was their first priority' (p.41).

In Scotland, the sole Gaelic (and thus Celtic) work which is directly relevant to the Reformation, namely John Carswell's translation of the *Book of Common Order* published in 1567, makes no mention whatsoever of any earlier proto-Protestant expression of the faith which could act as a model for the reformed church. Carswell compares his patron, the fifth Earl of Argyll, to Old Testament kings, and not to Celtic saints. His approach appears to be broadly consistent with the views of the first generation of Scottish reformers, whose model for the church was derived from the Bible, and pre-eminently from the New Testament. Celtic saints were irrelevant. What mattered was the restoration of what the reformers, including John Knox, regarded as the true church, exhibiting the 'notes' of 'true' preaching of the word, 'right' administration of the sacraments, and discipline uprightly administered. The reformers saw no need for church traditions, medieval accretions, or lineal succession. The only succession - which was, perhaps, more strictly a rediscovery on their part - was the transmission of doctrine through the ages, to be tested by the application of scriptural exegesis.

Nevertheless, an interest in the 'Celtic Church' and its saints began to appear among Scottish Protestants by the second quarter of the seventeenth century, when matters of church polity assumed importance, and the Reformation was no longer an issue. On the episcopal side, Archbishop John Spottiswoode (1565-1639) claimed in his *History of the Church of Scotland* (written c.1638-39, but published in 1655), when discussing St Ninian, that the church in Scotland had been founded by bishops and not by presbyters and monks. This counteracted the presbyterian view, put forward by David Calderwood (1575-1651) in his *True History of the Church of Scotland* (completed in 1631, though not published until 1678), that Columba was a presbyter and not a bishop, and that the reformed church had its roots among the Culdees, who, according to Calderwood, were not monks, but holy men who taught the people how to worship God. Calderwood's Culdees had their starting-point, not in post-Reformation partisanship, but in the mistakes made by the sixteeenth-century Scottish historian, Hector Boece (c.1470-1536), first Principal of the University of Aberdeen. Misled by much earlier misinterpretations, Boece confused the *Scotti* ('Irish') with the Scots, and thought that Palladius had been sent to Scotland, not Ireland. Professor John Duke (*The Columban Church*, pp.165-6) summarises this argument as follows:

> Boece wrote in the beginning of the sixteenth century - the century in which the Reformation swept over Scotland - and his description of the Culdees, as they came to be called, accepted as history, was eagerly acclaimed by Protestant

writers, and pressed into the controversy which had broken out with the Church of Rome. The argument, which was based upon Boece, was something as follows: if Palladius was the first Bishop who was sent to Scotland, and if there were Christians in Scotland for more than two hundred years before his arrival, then these Christians must have been Presbyterians: the earliest Church in Scotland was therefore Presbyterian, and not Episcopal; and its ministers were these Culdees - the argument seemed irrefutable; and so the fable grew. A still further development took place when the Culdees came to be identified with the followers of St Columba. The argument proceeded as follows: St Columba, as was well known, Bede being witness, was a Presbyter, and never held the rank of Bishop; and, if a Presbyter, then he and all his monks must have been Presbyterians; and between Presbyterian Culdees, who already existed in Scotland before St Columba, and the Presbyterian followers of St Columba, there was small difference. When the Columban Church went down before the Church of Rome in the eighth century, the nonconformists who remained faithful to the old Presbyterian traditions of the Church of Scotland were the Culdees. The Reformation of the Church of Scotland in the sixteenth century was but the restoration of the Church of Scotland to its original state of purity and simplicity, which it had enjoyed under the early Culdees, before it had been corrupted by the inventions and errors of Rome.

The role of Columba was affirmed by Scottish Presbyterians at home and abroad. Alexander Petrie (c.1594-1662), a Presbyterian who became minister of the Scots kirk at Rotterdam, in his *Compendious History of the Catholick Church from the year 600 untill the year 1600*, published in The Hague in 1662, stressed the importance of Columba, 'a man of excellent holiness and learning', who made Iona 'a most famous seminary of learning' which 'did resist the beginnings of antichristian pride at home and in our neighbour country.'

In Ireland in the first half of the seventeenth century, the early 'Celtic Church' was similarly enlisted to give support to the Protestant cause, in an episcopal context. James Ussher (1581-1656), who became Archbishop of Armagh in 1625, was engaged in a campaign to demonstrate that the Church of Ireland was the descendant of a Protestant form of the 'Celtic Church'. In his *Discourse on the Religion Anciently Professed by the Irish and the British* (1623), Ussher set out his main arguments, claiming in the dedicatory epistle that 'the religion professed by the ancient bishops, priests, monks and other Christians in this land, was for substance the very same with that which now by public authority is maintained therein against the foreign doctrine brought in thither in latter times by the bishop of Rome's followers.' Ussher argued the case for an Irish church which did not believe in purgatory, and did not employ prayers for the dead. As Professor Alan Ford has shown ('Ussher and Irish Identity', pp.201-2), Ussher 'contrasted the deeply religious Celtic monks with the "hypocrisy, pride, idleness, and uncleannness of those evil beasts and slothful bellies that afterward succeeded in their room"'.

In England, where the Reformation achieved a less complete break with the Catholic past, later reformers such as Matthew Parker, Archbishop of Canterbury under Elizabeth I and a noted antiquarian and collector of manuscripts, dug into antiquity to find a precedent for Anglicanism. So too did his colleague John Jewel, Bishop of Salisbury, who published his *Apologia Ecclesiae Anglicanae* in 1562. Within Anglicanism the ground was probably more fertile for the presentation of a 'Celtic Church' which was more 'catholic' than would be acceptable in Scotland, Ireland or Wales. The question of respectable roots for English Protestantism encouraged invention. A thirteenth-century legend which linked Joseph of Arimathea with Glastonbury, an ecclesiastical site notorious for its self-interested cult-collecting, raised the possibility of an early connection between the apostles (and even Christ himself) and England, and surfaced in both Welsh and English contexts. The legend has never been entirely eliminated from more speculative minds, and continues to have its advocates in the present day. This is exemplified most recently in Gordon Strachan's remarkable volume, *Jesus the Master Builder* (1998), a complex but entertaining work containing much ingenious theorising, best understood by numerologists and Pythagorean enthusiasts. In fact, the introduction of Joseph of Arimathea to the British scene owes less to druids or numerology or historical fact than it does to Arthurian legends which were intended to christianise Arthur and his court by associating them with the quest for the Grail. Dr Strachan conspicuously fails to address this legendary context, and largely overlooks the dynamics of an essentially literary motif which interacted with church politics and the claims of Glastonbury.

The 'Celtic Church' continued to have a validating role within the Anglican Church. When the Oxford Movement emerged among 'high' Anglicans in the first half of the nineteenth century and led to defections to Rome, one of its participants, a Welshman named Isaac Williams (1802-65), who is best known as a romantic poet strongly influenced by Wordsworth, 'remained in Anglicanism and defended its catholicity by delving into the history of the ancient Celtic Church'

(R. Chapman, *Faith and Revolt*, pp.35-6). The appeal of the 'Celtic Church' within Anglicanism has undoubtedly been helped by the broad catholicity of the latter, which it ascribes to the former. This 'catholic' vision is surely one of the factors which facilitates the current mania for the reinvention of 'Celtic Christianity' within the Anglican communion. Nevertheless, avowedly Protestant and Reformed bodies also exist in England outside the pale of Anglicanism. When these show an interest in the 'Celtic Church', they tend to espouse the much less 'catholic' and much more vigorously pre-Reformation Protestant model.

Since the mid-1980s, the 'Celtic Church' has been reclaimed particularly strongly by Anglican clergy, notably in the archdiocese of York, who have espoused 'Celtic Christianity' with enthusiasm and appear to be anxious to find for their church a pedigree which leans away from Canterbury and Anglo-Saxon culture. In the course of constructing this Anglo-Saxon 'bypass' (see Chapter 7), the new builders enlist the support of the 'Celtic Church', apparently seeing it as an institution which is broadly 'British' and represents an underlying 'Celtic' culture which was not only well represented in Northumbria, but was also distributed across the British Isles before the Anglo-Saxons invaded the land. In such a reconstruction, indigenous catholicity becomes native, 'Celtic' and tolerant; formal Anglicanism becomes alien, 'Roman' and dictatorial. Thus, in order to distance themselves from the constrictive claims of prelacy, modern Anglicans who are chafing under the yoke of Canterbury take refuge in a version of the 'Celtic Church' pedigree which was once manufactured by their ancestors in the sixteenth and seventeenth centuries to justify their break with Rome and to present the doctrines of the Reformation as a return to an earlier, indigenous model of faith and practice.

The denominational 'Celtic Church'

As the Anglican version shows, the pre-Reformation Protestant model of the 'Celtic Church' can be fine-tuned to meet the needs of particular denominations or ecclesiological positions within Protestantism. Within Presbyterianism, as it has fractured and remoulded itself across the centuries, the question of which part is the 'real' church has vexed 'seceders' and 'remainers' alike. Consequently particular churches, or parts of churches, have tried to lay closer claims than others to a pedigree based on the 'Celtic Church'. It was a minister of the post-Disruption Free Church of Scotland, the Revd Dr Thomas McLauchlan (1815-86), who, in his *Early Scottish Church* (1865), gave one of the biggest nineteenth-century boosts to the myths surrounding the Culdees. To him the 'ancient Culdee Church' represented the indigenous Scottish wing of the ideal 'Celtic

Church'. He was also among the earliest modern writers of conservative
Presbyterianism to reiterate the perspectives of Bede (see Chapter 7)
to denominational advantage. Following Bede, he envisaged a clear,
unequivocal distinction between the early 'Celtic' missionaries and
their 'Roman' counterparts who had come to the British Isles wth
Augustine, the one group being humble and self-denying, and the
other proud and ambitious (p.221):

> The king [Oswald of Northumbria] appointed Aidan the
> island of Lindisfarne, or Holy Isle on the east coast of
> Northumberland, as his residence. This may have been done
> at the request of the missionary himself, for these men always
> sought such retreats, and in selecting Lindisfarne, Aidan
> followed the example of Columba in choosing Iona, and of
> Baithean in choosing Tyree. How different from the Roman
> emissaries Augustine and Paulinus! The one chose Canterbury,
> the other York; fit emblem of the ambition of one religious
> system, and the humility and self-denial of the other.

McLauchlan's distinction, firmly drawn in order to set Scottish
Presbyterianism (and presumably the Free Church in particular) apart
from 'Rome' and closer to Columba, has been rediscovered and re-
articulated many times, not because people are reading McLauchlan's
tedious tome, but because the contrast is deeply engrained in the
popular mind. It lies at the heart of much of the current fad for 'Celtic
Christianity' in England, and forms part of popular ecclesiology in
Scotland.

The notion that the Free Church of Scotland was a reincarnation
of the 'Celtic Church' was particularly potent in the later nineteenth
century. In 1892, on the eve of the emergence of the Free Presyterian
Church from the Free Church in 1893, Nigel MacNeill (*The Literature
of the Highlands*, pp.120-1) expressed the view that the 'Celtic Church'
was in effect the 'early Free Church'. Its radiant, early witness had been
obscured by the pall of Roman Catholicism, and did not re-emerge
until 1843:

> In order to reach the heart of this Church, we must pierce
> through that belt of ecclesiastical and religious darkness
> which Papal Rome wove round the body of our national life
> during the four centuries which preceded the Reformation.
> Beyond these centuries we are enabled at once to grasp that
> one outstanding fact in our early annals, that from the days
> of Ninian, in the beginning of the fifth century, to the
> accession of the 'Sair Saint' King David, in 1124, a Free
> Church, comparatively evangelical and aggressive, existed in
> Scotland for a period of 700 years. No definite attempt has

been made to show the full national significance of this fact. If we contrast that period of 700 years with the following period of similar length, we find that during the first half of the latter, decay and death prevailed; and that even during the second half, with all the advantages attendant on post-Reformation times, large tracts of our country, once aglow with gospel life, remained practically heathen until the lost ground began to be reconquered and reclaimed by the modern Free Church of Scotland.

Within the Free Church of Scotland in more recent times, some have continued to regard the 'Celtic Church' as the ancestor of their denomination, and have even been prepared to suggest that it had a very similar missionary purpose. Douglas MacMillan (d.1991), formerly Professor of Church History in the Free Church College in Edinburgh, echoes the views of Nigel MacNeill in his wistful depiction of the life and demise of the 'old Celtic Church':

> Though many earnest missionaries worked northwards from Whithorn in the fifth century, the name which stands out most prominently in the emergence of the Celtic Church is that of Columba who landed on the island of Iona on 12th May 563. The teaching of this zealous missionary who, with his disciples, had crossed over the Irish sea, was warmly evangelical and under his labours the North and the West of Scotland became the cradle of a robust, literate Church which in its best days sent many Christian scholars and preachers out across Europe.
>
> This is not the place to dwell on the forces which eventually obscured, and almost extinguished, the witness of that old Celtic Church. It is enough to say that under the invasion of Norse paganism, and medieval Roman Catholicism, the darkness of a long spiritual night settled over the Scottish Highlands. The Word of God became a closed book to the people, and many of their instructors in spiritual things were not only ignorant of Scripture in the letter, but were without any experience of its sanctifying power (Campbell, *Gleanings of Highland Harvest*, p.130):

Here, as in MacNeill's account, a clear contrast is envisaged between the 'old Celtic Church' and Roman Catholicism, which is perceived to be on a par with Norse paganism. A contrast is also drawn between spiritual enlightenment, offered by the 'Celtic Church', and general ignorance after its eclipse. The 'Celtic Church' continues to be seen, in some Presbyterian circles, as the pre-Reformation torch-bearer of truth.

Beyond Presbyterianism, nonconformists have occasionally cast an eye at the 'Celtic Church', and have used it for their own ends. Baptists, for instance, have invoked the 'Celtic Church' as an example of independency and voluntaryism, and, in support of the case for 'adult baptism' (strictly 'believer's baptism'), they have sometimes alluded to the example of Columba in baptising adults. By this argument, the 'Celtic Church' is perceived to be an early 'Baptist Church'. In 1872, William Fraser, a native of Strathspey who served as minister of Tiverton Baptist Church, Bruce Co., Ontario, published an apologetic booklet, *A Historical Sketch of the Baptist Body all the way down from the Apostolic Age*. Fraser used his perception of the 'Celtic Church' to emphasise the voluntaryist nature of the body to which he belonged. Michael Haykin notes (*The Believers Church*, p.49):

> What is unique about Fraser's *Historical Sketch* is the lengthy section devoted to showing that the Celtic Church in Britain was actually a Baptist body. This interest was obviously linked to Fraser's background. The Celtic Church, the writer asserted, 'had no connections with the state, therefore it was more simple, pure and scriptural in faith and practice.' No pastor claimed lordship over another, 'for they were all brethren'. They rejected infant baptism, a claim Fraser based on his own observation of a baptistery in Iona. Moveover, the Celts' long isolation from ecclesial developments on the European continent 'naturally served to strengthen and confirm in them the spirit of ecclesiastical freedom.'

The concepts underlying the Protestant models of the 'Celtic Church' outlined above have a long history, dating back to at least the time of Spottiswoode, Calderwood and Ussher. However, the retrospective repossession of the past, in accordance with the needs of the present, still possesses creative energy. Further models of the 'Celtic Church' have been elaborated and presented in some of the recent writing on 'Celtic Christianity'.

The charismatic 'Celtic Church'

This is perhaps the most obvious attempt to re-interpret the 'Celtic Church' in a manner which accords with the preferred ecclesiology and theology of a particularly potent trend within modern church life. By this reformulation, the 'Celtic Church' becomes either a collection of small churches or a single 'community' of a type which appears to reflect the cell model characteristic of the charismatic movement. It is ironic that in his wistful book, *Restoring the Woven Cord: Strands of Celtic Christianity for the Church Today*, Michael Mitton should observe that:

> So many are approaching the Celtic church interested only in
> their own agendas. It would be all too easy for me, as someone
> who is closely involved in charismatic renewal, to pick out the
> charismatic strands and ignore some of the others which
> challenge me.

Having recognised the problem, he proceeds to portray the 'Celtic Church' in terms which are closely reminiscent of the language of charismatic 'renewal'. In fact, Mitton perceives the 'Celtic Church' as the debtor of a 'renewal movement', that of the 'Desert Fathers and Mothers who were a great inspiration to the Celtic church' (p.43). This is correct in broad terms, since it is acknowledged that the form of eremitic monasticism which was one of the strands of early Irish and British monasticism appears to have been influenced by the practices of the so-called Desert Fathers. One might, however, argue much more cogently that this was a movement of 'rejection' (i.e. rejection of existing ecclesiastical practices) rather than one of 'renewal'.

But what should one make of the contribution of the 'Desert Mothers' to the 'Celtic Church'? Although it is known that women did form part of some 'communities in the desert' in the fourth century A.D., when a coenobitic element was introduced, it is most unlikely that there were any 'Desert Mothers' who contributed anything to the development of the 'Celtic Church'. Their alleged influence is no more than a mirage in the modern desert of wish-fulfilment, consistent with the aspirations of those who want to be politically correct, even when that means being historically incorrect, and adjusting the facts to suit the theory. Overlaying the real evidence with political correctness in this way is part of the process by which much of the modern 'Celtic Church' has been produced, and by which it becomes relevant to all modern issues, including the desire to grant clerical recognition and status to women - another of the bones of ecclesiastical contention which dominate our institutional, angst-ridden age.

Although the early churches of Britain and Ireland admitted women as nuns, they did not grant them independent legal status. Society was avowedly patriarchal, and women who 'made it to the top' as abbesses were the exceptions that proved the rule. As Professor Fergus Kelly argues (*Early Irish Law*, p.77) it is likely that the church helped to raise the status of women in early Ireland, but this does not mean that it emancipated them; in the words of an early Irish law tract, a woman remained incapable 'of sale or purchase or transaction without the authorization of one of her superiors' *(ibid.,* p.76) and such superiors were normally men. The 'Celtic Church' offered no escape from, or counterbalance to, the claims of patriarchy. The 'feminist Celtic Church' is thus another figment of contemporary counter-cultural imagination.

The counter-cultural 'Celtic Church'

One of the main functions of the modern, reconstructed 'Celtic Church' is to provide a counterbalance to the various established or denominational churches with which the writer is out of sympathy. Not infrequently the 'Celtic Church' is portrayed as a contrast to the excesses of modern church life, regardless of denomination. Thus Michael Mitton tells us (*Woven Cord*, p.19):

> The Celtic church would have been appalled by anything to do with the so-called 'prosperity gospel' teaching of the smart-suited tele-evangelists who promise wealth and success. It also challenges the church's use of power and wealth at every level.

This claim is, of course, unsustainable, as is amply demonstrated by the manner in which early Irish monasteries and clergy were able to grow rich on the basis of their close links with secular society, through clientship and the various offerings given to the church by the laity (see Chapter 8). As Professor Fergus Kelly of the Dublin Institute for Advanced Studies has written (*Early Irish Law*, p.3), 'The result is a very wealthy Church, with the resources to fund the scholarship and craftsmanship for which Early Christian Ireland is renowned.' Power and wealth thus resided in the 'Celtic Church' to a significant degree. The simple fact that Vikings made a bee-line for the Irish monasteries shows that they had something of a reputation as repositories of splendid loot. The Irish monasteries did, of course, accommodate hermits and anchorites who renounced the world and (sometimes) the monastery, but this was not the only way of living the holy life in early Ireland (see Chapter 9).

The ecumenical 'Celtic Church'

The 'Celtic Church' has come to be associated with ecumenism, largely because a certain strand of retrospective reconstructionism has emanated from communities which seek to encourage the interaction of different denominations and faiths. This approach to the 'Celtic Church' is exemplified in the thinking of the Revd George MacLeod, founder of the Iona Community. It is also evident in other communities, such as the Nether Springs in Northumbria.

Like most of the ideals ascribed to the supposed 'Celtic Church' by modern revampers, this is somewhat anachronistic. When the 'Celtic Church' was in existence prior to 1100, there was no other church which differed from it substantially in the basic doctrines of the faith, or with which it needed, or desired, to achieve unity. The early medieval church, in different parts of Europe, placed different emphases on matters of practice and expression, as required or created by various social contexts, but there were no major divergences between its 'parts' in matters of belief (see Chapter 5 for fuller discussion of this theme).

Overview

Reviewing the interpretations of the 'Celtic Church' across the centuries, we may justly conclude that it has acted as the ecclesiastical 'comforter' of those who wish to find a suitable pedigree for a new foundation, or to provide an existing institution with a strong historical precedent, or to create a church which has none of the vices of the more recent institution(s) with which they are familiar. Although there is considerable variety in their presentations of the so-called 'Celtic Church', all the interpreters perceive it as the fountain-head of whatever form of purity is required to reinforce recent foundations or to counteract the ecclesiastical ills of the present time or the immediate past. By choosing the most attractive building-blocks, while deftly ignoring those that do not fit the model, the reconstructors can guarantee that the faith as well as the practice of the old but ever-new 'Celtic Church' will be in tune with their views of the past and their aspirations for the future. The re-imagined 'Celtic Church' thus fulfils ancestral, validatory and therapeutic roles relative to modern church structures, especially at times of anxiety, stress or fracture within the larger denominations.

Yet it is not enough to deconstruct modern notions of the 'Celtic Church' and 'Celtic Christianity'. We must also ask how the 'Celtic Church' and 'Celtic Christianity' square with the historical record. What was the complexion of the Christian faith in the British Isles, including its structures and its response to culture, really like, and how do we access it accurately? By what means did the faith come to these islands, and how was it propagated? What changes have taken place across the centuries, and how have these affected the alleged 'Celtic' continuum? These are the questions to which we must now turn.

CHAPTER 7
APOSTLES AND ABORIGINALS:
THE ORIGINS AND DISSEMINATION
OF THE CHRISTIAN FAITH
IN BRITAIN AND IRELAND

At this point we change perspective, and explore the validity of 'Celtic Christianity' more specifically from the farther end, that is to say, beginning from c. 400 A.D. and travelling onwards into the later Middle Ages. As has been argued in previous chapters, 'Celtic Christianity' carries a substantial load of modern presuppositions, some of them deriving from nineteenth-century reconstructions of the Celts, and others from the closing years of the twentieth century. It is not intended that the following chapters should provide a detailed account of the history of the Christian faith in these islands, since such accounts are readily available elsewhere (see the Bibliography); rather, they will offer summaries of the main patterns, and attempt to clarify areas of confusion and misconception which have contributed to the profile of contemporary, reconstructed 'Celtic Christianity'. Some of these areas have been mentioned briefly in earlier discussion (especially in Chapters 5 and 6).

In this chapter we shall tackle the broad theme of the arrival of Christianity in the British Isles. This is an important issue within 'Celtic Christianity', since the general view is that 'Celtic Christians' had a pre-eminent, if not a largely exclusive, role in the evangelisation of these islands. There is also more than a hint in the designation of some of the saints as 'our aboriginal apostles' that the 'Celts' were somehow able to tap into a stream of Christianity which had not been sullied by transmission through other agencies.

We shall also look at the ways in which early Christian 'missionaries' took the faith to various parts of these islands. We shall assess briefly the careers of Ninian (Nynia), Patrick (a plurality of Patricks, in fact), and glance quickly at another well-known early Briton, Pelagius, who is frequently mentioned by writers on 'Celtic Christianity'. The contribution of Irish monks and 'missionaries' (including Columba) will be considered, and so too will the mission which Pope Gregory the Great initiated when he sent Augustine to England in 597, the year in which Columba died. The attitudes and relationships of the British and Gaelic Christians to one another and to the Anglo-Saxon world will be assessed. How these different

James Macpherson (1736–96)

Ernest Renan (1823–92)

Matthew Arnold (1822–88)

Kuno Myer (1858–1919)

Douglas Hyde (1860–1949)

Alexander Carmichael (1832–1912)

groups related to Rome is another critical issue which requires to be discussed, since it is a particularly fruitful source of misunderstanding among the promoters of 'Celtic Christianity'.

Sources

It is important to urge a strong note of caution at the very beginning. Not only do we have much less in the way of source material than we would wish, but a great deal of it is also very difficult to interpret. The sources for the early ecclesiastical history of the Celtic areas of the British Isles are not by any means treasure-troves of hard fact, filled with transparent information which is immediately accessible to the enthusiast. They represent particular genres of literary and historical recording, and are subject to the conventions which distinguish these genres. Early annalistic sources, for example, are notoriously terse, and are shaped by the plenitude or paucity of the knowledge available to the annalist; they are also the victim of the annalist's biases, both political and ecclesiastical. Sermons and extended reflections on 'the state of the church' (as in Gildas's famous tirade against contemporary ills) have their own agendas, and these tend to over-ride and to submerge the historical fact-base. This process of 'being creative with the facts' is also very evident in the writings which describe the Lives of the saints - the Latin *vitae* which constitute the genre known as hagiography. The *vitae* were composed not only to extol the saint, but frequently to bring prestige and power to his successors, their churches and their wider political causes. The *vitae* also followed well established conventions, and not infrequently borrowed incidents from one another. Two foundationally important early saints' Lives, Athanasius's Life of Antony, and Sulpicius Severus's Life of Martin, have influenced both the shape and some of the content of Adomnán's Life of Columba, for example. Writers of saints' Lives operated by the literary modes of their own time, and did not always distinguish clearly between 'legend' and 'history' in telling their story. Adomnán was comparatively unusual in taking pains to identify some of the sources which supplied information about Columba. The interaction of legend and history is also evident in other genres, and can be seen even in annals.

The Celtic areas of the British Isles lack an early, single-volume history of the faith in these parts. On the Anglo-Saxon side, however, Bede's *Historia Ecclesiastica Gentis Anglorum* ('Ecclesiastical History of the English People'), composed around 731, furnishes a major source for the Anglo-Saxon dimensions and certain aspects of the Celtic contribution. Bede provides some of the earliest information about several very shadowy Celtic saints, such as Ninian. He is also particularly well informed about the history of the faith in the north-east of England, as we might expect from a monk who was located in Jarrow. Much of our knowledge of the mission which emanated from Iona, and, in the person of Aidan, reached Lindisfarne and beyond, is derived primarily from Bede. Bede, however, is not without his own biases; while sympathetic to Iona, for example, he is glad to berate the British (i.e. the early Welsh-speaking Britons) for their failure to evangelise the Anglo-Saxons. Bede's great story is justly held together by his admiration for the mission of Augustine, beginning in Kent in 597 A.D.

The difficulties in interpreting the sources, and in making the various bits and pieces of evidence fit together convincingly, are recognised by the scholars who explore the original texts. Nor are scholars themselves free from bias, and rival theories are not unknown; the available material offers much scope for differing interpretations. There have been numerous attempts, ancient and modern, to interpret the early founding figures of Christianity in such a way as to score points for a particular theory, for a denominational stance, or for the national or local image. Both Ninian and Patrick, for example, are surrounded in academic controversy. The controversy concerns their origins, dates, roles and achievements - in fact, just about everything that has to do with their lives. There have been occasions too when the academic controversy has flared into rather more of a feud, especially in the case of Patrick, and, as a result, these saintly figures have generated much more heat than light. In contrast to the painstaking, and often painful, explorations of scholars who wrestle with the sources at first hand, and dispute one another's findings in proper academic debate, writers on 'Celtic Christianity' frequently supply very simple, very clear 'answers', where there are *no* simple or clear answers. The modern writers are often in no doubt as to when Ninian founded his church or when he travelled to the Picts or when he went to Rome. Doubt is absent, not because new evidence has come to light, but because there is no meaningful interaction with the original primary sources. Writers on popular 'Celtic Christianity' often go boldly where angels, even academic angels, fear to tread.

Roman remains

The beginnings of the Christian faith in the British Isles take us back to the Roman occupation of Britain and to the years before 410 A.D. The importance of the Roman presence in creating a structure conducive to the introduction of Christianity to these islands cannot be over-emphasised. Any attempt to dismiss it and to afford a primary place to 'our aboriginal apostles' cannot be supported by the evidence. Christianity was doubtless among the motley gathering of 'cults' that the Romans and their camp-followers introduced to Britain.

Christianity is detectable at various levels in Romano-British society. Nevertheless, this is applicable only to certain parts of Britain and to certain levels of society. There is no case for believing that Christianity was uniformly spread throughout Britain during the time of the Roman occupation. This requires to be emphasised because certain scholars have occasionally gone further than the evidence warrants by arguing that, in early Britain, there were diocesan structures (i.e. bishops and their sees) based on tribal kingdoms and cathedral cities. We do know that there were three British bishops present at the the the Council of Arles in 314 A.D. - from London, York and, possibly, Lincoln - but that does not prove that Christianity was rooted at all, far less structured in a diocesan form, in other parts of Britain. It does, however, show clearly enough that there was some structure, and that British clergy interacted with those beyond their own shores.

In general terms, the evidence tends to show that Christianity in the Roman and sub-Roman period was apparently most firmly attested in the Lowland Zone in the south and south-east of Britain, including south-east Wales (present-day Gwent), and in the region at the western end of Hadrian's Wall, that is to say in the area around the Solway Firth, around Carlisle, including parts of Galloway. It has been argued from this that there may have been a diocese here, based on the old tribal kingdom of Rheged, with a bishop's seat at Carlisle by the later fourth century. It is generally accepted that there was a tendency within the Roman Empire to create bishoprics at important centres of population, forts or frontier stations, and it is argued that Carlisle would suit this context.

The evidence for the late Roman period falls within the following categories.

(1) Archaeological: The spade and trowel help us to some extent, by the slow process of unearthing artefacts and outlines of buildings which point to the presence of Christianity in certain areas of Britain.

(a) Artefacts: Archaeologists stress the danger of drawing too many conclusions from artefacts, particularly if they are portable, and could have been carried by travellers or merchants or formed part of a loot. However, there have been some recent discoveries of hoards of silver plate, consisting of vessels used in Christian ritual, and some of these discoveries at least may point to a relatively stable Christianity community in the vicinity of the find-spot. For example, a hoard of such vessels (28 objects) was found in 1975 at Water Newton in Cambridgeshire, apparently within the boundaries of the Roman town of Durobrivae. The evidence for a Christian use is furnished by the prevalence of the *chi-rho* symbol on the items: there are fifteen examples of the Constantinian form of the *chi-rho*. One inscribed cup bears testimony to the presence of a sanctuary or church. Other finds are more arguable in terms of their local significance, and we must always bear in mind that the *chi-rho* may have been no more than a kind of logo in some instances. Discoveries of artefacts which have the *chi-rho* on at least one item have been made at Appleshaw, Hampshire (pewter vessels) and Biddulph, Staffordshire. Another artefact with Christian connotations is the lead tank, known as the Wigginholt tank, which was apparently used for baptisms. Tanks of this kind have been found at several locations in East Anglia.

(b) Buildings: We are on firmer ground here, of course, because buildings were not portable. There are two sorts of evidence. First, there is the clear witness provided by the preservation of a church on a small basilican plan, as at Silchester in Hampshire. Another of similar type is found at St Albans, the town where Albanus was martyred, possibly during the Diocletian persecution. Second, there is the apparent use of a suite of rooms within a villa for private devotions. Thus, at a villa in Lullingstone in Kent by the mid-fourth century A.D., two rooms had Christian wall-paintings, with motifs including the *chi-rho* monogram, the alpha and omega, and praying figures. Two other villas, this time in Dorset, have important evidence: a mosaic decorated with an encircled *chi-rho* at Frampton, and the mosaic of the male head, with a *chi-rho* above it, at Hinton St Mary. This is generally thought to be a portrait of Christ.

(c) Tombstones and slabs: A few tombstones, or parts of tombstones, suggestive of a Christian presence are found in the district of Carlisle and in Cumbria. For example, there is a tombstone to Flavius Antigonus Papias at Carlisle, and it is thought that he may have been a Christianised Greek.

(2) Linguistic: The British people borrowed terminology for the expression of Christian ideas current in the Latin language; the range of borrowing covered most aspects of the life of the Christian community, including the word for 'church', Modern Welsh *eglwys*, from Latin *ecclesia*. We need not suppose that such borrowing took place consistently throughout the Celtic regions. More probably this is a manifestation of the interaction between indigenous British culture and *romanitas* within the relatively well-to-do villas and more urbanised settings of south-east Britain and south-east Wales. In the hills and fastnesses of the Highland Zone, there would be little scope for interaction of this kind, and probably little scope for Christianity to take root. The 'pagans' (i.e. country people, dwellers in the rural area) were likely to remain 'pagans' in our more modern sense of that word.

The early British context

What happened to these faint flickers of Christianity after the Romans had left Britain? Were they extinguished, or did they survive long enough to flourish as an 'indigenous' form of the faith in later centuries? What evidence do we have for some degree of continuity? Much is uncertain, but there is some support for the latter view, even if it is, as usual, very arguable.

Archaeology furnishes a certain amount of knowledge. The region around Carlisle, extending westwards to Whithorn, is of great significance in this context, partly because of Ninian and Patrick. It offers evidence of continuity in the form of gravestones. At Whithorn a gravestone which is probably of fifth-century date commemorates a certain Latinus and his daughter. It is inscribed in Latin, and begins 'Te Dominum Laudamus', and then gives the names of those commemorated, together with that of the man who erected the tombstone. Farther west, at Kirkmadrine in the Rhinns of Galloway, there are two more tombstones which are artistically slightly more ambitious. Both carry encircled *chi-rho* symbols, and one of them has the alpha and omega on the top left-hand corner (facing). The one with the alpha/omega reads: 'HIC IACENT SANCTI ET PRAECIPUI SACERDOTES IDES [?] VIVENTIUS ET MAVORIVS' ('HERE LIE THE HOLY AND DISTINGUISHED PRIESTS, IDES [?] VIVENTIUS AND MAVORIUS'). The other carries two names, one of which is now illegible, while the second name can be read as FLORENTIVS. The date usually ascribed to these stones is 'before 500'. Elsewhere in southern Scotland, notably at Peebles and Yarrowkirk, there are stones of a similar type, though they are more difficult to interpret. Evidence of this kind is also found in south-west Wales. One of the most conspicuous pieces is a stone commemorating Vortipor, who was severely chastised by Gildas. The stone, inscribed MEMORIA VOTIPORIGIS PROTICTORIS ('IN MEMORY OF VO[R]TIPOREX PROTECTOR'), carries a form of *chi-rho* which is simply a linear cross within a circle.

Archaeological evidence takes us only part of the way. Some of the most famous figures in the early Christian period - Pelagius, Ninian and Patrick - are known chiefly from literary, rather than archaeological, sources. The difficulty, at least with Ninian and Patrick, is how to fit them into the scenarios that we can deduce from other evidence, both literary and archaeological. We shall first consider Pelagius and Ninian, and then we shall reflect on the vexed question of Patrick's mission.

Pelagius

Pelagius has gone down in history because he gave his name to Pelagianism, a system of belief which was regarded as a heresy. But who was Pelagius? The following brief account is given by J. Stevenson (*Creeds, Councils and Controversies*, p.368):

> Pelagius, b[orn] c. 355, a lay monk from Great Britain or Ireland, was in Rome for a long period up to 409. Later he was in Sicily and Africa (410), and in Palestine (from 411). He was the author of a Commentary on the Epistles of Paul (still extant). From c. 410 he was involved in the controversy about grace and free will, to which his name is attached. His views were attacked by Augustine (i.e. Augustine of Hippo in North Africa), Jerome and Orosius, and were finally condemned by the Council of Ephesus in 431.

The source of Pelagius's Christianity is unknown. His distinctive contribution to theology was his argument that humanity could, with effort, fulfil the law of God. He therefore denied the need for divine grace except as a means of instruction. In this his views conflicted with those of Augustine of Hippo. In Britain it would seem that Pelagius's views had a strong following, but his teaching met with severe disapproval beyond Britain in the years immediately before and after 431. In 429 Germanus, bishop of Auxerre, was dispatched to Britain by Pope Celestine in an attempt to root out the heresy. In this he was unsuccessful, and made a second visit about 436-7 to try to stop a revival of Pelagianism. It is said that Pelagianism was suppressed in the course of the fifth century. One must suppose that this applies to Pelagianism as a mass movement, since it certainly does not mean that the thoughts and influence of Pelagius were banned or destroyed; commentaries by Pelagius, often under more respectable names (e.g. Jerone) or expurgated, were read by ecclesiastics in the churches of Britain and Ireland many centuries later.

It is important to note that the British church did come under the wider jurisdiction of Rome at this stage. It was regarded as permissible for the Pope to send a bishop from Gaul to Britain to stamp out what was perceived to be harmful or erroneous teaching. In terms of ecclesiastical structure, this squares with the overall picture of strong *Romanitas* given by Gildas a century later.

Ninian

We now turn to Nynia or Ninian, who is closely associated with Whithorn in Galloway. Many troubles await us in our search for his identity. Our earliest source for the life and work of Ninian is Bede's *Historia Ecclesiasica* (III: iv) of c.731. Bede provides a passage which appears to have been a relatively late insertion into the text of the History:

> The southern Picts who live on this side of the mountains had, it is said, long ago given up the error of idolatry and received the true faith through the preaching of the Word by that revered and saintly man Bishop Nynia, a Briton by birth, who had received orthodox instruction at Rome in the faith and mystery of the truth. His espiscopal see is distinguished by the name and church of St Martin the bishop, and there his body lies along with those of many saints; this see now belongs to the English race. This place, belonging to the province of the Bernicians, is commonly called 'at the white house' [*Ad Candidam Casam*] inasmuch as he built there a church of stone in a manner unusual among the Britons.

Yet we do not know much about Nynia or Ninian beyond what Bede says. Bede's evidence is difficult to interpret, causing historians to scratch their heads and write very complicated books. Who were the 'southern Picts', and where were they located? Current views seem to agree that they were not located in Galloway, and that they are likely to have been the southern grouping of the Picts, namely the Verturiones in the general area of Fortriu. Thus we have the prospect of a bishop, with his see (if he had one!) in Galloway, going all the way to the district north of the Forth and achieving (single-handedly?) the conversion of a major group of Celts - and as Bede makes quite clear, this happened 'long before' [*multo ante tempore*] Columba came to Iona.

Much ink has been spilt on the phrase, 'long before'. How long before Columba? Until recently scholarly opinion placed Ninian in the early fifth century, but at least one historian, Dr Alan Macquarrie, has now argued for a late fifth, early sixth century, date for his floruit, but he has been challenged by Professor John MacQueen, who argues still for the earlier date.

What about Ninian's link with Rome? This possibility is scarcely too contentious, although some have contended it. Rome was prestigious enough, and so was the Papacy, to attract a British cleric; Pelagius had likewise ventured to Rome. What of Ninian's connection with St Martin? This is Martin of Tours (died 397), and Bede tells us only that Ninian's church was dedicated to Martin by the eighth century. Again, there is a hint that a cult had started to gather around Ninian himself by this stage; his body lay at Whithorn 'along with those of many saints'. Do we know anything about his ecclesiastical polity? Did he have a monastery or not? Bede does not say. What he does say is that he had a church of stone, which was architecturally unusual in its day.

There are numerous wider questions here. Why was Bede so interested in Whithorn? The more obvious answer is that it had been erected very recently into a see of the English church of which he formed a part, and it was perhaps natural that he should have drawn attention to it, by way of providing a Christian origin legend for the foundation. Perhaps, in so doing, Bede was anxious to find a pre-Columban strand of history that would affirm the greater antiquity of that part of the English church. It is thus possible that Bede's words contain a hint of a counterblast to the developing cult of Columba, of which the writing of Adomnán's Life of Columba was an important part. Competition between the cults of saints was part of the ecclesiastical life of the early Middle Ages.

Christianity in early Wales

The emergence of the Christian faith in Wales is shrouded in obscurity. It is possible that the roots of Christianity in the region in the sixth century can be traced back to the strong influence of the Roman occupation of the south-eastern part of the country, which contains the greatest concentration of later Christian foundations. Historians face considerable difficulty in assessing the extent and vitality of the faith throughout Wales after the Roman period. Although there is clear evidence, beyond the twelfth-century Llandaff charters, of the creation of at least thirty-five religious foundations before the Norman Conquest, it is by no means easy to determine when these foundations came into existence. The majority of these are located in the south and south-east of Wales, with a lesser number situated on the coast and on the Welsh marches. As Professor Wendy Davies notes (*Wales in the Early Middle Ages*, p.143), the Llandaff charters refer to thirty-six monasteries in the south-east, and a further thirty-eight *ecclesiae*.

Monastic life was thus fairly well established in the south-eastern part of Wales, but it is not at all clear that such vigour was found in other parts of the country. The religious sites best attested earlier than the tenth and eleventh centuries are St David's (eighth-century evidence), Bangor on Dee, Caldey and Llantwit (Llanilltud) (seventh and eighth-century evidence). The large monastery at Llanilltud is said to have been influential in the careers of early Welsh saints, among them Samson, who moved from Llanilltud to a more ascetic existence on Caldey Island, before travelling to Cornwall, where he is said to have founded monasteries, and onwards to Brittany, where his *Vita* was written in the seventh century. The Life of Samson is of great importance in underlining the early significance of monasticism as a movement in Wales. It also preserves memory of some of the early abbots, including Illtud, who is associated with Llanilltud.

It was not, however, until the eleventh and twelfth centuries that most of the lives of the Welsh saints were written, including (at the end of the eleventh century) Rhigyfarch's Life of David, the patron saint of Wales, about whom relatively little is actually known. There are thus formidable gaps in our knowledge of how Christianity was both established and developed in Wales. A tantalising glimpse of monasticism in early Wales is offered by the early sixth-century writer, Gildas. His Latin work, *De Excidio et Conquestu Britanniae* ('On the Ruin and Conquest of Britain'), depicts a decadent church in which there were only a few men who lived up to their calling as monks (see Chapter 8).

Patrick, Palladius and Ireland

Patrick is one of the best known saints in the British Isles, but the surviving accounts of his work, including those apparently written by himself, are among the most perplexing and cryptic documents that we have. In his death, as in his life, he has presented scholars with many challenges. The troubles are manifold. The most important point that we need to note is the possibility, indeed the probability, that Patrick was not the first Christian missionary to Ireland. The rise of Patrick to pre-eminence in Ireland is very largely the result of skilful propaganda, written to enhance the status of the church at Armagh, with which Patrick was associated.

The chronicle of Prosper of Aquitaine notes a very significant event under the year 431: '*Ad Scottos in Christum credentes ordinatus a papa Caelestino Palladius primus episcopus mittitur*' ('Consecrated by Pope Celestine, Palladius is sent as the first bishop to the Irish who believe in Christ').

At its simplest, this means that the first bishop sent to the people of Ireland was a man named Palladius, not Patrick, and it is quite explicit that there were Christians already among the *Scotti* before Palladius was dispatched to Ireland.

At its most complex, this statement raises a thicket of questions. What do we know about Palladius's work in Ireland? We have no contemporary detail. The ninth- or tenth-century Irish 'Life of Patrick' (*Betha Phátraic*) tells us that 'He (Palladius) founded three churches, *Cell Fine*, in which he left his books, the casket with the relics of Paul and Peter and the board on which he used to write, *Tech na Rómán* (House of the Romans) and *Domnach Airte* containing Sylvester and Solinus' (probably two of his followers). These three churches are in Leinster, and this has prompted speculation that Palladius was sent to Ireland via Wales, because of the links between Wales and Leinster.

As for Patrick himself, one of the recensions of the Irish Annals tells us that he came to the Irish in 432, but this date, needless to say, is debated. Everything about Patrick is debated, of course; and the fact that the Annals also give two possible dates for his death has led to the creation of the theory of the 'two Patricks', the one operating in Ireland slightly earlier than the other.

What we know about the 'historical' Patrick is derived from his own writings (or at least they are generally accepted as his own, though it need hardly be said that their authenticity has been doubted by some). His writings include his Confession and his letter to Coroticus, who is usually regarded as a king in Britain, probably king of Strathclyde. Professor Michael Richter (*Medieval Ireland*, pp.44-45) summarises Patrick's career thus:

> He was born in Britain, a freeman. His father held the position of a decurio, a Roman civil servant. When he was fifteen years of age, and at that time not yet a Christian (it is uncertain whether this means that he had not yet been baptised or that he had not yet emphatically professed his Christianity), he was abducted by raiders and taken to Ireland where he worked in captivity as a herdsman. During his first stay in the country, lasting approximately six years, he devoted himself to Christianity, being moved by visions, and prayed long and often. He eventually managed to escape and return to Britain. Some years later he again had a vision in which he was called upon to convert the Irish. He worked for many years among people who had never had any contact with Christianity, became a bishop, baptised many thousands and travelled, in the course of his missionary work, to the outer limits of the inhabited world. He encouraged those he met to turn towards monastic life. He refers more frequently to monks and nuns than he does to ordinary baptised people and was especially proud of the fact that he was able to win over the children of several pagan kings (reguli) to monastic life.

The capture of Patrick by raiders reflects the unsettled conditions pertaining in the fourth and fifth centuries when raiding parties operated regularly, in both directions, across the Irish Sea. It is particularly interesting that, later in life, Patrick chose to respond to a vision in which he was asked to return to Ireland to preach. By responding in this way, he became the first known 'missionary' to venture forth of his own accord to evangelise 'pagans' beyond the established towns of the Roman and sub-Roman areas.

It is possible that both Palladius and Patrick were working in Ireland around the same time, but in different parts. Patrick is usually thought to have been active among the *Ulaid* (in the north of Ireland) and in north Connacht, while Palladius may have been active in the Leinster area. Ireland was big enough for them both.

Summarising the life of Patrick, we may conclude that he was a bishop, but that he also encouraged people to turn to the monastic life. In other words, there was an episcopal/diocesan dimension to his labours, and it is believed that the early churches founded through his efforts and those of his followers functioned on a similar basis. Monastic life flourished in Ireland after Patrick's time, but bishops also played a prominent part in the work of the church. We must not be trapped into the common error of believing that monasticism was the sole form of Christian organisation in the country.

Christianity in Ireland after Patrick

The evidence furnished by Prosper of Aquitaine indicates that there were Christians in Ireland before Palladius was sent there in 431. His move to Ireland followed the standard pattern within the Roman Empire whereby a bishop was provided to give oversight to an existing body of Christians. The likely sources for Christian influence on Ireland include Roman Britain itself, which provided Patrick; Wales, where some early Irish monastic founders were evidently trained; and Gaul, with which the Irish had trading links. Thus, Ireland cannot be seen in isolation from its neighbours; although it was never invaded by Rome, it was influenced by Rome in various ways, and evidence to that effect is gradually being gathered. The arrival of Christianity was destined to broaden and reinforce the spiritual, cultural and intellectual links between Ireland and the wider post-Roman world.

The growth of Christianity in Ireland in the fifth and sixth centuries appears to have been rapid. The picture of a uniformly monastic church from the sixth century onwards is now no longer fashionable among scholars, but it is certainly clear that monasticism was a significant component in the ecclesiastical configuration of early Ireland. Through the desire of some Irish monks to undertake the testing and self-denying voyage to find God in the depths of solitude, known as *peregrinatio*, further communities of monks were planted beyond Irish shores, from Scotland to Lombardy (see Chapter 9). Among the major monastic founders were Columba, later to become abbot of Iona, where he established himself in 563, and Columbanus, who reached as far as Bobbio in the north of Italy. It is debatable whether such expeditions always amounted to mission in our sense of the word, but it is clear that the monasteries established by such men had (in Richard Fletcher's phrase) 'diffusive potential' in spreading the message of Christianity and permeating society with the Christian ethic.

Augustine and the Anglo-Saxons

Christianity reached the western edges of the Roman Empire by a variety of means, most of them fairly informal. Wherever it took root, communities of believers began to alter the spiritual complexion of their immediate locations, and sometimes moved farther afield. 'Cumulative Christianisation' perhaps summarises the overall process; as far as we can judge, it was largely unplanned and haphazard at the human level, a by-product of the dispersal of people through military strategy, business and trade. Yet there were also more deliberate, targeted attempts to disseminate the Christian faith. We have already noted the remarkable initiative of Patrick, who was responsive to a divine call to go to Ireland, and was not dispatched by Pope or church. This was undoubtedly 'mission' of a form which corresponds more closely (though not precisely) to what we would understand by the term today.

A still more remarkable mission which reached the British Isles was that of Augustine, who arrived in Kent in the spring or summer of 597. The initiative came from Pope Gregory I, or Gregory the Great, as he is frequently known. Gregory had a strong interest in pastoral care, the foundation of monasteries and the spreading of the Christian faith. Augustine was an Italian, and prior of Gregory's monastery in Rome. When Augustine arrived in Kent, he was able to draw on the support of the queen, Bertha, who was of Frankish origin and already a Christian. She had married Aethelberht, who ruled Kent jointly with his brothers, on the understanding that she would be able to practise her faith although her husband was a pagan. She was accompanied to Kent by her chaplain, Liudhard. Pope Gregory was apparently well aware of the importance of Bertha's presence in Kent as a stepping-stone in the evangelisation of the Anglo-Saxons, who were by then resident in what came to be known as England. He encouraged both the king and queen to support this major missionary venture, and it appears that they did so. Aethelbert later became a Christian. Augustine established his archiepiscopal see at Canterbury.

Royal marriage to a Christian princess was one of the ways by which the faith was implanted in Anglo-Saxon England, and this process was set to repeat itself. Aethelburh, daughter of Aethelberht and Bertha, was soon to emulate her mother's example. When she married Edwin, king of Northumbria, in 625, she was accompanied to Northumbria by her chaplain, Paulinus, an Italian who had come to Kent with Augustine. Paulinus's work led to the conversion and baptism of Edwin in 627, and also to mass baptisms of converts in different parts of the kingdom. When he became bishop of Northumbria, Paulinus established his see in York. He returned to Kent in 633, when Edwin was killed by Cadwallon, king of Gwynedd, in the battle of Hatfield Chase. The kingdom of Northumbria then divided temporarily into its two constituent parts, Deira and Bernicia, before being reunited by Oswald, who returned from exile 'among the Scotti' after Edwin's death. Though Bede states that the kingdom reverted to paganism, Christian witness was not snuffed out with the departure of Paulinus; it was maintained at York by James the Deacon.

Aidan's contribution and legacy

The Christian presence in Northumbria, maintained precariously by James the Deacon, was strengthened greatly by the arrival of a Gaelic monk, Aidan, from Iona in 635. Oswald and his brothers, who were forced into exile when Edwin took control of Northumbria, were evidently living among the Gaelic people of Dál Riata, the foundational Gaelic kingdom in the west of present-day Scotland. They had close links with Iona, and Oswald, on his return to Northumbria, asked the Iona house to provide a bishop for the Northumbrians. Aidan was able to take up the challenge. Jane Hawkes (*The Golden Age of Northumbria*, p.42) summarises Aidan's career as follows:

> On his arrival in Northumbria in 635 Aidan established a bishopric at Lindisfarne close to the chief royal residence of Bamburgh on the land granted by Oswald, and during the next sixteen years oversaw the establishment of the Church in Northumbria through the foundation of a series of monasteries on land donated by members of the Northumbrian aristocracy. In many cases he selected the (royal) abbots and abbesses personally. In this work Aidan never lost the support of the rulers of Northumbria. He involved them in his mission, even to the extent of using Oswald as his interpreter when addressing the members of the Anglo-Saxon court. He was often in attendance at the royal courts, particularly when the king was in residence at Bamburgh; he was present at Oswald's feast on Easter Day when the food and silver plate from the royal table were distributed to the poor; and he was outside the church in Bamburgh when he died [in 651].

Bede fashioned a highly sympathetic picture of Bishop Aidan, a picture which has become the identikit of the 'typical Celtic Christian monk':

> Such were his love of peace and charity, temperance and humility; his soul, which triumphed over anger and greed and at the same time despised pride and vainglory; his industry in carrying out and teaching the divine commandments, his diligence in study and keeping vigil; his authority, such as became a priest, in reproving the proud

and mighty; and his tenderness in comforting the weak, in relieving and protecting the poor (Colgrave and Mynors, p.267).

In depicting Aidan in this manner, Bede was by no means a disinterested commentator. It seems highly likely that he had his sights on the pompous clergy of his own day, and that Aidan was, for him, the model bishop. Thus Bede, by choosing to present the Gaelic Aidan in a flattering mould, was perhaps the earliest creator of one of the most enduring myths of 'Celtic Christianity', namely that of the unworldly, self-effacing cleric whose life was a rebuke to those of a later generation. For every Aidan, there were, unfortunately, many, many more 'Celtic' clerics whose lives contradicted the virtues exemplified by him.

Bede and the British clergy

Despite his affection for Aidan, Bede appears to have had no meaningful concept of 'Celtic Christianity' as an entity embracing the Irish, the Scots and the Welsh. Bishop Aidan and those who had sent him to evangelise the Anglo-Saxons of Northumbria were highly regarded by Bede, but his esteem for the Gaelic monks of Iona was not matched by similar affection for their Welsh counterparts. The Welsh, who are termed 'British' in this period, had obtained knowledge of the Christian faith before Augustine arrived in England, but they committed a cardinal sin in Bede's eyes; they did not try to extend the benefits of Christianity to the Anglo-Saxons. Their guilt was not lessened by the merits of the Iona church or on the grounds of their being part of a wider family of 'Celtic Christians'.

Bede relates how in 603 Augustine, with the help of King Aethelberht, summoned 'the bishops and teachers of the neighbouring British kingdom' to a conference at a place called Augustine's Oak, possibly in the Worcester area, and implored them 'that they should preserve catholic peace with him and undertake the joint labour of evangelizing the heathen for the Lord's sake.' Bede cites some of the differences between the British and 'Roman' interpretations of the faith: these included the timing of Easter 'and other things too which were not in keeping with the unity of the Church', including a difference over the sacrament of baptism. The British clergy refused to comply after what Bede describes as 'a long and wearisome struggle' to persuade them otherwise. A second conference was requested by the Britons, and attended by 'seven British bishops and learned men' from the monastery of Bangor Iscoed. Briefed by a hermit to look for signs of meekness in Augustine's character before accepting his terms, the British once again refused; Augustine remained seated as they entered the room, and they interpreted this as a sign of his overbearing nature and inclination to despise their ways. As a consequence, Bede records, Augustine prophesied that 'war from their enemies' would come upon the British, and, according to Bede, 'this, through the workings of divine judgement, came to pass in every particular as he had foretold'. King Aethelfrith of Northumbria went to besiege Chester with a great army in 613, 'and made a great slaughter of that nation of heretics'. Priests from Bangor had come to Chester to pray against Aethelfrith, and, as a consequence Aethelfrith attacked the 'prayer warriors', killing 'twelve hundred men...who had come to pray and only fifty escaped by flight' (Colgrave and Mynors, pp.138-43).

Bede's sense of divine justice is sharply, even mercilessly, conveyed, and leaves the reader in no doubt that, for him, failure to recognise, and to comply with, the wider concept of 'the unity of the Church' was a serious crime, tantamount to heresy. It is common among modern commentators to lay the blame for the failure to reach agreement at Augustine's door, but events demonstrate that the British clergy would not budge easily from their own opinions; they were not of an accommodating disposition, especially where the Anglo-Saxons were involved, any more than were the Gaelic clergy who clashed with the 'Roman' party at Whitby. The Easter question, which was part of the problem addressed at Augustine's Oak, continued to be a cause of disunity, and disagreement on this issue was, to Bede, as big a crime as failure to evangelise the Anglo-Saxons.

Celts versus Romans? Putting Whitby in perspective

As a consequence of Aidan's work, the Christian faith was strengthened in Northumbria, and was represented in two strands, the 'Gaelic' strand as characterised by Aidan, and the 'Anglo-Saxon' strand which derived from Augustine's wider mission. These strands interacted in various ways, and influenced one another. There was, however, one area of potential conflict. This, as seen by Bede, was based on a major defect in Aidan's understanding, and in that of his fellow Gaelic monks; Bede emphasised that his portrait of Aidan was not constructed 'by any means commending or praising his lack of knowledge in the matter of the observance of Easter; indeed, I heartily detest it...' The Gaelic monks celebrated Easter at a different date from their Anglo-Saxon brethren, because they were using an older 84-year cycle, rather than the 19-year Dionysian cycle, which had been adopted gradually by various other churches within Christendom. In the Gaelic west itself, some churches had already moved to the 19-year cycle; by 633, the so-called *Romani* ('Roman party') in the south of Ireland had changed to the Dionysian cycle, thus indicating that there was no agreement on the matter within the so-called 'Celtic Church'. The Welsh churches did not adopt the Dionysian method of calculating the date of Easter until 768, more than a century after the Synod of Whitby.

The Synod of Whitby, held in 664 to settle the Easter question in Northumbria, is depicted at great length by Bede. The Gaelic churchmen are seen to be pitted against their Anglo-Saxon counterparts, presided over by Bishop Wilfrid, who had long accepted the 19-year cycle. The Gaelic contingent lost the argument, and Colman, an Irishman who was by then bishop of Northumbria, left the kingdom. In the account presented by Bede, the Roman (and Anglo-Saxon) camp is seen to triumph, and the Irish camp loses out. The tendency of later scholars and romanticisers to equate the *Scotti* ('Gaels, Irish') with 'Celts' has further befuddled the issue. Bede had no concept of a 'Celtic Church'. Furthermore, by 664 there was no single 'Celtic system of reckoning the date of Easter' (*pace* Williams, Smyth and Kirby, p.84), and no single view on 'opting in' to the widening sector of Christendom which had adopted the 19-year cycle. Much was determined by church leaders in their own areas, though even they could not persuade their colleagues to follow their examples in 'opting in' or 'out'; Wales, the north of Ireland and Iona (loyal to Columba, despite the endeavours of Adomnán) were 'late conformers'. There were committed traditionalists as well as modernisers within the various churches, and neat boundaries between traditionalists and modernisers cannot be exclusively drawn in terms of group identity.

Whitby is portrayed in different ways by modern commentators, but chiefly in terms of a kind of Armageddon between an overbearing, bureaucratic 'Roman Church' on the one hand and a small, self-effacing 'Celtic Church' on the other. The more deluded modern writers on the theme seem to believe that the 'Celtic Church' was extinguished at Whitby, but Whitby was, in reality, far less of a disaster than the terrible slaughter at Chester. There was no killing at Whitby, and Irish monks continued to be very active in Anglo-Saxon England long after 664. Again, the encounter is sometimes seen as a 'culture clash'. In reality, it does not fit any of these interpretations. It was part of an ongoing attempt to bring uniformity to the diverse practices of Christendom. The desire for uniformity on a single issue had painful consequences, causing disagreements and tensions at various levels. Movements which strive to achieve uniformity all too often result in conflict, and reinforce or create division in churches. That, it seems, is the moral of Whitby; it is not the lesson that popular writers on 'Celtic Christianity' want to transmit, but it is undoubtedly the one that is fairest to the overall evidence.

Biases and bypasses

The evidence gathered in this chapter shows that the Christian faith appears to have entered the British Isles, and to have been disseminated, through a number of different channels. The facilitating role of the

Roman Empire is of critical importance to the first plantings of the seed. In the century after the Romans departed from Britain in 410, Christianity appears to have been maintained to some extent in certain parts of Britain and Ireland. The extension of the faith to 'Celtic Britain' (since Britain prior to the coming of the Anglo-Saxons was inhabited by tribes generally regarded as 'Celtic') was thus dependent on the Roman Empire, which provided a massive infrastructure of roads, routes and amenities across wide tracts of Europe. These routes carried cults and philosophies as well as people. It is therefore impossible to divorce the arrival of Christianity in Britain and Ireland from the Roman contribution. Even monasticism itself developed as a response to the manner in which Christianity was accommodated within the Empire after Constantine (see Chapter 8). Gildas (c. 550) bears witness to the existence of an organised church (or sets of churches) in Wales and south-west Britain. After 597 the presence of Augustine's mission added another Roman dimension to the propagation of the faith. We may reasonably suppose that 'Celts' would have come into contact with Christianity as it was taught and expressed by different advocates in different contexts. If there ever was such a thing as 'Celtic Christianity', it must have taken a variety of forms in different parts of the country at different times, and it is unlikely to have been a pure, self-contained product. Bede was clearly unaware of its existence, even though he (unlike us) had first-hand knowledge of the 'common factor' of divergence over the timing of Easter, and was much closer to the 'real thing' than we will ever be.

Yet in modern writings on 'Celtic Christianity', Christianity is seen to be pre-eminently a 'Celtic' construct in its form and, as far as possible, in its origin. To achieve this picture, writers resort, sometimes innocently and ignorantly, but sometimes (one suspects) disingenuously, to journeys along one (or more) of the following 'bypasses'. First, on the Roman bypass, the driver steers well to the south and west, and avoids colliding with any fragment of Latinity between Rome and the North Channel. The role of Rome is 'dumbed down' to the point of being of little practical importance or influence, or it is presented as a preface before the 'real thing' emerges. It may even be expunged from the record. This route is neatly exemplified by Esther de Waal's misleading claim (*World Made Whole*, p.13) that::

> Here was a Christianity which was not Mediterranean-based, but forged anew on the fringes of Europe by a people who knew nothing of Rome or of urban civilisation.

Second, there is the option of travelling 'the Celtic way' by the 'British bypass', which follows the line of Offa's Dyke. The traveller on this route nods towards the notion of early British churches, especially in Wales, but these are glimpsed only in passing, and their significance is either deftly underplayed or seen to be ineffective because of the pride of Augustine, who (according to Bede) refused to show respect to the British clergy at Augustine's Oak in 603.

Third, there is the super-highway of the 'Anglo-Saxon bypass'. This mental motorway with a 'Celtic' camber whisks the spiritual tourist well clear of the mission of Augustine, which is either presented in sharp contrast to the 'Celtic' expression of the faith (with a great showdown at Whitby) or excluded from consideration. The remarkable achievements of the Christian faith in Anglo-Saxon England vanish swiftly over the horizon, though occasionally the traveller may glimpse Anglo-Saxons togged out as 'Celts' at certain service-stations. Popular writers generally hanker after the possibility that, somehow or other, the 'Celts' had absorbed the Christian faith without Roman or any other intermediaries, and thereafter succeeded in maintaining it in its pristine 'Celtic' condition across the centuries. If the Anglo-Saxons have to be disguised to tell the tale, it is a price worth paying for the 'Celtic' perspective on history.

Given the real cultural complexities of the time, the hope of discovering 'our [Celtic] aboriginal apostles' seems slim indeed. The truth is that whatever was 'Celtic' interacted with other expressions of Christianity within the British Isles. Northumbria in particular was a potent meeting point of different traditions, and each of these contributed to the remarkable flowering of secular and ecclesiastical culture in the region in the seventh and eighth centuries. At the same time, the different vernacular languages and cultures in the various areas of the British Isles - Anglo-Saxon in England, Gaelic in Ireland, Scotland and Man, Welsh in Wales, and Cornish in Cornwall - imparted a distinctive profile to individual strands of the tradition. Yet, below the surface there is often an underlying similarity. The differentiation of the 'Celtic' from the 'Anglo-Saxon' element in Northumbria is particularly difficult in the arts and crafts. Even the Anglo-Saxon expression of the faith shares many points with the 'Celtic' form. In such ways common ground can be detected, as well as areas of differentiation. Who borrowed from whom, when and under what circumstances, is often hard, if not impossible, to determine. Sometimes it seems as if 'Celtic Christianity' and 'Anglo-Saxon Christianity' have as much in common as they have in the way of distinctiveness. We now turn to explore the question of the relationship of Christianity and culture in the early British Isles, and especially in Ireland.

CHAPTER 8

THE WORLD, THE FLESH AND THE DRUID: CHRISTIANITY AND CULTURE IN EARLY BRITAIN AND IRELAND

Enthusiasts of 'Celtic Christianity' draw much attention to what they regard as the broadly harmonious relationship which allegedly existed between 'Celtic Christianity' and secular culture. The rapprochement between faith and culture, thus perceived, is largely an extension of the notion that the material and spiritual worlds in the 'Celtic' context were not placed in separate compartments, but mixed freely. In its most uncritical form, this perception sees no meaningful boundary between 'paganism' and 'Celtic Christianity'. The two, it is argued, blend together and interact without enmity, on the integrationist model allegedly reflected in Carmichael's *Carmina Gadelica* and (earlier) in Renan's concept of the church in the 'Celtic' areas (see Chapter 3). Seen through the lens of the nineteenth-century texts of the *Carmina*, the pagan past wears a rosy hue, and the 'Celtic Church' is happily syncretistic. Thus the 'Celtic saints' are frequently portrayed by modern writers as the successors of the druids, having uncontentiously absorbed the principles of 'druidism' into the new faith. Columba is sometimes regarded as a 'Christian druid'. Within this frame, the 'Celtic Church' itself becomes little more than a pagan institution with a Christian veneer.

Few aspects of 'Celtic Christianity' give such a vivid impression of the superficial manner in which modern enthusiasts approach the supposed 'Celtic' past. The simplicity of the model represents little more than naive make-believe; the 'Celtic Church' is reduced to something approximating to a single-cell organism, stuck in a time-warp. We have already noted that, in reality, the so-called 'Celtic Church' consisted of a considerable number of different strands (Chapter 6). It would be sensible to suppose that different attitudes to culture would be attested within each strand; the view of contemporary culture espoused by the ascetic, perched on a rocky island or on an isolated promontory, or in the hut at the bottom of the monastic garden, might be expected to be quite different from that of the more outward-going monk in a prosperous and wealthy monastery. Indeed, some monasteries, such as Llanilltud in Wales, had a reputation for compromise and comparative luxury; monks who were intent on asceticism, like Samson of Dol, forsook Llanilltud in favour of Caldey Island. Even there, however, some brethren had 'problems'; isolation was not necessarily a cure for over-indulgence. Perhaps, in some cases, it may have intensified the difficulty. Samson's abbot in Caldey was addicted to alcohol, and, as a result, he fell down a well and met his death. The personnel of the 'Celtic' churches were not all paragons of spiritual perfection, communing innocently with nature; compromise with the world was an ever-present danger on the rocky island retreat as well as in the plush monastery. That is why penitentials were necessary. Those who presided over 'Celtic' monasteries were realists, and laid down severe penances for deviation from the monastic rule. Thus, the penitential attributed to the sixth-century Welsh monk, Gildas, begins by calling a sin a sin (Winterbottom, p.84):

> A presbyter or deacon committing natural fornication or sodomy who has previously taken a monastic vow shall do penance for three years. He shall seek pardon every hour and keep a special fast once every week except during the fifty days following the Passion...After a year and half he may receive the eucharist and come for the kiss of peace and sing the psalms with his brethren, lest his soul perish utterly from lacking so long a time the celestial medicine.

Not only do we have to be aware that human nature was as hard to manage in the 'Celtic' era as in the present day, we also have to bear in mind that the period of the supposed 'Celtic Church' covers about five centuries, and it would not be surprising to find that attitudes to 'the world' and its culture changed across the years. We might expect that the churches' earliest encounters with paganism would be confrontational, but that their attitudes to it might become more mellow as they conquered more of the secular world. It is noticeable that several saints, including Patrick, Columba and Samson, are depicted in their earliest Lives as having sharp encounters with paganism at the outset of their endeavours. The triumphs of the saints led to other dangers. In the course of their conquest of the secular world, Christian communities, however large or small, as well as their inmates, might fall victim to sin and syncretism, and require to be called back to a greater spiritual devotion. Such devotion would tend to intensify the battle with the world, the flesh and the Devil - perceived by Christians across the centuries as the three great enemies of the soul.

If it is wrong to believe that the 'Celtic Church' was soft on paganism, it is also misleading to suppose that the attitude to paganism and secular culture found within it was somehow or other peculiar to, or distinctive of, that 'church'. The Christian church throughout

Europe encountered paganism, and had to address the question of its relationship to it. Confrontation and accommodation, to various degrees, are therefore attested at different stages in non-Celtic contexts. There were times when pagan temples, abandoned and discredited by those who had discovered the Christian faith, were left to decay gently, and were even visited as tourist attractions; at other times, Christians conducted crusades against pagan sites, and occasionally wrecked them. 'Celtic' enthusiasts make much of the manner in which the 'Celtic Church' allegedly re-used pagan shrines and temples for Christian purposes, but this likewise was by no means a peculiarly 'Celtic' practice. One of the clearest statements of how Christians ought to appropriate pagan shrines for Christian purposes was made by Gregory the Great in the context of his mission to Anglo-Saxon England. He sent an emissary with the following message for Augustine (Colgrave and Mynors, p.107):

> Tell him what I have decided after long deliberation about the English people, namely that the idol temples of that race should by no means be destroyed, but only the idols in them. Take holy water and sprinkle it in these shrines, build altars and place relics in them. For if the shrines are well built, it is essential that they should be changed from the worship of devils to the service of the true God. When the people see that their shrines are not destroyed they will be able to banish error from their hearts and be more ready to come to the places they are familiar with, but now recognizing and worshipping the true God.

How very 'Celtic' and un-Roman, one might think! Yet this remarkably irenic approach to pagan temples emanates from Rome. In fact, the Christian faith in Anglo-Saxon England is contextualised in contemporary culture in a manner not at all dissimilar to the Celtic areas. The details undoubtedly differ, but the wider patterns are comparable. The evidence for Anglo-Saxon England shows early use of the vernacular (Old English) language for transmitting the Christian message in song (as is attested in Caedmon's hymn) and in sermons (such as those of Aelfric and Wulfstan). Anglo-Saxon Christians produced illuminated Gospel books, built beautiful, unpretentious stone churches, several of which survive to the present day (as at Bishop Auckland, for example), and erected fine stone crosses which combined secular and Christian art styles. The best known of these is the splendid Ruthwell Cross (at Ruthwell, Dumfries-shire). The Ruthwell Cross is an outstanding tribute to, and reflection of, the manner in which the Christian faith interacted with Anglo-Saxon culture, since it carries an extract from 'The Dream of the Rood', perhaps the finest of all Old English Christian poems. It describes the heroic act of Christ in ascending the cross, and tells the story from the perspective of the cross. The extract is inscribed on the Ruthwell Cross using runes, an alphabet which was common to both the Anglo-Saxons and the Norse. Runic script had its 'Celtic' counterpart in Ogam. The origins of Ogam (whether in south-west Ireland or the south of Wales) and the manner of its transmission are still debated.

The lack of appreciation of their own Anglo-Saxon heritage shown by 'Celtic' devotees in late twentieth-century England is the clearest possible evidence of the existence of 'the Anglo-Saxon bypass' to which we have alluded (Chapter 7). It remains something of a mystery why 'Celtic' devotees in England seem so incorrigibly oblivious to the riches of early Christian culture on their own doorsteps, and to the clear witness which it bears to the contextualisation of the Christian faith in Anglo-Saxon England. The notion that the faith was contextualised effectively only in the Celtic areas reflects an over-emphasis on the differences between the 'Celtic Fringe' and other regions.

Points of contact

It is important to consider the points at which the Christian faith would have come into contact with the wider, secular culture of Britain and Ireland. These were, of course, many and varied; a priest going about his daily business could scarcely shut himself off from society. Nor were ecclesiastical institutions isolated from the world around them. Then as now, this posed a serious threat to the spiritual health of the institutions. It is quite evident that, in some cases, they fought a losing battle with the ways of the world. Gildas, who was writing about 550 A.D., somewhere in Wales or in its vicinity, and knew south-west Britain very well, has left graphic pictures of institutions which had been seriously compromised through contact with secular society. He himself was a monk, steeped in Latin, and he was addressing himself to a society in south-western Britain in which there was some obvious Christian structure and ecclesiastical organisation, as the following passage shows (Winterbottom, p.52):

> Britain has priests [*Sacerdotes habet Britannia*], but they are fools; very many ministers, but they are shameless; clerics, but they are treacherous grabbers. They are called shepherds [*pastores*], but they are wolves, all ready to slaughter souls. They do not look to the good of the people, but to the filling of their own bellies. They have church buildings, but go to them for the sake of base profit. They teach the people - but by giving them the worst of examples, vice and bad character. Rarely do they sacrifice and never do they stand with pure

heart amid the altars. They do not reprimand the people for
their sins; indeed they do the same things themselves...

Gildas also refers to bishops and to simony in the procurement of
ecclesiastical offices. The picture here, then, is scarcely one of a happy
marriage between 'the world' and 'the church'. It is one of a decadent
ecclesiastical structure, whose main officers were operating by a
double standard. In addition, we have evidence from Gildas that
monasticism was found in certain parts of Britain by 550. For
example, Gildas tells how Maglocunus, i.e., Maelgwn of Gwynedd,
went into a monastery for a spell and then came out again ('You
vowed to be a monk for ever, with (as you said) no thought of going
back on your promise'), preferring the ranting and foaming phlegm
of the secular bards to the praise of God. Gildas mentions those who
are living lives which are exceptions to his general picture of spiritual
and moral declension.

We can perhaps deduce from Gildas too that in some parts of
Britain there was no more and no less than a nominal adherence to the
Christian faith, and (if we can go by Maglocunus's example) some
rulers were attracted temporarily by the challenge of monasticism. At
least part of this scenario may attest some continuity with Roman
models, although the coming of monasticism is another story, to
which we must now turn.

The monastic ideal

In Britain and Ireland, as Christianity took root, it came to be
represented very strongly in terms of monks and monasteries. We
must be careful not to confuse monasteries and monks in this context
with the form of monasticism that came to the fore in the later Middle
Ages, with large, very widespread groups of monasteries following
(for instance) the Rule of the Benedictine order (see Chapter 11).

Although monasticism was well established by the early fourth
century, the type of monasticism that flourished in Britain and Ireland
(where it was particularly popular) was stimulated by the secularisation
of the church following the conversion of Constantine in 312 A.D.
and the consequent 'officialising' of Christianity. In time, a reaction
occurred against the decadence and worldliness of this state-sponsored
brand of Christianity, and the outworking of that reaction strengthened
the cause of monasticism. The persecutions of the church by apostate
emperors also aided the process. We can observe monasticism
developing in three stages, and coming into existence in the western
Mediterranean regions of the Roman Empire (see also Wand, *History
of the Early Church*, pp.192-205):

(1) Eremitic. The first stage was the development of solitariness, with the hermit seeking out a lonely place where he could liberate himself from the clutches of worldliness. The first known was Paul of Thebes, who retired to a grotto on the Egyptian coast of the Red Sea. He was followed by St Antony (251-356), a Copt (i.e. an Egyptian Christian, speaking the Christian vernacular, Coptic), who took to living in a tomb, and was renowned for his self-denying struggles. The movement spread from Egypt to Syria and Mesopotamia. It produced remarkable characters: some ate nothing but grass; others lived in trees; and some took to living on pillars (e.g. Simeon Stylites, 385-459), and were thus called 'pillar saints'.

(2) Semi-eremitic. Some of the hermits began to attract followers who came to live near their caves or grottos, and tried to imitate their life-style. This led to the appearance of many single huts called cells, forming a kind of colony. Members met together only for worship, on Saturdays or Sundays. There was no common rule or established authority. The ideal was contemplation, that is, seeking to know God and to get as close to him as possible through reflecting and thinking on him. St Antony appears to have started this trend; it became very common in Lower Egypt. The practice drove Simeon Stylites 'up the pole' in an attempt to get away from the crowds who came to follow his example.

(3) Coenobitic. This development led to the formation of a monastery in the proper sense. The origin of the coenobitic life is ascribed to Pachomius (c. 290-345), who founded a monastery at Tabennisi, thought to be in the region of the Upper Nile. Monks lived under several roofs but were placed under common authority. Poverty, chastity and obedience were enjoined, but observance left room for private experimentation. Pachomius founded eight monasteries, with thirty or forty monks in each. Modifications were introduced by Basil of Caesarea, one of the Cappadocian Fathers: monasteries tended to be placed by him near large cities, and not in the desert; and worship was regularised. Most importantly, learning and scholarship were introduced by Basil's reforms.

Coenobitic monasticism was gradually brought to the West from about 339, when Athanasius, a supporter of Antony, visited Rome. Martin of Tours introduced the practice to Gaul, founding a monastery near Poitiers in 360, which later moved to Marmoutier (*Martini monasterium*) outside Tours. Honoratus founded a monastery at Lerins in 410; Cassian, who drew up a monastic rule for Gaul, founded two monasteries, one for each sex, near Marseilles in 415.

Monasticism in the Celtic lands appears to have preserved features of all of these three stages, while placing strong emphasis on asceticism.

The ideals of the Egyptian desert fathers lasted long in the insular Celtic context as elsewhere in the West. The question, of course, is how these ideals came to be introduced to Britain and Ireland. It is quite unacceptable to see them as purely indigenous or unique to the Celtic areas. Some form of monastic ideal probably came in through the Roman channel, as Gildas's writing might suggest. We must also suppose that concepts and ideas could be picked up through travel, when British bishops and others visited the Continent. Contacts could have been established through trade with the Mediterranean world. We need to consider a wide context, or series of contexts, through which influences could move.

In the later period in Ireland, when the monastic movement was well established, Irish ecclesiastics looked back to links with Ninian of Whithorn and Cadoc of Wales, and thought that they owed no small debt to the Christian movement in mainland Britain. Indeed, Gildas came to be revered in Ireland in the sixth century, especially as an exemplar of piety and asceticism. The career of Patrick, that vexed and vexatious figure, at least points clearly to Britain.

However, we must not suppose that both Ireland and Wales took to monasticism in quite the same way or with the same enthusiasm. The evidence for monasteries in early Wales is relatively slight compared with that for Ireland. In Ireland, the monastic movement 'caught on' with great vigour, and produced what appear to be waves of monastic foundations. It seems that monasticism of this kind was very well suited to early Irish society, probably for a whole variety of reasons which we will consider at a later stage. Again, we must be wary of assuming that monasticism was the only form of ecclesiastical life in Ireland or Wales, nor must we forget that monasticism was very popular in continental Europe in the early Middle Ages.

Life and work in the monasteries

It is worth comparing the three phases found in the early Egyptian monastic context with what we find in Britain and Ireland. We cannot describe three such distinct phases of development for Ireland or Britain. Eremitic, semi-eremitic and coenobitic conventions are frequently found together, often at the same time, within monastic foundations. Certain monasteries had their hermitage, located in an isolated spot where the hermit could pursue his contemplation; sometimes hermits preferred to take off to live in total isolation; some monasteries were themselves perched on rocky islands (e.g. Skellig Michael in Ireland); others were relatively accessible; others again were small, while still others grew into what were very large aggregates of people, rivalling the concept of a city or large town. A few monasteries were double houses, accommodating both men and women. This was the case at Kildare in Ireland, where a monastery was established under Brigit. The brothers and sisters within monasteries would live under the Rule and guidance of the founder of the monastery and his/her successors.

The picture that we should have of a typical 'Celtic' monastery is not of a single, large building accommodating a large number of monks. Rather, we should imagine several small buildings, of stone or wattle, within an enclosing wall of stone or wood, just like the rath or 'ring-enclosure' of a secular noble. Some monasteries had outer and inner walls. Outside the main wall or *vallum*, as it was known in Latin, were the fields. Inside it there were all the various buildings: the cells for the brothers (or the sisters, in the case of a female house), the church, the refectory, the workshop and the scriptorium. In the workshop skilled craftsmen would make the vessels required for the church services, the goblets and chalices for the eucharist, like the Ardagh Chalice or the somewhat less ornate chalice discovered at Derrynaflan in 1980. The scriptorium, set close to, or possibly identical with, the library, was the place of writing, where the brothers (or sisters) would write and study, poring over the Scriptures or works by such scholars as Isidore of Seville, or perhaps illuminating a gospel-book to be placed in the church.

The corporate life of the monastery was usually controlled by the abbot, who was the 'head' of the *muinntir* ('household'). It needs to be said, however, that the popular view that the abbot superseded and eclipsed the bishop in the 'Celtic' context is not necessarily correct. The monastic movement, in the Celtic areas as commonly elsewhere, encouraged the type of structure in which the abbot came to the fore, but, equally in keeping with wider conventions, a monastery might also have a bishop-abbot who combined both roles. Where the roles were differentiated, a monastery would have a bishop within it, who discharged the special aspects of spiritual government required within a community of this kind, such as ordination. The bishop also exercised pastoral care over churches which came under the jurisdiction of the monastery, and he therefore remained a fairly powerful figure. There were priests too, ordained to celebrate the sacraments. Under the abbot would be a prior, who might be the head of another house within the monastic *familia* ('family' of the founder, consisting of his houses and the monks within them).

Much of the evidence for this chapter comes from Ireland. On the Welsh side, after Gildas's time, the evidence is much less plentiful, and we need to tread carefully. The indigenous record is sparse until the ninth century, and does not come on flow in any volume until the twelfth century. We can perhaps assume some broad similarities with Ireland, but we cannot yet prove them. There was certainly a monastic movement in Wales, but it does look as if it was less powerful than in Ireland, and it may be that the Roman inheritance in Britain maintained a rigidity which made it less easy to integrate church and society. In Ireland, close bonding between church and society led to a remarkable flowering of Christianity which interacted with, and helped to transform, secular culture. It was not, however, a flowering which was entirely without parallel elsewhere. Anglo-Saxon England, in the same period, produced treasures of Christian art which are all too easily overlooked by those who become fixated with 'Celtic Christianity'.

Early Irish society

Beyond the religious sphere, the ways and customs of society were permeated by ancient practices which would have been deeply engrained in people. Society would have had its own traditional rules and regulations, its own laws and its own structures in which individuals would have had a particular status, depending on their birth and their profession. Christianity did not come to a society which, in religious terms, was virgin soil, in either Britain or Ireland. There were already holy men and holy women in these countries, even if they were not of the Christian variety.

We may now consider the ways in which church and society, pagan beliefs and Christian religions, interacted in the Celtic areas of the British Isles, and particularly in Ireland in the early Middle Ages. Here again, Ireland will be the main focus of discussion since the evidence for Ireland is so plentiful. For the purpose of identifying the interaction of sacred and secular dimensions, it will be useful to provide a brief general sketch of the main features of early Irish society, because this will help us to understand not only Ireland itself but also something of the structure of Celtic society in the British Isles.

In a lecture on 'Secular Institutions' in Ireland given in 1953, the late Professor D.A. Binchy described the pattern of life in early Ireland as follows (Dillon, *Early Irish Society*, pp.53-4):

> It was a pattern of life that differed in almost every essential point from Irish society as we know it today. If you asked me to define its main characteristics, I should say that it was tribal, rural, hierarchical, and familiar (using this word in its oldest sense, to mean a society in which the family, not the individual, is the unit) - a complete contrast to the unitary, urbanized, egalitarian and individualistic society of our time.

Binchy's aphorism - 'tribal, rural, hierarchical and familiar' - may still serve as a convenient index of the key features of early Irish society. It is, however, important to understand that this does not mean that, in having these features, early Irish society was unique; broadly similar social structures can be found in Anglo-Saxon England, Wales and Scotland (both Gaelic and Pictish) in this period.

(1) Tribal: Early Ireland was divided into small kingdoms, each called individually a *túath*. The *túath* can be regarded as the basic political unit of early Ireland. It is reckoned that there were between 100 and 150 such units in fifth-century Ireland. Each was led by its own king, called the *rí túaithe* ('king of a *túath*'), with his nobles and clients, and a descending scale of importance through the free grades to the unfree. The *rí túaithe* in his turn would be in a type of client relationship to a higher king, who would have call on the services of more than one *túath*, probably a group of *túatha*. The king who held the group of *túatha* together in this way would be called a *ruirí*. This was not the end of the arrangement of royal clientship, if it can be so called. According to the law tracts, and as confirmed in practice, the *ruirí* was himself often found to be in an alliance with a still 'higher' king, the *rí ruirech*, who held him in clientship, and who was the top of the social pyramid. The latter could be the king of a province, who was in terms of Irish society the 'over-king' of the web of smaller units within the province.

Early Ireland comprised five chief provinces (and the oldest vernacular Irish term for a province, *cóiced*, means 'a fifth [part]'). These provinces were: *Ulaid* (Ulster) in the north, *Connacht* in the west, *Mumain* (Munster) in the south, *Laigin* (Leinster) in the south-east, and *Mide* (Meath), between Leinster and Ulster. Each of these provinces had its own sacral site, steeped in pagan ritual, especially that pertaining to kingship, and naturally associated with the ruling family of the province; thus *Emain Macha* and later *Ailech*, in Ulster; *Ailenn* in Leinster; and *Caisel* in Munster. Kingship and the inauguration of the king, performed at the sacral site, were particularly deeply linked with ancient ritual, in which the king was ceremonially 'mated' with the land.

(2) Rural: It is often claimed that Ireland did not have any major town life before the Viking settlements of the mid-ninth century. The latter may have introduced urban commercial centres, but before the Viking period there were certainly no towns as we know them today. The emergence of monasticism in Ireland, however, led to the concentration of population around the monasteries, thus creating substantial communities or aggregations of families. The very large early monasteries regarded themselves as 'cities', and we have to envisage that they created substantial settlements far beyond the popular concept of a monastery which we might carry in our heads nowadays. Nevertheless, 'cities' in our present-day sense of the word were unknown.

Across the country, units of land of varying size were occupied by individual families who would have lived in their 'forts' or *rátha*. These are sometimes called 'ring-forts' or 'ring-enclosures'. The latter is perhaps a better translation, since they consisted of an outer ring or stone wall, usually with a ditch, and this formed the main boundary mark and defence. The dwelling houses and other buildings would be inside the wall, within what was called the *lios*. Estimates of the number of raths in Ireland vary between 30,000 and 60,000. The raths were, of course, occupied by the well-to-do landholding - and free - grades. The unfree grades of serfs and slaves in early Ireland would have lived in poor huts, made of stone or wattle, within the land of their superiors.

The economy was predominantly pastoral, based on the grazing of cattle, but with the capacity for tilling the soil and producing essential crops. Well-to-do landholders ('lords') gave land to clients, who repaid them at a suitable level of produce, thus creating a structure of economic control. The *bó*, 'cow', was the principal unit of value, while the *bóaire*, 'cowman' or 'yeoman farmer', was the backbone of the early Irish farming system, and one of the best known characters in the law tracts. The larger unit of value in early Irish society was the *cumal*, 'female slave', equivalent to three cows.

(3) Hierarchical: Sufficient has been said to demonstrate the hierarchical nature of early Irish society in terms of its political structure. Hierarchical predilections are apparent in the social stratification of Ireland; the distinction between the free and unfree grades, and the different types of people within the free grades, each having the 'honour-price' due to his or her status. The 'honour-price' of each individual was used to calculate reparation due to the kin or the individual in the event of injury, death or insult.

(4) Familiar: The family, or more specifically the kin-group, was the basic decision-making unit; the buck stopped with the kin-group. There were several types of kin-group, depending on how far back in the ancestral line one was prepared to go, but for most purposes the *derbfine* ('proper kindred') was the principal unit. It consisted of all the living descendants of a common great-grandfather. The *derbfine* was very important in such matters as succession to kingship. If your kindred had royal links, and the king was from your kindred, you could stake your claim in the succession, and if you were stronger than the rest of your relatives, with more support at your command, you might well be designated as the king's successor, the *tánaise*, the 'one to whom [others] looked forward' or the 'tanist'. Succession was not necessarily from father to son, since it was not governed by primogeniture.

The influence of secular society on the church

To what extent did the Christian church fit into this kind of society? Did the secular world influence the church, or was it the other way about?

It is fair to say that the relationship of church and society was a two-way process, but that the strength lay with the Christian church. In contrast to early paganism, Christianity was well organised, and had a strong sense of mission. It possessed the power of literacy and the prestige of a learned literary caste. Yet we cannot ignore the significant ways in which early Irish secular society affected aspects of the development of the church. We may first consider this part of the process.

(1) Secular architecture influenced the physical shape of ecclesiastical units. This can be seen by observing the plans of the larger and more typical Irish monasteries. Usually they were constructed on the model of the ring-fort, just like the *ráth* of a noble, with all its main buildings inside a *vallum*. Sometimes a nobleman would give a piece of land or a fort to a monk or abbot, so that he could found a monastery there. The church benefited immensely through the bestowal of land and property by patrons and supporters, often within the kin-groups of the abbots.

(2) Secular, and even pagan, power sometimes influenced the location of monasteries and churches. It is noticeable that some of the most prestigious monasteries were situated alongside, or relatively close to, the centres of power or old sacral sites within the provinces: Armagh, which came to be dedicated to St Patrick, is close to Emain Macha, the old tribal centre of the *Ulaid* (Ulster); Brigit's monastery at Kildare was near to Knockaulin, which was a sacred site possibly associated with the Irish pagan goddess called Brigit (and here we may note the likelihood that the saint Brigit is a Christianised version of the pagan goddess). We can add further that *Cill Dara* (Kildare) itself means the 'church of oak tree/wood', and that there may be a chance that the site of the monastery was formerly that of a *bile*, an originally pagan sacred tree. There is some evidence to suggest that sacred trees may have helped to determine the location of other monasteries.

Against this, we have to set the fact that many Irish monasteries are nowhere near sacred sites of this kind. As for those monasteries which are located at, or close to, sacred sites, it is possible that such strategic locations are intended to show, not a happy compromise between paganism and Christianity, but the superiority of the Christian faith over earlier beliefs.

(3) The structure of society influenced the structure of the church. Clientship, based on the 'letting' of land, was practised by the monasteries. The bigger monasteries gathered many clients, known as *manaig* ('monks'), who lived on the land around the main enclosure, but were not in orders. They were laymen, and could be married with families. Large monasteries, often situated in fertile plains, owned correspondingly large amounts of land, and the lay monks would be employed in the fields - sowing, reaping, looking after cattle etc., and rendering tribute in kind to the monastery. A large monastery would require a small army of labourers of different types to maintain its life and work.

Monasteries could also have clients in the form of churches, and we must remember that there were various types of churches in this period. They were classed just like the grades in early Irish society as 'free' or 'unfree'; the 'unfree' churches were held under the control of a king or monastery. The 'free' churches were not bound by obligations to an original donor or founder. There was a considerable variety of such churches: some were family churches, surrounded by a simple graveyard; others were isolated chapels, tiny cells compared with the sprawling monasteries of the Irish Midlands.

Alongside clientship, the recognition of kinship had implications for the internal working of the monasteries. The kin-based nature of early Irish society was reflected in the appointments made to the leadership of the monasteries. For example, the founding abbot was frequently a well-to-do member of a powerful kindred, and succession to the abbacy would be determined, as far as possible, within the kin-group, like the choosing of a successor to a tribal king. It is quite evident that certain strong kin-groups dominated the life of certain monasteries. We may note, in passing, that the convention of choosing a successor from the abbot's kin was not peculiar to the 'Celtic' areas or to 'Celtic' monasteries. It was known in Anglo-Saxon England. When on his deathbed, Benedict Biscop, Bede's abbot and founder of the monasteries at Monkwearmouth and Jarrow, expressly forbade his monks to follow this practice, since he recognised that it would not be in the best interests of the monastery. The kin-based approach to abbatial succession was fraught with difficulties, not the least of which was the danger of secularising the monastic institution.

Irish monasteries were linked together in groups known as *familiae*, 'families', each of which was linked together by allegiance to a common founder. The prestige of the ancestral founding father was thus acknowledged, and the abbot of the principal house had control over the other houses of the *familia*. For example, Columba, founder and abbot of Iona, was the head of the monastic houses which he had founded, such as Durrow in Ireland, as well as monasteries founded in other parts of western Scotland. In terms of government, the nearest secular parallel to this convention is the arrangement whereby groups of *túatha* came together under the leadership of an overking. Like interconnected secular units, groups of monasteries under powerful leaders had considerable clout, and they could act like secular lords, aggregating land and prestige, and even going to war against one another.

(4) The clergy and monks were fitted into the value-system of Irish secular society. Clerics belonged to the prestigious free grade known as *nemed* ('holy, sacred persons'), embracing king, lord, cleric and poet, and they enjoyed special legal privileges. The term *nemed* itself provides a fascinating glimpse of the relationship between pagan and Christian aspects of society, since it is cognate with a Gaulish (Celtic) word *nemeton*, used of a holy place which would not originally have been Christian. Clerics were given honour-prices according to status. Thus, the abbot of a big, prestigious monastery would have the same honour-price as the king of a province, as would an archbishop, namely 14 *cumals*. It was expected that the clergy would discharge their duties as befitted the contract which, in broad terms, existed between the church and the secular world. The laity could take action against any cleric who was deemed to have acted in an unbecoming manner, such as harbouring thieves or robbers in his church.

Downgrading the druid

All of this indicates that, at several levels, the church was fitted closely into the structure of secular society in Ireland. However, this does not mean that the church came to terms gladly with the practices of pagan society; there were areas in which church and society were in tension, if not in outright conflict. Saints' Lives sometimes show considerable confrontation between the controllers of the pagan (or 'primal') rituals and the Christian saints (see Chapter 9), and this spirit of confrontation was taken abroad. Two saintly travellers to the Continent, namely Gall and Columbanus, contended stiffly with the forms of paganism which they encountered there in the late sixth century. When they reached Switzerland, they were attracted particularly by a great heathen festival at Tuggen, but 'when Gall had burnt temples and thrown offerings into the water, the party was firmly asked to leave' (Walker, *Sancti Columbani Opera*, p.xxviii).

Paganism was challenged in other, less overtly confrontational, ways. We can assert fairly confidently that, as Christianity advanced in Ireland and consolidated its position by means of canon law, earlier pagan practitioners of learning and religion suffered loss of status, and some even became outlaws in the eyes of the church. It is sometimes said or implied by writers on 'Celtic Christianity' that Christian clerics simply took over the teaching and the role of druids, but this claim lacks any meaningful foundation. It is certainly evident that clerics displaced druids, but there are no grounds for believing that displacement occurred because the church absorbed their teaching, so that they became redundant. Rather, the church held them in disdain; a treatise 'On the Miracles of the Holy Scripture', written in 655, refers to 'the laughable tales told by the druids, who say that their forebears flew through the ages in the form of birds' (Carey, *King of Mysteries*, p.58). The 'First Synod of Patrick', dating to approximately the sixth century, regarded them as unreliable witnesses; it states (Canon 14) that 'a Christian who has committed murder, or committed adultery, or sworn before a druid as pagans do, shall do a year's penance for each of these crimes.' Druidry is thus on a par with murder and adultery. Druidic knowledge was also downgraded. As the *suí litre* ('expert in letter', i.e ecclesiastical learning) became the top-rank scholar of early Ireland, with an honour-price equivalent of the king of a *túath*, the druid's profile as a man of learning was reduced, and his powers were gradually restricted; he came to be regarded (at best) as little more than a sorcerer whose honour-price, in practice, was apparently no higher than that of a yeoman farmer. Druids did not, however, cease to exert some degree of power in the sixth and seventh centuries; in Irish tales which portray early Irish society before the arrival of Patrick, druids function as teachers and wizards, and it is evident that after the coming of Christianity they continued to be feared, particularly for their magic spells, by which some were believed to have the capacity to turn the tide of a battle in favour of the weaker group. Protective prayers against malevolent powers, such as the celebrated 'Breastplate' associated with St Patrick, invoke God's various anthropomorphic characteristics (mind, eye, ear, word, hand, path, shield etc.):

> *against the black laws of paganism,*
> *against the crooked laws of heretics,*
> *against the encirclement of idolatry,*
> *against the spells of women and smiths and druids,*
> *against every knowledge which harms a man's body and soul..*
> (Carey, *King of Mysteries*, p.133)

The church even went so far as to classify druids alongside its chiefest enemy, namely the *díbergaig*, a term which embraced berserks, brigands and roving *fian*-warriors who were outside the pale of civilised society and did violence to the church itself (McCone, *Pagan Past*, pp.220-3). The druids are also commonly portrayed in saints' Lives as the inveterate opponents of Christianity, with whom the saints engage in set-piece preliminary contests to assert the superior power of the new faith. The druids in early Christian Ireland have left no records of their own, and we do not have a reliable picture of their pre-Christian function in the region; they are invariably perceived through the lens of Christianity, which has no doubt distorted their image. Nevertheless, the evidence gives little support to the common notion that they and their teachings were happily assimilated into the church. The opposite appears to have been the case.

The displacement of the druid was symptomatic of a far-reaching change in the spiritual complexion of Ireland. Oengus, Céle Dé, composing a poem in the early ninth century, thought that Christianity had achieved not a partial success, nor a compromise, but a complete triumph in the land. He stated:

Ro milled in genntlecht	*Paganism has been destroyed*
ciarbo lígdae lethan;	*though it was splendid and far-flung*
ro lín flaith Dé Athar	*the kingdom of God the Father*
nem, talam la trethan.	*has filled heaven, earth and sea.*

(Greene and O'Conor, *Golden Treasury*, pp.63,65)

The influence of the church on secular society

Perhaps Oengus overstated his case, since pockets of paganism appear to have lingered, but there can be no doubt that the church did make a massive impact on Ireland and on paganism. In what particular ways did the Christian faith influence Irish society, and bring about some degree of change?

(1) The Christian faith brought Latin literacy to early Irish society, but also provided means whereby tales and poems in the Irish/Gaelic language, hitherto transmitted orally, could be written down and preserved. We owe a considerable debt to the Christian church in this respect, and to the monks who spent hours copying down the material; we would be much the poorer if it were not for the labours of the clerics who wrote down the secular tales and other items. Most of the surviving manuscripts were copied in the eleventh and twelfth centuries (see Chapter 11), but the linguistic evidence indicates that the material often goes back to an earlier period, and reflects a process of copying and recopying.

(2) Christianity provided a new corpus of stories and tales to set alongside the traditional stock. These stories were to be found in the Old and New Testaments, and one can see themes from these sources interacting with the traditional tales. The Old Testament and the New provided new models for literary creation, most conspicuously in the biographies of saints. A kind of 'grafting' was practised, whereby the new Christian material was implanted into the native lore, sometimes offering an interpretative framework for genealogy

and secular history. There was creativity in all of this, and an element of 'give and take'; new stories were probably written 'from scratch' by some clerics.

(3) Christianity influenced some of the legal texts and perspectives of early Irish society. The Judaic laws of the Old Testament were sometimes employed to provide precedent for the early Irish jurists. The example of the Patriarchs was used to justify the concept of polygamy or polygyny, the custom of having more than one 'wife' and/or concubines. It would seem too that reformulation of legal codes was influenced significantly by the Christian faith. The Bible was used to affirm certain practices in early pre-Christian Ireland, but it was also used to reject others. Society expected forms of behaviour from clerics and churches which set them unequivocally apart from *gentes* (Latin for 'gentiles, pagans'). Thus the 'First Synod of Patrick' prohibited a cleric from acting as 'a surety for a pagan in whatsoever amount'; if he did so, and the pagan defaulted, he had to repay the debt from his own means; if he fought with the pagan, he would be in effect excommunicated (Canon 8). The church was also forbidden to accept 'alms offered by pagans' (Canon 13).

Certain famous churchmen promulgated particular laws which were intended to protect or strengthen certain sectors of society. The law of Adomnán, Columba's biographer, promulgated at Birr in 697, was intended to protect women and non-combatants in times of war, and was a significant humanitarian measure.

(4) Institutions were remoulded to a certain extent, perhaps not always deeply, but sufficiently for the purposes of outward conformity: for example, kingship, which continued to be steeped in pagan ritual into the later Middle Ages, is sometimes overlaid with Christian and Hebrew custom. Columba is depicted as consecrating Aedán mac Gabráin king of Scottish Dál Riata in the same way as Samuel had consecrated Saul and David. Traditional kingship in certain contexts was thus brought unobtrusively into line with Old Testament practice, at least in theory. The church too was able to take advantage of some of the underlying theories of kingship - especially the more retributive aspects associated with the 'unjust ruler' - to ensure that dues would be paid to it and to God. Failure to pay ecclesiastical dues would amount to a 'blemish' on the ruler concerned, and thus invite divine judgement. Christianity of this kind, which was determined to insist on its rights and give itself a place at the royal table, was hardly in the same league as the supposedly soft 'Celtic Christianity' of popular imagination.

(5) The church and the various monasteries provided a new form of patronage or (in today's terms) sponsorship. Thus the creative skills of early pagan Ireland were given a new force and direction, and the church undoubtedly became the greatest patron of the arts. This encouraged the

illumination of the great gospel-books that we know today as the Book of Kells and the Book of Durrow, as well as many other less famous volumes. Craftsmanship reached high points under the patronage of the monasteries and churches, as can be seen in such artefacts as the high crosses. Secular craftsmanship was thereby transformed for the service of God and his church. This is also true of other aspects of secular culture.

The overall evidence therefore suggests that the church was firmly contextualised within early Irish society. It took much of its outward, physical shape from that society, and its clergy were accommodated within the prevailing social hierarchy and value-system. Yet such assimilation does not necessarily imply the wholesale, no-holds-barred acceptance by the church of paganism/primalism on the scale that romantic devotees of 'Celtic Christianity' like to emphasise. Nor is there evidence which demonstrates the outright destruction of paganism. Instead, we find a range of responses, including the suppression of paganism and pagan sites, the drawing of boundaries between pagan and Christian practices, and a more subtle interaction of sacred and secular conventions (as in any normal society). The last-mentioned process resulted in the gradual transformation of certain key aspects of secular culture for Christian purposes, and extended to symbols of the old order, such as memorial stones, which could be overwritten with the cross, and also cultural practices (such as poetry) which could be readily cleansed from any previous taints. Transformation, rather than overall assimilation, is by far the more conspicuous approach.

Pagan, primal or Christian?

The manner in which Christianity may have transformed early Irish society generally - and that of early Britain in like manner - is a subject of considerable complexity. Although devotees of 'Celtic Christianity' may wish to believe, in all innocence, that the faith effortlessly absorbed, and thus was shaped by, the main features of existing pagan or primal religion, this is much too simple a solution. Nor is it wholly correct to suppose that Christianity easily defeated or expunged the pagan or primal inheritance. As has been argued in this chapter, the process of contextualising the Christian faith was likely to have been two-way, with some degree of variation over time.

The matter has been hotly debated in the context of the surviving literature from Ireland. For much of this century, scholars, with some notable exceptions, were more inclined to take what would now be seen as a 'primitivist' (or 'nativist') position with regard to the pre-Christian culture of Ireland, emphasising the existence of a substantial pre-Christian body of archaic lore and legend which was committed to writing by Christian scribes who were largely the passive recorders of large bodies of oral material. Some scholars were also inclined to stress the persistence and prominence of paganism in shaping early Irish culture, despite the remarkable success of the church. As has been noted at the outset of this chapter, grossly simplified versions of this latter view underly much of the popular writing on 'Celtic Christianity'.

These theories were first challenged in the early 1950s by Professor James Carney (1914-89), and some recent scholars, most notably Professors Donnchadh Ó Corráin and Kim McCone, have followed in his footsteps. The former has demonstrated the manner in which early Irish jurists were influenced by the Mosaic law. The latter, in his ground-breaking book, *Pagan Past and Christian Present in Early Irish Literature*, has argued forcefully that Christianity exercised a major influence on the literary activity and institutions of early Ireland; as happened elsewhere in medieval Europe, the Bible contributed very potently to the making and shaping of early Irish laws and tales and histories of Ireland's past. Although certain aspects of secular culture and customs survived, the controlling power, McCone argues, was that of the church, and the pagan past was remade to conform to models which matched those of Holy Writ.

McCone's arguments have been reviewed shrewdly by Professor Patrick Sims-Williams, who, like McCone, is concerned primarily with the literary evidence; he suggests that the reality may have been less starkly ecclesiastical, and that the relationship between sacred and secular may have varied with time. McCone's views have also been treated more confrontationally by Professor James Mackey, a persuasive advocate of 'Celtic Christianity' (see Chapter 1), who argues for the 'Christian past and primal present' in early Irish society, contending that 'primal religion' in early Ireland continued to exert a potent influence on Christianity. Even so, the evidence presented by McCone is writ large in the literature of the early Middle Ages, and is hard to gainsay in that context. However, while the church undoubtedly did 'rewrite' history and create a massively influential learned class, it did *not* invent the totality of early Irish literary tradition. It adjusted it, and preserved it in a certain form, and also supplemented it very significantly. The picture with regard to institutions such as kingship, steeped in traditional ritual predating Christianity, is even more complex, but it does not suggest that the church wholly eliminated pagan practices in that context.

Proper scholarly debate may not be of interest to the average devotee of highly reconstructed 'Celtic Christianity', but reference to it serves, at the very least, to demonstrate that there is much that is still very arguable in the field of Christianity and culture in the early British

Isles. The profiles of the Celtic saints, who concern us in the next chapter, were shaped at the interface of secular and Christian traditions, and are part of the ongoing debate.

CHAPTER 9
BETWEEN FAITH AND FICTION: THE PROFILES OF THE CELTIC SAINTS

Saints have a high profile in modern 'Celtic Christianity'. This is partly because earlier works on the 'Celtic Church' have laid great emphasis on the saints; Nora Chadwick entitled one of her most influential books *The Age of the Saints in the Early Celtic Church*, thus reinforcing the popular link between the saints and the 'Celtic Church'. Indeed, it seems likely that to many present-day minds the 'Celtic Church' and 'Celtic saints' are largely synonymous. The saints have also been associated with specific parts of the Celtic areas of Britain and Ireland; Ireland is sometimes designated the 'Isle of the Saints'. From such convenient labels myths arise.

Within popular 'Celtic Christianity', the saints are regarded with warmth and admiration. They are nearly always perceived to be friendly, helpful characters who are always at hand, and ready to provide kindly succour and advice. Like much else in 'Celtic Christianity', they are often delineated in contrast to the conventions of the rest of Christendom. They are, it is argued, very different from the cold, aloof saints of Catholic orthodoxy. Yet, when reading some of the popular accounts of the Celtic saints, one senses that they have lost many of their ancient powers as delineated in the surviving sources. The sanitising of the saints parallels the maner in which the 'Celtic Fringe' and its less saintly inhabitants have been transformed by modern seekers.

The significance of the saints

In some Christian traditions, notably Roman Catholicism, the saints have been invoked, celebrated and commemorated at a variety of popular levels across the centuries. This has led to the reshaping of saintly profiles to meet a broad range of needs, including changing fashions within both faith and community. In trying to assess the saints and give them a place in their modern worldviews, contemporary seekers maintain the tradition of popular pliability, and approach the subject in different ways, depending on what they want to get out of the saint. At the risk of oversimplifying, it can be said that what a Roman Catholic seeker expects to find in a 'saint' may be quite different from what a Protestant seeker may wish to find; but it is unlikely that there can be a single Roman Catholic approach or a single Protestant one. Nowadays, there may be many 'saint seekers' who have only the vaguest connection with Christianity in any form. Their reasons for seeking the saints may be quite diverse, in many cases unashamedly secular rather than devotedly sacred. As a result, the quest for the saints may be motivated by factors ranging from general curiosity to a special concern for the local economy or the environment. It is important to recognise the diversity of approaches within contemporary 'saint seeking', since the preconceived expectation will almost inevitably lead to a degree of reconstruction of the (rediscovered) saints. The saints, however, are no strangers to reconstruction. Their profiles have been rearranged by politicians, clerics and special pleaders since the earliest days, as we shall see in the case of Columba (Chapter 10).

The Celtic saints generally occupy a curiously peripheral, but at times very central, place within the structures of postmodern Christian belief. They are pulled from the periphery to the centre, or sometimes pushed out to the margins, as required, or even dropped off the edge of the popular record. Four centuries and more after the Reformation, even the most thoroughly reformed of Protestants still maintain an awareness of some of the saints, and are not averse to remembering them on special occasions. The most secular of people, too, trusting their lives utterly to Mammon, occasionally feel the need to slip their futures, their enterprises, and even their cheque-books, into the hands of the saints.

For this reason, the saints' claims to distinction have been modified skilfully in the course of the centuries. This is reflected in the endurance of their legends, and the very fact that their names exist at all. In the twentieth century, the saints have continued to be recreated, not so much to press the case for a monastic cause, but more to meet the needs of a whole variety of causes which, in some cases, might make the real saints rattle in their reliquaries. The profiles of the saints in the earlier texts (themselves created to meet the needs of a cause) have been refracted through lenses of different kinds, and all too often only parts of these profiles are used in modern representations of individual saints. Can we put the saints together again, so to speak, and should we even try to do so?

The temper of modern society suggests that anyone who tries to reverse the trends of modernism and postmodernism, to say nothing of the patterns of the centuries, is facing an up-hill struggle. Powerful forces - ecclesiastical partisanship, economic determinism, local pride, national and even nationalist aspirations, to name but a few - are ranged against the academic who calls attention to the problems inherent in discovering the identity and reality of any saint. Personal and public involvement with, and perspectives of, saints may also militate against any attempt to set the record straight. Most people who invoke the saints nowadays will not be concerned so much with the profile of the saints in the past; their main concern will be with the power and efficacy of the saints in the present. Saints are public property, and are in every sense 'popular' figures; they do not belong to scholars exclusively, and scholars cannot dictate the outlines of the saints' profiles.

The difficulty goes back to the origins of the saints; in the saints' ends were their beginnings. The practice of commemorating those who, like Polycarp of Smyrna (c. 69-c.155), had suffered martyrdom, had emerged by the middle of the second century A.D. By the fourth century, those considered to be saints, and esteemed as the 'holy dead', included not only martyrs, but also confessors (i.e. those who had survived suffering) and virgins. When people looked back, then as now, they believed that these ordinary men and women had many remarkable achievements to their credit, and they venerated them after their deaths. It was thought that God had used them greatly while on earth, and it was believed that human beings who were still alive could continue to benefit from their qualities, and not least from their ability to intercede with God. The 'holy dead' linked heaven and earth, and their special festival days were occasions on which entire communities, local and/or national, were brought together in remembrance and celebration across the centuries. Professor Hugh McLeod (*Religion and the People of Western Europe,* p.56) refers to the 'multitude of local saints in Catholic Europe, many of them unknown outside a particular parish or district - not to mention the necessarily unique holy places (springs, wells, rocks) which were local centres of pilgrimage by anxious individuals throughout the year, and by whole communities on a given day.'

The cults of the saints and martyrs led to the writing of saintly biographies, the creation of legends, statues, and invocations, and the use of saints' names in a range of circumstances, to bring blessing, to add validity, and to secure spiritual, ecclesiastical and other enterprises. The Celtic saints formed part of this wider pattern of veneration, and were not (as many would wish to believe) somehow without parallel elsewhere. Given the extent of the refashioning that has occurred across the centuries, it is unlikely that we will rediscover the full historical reality of any saint, Celtic or otherwise. The same applies to most figures from the early Middle Ages. In the case of the saints, hindsight has been too thoroughly spiritualised, and has become the main driving-force of saintly business. The patterns of retrospective reconstruction of saints' lives, which the scholar may use to illustrate the challenge of discovering the historical saints, have a momentum which defies any attempt to set out 'the truth' about saints, even if that 'truth' is that we cannot know 'the truth'.

The popularising of the stories of the saints, and the extraction of 'wisdom' from their words and deeds in the closing years of the twentieth century, is, to some extent, the largely secular version of this centuries-old process. Yet it could be argued that it is not fair to the saints, or to ourselves, to allow what remains of their 'real' profiles to be shaped out of existence by the demands of new management techniques, or by economic exigencies or political opportunism, local or national. On the threshold of a new millennium, we need to recover the cutting edge of our reason, and apply that to the evidence. Even if the earliest sources are biased, it is worth using these sources to check, and, where necessary, to correct contemporary, modernist biases. We may begin our attempt to 'recover' the saints by cutting through the various layers of reinterpretation which have been deposited on top of the 'historical' saints, so that we may hope to arrive at the earliest level of interpretation.

The place of the saints

It is popularly thought that, within the various churches of the Celtic lands, there were three conspicuous categories of holy people - saints, monks and hermits. In retrospect, the saints appear to have been 'a class apart', since their designation suggests that they had major significance within the structures of Christian belief in these regions. Yet 'saints', in their earthly lives, were not in a different league from 'monks' and 'hermits'. A 'saint', later esteemed and venerated by the faithful, might have begun his/her career as a monk, nun or hermit. Indeed, the particular qualities of the hermit or anchorite might be among those that were specially valuable in making a person a saint. Hermits and anchorites lived abstemious lives, and were committed to abstinence from the wiles and temptations of the world, fighting against the three great enemies of the soul - the world, the flesh and the Devil.

What are the other preconceptions which may govern our approach to the word 'saint' in our modern secular world? Perhaps we automatically think of saints as weaklings, men and women who are soft and fey, both now and then. Perhaps we believe them to have been detached from reality, not involved in the mundane and the secular affairs of the world. Again, we may consider that saints are honorific characters, in the sense that their sanctity is created by a central body with committees that examine their miracles to see if they are significant. If the candidate has a credible and creditable *curriculum vitae*, he or she will be allowed into the 'hall of heaven', and counted among those who have achieved heaven and have a great reservoir of virtue, or 'merit', which can be used in intercession for others. Nowadays, primarily within the Roman Catholic Church, a 'saintly' stage preceding canonisation is recognised, namely beatification, but if we bring such concepts into the Celtic world of the early Middle Ages, we may run the risk of severely misunderstanding sainthood and the manner of its recognition. Our Celtic sources conceived of people who were *sanctus/-a* and *beatus/-a* in quite different ways from the organised structures of the modern Roman Catholic Church. Of course, some Celtic saints did 'make it' into the ecclesiastical records, and were canonised by official procedure. But the Celtic world contains many saints who were never recognised in this way at all. In this respect, the Celtic saints are (again) no different from those of the rest of early medieval Christendom, including the apostles and the writers of the Gospels. No official machinery for canonisation existed before the tenth century, and its creation rested largely on the initiative of Rome.

The making of the saints

How, then, were saints 'made' in the Celtic world? How were they recognised as such? There were several criteria. These were based on how the person was perceived after his or her death, but it is fair to say that it was what the saint did, or was believed to have done, while alive that really made the difference. Of course, after the saint's death, there was the possibility of the development of a cult around his/her name, and this could lead to considerable elaboration of the stories of the saint's powers. Many saints gained their real reputations after their deaths, when their cults were established, their lives were written in biographies, and churches were founded bearing their names. We have to be very much aware of such developments, and we shall consider further aspects of this matter later in the chapter. But, for the present, we can explore the special qualities that were recognised as equipping their owner for the Celtic hall of religious fame.

The quality of the saint's purity and moral stature was the first consideration. Christianity in the Celtic world, as elsewhere in Europe, generally placed very heavy emphasis on the ability of the 'holy person' to live an unblemished life, in which great discipline was exercised and the body was kept firmly under control. Some saints appear to have qualified for veneration because of this quality alone: for example, St Gall was an Irish saint who was renowned for his asceticism, and, when he went to the continent of Europe, a monastery was established in the location of his cell by those who had come to emulate his holy life. St Cuthbert, associated with the monastery at Melrose on the Tweed, was another who laid great stress on mortification, i.e. on the 'putting to death' of the body and its desires, and he did so by bathing in the Tweed when the ice was floating in the river.

The saint's purity was related to his/her ability to receive power from, and be in communication with, God. The cleaner the life, the more suppression there was of the desires of the flesh, and the greater the opportunity for God's power to flow through that person.

The power of the saints

Power, representing proximity to God, was exemplified in various ways in the life of the holy person:
(1) the ability to tell the future;
(2) the capacity to see into the mind of an evil or good person so that he/she was realistically assessed;
(3) command over the elements - Columba could bring about good or bad weather;
(4) control over the animal world - Columba defeated the water-beast in the River Ness;
(5) the capacity to perform miracles of healing, etc.

Not least significant was the potency of the saint's blessing and cursing, as if the holy person were able to affect the way matters proceeded simply by an utterance or pronouncement. Celtic saints are often portrayed rather romantically in 'Celtic Christianity' as having great benedictive power, and as wonderful sources of blessing; but they were also capable of very strong curses, and some were much better known for their maledictions than their benedictions.

Welsh sources furnish us with particularly good instances of maledictive saints. These have been conveniently summarised by Professor Wendy Davies (*Wales in the Early Middle Ages*, pp.177-8):

'David cursed the bees that followed Modomnoc so that they never again flourished in his settlement, and he withered the hand of the man about to strike the saint. Cadog caused the barn and its attendant servant to be consumed by fire, for insubordination; he occasioned the death of two disciples of his when they carelessly left his book behind on Flatholm; he killed his steward for dereliction of duty and deficiency in looking after the resources of the community...By the agency of St Germanus the tyrant Benlli was consumed by fire which fell from heaven...'

In medieval Irish hagiography, its saints are portrayed as no less ferocious in their response to the perpetrators of injustice and oppression, the representatives of evil (be they human or animal), and those earthly potentates who stood in their way. The potency of the holy person's life is thus shown very clearly not only in the facilitation of God's blessing through his/her agency, but also in the holy person's ability to stop evil in its tracks. The saints were the moral and spiritual police of their time, and it was their duty to catch 'criminals'. The application of spiritual power, in both its positive and negative aspects, was what made a person a 'saint', indeed a 'hero', in the eyes of later admirers.

The fight of the saints

The common perception of the 'Celtic' man or woman of God was indeed that of the *miles Christianus*, the Christian soldier, who fought a battle against the forces of evil. For example, in the case of Columba of Iona, an Old Irish poem was composed on his death, the *Amra Choluimb Chille* ('Song/Hymn on Colum Cille' c.600). Stressing Columba's nobility and learning, the poet employs the imagery of warfare; the 'heroic code' of descriptions used of a secular warrior and his war-band is applied to the saint (Clancy and Márkus, pp.110-1) :

> *The guardian of a hundred churches...*
> *A mighty hero, no idolator,*
> *he did not assemble a crooked company*
> *who scattered under instruction...*
> *He fought a long and noble battle against flesh...*

This was precisely the theme that Adomnán took up in his biography of the saint, written a century after his death. Columba, he tells us, lived as an *insulanus miles*, 'an island-based soldier', for thirty-four years, and, according to Adomnán, he 'repulsed innumerable hostile bands of demons making war against him, visible to his bodily eyes, and preparing to inflict deadly diseases upon his community of monks'. We need to remind ourselves, nevertheless, that the battling Celtic saints had their counterparts in other cultures; the Anglo-Saxon saint, Guthlac, was particularly well known for his struggle against demons when he lived in isolation in the fens of East Anglia.

Heroic, and often regal, imagery was applied to the Celtic saints by poets and biographers. Even female saints, such as the celebrated Brigit of Kildare, were honoured by the poets in this heroic strain, though the warrior imagery was (suitably) less conspicuous:

> *Sit safely, Brigit, in triumph*
> *on Liffey's cheek to the strand of the sea;*
> *you are the princess with ranked hosts*
> *above the children of Cathair Mór...*
>
> *Brigit in the land I behold,*
> *where each in turn has lived,*
> *your fame has proved greater*
> *than that of the king; you are superior to them.*
>
> *You have an everlasting principality with the King,*
> *apart from the land where your sanctuary is;*
> *grand-daughter of Bressal, son of Dian,*
> *sit safely, Brigit, in triumph.*   (Greene and O'Connor, pp.69-70)

Since the truly great 'holy men' and 'holy women' achieved the status of heroes and heroines, their doings became the religious equivalents of the heroic deeds in the secular tales and sagas. When the Lives of the saints came to be written down by admiring biographers after their deaths, these Lives - the *vitae* - formed the religious counterparts of the secular 'heroic biographies' in which the lives of the great Celtic heroes were commemorated.

The stories of the saints

The biographies of the saints are found in the type of literature commonly called 'hagiography'. This literature, recording the great deeds of the saints, follows certain standard conventions and patterns in the manner in which it portrays the saints, from their birth through to their deaths: not all saints' Lives follow the same pattern, nor do they include the same features, but if they are taken together they do seem to show recurrent themes. These have been identified as follows by Dr Elissa Henken ('The Saint as Folk Hero: Biographical Patterning in Welsh Hagiography'):

(1) The conception of saints is dramatic or unusual, accompanied by strange phenomena;

(2) They are often of royal lineage. St David of Wales, for example, was said to be the son of Sant, king of Ceridigion;

(3) Their birth is prophesied. David of Wales's birth was prophesied thirty years in advance.

(4) They are very precocious as children: they speak in their infancy, learn to read in one day, study Scripture, and argue with their elders about theology. (Here we may compare the New Testament story of Christ in the temple. It is evident that the pattern for the saint's life sometimes follows the life of Christ, as portrayed in the New Testament.)

(5) They perform childhood deeds, like herding swift-moving forest creatures. (We may compare the Irish hero, Cú Chulainn, who catches a wild stag on the day he takes up arms.)

(6) They perform a special miracle, indicative of maturity.

(7) They go out into the world, and find disciples (cf. the warband of the secular leader). They acquire powerful objects, bell, crozier etc.

(8) They travel by miraculous means, sometimes sailing on a stone over the ocean.

(9) They establish their authority, fighting with magicians, monsters or druids; they carry strong spiritual weapons, which can strike the opponent with a debilitating physical illness (e.g blindness).

(10) They die in a way that indicates their readiness to go to heaven, and heaven awaits them. Their power, however, can live on through their relics, their mortal remains or objects associated with them - staffs, bells, book satchels - which can function as conduits of the saints' power after death. One scholar points out very shrewdly that, in the ability of the saints' power to continue beyond their deaths, there lies a major difference between them and secular heroes; and one might say further that in this lay the ultimate triumph of the saints.

Much of what we know about the early saints of the Celtic churches is derived from hagiography of this kind, often constructed long after the saint's death, and the historian has to engage in a detailed sifting of the evidence, to ascertain if it is possible to extract a core of facts about the saint from the accumulation of legend. This can be done fairly successfully in some instances, depending on the historical base of the writer. One of the finest examples that we have of a well-based Life of a saint is Adomnán's *Vita Columbae*, the biography that we have already mentioned, compiled about a century after the saint's death. The latest study of the *Vita Columbae*, by Professor Máire Herbert, argues that Adomnán used an earlier collection of material about the saint that had been collected in Iona, *Liber de Virtutibus Sancti Columbae* - 'The Book of the Powers of Saint Columba'. Even when one strips out the miracles and the later yarns about Columba, one is left with a picture of a very powerful figure who had a great influence on the life of early Dál Riata, through his association with the rulers of the kingdom and his own royal status in Irish society. His influence is reflected in his presence at the conference of kings at Druim Cett (see Chapter 10).

The cities of the saints

Spiritual power, then, was an important aspect of the saint's persona, and won the status of a hero for the greatest saint. Another criterion was the foundational role of the saint in establishing a monastery or a family of monasteries. In the case of Columba, several monasteries were ascribed to him, but there were other saints who had no less impressive track records as founders of monasteries and made an impact on religious practice far beyond Britain and Ireland. We have the example of Columbanus (whose name should not be confused with that of Columba). Columbanus studied at the monastery of Bangor, in the north of Ireland, and set off for the Continent in 591. In France, Columbanus established a monastic house at Annegray in the Vosges mountains, at the site of an old Roman fort. He founded a second monastery at Luxeuil, and a third at Fontaines, near to Luxeuil. Following bitter disputes with French bishops and secular authorities, Columbanus pressed on over the Alps, and ended his days (615 A.D.) at Bobbio, where he established another monastic house. The record of the achievements of Columbanus is particularly full, since we know a great deal about him beyond the Life written by his follower, Jonas. He has left letters and other documents, including a penitential. He was a severely ascetic man, whose grim determination is writ large in the record of his foundations and in his dealings with other people.

As we have already noted, saints had the power to 'live on' after their deaths, and, allegedly, to work miracles through their relics. Something similar applies to their ability to found religious houses after their deaths. The cults of the saints, promoted by their followers, included the dedication of new churches in their honour. Thus, for example, the name of Cainnech of Achad Bó in Ireland became well known in Scotland, through dedications of churches. The common feature of dedications of this kind is the use of the term *cill/cell* (from the Latin *cella*), 'monastic cell', followed by the name of the saint (as in *Cille Choinnich*, in the case of Cainnech, and in *Cill Mo-Luaig*, in the case of Mo-Luag). One has to be very careful in using these dedications as reliable historical evidence about the presence of the saint at that site. The name of the saint - the name alone - had power and prestige, and was regarded as a suitable marker of saintly authority. In Wales, the most popular ecclesiastical term found in such dedications is *llan*, of which the country has an abundance, following patterns of commemoration similar to *cill-* names in Scotland.

The journeys of the saints

Hermits were mentioned earlier in this chapter, but we have almost lost track of them. They themselves would no doubt appreciate this, since their aim was frequently to escape from human attention in order to engage in an intense pursuit after holiness. Different types of hermit or anchorite were associated with the Christian movements in the Celtic lands. Some stayed put on a lonely spot in their homeland for most of their lives, while others journeyed off into the unknown oceans to seek for a *desertum*, an isolated place where they could contemplate God. Wandering monks of this sort, who did not undertake a purposeful peregrination of the kind that took Columbanus - and also St Gall, and a considerable number of other saints - to the Continent, were to be found moving through the western seas. The Norse referred to them as *papar*, because the Norsemen sometimes discovered these remarkable men installed in seclusion in remote islands. The word the Norsemen used apparently comes into their language from Early Irish *pupu, popa* ('father, priest'), which seems to have had a secondary meaning of 'anchorite'. The *papar* have left their mark on place-names in Skye and the Outer Hebrides and also in Orkney and Shetland; Pabbay, Bayble, Papa Westray and similar place-name forms derive from *Papar-ay,* 'Anchorites'/'Priests' Island'. Unfortunately the surviving historical record does not allow us to reconstruct the lives of such men in any detail.

It is important to note that wandering monks who went off into the unknown were not, in fact, a central feature of Christianity in the Celtic lands in the early Middle Ages. It is all too common to encounter the view that 'Celtic Christianity' was, in essence, a constant process of journeying, involving *peregrini* ('pilgrims') who 'popped off' somewhat casually to undertake 'spiritual journeys' with which we today can readily identify. There was indeed an element of 'drop-out' journeying in the Celtic expressions of the faith, but this was not peculiarly a Celtic phenomenon; its roots lay in the Egyptian deserts (see Chapter 8). Nor was it something that was undertaken lightly as a matter of course. It was often brutally hard. When a monk left settled monastic life, he became a *deorad* ('stranger') who forfeited his legal rights and kin. The custom was also very strictly regulated, since it was all too easy for *peregrini* to become *vagabundi.* Abbots were generally not too happy to see their monks going off in a vague search for God, and some made the point that those who had not already found God at home in Ireland were unlikely to find him elsewhere. Loss of monks also meant diminution of the monastic community - and stable communities were vitally important to the success and influence of the church, then as now. It was thus important that *peregrini* should have the permission of their abbots before they could embark on their wayward adventures.

In addition to the 'high achievers' like Columba and Columbanus, and the drop-outs who bobbed around in boats and could be washed up anywhere between Kent and St Kilda, there were other holy men who went 'on pilgrimage', in much the same sense as we would understand the term today. Their journeys had a clear purpose; Irish monks were glad to travel to Rome, and to experience Peter's great city. As a result, they reinforced their links with the Holy See, and brought home sacred souvenirs - relics and treasures which enhanced the status of their churches and monasteries.

The search for the saints

We have considered the profile of the saints, but how should we approach the task of identifying the faith of the saints? Some may consider that the recovery of the historical profile of a saint is a task for a trained historian, in the first instance. If we regard ourselves as non-specialists, looking for inspiration for our own time, how should we seek to interpret the saints of the early churches in these islands?

Do the saints belong only to Roman Catholics? What (if any) relevance do they have for Christians who are members of Protestant churches, and who would deny the role of the saints as intercessors with God? Can they dare to claim the saints as their own kith and kin? Can they do so without misrepresenting them, or without forfeiting their Protestant perspectives?

At the very outset, it needs to be acknowledged that the saints had, and continue to have, an earthly function as examples and role-models for the faithful. Protestantism too maintains a very strong awareness of the need for such role-models, and has recognised its own succession of exemplary men and women, who are likewise memorialised in biographies of various kinds, oral and written (see Chapter 12). Nevertheless, in seeking to identify with the pre-Reformation saints, Protestants may need to free their minds from modern prejudices and preconceptions. As has been shown in Chapter 6, enthusiasts sometimes think that the so-called 'Celtic Church' was different from the 'Roman Church', and that it was a precursor of the Reformation. This understanding of the past cannot be sustained on the evidence. There were certainly matters of divergence between the so-called 'Celtic tradition' and the practice of the wider 'church universal', but these were gradually eliminated. A similar notion exists about the saints; Columba is often regarded as a pre-Reformation Protestant (see Chapter 10). Yet, the saints were not pre-Reformation Protestants. If Protestants seek to be true to the existing evidence, they are not at liberty to re-interpret Celtic saints to suit themselves in this way; the saints were not proto-Presbyterians, proto-Baptists or proto-Brethren. They were part of the Catholic church of their time, and require to be seen in that context.

Celtic saints must therefore be accepted with all their 'faults', as these faults may be perceived from various modern denominational vantage-points. They may have been a motley crew, with good and bad among them, but they cannot be dismissed simply because they had the 'misfortune' to live before the Reformation, and adhered to pre-Reformation doctrines. Nor can they be sanitised into an uneasy conformity with post-Reformation practices. Instead of condemning the saints outright or remaking them in a 'more orthodox' image, the primary aim of all concerned with elucidating the role of the saints ought to be to understand their place in the spirituality of the early Middle Ages. While we may not be able to recover the full historical facts about any saint, we may be able to identify what early medieval people regarded as the hallmarks of sanctity.

What did the Celtic writers generally perceive to be the driving force of sainthood? What were the special qualities which, in the opinion of the faithful, made the saints 'tick'? These quailities can be identified in different ways, using different criteria. We have already considered some of the wider European perspectives, and the formal biographical themes which are most frequently pursued by hagiographers. We could also focus on the secular or political aspects of the saints, portrayed according to the desires and ambitions of their biographers; and we could equally easily concentrate on the heroic characteristics of the saints. Yet, in the very essence of their being, these were men and women of faith, a rugged and, at times, erratic faith - but men and women of faith nevertheless.

The spirituality of the saints

Most people who are interested in 'Celtic Christianity' will be concerned with the spirituality of the saints. They will wish to observe the faith of the saints, and see how it looks, with a view to emulating that faith today. When they do that honestly, however, they will see a faith very different from the kind that modern 'Celtic Christianity' frequently represents. It is unwise to draw general conclusions, since there are always exceptions to any rule, and not least to spiritual rules; but there are at least some common features that embrace a considerable proportion of the Celtic saints. How we perceive these common features, however, will depend to some extent on what we are looking for. An evangelical picture of the saints, which places its emphasis on their exemplary lives, would proceed as follows:

First and foremost, the sources suggest, most Celtic saints devoted themselves to Christ. Some of the saints went through very deep spiritual experiences. They were aware of the call to follow Christ as pilgrims and, in some cases, as missionaries. Patrick, the patron saint of Ireland, has left us his own testimony. As we have seen in Chapter 7, Patrick was a Briton who, in the early fifth century, was captured by a band of raiders and taken away to Ireland. He later returned to Britain, and then found that God was calling him back to Ireland. He has also given an account of the remarkable ways in which the Lord spoke to him, encouraged him, and commissioned him as a missionary to the Irish. Patrick's account of his calling to serve Christ is very moving, and its theology resonates with much of Protestant thought. He lays great emphasis on his awareness of God's grace in calling him, and on his sense of mission.

Not all saints were called to be missionaries like Patrick. Some spent their lives in a single monastery, and others went on *peregrinatio*, but most were determined to spend their lives in a manner which glorified Christ. When Adomnán wrote his biography of Columba, he drew attention pre-eminently to the way in which Columba's life reflected that of Christ.

Second, the Celtic saints devoted themselves to holy living. The best among them were believed to have lived godly lives. Godly living was greatly admired, and many subjected their bodies to very harsh circumstances while they conducted their devotions, including prayer and other vigils. Several saints made a point of seeking solitude to commune with God. Columba went to lonely places in Iona, and engaged in intercession and prayer. In order to be alone with God, he often went to another island called *Hinba* (probably to be identified with Oronsay, south of Colonsay).

Third, the saints devoted themselves to the study of the Scriptures. They loved the Scriptures. Columba, for example, is portrayed by Adomnán as being particularly fond of the Psalms. The last piece of Scripture which he copied before his death was the 34th Psalm. Adomnán himself, who wrote the Life of Columba, was steeped in the Bible. The 'Confession of St Patrick' also demonstrates that Patrick knew his Bible thoroughly; he quotes directly from it, and echoes it frequently. Love of the Scriptures - though not always sufficient in itself to ensure accurate transcriptions - is attested in lavishly illuminated gospel-books such as the Book of Kells, possibly begun at Iona. It is evident too on the Celtic crosses, and particularly on panels which represent particular scenes from the Gospels.

Fourth, the saints devoted themselves to demonstrating the power of God in the land. The power gained by living a life close to God was manifested in various ways in the life of the holy person. The power of God stood opposed to the power of paganism. Columba's Life depicts him as travelling from Iona to the King of the Picts in the Inverness area, where he challenged Pictish magicians in a contest of power. Columba won the contest, and vindicated the name of God in the land. This is an important point, since (as we have noted in Chapter 5) the emphasis in much modern 'Celtic Christianity' is on how the faith made friends with paganism. This interpretation plays down the need for confrontation and conversion.

Fifth, and by way of a summary, we can assert that the saints devoted themselves to the extension of Christ's kingdom. They did so in different ways. The sources depict them as presenting the Christian gospel to pagans, exercising strict discipline, and establishing a monastery or a family of monasteries. Not all were missionaries, not all were disciplinarians, and not all founded monasteries, though many did. In the case of Columba, several monasteries were ascribed to him, and we know that he founded monasteries at Durrow in Ireland and in Iona and Tiree in the Hebrides. Other saints had strengths as missionaries, hearing the call of God to evangelise different places. Patrick of Ireland is the classic example of a man who was obedient to God's word, and, despite difficult circumstances, worked to evangelise the country. He was not the only missionary who was active in the evangelisation of Ireland; others had preceded him in the task, and had made their own contributions, but his writings ensure that his mission is the most memorable.

The Lives of the Celtic saints reveal a very robust spirituality, demonstrating forcefully that they were not soft-centred people, always making friends with paganism, or acting gently when there was need to be strong. They were tuned to another wavelength altogether. The factor which appears to be common to all of them is that they were devoted to Christ - devoted to knowing him better and to extending his kingdom.

Being fair to the saints

Yet, if we insist on deriving spiritual lessons and moral messages from the saints, we have to accept that there was also (in our terms) a 'down' side to their spiritual profiles - and that side is much harder to portray in contemporary evangelical sermons. They were 'earthy' as well as 'heavenly' people. They were sometimes instruments of malediction, meting out judgements that may seem harsh to us today. It is easy to forget about, or set aside, the unpalatable aspects of the saints' lives as recorded by their biographers. We can explain these 'deviations' by supposing that their biographers were investing the saints with some of the more fearsome properties of the secular heroes, including vengeance on the enemies of the tribal group (who would correspond to opponents of the saints' causes). But the appeal to secular conventions is not enough. We need to face the fact that even Old Testament prophets had a darker side to their characters - and Old Testament models were much in the minds of certain hagiographers. It is, however, no less evident that the New Testament provides clear examples of Christians who challenged, with strong words and equally strong actions, the injustices, exploitative structures and theological 'errors' of their time. Christ himself cursed the barren fig-tree, cast the money-lenders out of the temple, and addressed the Pharisees as 'a brood of vipers'. The Apostle Peter condemned the actions of two individuals, a husband and wife, who had deceived the early church in matters pertaining to money, and he witnessed their immediate deaths.

In acknowledging the robust spirituality of the Celtic saints, we must seek to avoid the constant temptation to cover our religious heroes and heroines with a romantic gloss. Celtic saints - despite the 'Celtic' label - were not perfect people. They functioned in imperfect churches, in an imperfect world, with other imperfect human beings. They were also prepared to indulge in practices which the Reformed tradition and even later Catholicism might well regard as unacceptable, but which were entirely orthodox in 'the age of the saints'. Even if we avoid romanticism, we can deceive ourselves just as easily, if, on the score of differences and 'errors' which were regarded as such after 1500, we dismiss the saints. Rather than play hide-and-seek with the evidence of existing records, we should accept that the saints operated in the light of the Christian revelation that was given to them and to their churches in their own day. In those contexts, they faced up to the challenges of their time. Without such saints, firm in the faith, ready to condemn the evils of the world, and prepared to suffer to the point of death, there would have been no church and no Christianity, 'Celtic' or otherwise.

As we pay due respect to the saints, we nevertheless need to consider the manner in which perceptions of the saints have changed across the years in accordance with contemporary expectations. Depending on where we look, we will find different emphases on the value or function of the saint concerned. Sanctity, as perceived by human beings, is not a wholly static concept, and can become the servant of, rather than the model for, human aspirations. Indeed, the saints are so pliable in human minds that it is dangerous to make general statements about their faith or achievements. All too often such generalisation conforms to our preferred stereotype of sanctity, which is conditioned by our own particular understanding of the faith. As a result, we find, and even create, not 'the saints as they were', but 'the saints as we want them to be'. If we wish to observe the manner in which the profile of a saint can be reconstructed at different stages of history, we can do no better than to reflect on changing perceptions of one of the most famous of them all - no less a saint than Columba.

CHAPTER 10

A SAINT FOR ALL CENTURIES:
CHANGING PERCEPTIONS OF COLUMBA

The 1400th anniversary of St Columba's death was celebrated across Britain and Ireland in 1997 in grand style - and gave 'Celtic Christianity' a huge publicity boost. The celebrations included major and minor conferences, pilgrimages to Iona and to other 'Celtic' monastic sites, flying visits to these and other locations by influential political figures, and a whole harvest of books and articles by scholars across the British Isles. For a brief period, Columba was well out in front in the popular marathon of the saints, while Augustine of Canterbury, always a slow starter in 'Celtic' eyes, turning up when Columba expired, only just managed to hold his place. Ninian also ran. But who was this saintly fast-tracker, Columba? Did everyone celebrate the same Columba? Is Columba the same today as he was last century? Like most 'Celtic' saints, Columba has what could be termed a 'moving' biography, since new chapters are added at regular intervals.

The coming of Columba

Around the year 563 a small boat left the coast of Ireland. It may have made its initial landfall elsewhere in the Hebrides, but it eventually reached the shores of Iona. As far as we are aware, nobody was there to greet its arrival; we can presume that the main observers of this historic landing would have been the seagulls and the other birds wheeling overhead. Perhaps an occasional inquisitive seal popped his smooth head and bristling whiskers above the water. These creatures of the sea were likely to have been quite familiar with the appearance of little vessels of this kind - the wooden-framed leather coracles which were the principal means of transport between the islands and around the shores of Ireland and Scotland. There was nothing out of the ordinary in a landing of this kind. It was only in retrospect that the event would have been seen to have had any particular significance.

The men on board the coracle were also quite ordinary to all appearances - twelve in mumber, with a thirteenth who was to become their leader and the founder of a new monastic community in Iona. We can only speculate as to what Columba looked like: there are no contemporary pictures of him, in stone or in word. In the course of the centuries, however, Columba was to be portrayed by many composers and writers, in Latin and in early Gaelic, in English and in modern Gaelic, each one trying to capture the essence of the man, and recreating him in the most appropriate forms that they knew.

Early visions of the saint

The earliest surviving full-scale Latin Life of the saint was attempted a century after his death, but it was by no means a neutral account. This is the *Vita Columbae* ('The Life of Columba'), written by Adomnán, the ninth abbot of Iona. The evidence on which it was based was probably massaged rather gently by the composer or his informant(s), in an attempt to construct a particular image of Columba, as a rather fearsome, miracle-working, powerful holy man who commanded an awesome respect, and by whose authority the Iona monastery and other monasteries within the Columban group still stood.

Book One of the *Vita Columbae* describes a number of Columba's prophecies, some of which make grim reading. These prophecies, demonstrating the saint's ability to foresee God's plan, often foretold dire retributions which awaited those who had committed crimes against their own relatives and kindreds, and against the church itself. Although Columba undoubtedly had his kinder attributes, this is no gentle, Celtic saint in the modern romantic mould; rather, Columba appears as a man who did not shrink from prophesying the most severe penances for malefactors.

Some people had the privilege of seeing Columba in great visions after his death, particularly before battles, as if there were a connection between this godly man and the forces of evil and disaster. Adomnán tells us a splendid story about Oswald, the Anglo-Saxon king of Northumbria, on the day before he was going to fight a powerful king, Cadwallon, the ruler of Gwynedd (Anderson and Anderson, *Adomnán's Life of Columba*, pp.14-15):

> One day when king Oswald was encamped in readiness for battle, sleeping on his pillow in his tent he saw in a vision Saint Columba, radiant in angelic form, whose lofty height seemed with its head to touch the clouds. The blessed man revealed his own name to the king, and standing in the midst of the camp he covered it with his shining raiment, all but a small remote part; and gave him these words of encouragement, the same that the Lord spoke to Joshua ben-Nun before the crossing of the Jordan, after the death of Moses, saying: 'Be strong, and act manfully; behold I will be with you', and so on. Thus in the vision Saint Columba spoke to the king, and added: 'This coming night, go forth from the camp to battle; for the Lord has granted to me that

at this time your enemies and your adversary Catlon [i.e. Cadwallon] shall be delivered into your hands. And after the battle you shall return victorious and reign happily.

King Oswald did win the Battle of Heavenfield in 633, and Cadwallon, king of Gwynedd, was killed.

We may be inclined to dismiss this as a pretentious piece of fiction, indebted not only to the Old Testament narrative of the initiation of Joshua as the new leader of the Hebrews, but also to the vision of the cross which was seen by the Roman Emperor, Constantine, before he defeated his rival, Maxentius, at the battle of the Milvian Bridge in 312 A.D., thereafter becoming the first Christian Emperor of the Roman world. Whatever the literary antecedents of the account, it tells us much about how Columba was regarded after his death. A figure of massive stature has emerged by the end of the seventh century: he is larger than life, indeed almost cosmic in scope, his head seeming to touch the clouds; he is able to perceive the course of battles, and also to affect, by implication, the destiny of nations. He acts as a mediator between an earthly king and God.

This vision also helps to provide perspectives on the relationship between culture, politics and ecclesiastical matters in the period concerned. Because Cadwallon was king of Gwynedd, the northern kingdom in Wales, he would be regarded by some today as a 'Celtic' ruler. Columba, as a saint from the Hebrides, would similarly be considered to be 'Celtic', and, in terms of our modern understanding of the Celtic countries, one might have expected him to have sided with Cadwallon rather than Oswald. However, cultural links of this kind would not have been of any significance to Adomnán or Columba; what mattered was the connection which had been made through the mission of Aidan, a monk from Iona who went to Northumbria in the early seventh century (see Chapter 7). There is therefore no contradiction in the role of Columba as a helper of the Anglo-Saxons rather than the Welsh; Cadwallon was seen to be an evil ruler.

By the late seventh century, Columba was becoming a major figure in the gallery of the saints. It was one of Adomnán's primary aims that he (and Iona) should achieve an even greater reputation as a result of the writing of the *Vita*. But who was this Columba, and why had he come to Iona?

The making of the monk

We have some information about Columba's pedigree and background. He was a native of Donegal, born, according to tradition, in a small village called Gartan in the north of Donegal about the year 521. His father was Fedelmid mac Fergusa, who was himself the grandson of a famous Irish hero, Conall Gulban ('Conall of the Snout'), who gave his name to the part of Donegal called *Tír Chonaill* (Tirconnell). Conall Gulban, Columba's great-grandfather, also achieved legendary status; tales were told about him both in Ireland and in Gaelic Scotland. Columba did the same in the spiritual realm. Great founders were produced by that family, great political and religious founders. The family belonged to the Uí Néill, an increasingly powerful kindred in the north of Ireland. So Columba was 'well connected', right from the start. These connections, with the families who mattered, gave Columba a firm foundation on which to build his own kingdom of spiritual power.

According to medieval Irish tradition, Columba was originally called Crimthann, and later given his name 'Columba' ('Dove') for monastic use. In Irish he became 'Colum Cille' ('Dove of the Church'). His Latin Life records that he was fostered out with a priest, and then his training as a deacon was undertaken with a bishop called Finnio whose identity is uncertain, but who may be equated with the famous Finian of Clonard, a monastic founder renowned for his hard-line discipline. Columba himself became another hard-liner when it came to making people pay for their sins and doing penance. These Irish saints were anything but a 'soft touch'.

Well-connected and heading for a good career in the boom-time of Irish monastic development - that was the way Columba's early life seemed to be going. A new religious movement which was productive of many monasteries was on the point of achieving phenomenal growth in Ireland after 550, and Columba would seem to have become a founder of monasteries in Ireland itself (see Chapter 7). But why did he come to Iona, and why did he make that island his headquarters? Would he not have been better to have stayed at home?

Adomnán records for us, in a rather cagey way, that there was an episode of some kind in Columba's early days that put him temporarily out of favour with the leaders of the churches in Ireland. In fact, he was excommunicated for what Adomnán considers to have been relatively minor offences. The sentence of excommunication was reversed at Teltown (where it was probably imposed), because, states Adomnán, another saint had a vision of the impending greatness of Columba. Adomnán also indicates that Columba came to Iona two years after a battle called *Cúl drebene*, in which Columba's relatives, the Uí Néill, were heavily involved. Victory went to the northern branch of the family, and this victory was later ascribed to Columba's prayers.

It is very difficult to be sure what Columba's role was in the battle, or whether it caused him to uproot himself from Ireland. The early days of the saint in Ireland are not well covered by Adomnán.

However, it is quite clear from his later deeds in Scotland that Columba was a very forceful figure indeed, and that he liked to be involved in politics. He was probably a kind of stormy petrel, who perched on a tight-rope between the sacred and secular roles of the new breed of monastic leaders who were emerging in Ireland. We are given the impression that these founding fathers had strong personalities, and that they needed to give one another plenty of room. What Adomnán says about Columba and *Cúl drebene* is very allusive and non-specific (Anderson and Anderson, pp.6-7): 'In the second year after the battle of Cul drebene, the forty-second of his age, Columba sailed away from Ireland to Britain, wishing to be a pilgrim for Christ (*pro Christo perigrinari volens*).'

Adomnán thus sees Columba's departure from Ireland as a very positive matter - a 'peregrination' for the sake of Christ.

Power and politics
It seems likely that even if Columba did leave Ireland for the sake of Christ, his aristocratic links would have made him a very powerful person wherever he went, and there may have been those in Scottish Dál Riata who shuddered at the prospect of his arrival because of its political implications. We must remember that he was closely related to the main branch of the Uí Néill kindred in the north of Ireland, and that the Uí Néill were in the ascendant at the time of his arrival in Iona. In fact, they were beginning to squeeze the *Ulaid* (including Irish Dál Riata) very hard indeed, and trying to exert overlordship. It is possible that Columba exerted a form of personal overlordship in Scottish Dál Riata after he arrived, and that he did it to the advantage of his kinsmen, the Uí Néill.

How otherwise do we explain the forceful manner in which he acted with the kings of Scottish Dál Riata? Columba is said to have consecrated Aedán mac Gabráin as the king of Dál Riata, and then around 575 he went to a 'summit' conference with Aedán. This conference was held in the north of Ireland, at Druim Cett near Limavady, and according to later Irish tradition Aedán mac Gabráin, king of Scottish Dál Riata, had to sort out his position relative to Irish Dál Riata on the one hand and the king of the northern Uí Néill on the other. Whatever the reason, it is very interesting indeed that Columba had to accompany Aedán. In the opinion of Professor F. J. Byrne (*Irish Kings*, pp.110-1), one result of the conference was the formation of an alliance which bound Aedán more closely to the king of the Northern Uí Néill, and set him against the king of the Ulaid, Baetán mac Cairill. To ensure that the agreement was maintained, we have it on Adomnán's authority that Columba prophesied disaster to Dál Riata if this alliance were broken.

Once in Scotland, Columba was able to influence kings beyond Dál Riata. Adomnán's Life of the saint records that he crossed into Pictland on occasions, and that he had a memorable encounter with Bruide, the king of the Picts, at his fortress near Inverness. There he engaged in exciting feats of power with Bruide's magician, and was able to impress the Pictish king with his ability to open a locked gate; as Adomnán tells us, the result was that 'from that day onwards, throughout the rest of his life, that ruler greatly honoured the holy and venerable man, as was fitting, with high esteem'.

It looks as if Columba succeeded, then, in establishing a personal spiritual overlordship in Pictland, so that he was given a place of great honour. Yet there is no convincing evidence in Adomnán that Columba converted the Picts, as is often thought. In fact, there is no evidence that he even converted the Pictish king, Bruide. His achievement was to establish himself in a position of power relative to the Picts. He showed them that he had the real 'magic' and that they would need to bend the spiritual knee to him. This must have worked to the long-term political advantage of Scottish Dál Riata.

So was Columba more of a politician than a saint? Was his little outpost in Iona really an Uí Néill colony in disguise? It is fair to conclude that politics and sanctity went closely together in this man and probably in his followers. It is quite evident that Columba kept a very keen eye on events in Ireland, especially those relating to his own kindred. Nevertheless, there are other pictures of Columba in Adomnán's biography. We see him at work looking after the day-to-day affairs of the monastery, engaging in prayer, visiting penitents (especially in *Hinba*, an island where there was a monastery and penitentiary), transcribing manuscripts, and, prior to his death, transcribing the Psalter. It is hard to escape the conclusion that, whatever Columba's involvement in secular society, it was Adomnán's intention to portray him as a Christ-like saint, and, indeed, one of exceptional piety. Yet Columba may have had a belligerent streak in his nature which could have compelled him to leave Ireland, and that side of his character was to emerge strongly in the course of the Middle Ages, since he is often represented as a fighter, in spirit, against the invaders of his homeland.

Columba and the Vikings

The arrival of the Vikings in the late eighth century posed a serious threat to the life of monasteries such as Iona (see Chapter 11). Though it is evident that active monastic life at Iona did not cease with the coming of the marauders from the north, the monastic community in Iona was subjected to several onslaughts, and in one of these - in 825 - the shrine of Columba was attacked. It was defended by a certain

Blathmac, whose bravery reached the ears of Walafrid Strabo, abbot of Reichenau (838-49), who composed a Latin poem in his honour and in commemoration of his martyr's death (Anderson, *Early Sources*, Vol. 1, p.265):

> The violent cursed host came rushing through the open buildings, threatening cruel perils to the blessed men, and after slaying with mad savagery the rest of the associates, they approached the holy father, to compel him to give up the precious metals wherein lie the bones of St Columba, but the monks had lifted the shrine from its pediments, and had placed it in the earth, in a hollowed barrow, under a thick layer of turf...This booty the Danes [*sic*] desired; but the saint remained with unarmed hand, and with unshaken purpose of mind, trained to stand against the foe, and to arouse the fight, and unused to yield.

We are confronted once again with the recurrent theme of the *miles Christianus*, so closely associated with Columba himself, but here it recovers something of its active warrior perspective, in the last stand of Blathmac protecting the founder's relics at Iona.

By the middle of the ninth century, some of Columba's relics had been moved from Iona. In 849, soon after Kenneth mac Alpin was recognised as king of both the Picts and the Scots, the relics of Columba were taken to Dunkeld. This indicates that Columba's prestige was high, since he was being associated with the main Scottish dynasty and with its principal ecclesiastical foundation.

Because of the Viking attacks, Columba was viewed increasingly as protector of Gaelic groups, regions and even nations. He is portrayed as assisting 'the men of Alba' against the Vikings on two occasions, on the first through the power of his crozier as a battle-standard, henceforth known as the *Cathbhuaid* ('Battle-Triumph'), and on the second through his response to the men's prayers (Clancy, 'Cult of Saints', p.27). In military contexts, his insignia - reliquaries and crozier in particular - are said to have bestowed much favour on the Scots. Towards the end of the turmoils of the Viking Age, Columba appears to have been sufficiently respected, even by the Norse, to give pause for thought to the most violent of their kings. In 1098, the Norse king, Magnus Barelegs, arrived in the Hebrides on a major harrying expedition (McDonald, *Kingdom of the Isles*, p.35). He plundered extensively in the Isles, but when he arrived at Iona, Magnus, we are told,

> wished to open the small church of Columcille; and the king did not go in, but closed the door again immediately, and immediately locked it, and said that none should be so daring thenceforward as to go into that church.

Later, the Norsemen themselves felt that it was opportune to portray, and perhaps even to invoke, Columba as the protector of the Hebrides against the expansive power of Alexander II, which came to an end when Alexander died at Kerrera in 1249. According to a Norse saga, the king had a dream, which the saga-teller relates as follows (Anderson, *Early Sources*, Vol. 2, pp.556-7):

> When Alexander lay in Kerrera sound, he dreamed a dream: and he thought that three men came to him. He thought that one wore royal apparel; this man was very frowning, and red-faced, and stout in figure. The second man seemed to him tall, and slender, and youthful; the fairest of men, and nobly dressed. The third was by far the largest in figure, and the most frowning, of them all. He was very bald in front. He spoke to the king, and asked whether he intended to go plundering in the Hebrides. He thought he answered that that was certain. The dream-man bade him turn back, and said to him that they would not hear of anything else.
>
> The king told his dream; and men begged him to turn back, but he would not do that. And a little later he fell ill, and died. Then the Scots broke up the levy, and conveyed the king's body up into Scotland. The Hebrideans say that these men who appeared to the king in his sleep must have been St Olaf, king of Norway; and St Magnus, earl of the Orkneys; and St Columba.

Here Columba is allied not only with the Hebrideans, but also with two great Norse saints, against the aggrandising intentions of Scottish kings. His capacity to meet the needs of all parties as a powerful and protective 'dream man' (in a more modern sense) was thus well established by the end of the thirteenth century (see further McDonald, *Kingdom of the Isles*, pp.229-30).

By the fourteenth century, Columba's protective powers on behalf of his own people were acknowledged from one side of Scotland to the other. At the monastery of Inchcolm, in the Firth of Forth, he was invoked (in the *Inchcolm Antiphoner*) as the defender of the community against the attacks of the English, and as *Spes Scotorum* ('Hope of Scots'):

> *Father Columba, splendour of our ways,*
> *receive your servants' offerings.*
> *Save the choir which sings your praise*
> *from the assaults of Englishmen*
> *and from the taunts of foes.*
>
> (Clancy, *The Triumph Tree*, p.318)

Within the Hebrides, Columba's shrine in Iona was astutely patronised by the Lords of the Isles; Donald, Lord of the Isles, commissioned a shrine 'of gold and silver for the relic of the hand of Columba' (Bannerman, 'The Lordship of the Isles', p.229). Columba functioned as the defender of the region and as the protector of its churches. In Tiree, for example, two churches bore his name, in the parishes of Kirkapol and Soroby respectively. The church in Kirkapol is described in 1375 as 'the parish church of Saint Columba of Kirkapol of the diocese of Sodor'.

The Columba of medieval literature

Columba's name continued to be associated with literary activities throughout the Middle Ages. He was linked increasingly closely with the composition of poetry and prose in Gaelic, functioning as the defender of the poets against oppression, and also as the subject of prose and verse and (supposedly) as a creative 'voice' within the verse tradition. In the eleventh and twelfth centuries, Irish poets ascribed much verse to him, in which he was often depicted lamenting his departure from Ireland, and longing wistfully to return. Some of the verse uses imagery very similar to that of the early 'nature poetry' allegedly composed by 'hermits' (see Chapter 5):

It would be delightful, Son of Mary,
in strange journeys
to travel over the sea, the well of floods,
to Ireland...

The host of the seagulls would rejoice
at our swift sail
if the dewy Derg [his ship]
were to reach welcoming Port na bhFearg.

Sorrow filled me leaving Ireland
when I was powerful,
so that mournful grief came to me
in the foreign land.

Wretched the journey that was imposed on me,
O King of Mysteries -
ah!, would that I had never gone to the battle
of Cúl Dremne!

Lucky for the son of Dimma
in his pious cell,
where I used to hear westwards in Durrow
the delight of my mind:

The sound of the wind in the elm-tree,
playing music to us,
and the cry of the blackbird with pleasure
when it had clapped its wings.

To listen early in Ros Grencha
to the stags,
and the cuckoos calling from the woods
on the brink of summer.

(Greene and O'Connor, *Golden Treasury*, p.183)

Columba was given a vernacular Life, written in Middle Irish, in the middle of the twelfth century by an admirer in (probably) the monastery of Derry. This Life casts him in a frame which is close to that of the Old Testament patriarchs (and especially Abraham). He is also presented as the founder of many churches in Ireland prior to his departure to Iona. In the late Middle Ages, Columba's cult was sufficiently strong to encourage the writing of yet another Life, this time in Classical Gaelic, which was commissioned by Manus Ó Domhnaill of Tirconnell and completed in 1532. As an extended biography, it resembles a compendium, since it draws on Adomnán's earlier *Vita* and the Middle Irish Life, but adds many more legends about the saint (see further Lacey, *Life of Colum Cille*).

The urge to write Columba's Life in Latin resurfaced in the sixteenth century, when Roderick MacLean, bishop of the Isles from 1550 to c. 1553, composed a work which contains poems on the saint in sixteen different forms of Latin verse. It was published as a book in Rome in May 1549, thereby bringing the saint's name directly into St Peter's city, but also into the world of the printing-press. It looks as if the saint, or at least the printing of this latest Life, may have helped to promote the interests of Roderick MacLean prior to his appointment as bishop of the Isles. The saint was, no doubt, meeting the needs of the hour in his usual compliant manner.

The Columba of modern lore and legend

Columba's place in literature, Gaelic and Latin, was thus firmly assured, but his memory also entered folk tradition, where it was well preserved as late as the beginning of the twentieth century. A 'folk memory' has been maintained to some extent throughout the century, but it would be wrong to suppose that a 'Columba consciousness' is still pervasive in the Highlands and Islands. The gradual attrition of the Gaelic communities has affected the saints as well as the sinners. Columba's memory has been preserved in these communities and beyond partly because of the folklore-collecting ventures of the second half of the nineteenth century, especially the work of Alexander

Carmichael. These ventures came off the presses at the very beginning of this century. Carmichael's *Carmina Gadelica* began to be published in 1900, and ensured that the twentieth century would be well supplied with a store of popular belief which has enjoyed some degree of artificial revival in the last twenty-five years. Other late nineteenth- and early twentieth-century collectors, notably Duncan MacGregor Campbell and Kenneth MacLeod (see Chapter 3), also recorded fragments of lore relating to Columba. Such sayings and fragments indicate that, during the centuries, Columba became a figure of invocation, in proverbs and rhymes. These have been particularly well preserved in the Roman Catholic communities of the Hebrides, though the saint is also remembered in the Protestant islands.

Columba's role as a spiritual warrior, efficacious in prayer and triumphant in worsting the Devil, is well attested in traditional Gaelic lore, but he is most frequently portrayed as a protector of the weak and as a facilitator of the regular tasks of life. His festival day (officially 9th June, but falling on the second Thursday of June, according to Gaelic tradition) has long been regarded as an auspicious day for undertaking new ventures (Meek, *Campbell Collection*, p.80):

Diardaoin, Là Chaluim Chille chaoimh,
Là chur chaorach air seilbh;
Là deilbh 's a chur bà air laogh.

(Thursday is gentle St Columba's Day;
the day to send sheep to pasture,
the day to lay warp, and to give a calf a foster-mother.)

For Hebrideans at the beginning of the twentieth century, Columba was generally a benign figure. This aspect of his character was manifested in the regular application of the Gaelic adjective *caomh* ('gentle') in neat alliteration with his Gaelic name, as the above saying bears witness. The regularity of the epithet might suggest that there was once a darker side to Columba which needed to be placated. The Hebridean designation, tinged with cultural romanticism, is echoed in the verse of a modern Gaelic poet, George Campbell Hay (1915-84). Expressing his deep affection for his 'homeland' of Kintyre, Hay imagines the days when Columba visited its harbours (*Fuaran Slèibh*, p.16):

Is domhain a chaidh freumh do sheanchais,
luingeas Lochlainn, airm is trod,
Clanna Lir air Sruth na Maoile,
Calum Cille caomh 'nad phort.

(Deep went the root of your story,
ships of Lochlann, arms and strife,
the Children of Lir on the Mull Race   [between Ireland and the Mull
gentle Calum Cille in your port.)   of Kintyre]

Hay, who appears to have regarded Columba as a legendary figure on a par with the mythological Children of Lir, places him in the context of the traditional Gaelic cultural links between Ireland and Scotland. The image of the saint as 'bond and bridge' across the North Channel was to reappear in potent and productive guise later in the century.

The generally kind Hebridean portrait of the saint stands in contrast to the manner in which he has been remembered in Donegal, where he looms large as a somewhat sinister figure. Only occasionally does a less attractive dimension of Columba's character surface in the Hebrides, notably in Tiree tradition. There he is still remembered for his powers of cursing, commemorated in local *dindshenchas* ('the lore of famous places'). The rock *Mallachdag* ('The Little Cursed One') in Gott Bay is said to have been at the receiving end of the saint's wrath because its seaweed failed to provide adequate mooring for his coracle. When he returned to the bay, at the end of his visit to the island, he found that his little ship had drifted out to sea. As a result of the saint's curse, the rock failed to produce or attract any more seaweed. Later maritime enterprise evidently forgot the saint's unhappy encounters with boats, and his name was used benevolently on at least three vessels of the MacBrayne (later Caledonian MacBrayne) fleet. Despite the application of his name, these ships were not entirely saintly in maintaining their schedules. Yet Columba, it would seem, missed not only his own boat but also the opportunity to become the patron saint of the ferry-frustrated passengers of the Hebrides.

The Columba of modern ecclesiology

In Hebridean folklore, Columba's memory was preserved mainly in prayers and sayings relating to daily work on the crofts. In the churches, both Scottish and Highland, he has been remembered rather more as the exemplar of orthodoxy, defined from the position of the church or denomination concerned.

In particular, Columba has had a long and seemingly paradoxical link with Presbyterianism. Within Scottish Protestantism more generally, the commemoration of saints has varied depending on the extent to which each form of Protestantism has (or has not) disavowed its pre-Reformation past. Although most forms of Protestantism would be uneasy with the invocation of the saints, many Protestant churches and individuals have maintained a lively interest in the saints, and Columba in particular has bucked the Protestant trend. This is largely because he was understood by medieval historians and propagandists to be a presbyter, rather than a bishop, within the ecclesiastical structure. He thus failed to make a major niche for himself within the episcopal ecclesiology of pre-Reformation Scotland.

Following the Reformation, however, as seventeenth-century historians struggled to find an appropriate cultural and spiritual lineage for Presbyterian polity (see Chapter 6), Columba's support was gladly enlisted. He remains something of a saintly comforter in times of disruption and anomie. Even today, Columba may be vaguely regarded by denominational apologists as a Puritan of Puritans, a Knox of Knoxes, a Calvin of Calvinists, belonging to that consoling stream called 'Pre-Reformation Protestantism'. From time to time in the present century, he has been given at least a kindly and admiring pat on the head by evangelical Presbyterians, particularly within the Free Church of Scotland.

The wistful 'backward look' of Scottish Protestantism finds expression in ecclesiastical nomenclature. A considerable number of Protestant (often Presbyterian) church buildings have been dignified with the names of saints; in this respect, Columba is probably more popular in Scottish Protestant practice than in Scottish Catholic tradition. This simple act of Presbyterian pietas may have contributed to the reshaping of the profile of the saint. Since his name is used on church buildings belonging to the Church of Scotland (in Glasgow) and the Free Church of Scotland (in Edinburgh), it may be tacitly assumed by those who enter the hallowed portals that the saint thus commemorated had all the qualities and ideals which the denomination itself aspires to have (see Chapter 6).

Such wishful thinking (which overlooks such minor religious differences as the mass, relics, penance, etc.) is sometimes assisted by the well-meaning but misleading efforts of those romantic historians who manage to see 'the legacy of Columba' in every aspect of Highland ecclesiastical practice. The austerity of the conservative Presbyterian Churches, the Reformed tradition of unaccompanied psalm-singing and the rejection of certain aspects of secular culture, may somehow be seen as deriving strength and even validation from the earlier example of Columba (see Chapters 11-12). The forces and processes which created the much more recent religious complexion of the Highlands are forgotten, and Columba becomes an ecclesiastical father figure who transcends not only time, but also modern denominational divisions and theological disputes.

The Columba of 'Celtic Christianity'

The Celtic saints have been reinterpreted to suit the trends of contemporary 'Celtic Christianity'. As we have observed in Chapter 9, they are often seen to be approachable and near at hand, in contrast to other European saints, who are cold and stand-offish in their shrines; they are environmentally-friendly folk, always ready to show kindness to human or animal.

Columba has not been immune from plastic surgery of this kind, and regularly changes shape to appeal to the current fad. Thus, to take but one example, his concern for a sick crane which has flown from his own homeland in the north of Ireland and lands, weak and tired, in Iona - an incident famously described in Adomnán's Life of the saint - is regularly interpreted by modern romanticisers as an indication of his environmental kindness. In fact, as Adomnán makes abundantly clear, Columba's concern is not for the bird as such, but for a creature which represents his native region. In Adomnán's portrait, as Columba moves beyond the circles of kin and culture, he becomes an altogether more aggressive figure. Thus, by his very word, he slays a boar in Skye - an incident which (for some reason) scarcely figures in the frame of modern Christian Celtophiles (see further Broun and Clancy, *Spes Scotorum*, pp.115-38).

Again, Columba is frequently portrayed as a Christian druid, taking on the offices of the pre-Christian druids of the early Gaelic world. Such an interpretation panders to the tastes of those who wish to argue that 'Celtic Christianity', unlike modern Christianity, was tolerant of pagan belief and practice. The more evidently biblical and confrontationally Christian dimensions of the saint are often played down when making a pitch for the attention of modern neo-paganism.

Columba's *persona* undergoes reconstruction not only in the context of popular perceptions of modern problems, but also in the services of worthy causes. He has been associated (inevitably) with the Iona Community since its inception in 1938, and has given good service as a figurehead and validator of its aspirations. He has been a focal point in the ecumenism which lies at the heart of the movement; his arrival in Iona in 563, like his death in the island in 597, has been the occasion for great ecumenical gatherings. If we can accept the argument recently put forward by Dr Ian Bradley (*Pilgrim and Penitent*, pp.102-3), Columba has much in common with the founder of the Iona Community, Lord George MacLeod of Fuinary. What MacLeod and Columba do not have in common, of course, is the Gaelic language and the deeply Gaelic profile of the latter. Gaelic culture does not seem to be central to the modern Iona Community.

The Columba of culture and heritage

The Celtic saints are purposefully reconstructed not only by churches and wishful thinkers, they are also big business nowadays for the heritage industry. Heritage centres - all too often potent reminders of the retreat of Gaelic culture into the glitzy, non-Gaelic world of the cellophane package and the perfume flask - are increasingly popular in the Highlands and Islands. Because 'heritage' is itself a contemporary buzz-word, and also because the pervasive Christian ethos of the earlier and later Middle Ages is hard to avoid in any quest for 'heritage', Christianity in various forms, real and imagined, is finding its way back into the mind of the people at large, sometimes packaged and marketed (like a neatly wrapped bar of soap) as a version of the more neutral and less offensive commodity called 'spirituality'.

In such centres, which sometimes allow push-button access to colourful interpretations of what was once 'culture', the local saint may be enjoying a timely resurrection. Such resurrection is occasionally achieved by recreating him on video; from the mists of modernity the video-saint beckons. His new electronic *vita* is generally low on fact, but high on graphic art and design, incorporating much mist, swirling low in Highland glens; his voice is deep and resonant, beckoning the New Age believer and the Old Age sceptic. Fillan, a saint associated with southern Perthshire, has been recreated in this way in Breadalbane Heritage Centre in Killin. Columba has yet to become a video-saint, but a centre devoted to him is now established in Fionnphort in the Ross of Mull. In such a context, saints like Fillan and Columba represent local awareness of a phase of history which is both prestigious and potentially beneficial in the present day.

It is clear that the most common use of Columba and other saints in the contemporary Gaelic context is to encourage economic and cultural renaissance. Columba's role as a potent symbol, capable of igniting new initiatives of this kind, is demonstrated in *Iomairt Chaluim Chille* ('The Columba Initiative'), which seeks to provide closer links between Gaelic-related enterprises in Ireland and Scotland. Here Columba's name alone is serving the wider cause of 'cultural connectionalism', by creating a bridge which reclaims the relationship between the Gaelic components of Scotland and Ireland. He himself, as a Donegal man resident in Iona, is perceived to have linked the two Gaidhealtachds (which constituted only one Gaidhealtachd in his time), and to have operated on both sides of the North Channel throughout his active career. This important aspect of the saint's life was emphasised by the President of Ireland, Mrs Mary Robinson, when she visited Sabhal Mòr Ostaig, the Gaelic College in Skye, on 9 June 1997, Columba's festival day, and also the day when *Iomairt Chaluim Chille* was publicly unveiled. She had been in Iona and Lewis prior to her arrival in Skye. Her sensitive and moving address had the theme of Gaelic culture at its heart, and opened with an appealing picture of Columba, uniting the two Gaidhealtachds (*Signatures on Our Own Frequency*, p.11):

> As prince, poet and priest he symbolises many of the links between these islands and between Scotland and Ireland. Of noble birth, he was regarded as a person of authority who could adjudicate in the political disputes between Ireland and the growing kingdom of Dal Riata....

As a poet he's representative of a society which took the
role of the poet seriously. Of the stories which are told about
him, two of the most famous concern literary disputes. His
exile from Ireland, it is claimed, was a result of his defeat in
the dispute about copying a manuscript. Later, at the
legendary convention of Drumcath (*sic*) in 575 he ensured
the privileged position of the bardic order in Gaelic society,
an order which was to retain its power and influence for a
thousand years.

As an exile for Christ he founded Iona, which was to
become a great monastic settlement, the centre of the Celtic
church in these islands and a beacon of learning in Europe,
and yesterday in Iona I had a sense of what had been founded
there and how relevant it is to our modern world. These
three strands of politics, learning and religion embodied in
Columba are intimately linked.

The power of the late medieval legend of Columba is graphically
illustrated by these words. He is perceived by President Robinson as
the pan-Gaelic protector of culture in a neat trinity of concerns. We
may wonder whether the saint, on his own, actually guaranteed the
special position of the poets. To what extent there was a single 'Celtic
church in these islands' may also be disputed by some scholars (see
Chapter 6), but the foundational role of Columba in Iona is not in
doubt. The President duly emphasises the spiritual dimension of the
saint, and alludes to 'how relevant it is to our modern world'. Yet, as
reconstructed by modern enterprise managers and image-makers,
Columba is very much a secular saint. *Iomairt Chaluim Chille*, while
using Calum Cille's saintly name, is concerned with developing
primarily secular links between Scotland and Ireland.

One wonders how the saint himself would have regarded the
ethos which has produced the range of fund-raising ventures now
found in the Highlands and Islands, notably in the monetarist (and
non-monastic) hard cells of local enterprise. Columba is given his
place in the matrix. His name is worth having at the mast-head, to
bring blessing on such ventures, and is more likely to be bestowed
nowadays on new buildings relating to heritage than on churches; but
it is open to question whether, for the promoters of Highland
enterprise generally, he represents more than a name. His person, thus
construed, may appear to contain more in the way of economic *élan*
than of spiritual power, but in *Iomairt Chaluim Chille* he is identified
with modern Gaelic culture in a context which will (we trust) respect
much more than his name.

The relevance of Columba for today

Columba is adaptable. He has shown a capacity to be relevant to the needs of many phases of history. Adomnán, his first Latin biographer whose work survives, obviously constructed his *Vita Columbae* in such a way as to make the exemplary nature of the saint's life clear to all who read his work. The purpose of Adomnán's portrait of Columba was in large measure commemorative, but he also raised the flag for Iona, and, in the bygoing, intended that others might be made in the mould of the saint. Of course, that mould was determined by Adomnán, and by the various strands of fact and folklore to which he had access and which he chose to use. The academic (always the sleepless spoiler of dreams) might say that we will learn more about Adomnán than about Columba by reading his account of the saint. Nowadays, modernity follows a similar course, bringing its own range of preconceptions to the saint and remaking him in its own image. The crucial difference is that Adomnán was some thirteen hundred years closer to Columba.

Adomnán's interpretation contains a timeless Christian message which has lost none of its potential relevance for those who wish to be so inspired. But is his perspective attractive in the present day? Is it in order to recover such a perspective that the average Islander, Highlander, Lowlander, Scot (or whoever) will remember, or reflect on, Columba? Sadly, one must respond in the negative. The picture of Columba that most average people have (if they have any at all) will seldom go beyond the saint's name, and perhaps a few generalities picked up from a passing acquaintance with lore and legend. This meagre mixture will be well garnished with generous helpings of public commemoration and personal preference. Such a recipe for 'making your own saint' guarantees the exclusion of inconvenient ingredients. The sharp-edged saintliness of the saint, as portrayed by Adomnán, is therefore unlikely to be a palatable pill for many in our modern day. His flesh-subduing austerity - not a prominent theme in modern 'Celtic Christianity' - stands in sharp contrast to the narcissism of contemporary popular philosophy. The Celtic saints of modernity are all too often recognisable as the 'cushion saints' of the middle-class comfort-zone.

The earliest records of the saint will therefore remain a challenge to popular (mis)understanding. It is only by taking these sources as our primary founts of knowledge that we will have any hope of encountering reality. But is reality what we want to discover in any saint? Is that what our ancestors wanted? It is hard to escape the conclusion that, since at least the first centenary of his death, Columba has been refashioned by a wide variety of seekers and, of course, finders who have not hesitated to use his good offices for their own earthly purposes. His great quality is his perennial availability. He exists to be of occasional service; otherwise he is forgotten by the world, and lives quietly in his heavenly *Hinba*. The relevance of Columba at the end of the twentieth century, some might say, comes into focus only when he 'clicks' with the latest good cause or the latest aspiration of contemporary society, in its sacred or secular aspects.

The process will doubtless continue into the next century, since it seems inevitable that he will be fashioned and refashioned to meet the needs of society after 2000. The possibility that he will in any way help to refashion society seems remote. Like 'Celtic Christianity' itself, the saint has been exposed to a process of continuous refashioning to ensure that he will be compatible with the dreams and visions, hopes and fears, of each successive generation. In this he is by no means exceptional, since most Celtic saints who have survived to the present day have retained their relevance partly by rearranging their profiles to meet the needs and pressures of 'modernity'. In all of the Celtic areas, the Christian church too has been remoulded to suit new centuries and new ideologies. To these wider changes we must now turn.

CHAPTER 11
CONVERSION, CONFLICT AND CONTINUITY: DEMYSTIFYING THE CELTIC MIDDLE AGES

Popular works, and even some 'scholarly' collections, on the subject of 'Celtic Christianity' tend to give the impression that 'Celtic Christianity' has endured unmolested into the present century as a vital form of faith in certain quarters, and that its rituals and tenets are still observed by some. Certain writers also argue, in somewhat broader terms, that a legacy from the days of 'Celtic Christianity' is detectable in the Celtic areas of the British Isles and even beyond. Recently Dr Ian Bradley has suggested that a Columban legacy can be traced in the worship of the Presbyterian churches of the Highlands and Islands. Thus, he ascribes the ascetic element and the love of psalmody characteristic of Highland Presbyterianism to Columban influence (*Columba: Pilgrim and Penitent*, pp.98-100).

Such a perspective on the history of the Highlands and Islands functions on much the same level as the notion that 'Columba was a Calvinist' (an idea that underpins one of the models of the 'Celtic Church' discussed in Chapter 6), but it operates in the opposite direction by implying that 'Calvin was a Columban'. Versions of this model have been espoused by evangelical Protestant writers (see Chapters 6 and 12) who would deny the 'continuity theory', and would argue instead that the 'Celtic Church' was destroyed by the Vikings and by the false doctrines of Rome. By this model, paganism and spiritual darkness reigned supreme until the Reformation brought the first rays of light. More focused, localised versions of this 'disjunction theory' can be found.

Flexibility with the facts, or (more worryingly) the failure to accommodate or appreciate different types and layers of evidence, produces a romantic, 'Celticised' historiography, with various doctrinal and political agendas, which does serious despite to the real history of the Highland area. This sort of reconstruction can be found not only among the devotees of 'Celtic Christianity', but also among those who dress the Highlands in tartan-trimmed Jacobitism, or who believe passionately that all emigration from the Highlands and Islands was caused by the Clearances. It springs from an obsession with a particular aspect of Highland history, an *idée fixe* which interprets in its own terms the character of everything that has ever happened in the region.

The 'Celtic Christian' model of Highland church history, regardless of denominational stripe, often either ignores large tracts of ecclesiastical development - in fact, virtually everything that has happened since the twelfth century - or remakes the past to conform to the preconceived pattern. This is part of the 'primitivist' perception of the 'Fringe', as an area in which stasis prevails, or where some major 'distinguishing feature', recently discovered by the writer, is seen to determine the course of all subsequent events. 'Innocent' readers of the books concerned, and also tourists who pay but the briefest of visits to influential heritage-centres, can be taken in all too easily by this simplified view of the past.

The truth is, of course, far from simple. The Scottish Highlands and Islands have undergone massive changes across the centuries. These changes have occurred at the political, social and (not least) the religious and ecclesiastical levels. Often political and social changes have had a bearing on the complexion of the church. This is equally true of the other Celtic areas: Ireland and Wales have been transformed likewise across the centuries. The aim of this chapter is to summarise some of those changes, especially in the ecclesiastical domain, and to consider how much (if any) of the earlier pre-1200 'Gaelic' type of Christianity and its associated cultural activity may have survived, and in what form, until the eve of the Reformation. The Middle Ages and the post-Reformation period constitute the two major 'black holes' in the minds of those who 'buy in' to 'Celtic Christianity'.

Incursions

The Middle Ages were a time when the Celtic world faced new challenges. These challenges came in different ways to the different countries, and we must beware of assuming that the pattern is the same for all. The new challenges sometimes came relatively quietly, creeping up almost by stealth on even the most conservative of practitioners; but they also came violently in some cases, backed by a firm use of political intrigue or brute force.

(1) The Vikings: In the year 795, and again in 806, the monastic community in Iona was visited by ships that had very unpleasant intentions. These were Viking longships, with their high, snake-like prows and curved sterns. We can imagine that the monks might have found them of interest, at least at first, but the interest would soon have turned to horror. The Vikings had come to wreak havoc and destruction in the island, and in 806 they put to the sword 68 of the monks there. Monasteries like Iona, conveniently situated for sea-borne raiders, were a ready target for bloodthirsty pirates of this kind.

Because of the patronage that they offered to craftsmen and others skilled in adorning the churches, such monasteries usually housed a considerable amount of treasure which could be taken as loot, either for melting down or for trading purposes; and the monks could readily be captured as galley-slaves, to row the longships across the ocean to inflict more damage on unsuspecting communities of one kind or another.

The arrival of the Vikings marked yet another phase in the restless, ongoing series of incursions into the Celtic lands by voyagers from across the sea. In a sense, this scenario was close to that by which the Anglo-Saxons had come to the shores of Britain: the Vikings were Germanic-speaking peoples from Scandinavia, who inhabited regions that were geographically fairly close to the Anglo-Saxon homeland, and they shared some of the characteristics of the Anglo-Saxons. For example, they too were skilled seamen and navigators, who had developed the galley, with its sharp keel, as a formidable means of transport across the seas. They had various types of ship for specific purposes, including trade, in which they had a particular interest. They also had fast ships - the longships proper. Replicas of the Viking longships, built on the lines of the clebrated Gokstad ship, could sail at speeds of up to 10 knots.

The Vikings were land-hungry people who had been forced to move out of their homelands probably because of a combination of population growth and political pressures. They were also, initially, pagans, who had no respect for the church or for Christianity. They had their own pantheon of northern gods, who, when interpreted through Roman eyes, showed similarities to the gods of the Celts.

Monks had every reason to fear for their lives when the pagan, treasure-hunting Vikings arrived on the scene. Nevertheless, the Vikings did not destroy the monasteries at one stroke, nor did they obliterate the achievements of the preceding centuries. We have to bear in mind that the sources that condemn Viking atrocities most vocally derive from those monasteries that bore the brunt of the initial attacks. Monasteries which were looted early in the Viking period might enjoy periods of peaceful and even productive existence after the initial raids were over. Life, in one form or another, did continue after those early Viking depradations, as happened at Iona. The Vikings who first struck Iona were Norsemen (i.e. Norwegians) rather than Danes; Strabo's reference to Danes (see Chapter 10) is a generalised 'external' view; Danes did come at a later stage. That would square with the general picture of Norse settlement in the islands. Danes were a later part of the general mayhem that came about, and the Danes fought against the Norsemen in subsequent phases of the occupation. The Vikings who harried the southern islands would have had staging-posts or bases in the Outer Hebrides, where there were many bays and inlets which would have been ideal for sheltering their ships and planting shore-camps (cf. the name 'Viking', which probably contains the element *vik-*, 'bay', thus implying that the Vikings are 'the bay people', i.e. raiders who shelter in the bays). It was from the Outer Hebrides that the Vikings sallied forth as they raided the west coast of Ireland, and, moving south, established further raiding-stations on the southern Irish coast.

Irish monasteries in such places as Inishbofin and Inishmurray suffered initially in much the same way as Iona did. The annalists who recorded the Viking onslaught referred to the Vikings as *genti*, 'gentiles'. The concept of 'gentiles' was, of course, rooted firmly in the Bible, in the Old and New Testaments, and its use provides an interesting perspective on how the Christian Irish viewed the raiders, and contextualised their own unpleasant experiences. They equated the raiders with godless pagans, beyond the bounds of the spiritual Israel, to which, by implication, they themselves belonged. This distinction is, however, earlier than the Viking era. The terms *genti, genntlidecht / gentliucht* had been used occasionally by Irish writers before the Vikings arrived, and to them the words meant respectively 'heathens, pagans' and 'heathen lore, paganism'. As we noted in Chapter 8, Oengus, Céle Dé, composed a poem in the early ninth century which celebrated the overthrow of paganism, and in which he boasted *'ro milled in genntlecht'* - 'gentiledom [i.e. paganism] has been destroyed'. Now, with the arrival of the Norsemen, it seemed that paganism had more than reasserted itself. The extent to which Christian values had permeated Irish and Gaelic society explains, in part, the unalloyed horror with which monks initially viewed the arrival of the pagan Vikings. The Christian community in Ireland and Scotland at the time of the Viking attacks was certainly not pagan-friendly, nor was it prepared to throw a happy, syncretistic tea-party to which 'gentiles' could be invited. Martyrdom was preferable.

The Vikings made an impact on Wales as well as on Ireland, but the raids on Wales came later than those on Scotland and Irleand. The Viking attacks on Wales came after 852, and were evidently launched, at least in part, from the eastern seaboard of Ireland, specifically from Dublin, after the latter became a major centre for Viking activity. The parts of Wales most seriously affected by the Vikings were Angelsey and Dyfed. St David's, where there was a distinguished monastery and bishop's seat, was a persistent focus for attack. In 1049, according to the Welsh annals, the whole of southern Wales was deserted 'for fear of the gentiles'. In Wales, as in Ireland, therefore, the main characteristic used in labelling the Vikings was their paganism - the fact that they were 'outside the fold' in terms of religious adherence.

We need not doubt that the arrival of the new, northern pagans had serious implications for the monasteries in the Celtic areas. This can be seen in the narrower context of Iona itself. The monastic community at Iona was not destroyed, and religious life was maintained for long, unbroken periods, but part at least of the community was forced to move to Ireland after the raid of 806, and it established itself at Kells. If it had not been for this, the beautiful gospel book which we call nowadays 'The Book of Kells' might have been called 'The Book of Iona' - but, of course, it might have been destroyed if it had remained in the island. Professor Proinsias Mac Cana notes ('The Influence of the Vikings on Celtic Literature', p.104) the wider literary impact of the Viking raids: possibly because of 'the Norse onslaught of the ninth century', the literary activity of the Irish monasteries appears to have moved 'from the older peripheral areas in Ulster, Leinster and Munster to the monasteries of the lower central plain'. In addition, many monks left Ireland for good, and made for the Continent, where Irish houses had already been established and where there was less chance of Viking raids. Latterly, from the late ninth century, the Norsemen in the Hebrides were gradually christianised, presumably under the influence of centres such as Iona and its satellites.

It says much for the strength of Christianity in the Gaelic west that the Norse were christianised, while the Gaels were not paganised. Once settled, the dreaded Norsemen came to follow similar conventions to the earlier inhabitants of these areas, and it seems possible that a Gaelic-Norse form of Christianity may have come into existence. Norse place-names of the islands record the location of *kirk*s and crosses (as in Kirkapol and Crossapol in Tiree), and several parish names are of Norse origin. It is also important to note that, within the Irish Sea area, and also in the Northern Isles, Norse/Gaelic polity appears to have aided the introduction of bishops in the continental mode - to Dublin, Waterford, Limerick and Orkney - at an earlier stage than is found elsewhere. A bishop of the Isles is attested from c. 1094, and from 1153 until c.1350 the diocese of the Isles (Sodor and Man) came under the jurisdiction of Trondheim (in Norway). The christianising of the Norsemen is thus likely to have broadened cultural and ecclesiastical horizons in the Gaelic west, while helping to change the formal organisation of the faith in these parts.

(2) Normans and Anglo-Normans: When William the Conqueror landed in England in 1066, it is doubtful whether the Celtic areas would even have noticed his arrival. In due time, however, the people of Wales and Ireland, and the Gaelic people in different parts of Scotland, were to feel the effect of the Normans, particularly in their Anglo-Norman guises. The Normans contributed much to the

changing complexion of the British Isles, and we must now consider some broad aspects of their arrival in, and impact on, the Celtic areas.

We can begin with Wales since this was the first of the Celtic areas to feel their influence. The securing of the Welsh border was one of the priorities of William the Conqueror and his followers, and so the Welsh Marcher lords came into existence - feudal barons to whom was entrusted the protection of this strategic border area. The Normans established themselves on the Welsh border and penetrated the south of Wales with comparatively little difficulty, encountering only slight resistance in the years up to 1095. Chester, Shrewsbury, Hereford and Gloucester became the centres from which they launched their expeditions into Wales. Their conquests were secured in Wales, as elsewhere, by the motte-and-bailey castle. The areas which lay beyond the immediate grasp of the Normans were the north of Wales and the mountainous areas, and it was from the north - from the kingdom of Gwynedd - that the stiffest resistance came. Under Llywelyn the Great (I, 1194-1240) and his grandson Llywelyn the Last (II, 1246-82), the kingdom of Gwynedd was strong, but resistance and resurgence crashed with the death of Llywelyn the Last, slain in 1282 in an encounter with Edward I of England.

The Anglo-Normans arrived in Ireland later than they did in Wales. For Ireland, the critical date is 1169, and their arrival was something of an accident or an unfortunate 'own goal' that the Irish managed to score - a by-product of the struggles that were going on in the twelfth centuries between the Irish kings. The tribal kings had long since given way to provincial kings, who vied with each other for the kingship of Ireland. In the prelude to the arrival of the Normans, the kings who were competing with one another for the supreme title were Ruaidrí Ua Conchobair, king of Connacht, and Diarmait Mac Murchada, king of Leinster, who had allied himself with Muirchertach Mac Lochlainn, king of the Uí Néill. When Mac Lochlainn died, Mac Murchada was left without a strong ally, and in response to pressure, he appealed to Henry II of England. The Pope gave Henry the right to rule Ireland in the interests of reforming the Irish church in the papal letter *Laudabiliter* (1155), but in the event the challenge of raising forces was left to Mac Murchada himself. Diarmait Mac Murchada then turned to south Wales, where he recruited Richard fitz Gilbert de Clare, Earl of Pembroke, who was glad to oblige - and became better known in later Irish history as 'Strongbow'. Strongbow led a group of followers to Ireland in support of the beleaguered king of Leinster. Leinster was secured for Mac Murchada's nephew, who succeeded him in 1166, but the price of the whole adventure was the gradual infiltration of Ireland by the Normans.

Perhaps Scotland is, in general terms, the most complicated of the three countries that we have examined, since the process of Normanisation was set in motion by relationships of kin, most notably through the marriage of Malcolm III (*Ceann Mór*) to Margaret, sister of Edgar the Atheling, son of a refugee of English royal blood. Suffice it to say that, although brought up in Hungary, Margaret found her way to England and thence to Scotland. Her sons by Malcolm who were later to rule Scotland (1097-1153) - Edgar, Alexander and David - were decidedly pro-Norman in their sympathies, and it was through them that the door was opened to the arrival of Flemings and Normans in Scotland. David I gave a feudal grant of lands to an ex-patriate Frenchman who had already gained estates in England - no less a person than the first Robert de Brus, as good a Norman as ever came out of Normandy and a 'settler' from England in the bygoing.

The Flemings and Normans who settled in Scotland did so mainly in the south, coming into Galloway and Nithsdale, Kyle and Carrick. With the Norman knights came motte-and-bailey castles, new styles of architecture in the more permanent stone structures, the allocation of land in exchange for knight service and fealty, and the French language - to note but a few of the changes. The cultural implications were perhaps the most profound in the long term, since they set the stage for the gradual transformation of the Celtic areas, and brought the spear-point of English (and of the English people) into the northern and western fastnesses. However, we should not ignore the very real likelihood that established Gaelic practices may have exerted considerable influence on the shape of the new society in Scotland.

Reforming the 'Celtic Churches'

We must also be wary of ascribing all of the challenges or the changes in the Celtic areas to the Normans (or even the Vikings). The fact is that the Celtic countries were never an isolated backwater, somewhere in the west; by the eleventh and twelfth centuries they were playing an even stronger part than before in the wider world of European ecclesiastical and secular culture, and steps were being taken, without external pressure and prior to the arrival of the Normans, to change the older patterns.

In the Irish church, for example, monastic reformers appeared as early as the eighth century in response to the danger of secularisation. Further reforms followed. The early twelfth century witnessed a major restructuring of the Irish church. As we have observed elsewhere (Chapter 8), the early Irish monasteries functioned on the basis of the *familia*, and much power resided with the abbot. This type of arrangement led to laicisation and the abuse of power, and was ripe for reformation by 1100. There was no national diocesan structure in early Ireland; the monasteries and their associated churches functioned on a decentralised, localised basis. The whole 'non-system' was given a thorough overhaul in three synods: Cashel (1101), Ráth Bresail (1111) and Kells-Mellifont (1152), thus creating what was in effect a national church under the control of Armagh as metropolitan. The background to this is, of course, the wider connection that Ireland had with England and the Continent. The zeal to reform the Irish church formed part of a much broader monastic revival. Irishmen were familiar with, and influenced by, the continental monastic movements. Through this channel the monastic orders of medieval Europe - Benedictines, Cistercians and Augustinians - found a firm foothold in Ireland. Of these the most significant were the Cistercians, introduced by Malachy of Armagh in 1142.

In Ireland, the changes in the church were far advanced before the Anglo-Normans arrived in 1169. In Wales, the adoption of the new orders was part of the harder, firmer Norman drive into the country, and the new communities, the abbeys with their monks, were often situated close to Norman castles and positions of strength. In Wales, as in Ireland, the older so-called Celtic saints were in certain cases knocked off their pedestals, but, more commonly, they were allowed to stand alongside a new gallery of imported saints.

As happened in Ireland and Wales, the continental orders found a place in Scotland. Benedictines were introduced to Dunfermline by Margaret in 1070, and Cistercians came to Melrose in 1136. In the Gaelic west, they gradually established themselves within the bounds of the Lordship of the Isles. The Lords of the Isles controlled the western seaboard and islands of Scotland from the twelfth century until c.1493, and helped to introduce the new orders. Benedictines settled at Iona (c.1203), Cistercians (brought from Mellifont in Ireland) at Saddell in Kintyre (c.1207), Augustinians at Oronsay (c.1353), and the Valliscaulians, a very severe French order, at Ardchattan on the Argyll mainland, and at Beauly, west of Inverness (c.1230). In due time, the new houses were patronised by the local aristocracy and magnates. The patronage bestowed on these orders by the Lords of the Isles conforms to a wider pattern also found in Ireland, whereby secular kings played a prominent part in endowing the new orders and in funding the surge of Romanesque building that emerged in their wake.

The arrival of the continental orders led gradually to the absorption or reorganising of the older, surviving Céli Dé communities in Scotland, as at Abernethy in Perthshire, which became Augustinian c.1172. Yet the transition was not always smooth, since earlier kin-based concepts of the monastic community sometimes came into collision with these innovations. At Iona in 1204, for example, the

Benedictine monastery founded with the patronage of Reginald, son of Somerled of Argyll, was destroyed by a band of clergy from the north of Ireland, who were loyal to Columban tradition, and claimed that it had been built 'without any right, in dishonour of the community of Iona'. By 1230 Benedictines had been restored to Iona.

The replacement of the earlier 'Celtic' monasteries by the houses of the new orders had implications for the development of 'Celtic' culture. According to one historian, their arrival was a 'disaster' for Irish learning and the transmission of native Irish literature, since, by this view, the new monks were much less sympathetic to Irish culture. The Cistercians, for example, had their roots in France, and insisted on the use of French by monks in Mellifont in the thirteenth century. The new orders were associated originally with the Continent and England, and not with Ireland. Those who admitted them, such as Malachy of Armagh, are sometimes seen in later history as traitors to the 'Celtic' cause. A less negative interpretation might argue that generally within the Gaelic west there was a growing recognition that the old ecclesiastical structures had served their day and that reform was necessary. Nor was the antipathy of the new orders to Gaelic culture sustained indefinitely. After an initial stand-off, some at least of the new orders gradually came to terms with Irish culture; the mendicant orders of Dominicans and Franciscans, for instance, were accused in a Royal Commission report of 1284-5 of making 'too much use of that [Irish] language' (Conlan, *Franciscan Ireland*, p.14). The Franciscans, in particular, became strongly supportive of indigenous Irish culture, and contributed much to the subsequent recording and preservation of literature in Irish. Nevertheless, the ecclesiastical and political changes taking place after 1100 forced some degree of realignment in the cultivation of learning, since the preservation of native tradition after the twelfth century came to depend much more on the secular orders of poets, physicians and craftsmen.

Cultural continuities

Literary activity did not cease in the Celtic areas with the coming of the Vikings, the arrival of the Normans and the reorganising of the church. In Ireland, in fact, we can see the opposite; it is evident that the eleventh and twelfth centuries were a time of great literary ferment, especially within the monasteries and the scriptoria. Indeed, the earliest manuscripts that we have of the sagas and poems from Ireland were written down in this period. Of course, they contained material that was earlier than the eleventh century, and an earlier literary tradition intermingles with later medieval practices.

One of the most important compendia from this period is the manuscript called *Lebor na hUidre*, 'The Book of the Dun Cow' - an intriguing name, which is said to derive from the 'dun cow' that followed Ciaran of Clonmacnoise to school. Sadly, in due time the cow went the way of all flesh, and its hide was turned into vellum for a manuscript - perhaps this manuscript. (Vellum was often regarded as sacred and special, and this is a tradition associated with a special book.) The Book of the Dun Cow was probably compiled at Clonmacnoise. One of its scribes, called Mael-Muire, is thought to have been killed by marauders in 1106. The manuscript contains, among other things, a very early version of the greatest of all Irish epic sagas, *Táin Bó Cuailnge*, 'The Cattle Raid of Cooley'. The compilers of the manuscript appear to have been drawing on other manuscripts, perhaps from other leading Irish monasteries, like Armagh, Durrow and Monasterboice.

Other famous Irish manuscripts also originate from this period. One of these is the Book of Leinster, largely compiled, it would seem, in the second half of the twelfth century. Again, this manuscript seems to draw on earlier manuscript sources, assembled for Find, Bishop of Kildare, and Aed, abbot of Terryglass. Find describes Aed as 'the chief historian of Leinster in wisdom, knowledge, cultivation of books, learning and study'. This great manuscript also contains a version of *Táin Bó Cuailnge*, as well as a version of the *Lebor Gabála* ('The Book of Invasions') as its first item, followed by king-lists, genealogies, stories about famous places, and also poems.

The list of contents in the Book of Leinster does tend to suggest that this was a time when scribes were particularly anxious to gather the native tradition into manuscripts. It is also evident that stories and tales on particular themes were themselves gathered into larger compendia of anecdotes. In the course of the gathering, the various smaller items could be recast, and tempered into an alloy of new form. These recycled tales included pre-eminently stories about the secular hero Fionn and his warrior-bands of Fiana, which in Ireland were gathered into *Acallam na Senórach* ('The Conversation of the Old Men'). Here Oisín, the son of Fionn, and Caoilte tell stories about the Fiana to St Patrick. The structure of the 'Conversation' is that of journeys round Ireland, and, as the band of saint and heroes moves from place to place, the sites associated with Fionn evoke tales and reminiscences. This is the period, too, when narrative ballads about Fionn and the Fiana begin to make their appearance. Examples are found in the Book of Leinster. Narrative poetry is not usual in Ireland before this point, but thereafter heroic ballads about Fionn and the Fiana become relatively common. The inclusion of such material in twelfth-century compendia with an ecclesiastical flavour suggests that a more accommodating approach to the secular world was emerging; hitherto, Fionn and his Fiana - bands of rootless young men who sowed their wild oats as warriors and womanisers - had been long regarded with some considerable degree of horror and disdain by the church (see Chapter 8); only occasionally are their adventures recorded in written forms earlier than the twelfth century.

Across the water in Scotland, we find that there is some evidence of literary activity in at least one monastery. This is the monastery of Deer, in Aberdeenshire, which looked back to Columba as its founder. A little pocket gospel-book, now known as the Book of Deer, has survived from its scriptorium. Although we cannot be certain that the book itself originated at Deer, it was clearly very special to the monastic coummunity, since the monks used it to preserve a record of the land-grants and immunities that they were given by local landowners. These grants were recorded in the margins of the manuscript in the opening years of the twelfth century, in a form of medieval Gaelic which was shared with Ireland. The material affords very clear evidence of the emergence of a distinctive, Scottish form of Gaelic - an indication that, to some extent, the Gaelic world of Scotland was 'growing apart' from that of Ireland, although the common core of literary Gaelic shows that Scotland was still very much part of the wider Gaelic province embracing the two countries. There is much argument about other aspects of the book, especially its art-work and the implications of its apparently 'poor' figures of the evangelists.

If we turn to Wales, we find that there is evidence for considerable literary activity in the eleventh and twelfth centuries. The earliest extensive sample of Christian literature in Welsh goes back to the ninth century; the *Juvencus Englynion*, consisting of nine verses on the impossibility of praising adequately the achievements of God the Creator, are to be found in a manuscript in Cambridge University Library. There is a gap in the literary record until further religious poems are found in the Black Book of Carmarthen (thirteenth century), the Book of Taliesin (c.1325), the Red Book of Hergest (c.1382-c.1410) and the Hendregadredd Manuscript (c. 1300). The Latin Lives of the Welsh saints were written down in the twelfth century, and it would seem too that the tales known as 'The Four Branches of the Mabinogi' took their present shape in the twelfth century. Behind the 'Mabinogi' there lies a body of earlier material - tales about Pryderi and others - which is reworked into a new format, rather like what happened with material about the Fiana in Ireland. Christian poetry was composed vigorously in Welsh in the twelfth and thirteenth centuries by the *Gogynfeirdd*, the poets who were given patronage by the native princes, especially in North Wales.

The cultivation of literature, sacred and secular, as well as art styles, was maintained by the churches, and patronised by secular nobles, during the catholic Middle Ages in all the Celtic areas. The literary tradition continued powerfully until the time of the Reformation. Poets and storytellers of high quality flourished in Ireland, Scotland and Wales, and in the other Celtic countries. There are also numerous examples of clergy who preserved the native tradition in manuscript. In Scotland, for instance, at the very end of the Middle Ages, we can cite the contribution of James MacGregor, the Dean of Lismore, and his family, to whom we owe the famous Book of the Dean of Lismore, compiled probably in Perthshire between 1512 and 1542. This remarkable manuscript contains much of the cream of the Gaelic poetry of the Middle Ages, from both Scotland and Ireland. It includes fine specimens of formal bardic praise poems and religious verse (such as Muireadhach Albanach's poem on the Virgin Mary), and a representative sample of Gaelic narrative ballads about Fionn and the Fiana, as well as a considerable number of more ephemeral types of verse. These would have been composed originally in the formal type of Classical Gaelic used by poets and literary practitioners throughout Ireland and Scotland. In Wales, it was by no means unknown for the new abbots to act as patrons of the poets in the later Middle Ages, and it is quite clear that the abbeys and monasteries (particularly those of the Cistercians) did encourage the growth of indigenous learning and culture.

Christian creativity

The numerous changes which occurred in the Celtic areas in the course of the Middle Ages did not obliterate the achievements of earlier days. Memory of Celtic saints was preserved in quasi-historical writings and place-names, and not infrequently in creative literature. The structural remains of monasteries and other ecclesiastical buildings from the period before 1100 were preserved, and no doubt revisited in body and spirit by later generations. The evidence suggests that, even into the later Middle Ages, there was a significant degree of interaction with the Christian legacy of Columba, Patrick and David. Much of this, however, was retrospective and imaginative, and for that reason it is very dangerous to assume that practices and traditions of the 'Celtic' churches were preserved intact. The 'Celtic' past was given a commemorative and affirmative role, validating and confirming contemporary aspirations. The 'appeal to history' and the 'consolation of alleged continuity' were lively concepts, then as now. Within the medieval period, the creative use of the Christian 'Celtic' past, pre-eminently involving the saints, can be illustrated at various levels.

(1) Ecclesiastical origin legends: Origin legends were of considerable importance when individual churches laid claim to special privileges.

Thus, in the early twelfth century, the monastery at Deer in Aberdeenshire (not to be confused with the Cistercian abbey, founded in 1219 by William Comyn, earl of Buchan) wrote its own origin legend in Gaelic in the margins of the Book of Deer, cleverly making the case for the intervention of Columba in the assignation of a monastery which was already in existence before the creation of the legend (Jackson, *Gaelic Notes*, p.33):

> Columba and Drostán son of Coscrach, his disciple, came from Iona, as God guided them, to Aberdour; and Bede the Pict was mormaer of Buchan on their arrival; and it was he who bestowed on them that monastery, in freedom till Doomsday from mormaer and toísech. They came after that to the other monastery [Deer], and it pleased Columba, for it was full of the grace of God. And he begged the mormaer, that is, Bede, that he should give it to them, and he did not. And a son of his took a sickness, after the clerics had been refused, and was all but dead. Thereupon the mormaer went to beseech the clerics that they should make a prayer on behalf of the boy, that health might come to him; and he gave them [land] as a grant from *Cloch in Tiprat* as far as *Cloch Peitte Meic-Gartnait*. They made the prayer, and health came to him. Thereupon Columba gave Drostán that monastery, and blessed it, and left the curse that whoever should go against it should not be full of years or success. Drostán's tears [*déra*] came as he was parting from Columba. Columba said, 'Let Deer be its name from this on'.

This - the first Gaelic note in the Book of Deer - intermingles features of various literary genres. The writer was evidently aware of Columba's visits to Pictland, as described in Adomnán's Life, and probably of the alleged existence of Columban monasteries in the area. Columba's supreme authority, over secular and sacred rulers, is also evident, and this reveals the two contrasting dimensions of the Celtic saint, namely the powers to heal and to curse. The saint's curse is a weapon for the present, since it (allegedly) continues to affect 'whoever should go against' the monastery. The writer then moves from a hagiographical pose to the composition of a note in the form of 'popular etymology', purporting to describe how Columba gave the monastery its name. The element of popular etymology reflects the influence of the Gaelic tradition of *dindshenchas* ('lore of famous places'), which provided tales and stories about particular place-names, and often explained the origin of the names. It needs to be said, however, that this practice was by no means unique to the Gaelic world; it was common also in Wales, but it was equally common in Hebrew literature, as can be seen in the

Old Testament, with its many accounts of how famous places were given their names.

(2) Poetry in praise of, or invoking, the Celtic saints: Memory of Columba was well preserved in verse and prose of the Middle Ages and of later years, and Columba himself became a 'voice' to whom poems were ascribed (see Chapter 10). Other Celtic saints were similarly commemorated, and their good offices were sought in like manner. In Wales, the 'Poets of the Princes', who flourished in the twelfth and thirteenth centuries, addressed a number of poems to the native Welsh saints. Three of these - to Dewi (David), Cadfan and Tysilio - have survived. Dr Catherine A. MacKenna (*The Medieval Welsh Religious Lyric*, p.30) notes that, in the first of these, composed by Gwynfardd Brycheiniog, the poet regards Saint David as 'the greatest of God's saints, amplifying that praise with accounts of his miracles and missionary activities. Particularly striking, though, is the large number of references to churches throughout Wales dedicated to Saint David. These seem intended to advance politically the claim of the see of Saint David's to independence from Canterbury...' The poem to Cadfan, composed by Llywelyn Fardd, focuses on the church of Tywyn in Merionydd, which was dedicated to the saint. The poet makes much of the generosity of the abbot to the poets, reflecting the role of the new monastic orders in encouraging indigenous culture. The third Welsh poem in praise of a saint, namely Tysilio, is the work of Cynddelw, and draws attention to Tysilio's aristocratic lineage. It thus combines sacred and secular perspectives, and extols the qualities of the monastery allegedly founded by Tysylio at Meifod. The poems on the Welsh saints stand alongside others invoking biblical and international saintly figures, such as Michael and Mary.

In Gaelic tradition, there is a similar awareness of local, national and international saints. Patrick and Brigit appear regularly in medieval Gaelic (including Irish) verse, as do the biblical saints, Michael and Mary. Secular poets in both Ireland and Wales produced high-quality religious poetry praising the Virgin, and beseeching her and other saints to intercede on their behalf. The need to face God's judgement was a very conspicuous theme in the medieval poetry of the two countries, and the prospect of hell (so searingly portrayed in earlier 'Celtic' literature such as *Fís Adomnáin*: see Chapter 5) lost none of its terror for those of a later day with an awareness of human sinfulness. A remarkably deep sense of accountability, and the need to find saintly intermediaries, is perhaps the most consistent note that is sounded throughout the medieval corpus of Christian prose and verse in Gaelic/Irish and Welsh tradition. This picture certainly contrasts with the happy sentimentalism offered by present-day 'Celtic

Christianity', but it matches the mood for Europe as a whole, although (as happened elsewhere), indigenous features are evident in such practices as the invocation of local saints.

(3) Prose tales and secular verse involving the saints: The most prominent of the early saints were sometimes given a place not only in hagiography (see Chapter 9), but also in secular tales and verse. The saint who rose to pre-eminence in the broadly secular realm after 1100 was Patrick. He was represented as a key figure in *Acallam na Senórach* ('The Conversation of the Old Men'), composed c. 1175, in which he is brought face to face with a group of survivors from the Fiana of Fionn mac Cumhaill. The association of Patrick and the warriors of the Fiana is symbolic of a rapprochement between the church and a sector of society which had previously earned its disapproval. In the opening section of the text, the old warriors are portrayed as giants who have outlived their natural period (supposedly somewhere in the third century A.D.), so that they are able to meet the saint. The saint baptises the warriors, and thus incorporates them and their associated traditions into a Christian milieu. As we have already noted, the narrative envisages journeys round different parts of Ireland, in which Patrick seeks explanations of the significance of famous places which he and the warriors of the Fiana visit on their travels. These explanations are provided by the warriors Caílte and Oisín, usually in a good-humoured manner.

Patrick is not always portrayed in a good light, however. The *Acallam* contains occasional hints of some unease between the tradition of the Fiana and the church. This becomes even more explicit in the corpus of narrative ballads about the Fian which belong to the period 1200-1600, and are well attested in the Book of the Dean of Lismore. The most common framework for these ballads is a conversation between Patrick and Oisín. In several ballads, Patrick is pictured as the doughty opponent of the pagan, indulgent lifestyle of the warriors of the Fiana, and he denies that they will gain entrance to heaven. A vigorous debate with Oisín ensues, in which the old warrior puts the case for the excellence of his erstwhile colleagues, and insists that they should be admitted to the heavenly city.

Despite the good humour and the 'Punch and Judy' style of the confrontation, there is an underlying element of antipathy in the verse which appears to reflect resentment at Patrick's rise to ecclesiastical power and his curtailment of pagan cultural pleasures. In fact, Oisín is shown finally to be in thrall to Patrick, and ends his life as his slave, dragging stones to build his church, and lamenting the passing of the 'good old days' when he was part of the Fiana of Fionn mac Cumhaill and enjoyed, along with his colleagues, the delights of

the way of life of youthful rustic warriors. Retrospective nostalgia is
the keynote of a small poem in which the 'voice' of Oisín (Ossian in
Gaelic) bemoans his lot, imprisoned as he supposedly is in Elphin, Co.
Roscommon:

> *The night in Elphin goes slow,*
> *slowly too last night went by;*
> *though I felt today long,*
> *longer still was yesterday.*
>
> *Each day that comes wearies me;*
> *that is not how we once were,*
> *no fighting now and no raids,*
> *no learning of agile feats...*
>
> *No war-gear ever again,*
> *nor playing of games we loved,*
> *nor heroes swimming the loch:*
> *the night in Elphin is long.*
>
> *Alas for my worldly plight,*
> *I'm wretched, O God, as I am,*
> *alone, and gathering stones:*
> *the night in Elphin is long.*
>
> *The last of the famous Fian,*
> *great Ossian, the son of Fionn,*
> *listening to the baying of bells:*
> *the night in Elphin is long.*
>
> *Find out, O Patrick, from God*
> *word of the place I'll be in;*
> *may my soul be saved from harm:*
> *it's a long night in Elphin.*

(Derick Thomson, *Introduction to Gaelic Poetry*, pp.104-5)

The literary evidence, even in the late Middle Ages, perhaps as late as
1500, suggests that, despite what proponents of 'Celtic Christianity'
might wish us to believe, the gulf between the church and secular
culture was never completely bridged, although a significant degree of
healthy collaboration was achieved.

The enduring legacy of the Middle Ages

Reviewing the evidence for the Middle Ages (and we have looked at
only the merest fraction of that evidence in this chapter), we can see
clearly that the formal structures of the Christian faith did change,
most evidently in the twelfth century. There was much vigorous
interaction between the Celtic regions and the wider world, embracing

continental Europe. It is thus difficult to argue a case for any form of
'Celtic Christianity' which existed in a cultural enclave, occupied
only by itself and undisturbed by broader currents. It is also clear that
the replacement of the fondly admired 'Celtic Church' by the new
monastic orders and by wider reorganisation was not wholly
detrimental to cultural development. There were undoubtedly some
losses. In Ireland, the Cistercians were less than kindly disposed to the
use of the Irish language, and failed to promote the writing of Irish
annals or adherence (by laymen) to traditional law. Indeed, the rather
gloomy image of the Cistercians has been a factor in producing the
romantic notion of the culture-friendly 'Celtic' hermit (see Chapter
5). Yet there were gains too; it could be argued that literary horizons
were extended, and that a wider interaction of sacred and secular was
encouraged, after 1100. Since literary activity could survive the
scrapping of the older allegedly 'Celtic' structures, it is unnecessary to
invoke the continuing existence of the 'Celtic Church' as a form of
religious scaffolding for creativity beyond 1100. The Christians of the
Middle Ages had a very broad and healthy interest in the cultivation
of Celtic literature and art; indeed, the Middle Ages are perhaps the
period in which it is easiest to sustain an argument for the interaction
of sacred and secular aspects of culture and society. In Wales, some
Cistercian houses actively offered patronage to the poets. However,
to suggest (as some do) that these literary-minded Christians were
somehow participating in an ongoing stream of 'Celtic Christianity'
is to use the concept as little more than a form of cultural elastoplast
which covers all the gaps and cracks in the knowledge of the person
using the term. It is also potentially misleading to suppose that a clear-
cut boundary of some kind, around 1100, somehow separates the
'Celtic Christians' from the 'Catholic Christians'. Life went on, and
the streams, old and new, gradually flowed together.

   In the later Middle Ages clergy and *literati* alike would undoubtedly
have been aware of the legacy of the early Middle Ages, since it would
have been visible and audible all around them (as parts of it still are
today). Celtic saints, famous and obscure, were very well represented
in the place-names of all the Celtic countries. Indeed, place-names
probably acted, in their less obscure forms, as a commemorative index
of the saints, and, despite the tendency towards fiction in certain types
of names, they reflect the very real and lasting impact of the early
Christian faith on the secular society of these countries. The 'Celtic'
legacy would have been futher imprinted in the survival of older
churches and chapels within the parishes, some of these bearing the
names of saints such as Columba, Ninian, Brendan, Brigit (in the
Scottish Highlands and Ireland); David, Cybi, Tysilio and Cadfan (in
Wales); and Austell, Buryan, Mewan, and Morwenna (in Cornwall).

Yet none of this necessarily implies that 'Celtic Christianity' had conceptual or practical reality as a cohesive force between any of the countries concerned. A priest in Lewis, for instance, celebrating mass in a chapel like that at Eye, dedicated to Columba, is unlikely to have been aware of any wider 'Celtic' dimension of the dedication. We are not to know whether he would have perceived himself as the heir of Columba, but we can be fairly sure that he would not have regarded himself as part of a distinctive 'Celtic Church' embracing Ireland, Wales and Scotland. That concept came much later than his time.

There is, of course, a danger in the terminology itself, and in particular in the word 'Celtic', which needs to be re-emphasised at this point. When visiting one of the Celtic areas of the British Isles and observing the legacy of the earlier and later Middle Ages - perhaps the remains of a medieval chapel, now severely punished by the ravages of time, but retaining a romantic beauty in its moss-covered walls and sea-girt location - it is easy to imagine that, because a Celtic language was, or is (happily) still, spoken in the area, everything in the area is likewise 'Celtic', and that it can be ascribed automatically to Columba or some other foundational saint of his time. This, however, is to fall victim to an illusion which collapses the time-frames and reduces historical processes to an idealistic conflation of 'now and then'.

The connecting thread across the ages, if there is any, is likely to be the actual existence of a Celtic language, since Celtic languages (in the regions where they are still spoken) are perhaps the one continuous feature of Celtic cultures that we can trace with some certainty from the early period to the later. Languages often transcend historical phases and periods, and survive major upheavals in church and society. This is very clearly indicated by the manner in which the Gaelic and Welsh languages, for example, were embraced by the Protestant movements which took root in Scotland and Wales, though not so markedly in Ireland, after the Reformation. The Reformation provided new opportunities for diversifying the uses of the Celtic languages, and it also offered new frames of reference in which the people of the Celtic countries could view themselves, their churches and their cultures.

CHAPTER 12

RE-FORMING THE WILD WEST: PROTESTANT PERSPECTIVES ON THE CELTIC PAST

The notion of 'Celtic Christianity', as popularly applied, is potentially boundless. It can be used to cover the entire Christian experience of the areas of the British Isles which we would now regard as Celtic; it can embrace every movement within the period, although, as has been argued in Chapter 11, there may be immense gaps in the overall treatment. Whole sections of history may collapse or vanish, or be entirely reshaped to suit the broader concept. The Reformation and the accompanying process of 'protestantising' may be seen as part of the continuum, or as a fateful disjunction, or as a recovery of lost ideals which once flourished in the 'Celtic Church' of blessed memory. Is any one of these views of the Reformation correct, or do they all have some validity? How did the Reformation affect the views that Celts had of themselves and of the natural world around them? How was the image of the Celts modified to suit the perspectives of the Reformation?

Reforming the 'Celts'

Reformation was not an entirely novel concept to the churches within the Celtic areas of the British Isles. As we have seen in Chapter 11, the churches were given significant structural overhauls in the earlier and later Middle Ages. The Protestant Reformation was, however, a process very different from what had occurred earlier, since it challenged not only religious structures but also the doctrine proclaimed and practised within them. It began with, and concentrated on, the root, whereas earlier reforms had concentrated on the branch.

There is no uniformity in the manner in which the Celtic countries received, and responded to, the Reformation, although there are broad parallels in their attitudes to the past. In Scotland, the Reformation came later than in England, Wales or Ireland, but with the support of an influential sector of the nobility it was much more thorough-going. The Reformation Parliament met in 1560, and gave a measure of official countenance to the Reformation in Scotland. Reformed doctrine began to penetrate the southern edges of the Highlands and Islands, notably Argyll, almost immediately. John Carswell, reformed Superintendent of Argyll, published the first-ever

Gaelic printed book in 1567; this was his translation of the *Book of Common Order*. Carswell had the support of the fifth Earl of Argyll, and the attitude of clan chiefs was to be of great importance in furthering, or resisting, the Reformation elsewhere in the Highlands. Although reformed doctrine had reached Ross-shire as early as 1561, it did not enter all parts of the mainland Highlands and the Hebrides with such rapidity. Pockets of Roman Catholicism survived even in Lewis into the nineteenth century. In Ireland and Wales, the Reformation followed the English model, taking its lead from Henry VIII and Elizabeth I. In Ireland, Protestantism became the badge of the non-native (English or Scottish) occupiers of the key towns, and Catholicism was identified most strongly with the native people. In Wales, the progress of Protestantism was slow at the outset, but advanced more rapidly after the publication of the Welsh New Testament in 1567 and the entire Welsh Bible in 1588.

Wherever it took root, the Reformation represented both continuity and discontinuity with the past. Discontinuity was reflected in doctrine and ministry, which emphasised the centrality of the biblical Word as preached, and in the rejection of Catholic festivals, instrumental music, styles of worship and anything which might smack of 'Popery'; continuity was evident in the manner in which Protestants harnessed key aspects of pre-Reformation culture to proclaim their message. They retained some of the older church buildings, used traditional sites of meeting as preaching stations, and preserved aspects of monumental sculpture, sometimes with the more 'offensive' features (such as crucifixes) struck out. The dimension of culture most obviously maintained, and even reinforced, by the new church was language. In Scotland, John Carswell employed Classical Gaelic, the language of the poets, scholars and scribes in both Ireland and Scotland, for his translation of the *Book of Common Order*. In Wales, William Salesbury and William Morgan likewise followed the diction of the poets and literati in their translations of the New (1567) and Old (1588) Testaments. In Ireland, the translators of the New Testament (William Ó Domhnaill, 1602) and the Old Testament (William Bedell, 1685) similarly employed the classical language, and later Scottish translators drew on a modified form of the classical language for the Scottish Gaelic New Testament (1767) and the Old Testament (1801). Yet these texts in all countries were also fundamentally different from earlier models, since they were made available in print, and not in manuscript. Protestants introduced the printed book to the Celtic areas of the British Isles.

Reformers were very much aware of the need for precedent and continuity not only in matters of language, but also in ecclesiology. In Wales, they followed the English convention of claiming continuity with the values of the 'British Church', before it was subverted by Rome. Although John Carswell, the translator of the *Book of Common Order* into Gaelic (1567), made no such appeal to the 'Celtic' past, preferring instead to anchor his model of the Reformation in the example of the patriarchs of the Old Testament and the reforming kings of Israel and Judah, the 'Celtic Church' entered the Scottish Protestant consciousness, especially in the Lowlands, in the seventeenth century. Indeed, it could be argued (as has been done in Chapter 6) that the myth of a pure 'Celtic Church' and a delectable 'Celtic Christianity' is largely (though not exclusively) a non-Celtic Protestant invention - a fig-leaf to conceal both novelty and disjunction. As Protestants moved away from the Catholic past, and as their churches developed distinctive polities, it became important for them to discover a form of indigenised Christianity which historically validated their own cause, so that they could claim to have been 'here before'. New Testament primitivism served the purposes of the sixteenth-century Scottish reformers, but by the mid-seventeenth century 'Celtic' primitivism, which claimed some of the saints for Presbyterianism or episcopacy, was emerging.

Gradually, as the Reformation receded into the past, Scottish Protestants, suspicious and even dismissive of 'tradition' at the outset, also made their peace with the legacy of the Celtic period. They became the dominant religious force in parishes with names frequently derived from those of native saints, real or imagined, and ultimately they made use of buildings which carried the names of such saints (see Chapter 10). Memory of the 'Celtic' past was thus preserved by Protestantism, and some aspects of that past were revived, or even reinvented, to facilitate the spread of the reformed faith.

In the Scottish Highlands, Protestantism became the main religion of an area which had once been wholly Roman Catholic. By 1800 the strength of Roman Catholicism had been substantially reduced. It was now restricted mainly to the southern Outer Hebrides (Barra, Eriskay and South Uist), the Small Isles, the western edge of the mainland, and the eastern borders of the Gaelic area (west Aberdeenshire). The power of Catholicism was also curtailed in Wales, but not to any great extent in Ireland. The Catholic areas of the Hebrides were the primary sources of the material reproduced in Carmichael's *Carmina Gadelica*, although a small proportion of the charms, prayers and incantations was collected in Protestant communities. This suggests that, although they were once widely known throughout the Highlands, the *Carmina* had become (by 1850) largely the property of the Catholic communities. In the Protestant areas, they were no more than a small survival.

Civilising the savages

From at least the fifteenth century, attempts were made by Scottish central government to bring the 'Wild Scots' of the Highlands and Islands under its control. Both Wales and Ireland were subjected to similar processes by the English government. The dwellers on the 'Celtic Fringe' were seen to be barbarians, speaking uncouth languages, practising outlandish religions, and plotting against the forces of 'civilisation' and good government. In the Scottish Highlands, the reprisals taken after the Jacobite Rebellion of 1745 reduced the threat posed to 'civilisation' by the Highland menace, and brought the region more closely under the sway of what was by now the British government.

The Protestant church became one of the vehicles for the advancement of the policies of central government. It operated mainly through its own formal ecclesiastical machinery, but it enlisted the support of ancillary bodies such as the Society for the Promotion of Christian Knowledge (SPCK) in Wales, and the Society in Scotland for Propagating Christian Knowledge (SSPCK), established in Scotland in 1709, which were influential in the eighteenth century. These bodies were, in theory, initially hostile to the native languages, preferring to see English advanced as the language of civilisation. At the same time, they promulgated Protestant principles, driving them ever more deeply into the Welsh and Gaelic communities by means of translations of Puritan texts and the pedagogic power and authority of schoolmasters.

In the nineteenth century a desire to make the Welsh and the Gaels, and to a lesser extent the Irish, literate in their own language, so that they could read their vernacular Bibles, stimulated further missionary activity in these regions. Itinerant evangelists of various persuasions, including Baptists and Congregationalists, travelled extensively in the Highlands and Islands, and also in Wales. In Scotland, and especially in the Scottish Highlands, the evangelical movement produced a strong following which, in 1843, welcomed the arrival of the Free Church of Scotland. Unquestionably, the Gaelic culture of the area imparted a certain shape to the religious bodies, but this did not imply any close or continuous relationship to a 'Celtic' past. In Ireland, on the other hand, Protestantism, represented primarily by the Church of Ireland, was much less pervasive. Even in Ireland, the nineteenth century witnessed the extensive reshaping of Roman Catholicism, so that any argument for an unbroken continuum from the period of 'Celtic Christianity' must be questioned.

Although there are significant differences between the two regions, the influence of evangelicalism and the romantic movement in Wales offers some parallels to the Scottish Highlands. In Wales, the Evangelical

Awakening of the eighteenth century helped to produce a new perception of the country and its customs. Methodism and nonconformity set the spiritual tone, rejecting significant aspects of secular culture, while the conventional stereotypes, now so familiar to the outside world - harps, national costume, druids - were reconstructed in more appealing forms, as Dr Prys Morgan has demonstrated ('From a Death to a View: The Hunt for the Welsh Past in the Romantic Period'). The past was in effect remade for popular consumption. Through the influence of Macpherson's 'Ossian' and the romanticism of the nineteenth century, the Highlands and Islands - and Wales too - were seen in a new light (see Chapter 3), and repackaged for external marketing by writers and propagandists who wished to provide a better image of their hitherto despised inhabitants. These secular efforts had their spiritual counterparts in the work of Protestant religious movements. An intensely evangelical form of Christianity helped to transform the Celtic regions of Wales and Scotland after 1700, and it exerted an undeniably strong influence over the shape of the cultures. Its impact on Scottish Gaelic culture can be illustrated readily.

The spiritual warrior

The Presbyterian church in the Highlands of Scotland was involved, at various levels, in sustained initiatives which strove to break the people's link with the Catholic past. These initiatives had the making of the 'godly Gael' as their aim. This was a spiritual Gael who was different from the modern 'Celtic Christian' stereotype: the 'new creation' was a hard-headed Puritan rationalist who was able to subject his/her own body, desires and emotions to spiritual control.

The image of the Highland warrior who was a spiritual soldier, bearing the sword of the spirit rather than the sword of steel, was taken up in the mid-eighteenth century by religious poets such as Dugald Buchanan (1716-68), an SSPCK teacher and catechist stationed at Kinloch Rannoch, Perthshire. The spiritual soldier was an ideal to which people ought to aspire. As Buchanan wrote in the aftermath of the 'Forty-five (MacLean, *Spiritual Songs of Dugald Buchanan*, p.87:

Cha bu ghaisgeach Alasdair Mòr
No Cèasar, thug an Ròimh gu gèill,
Oir ged a thug iad buaidh air càch
Dh'fhan iad 'nan tràill' dam miannaibh fèin.

Cha ghaisg' na nì bhith liodairt dhaoin',
'S cha chliù bhith ann an caonnaig tric;
Chan uaisle inntinn àrdan borb,
'S cha threubhantas bhith garg gun iochd.

Ach 's gaisgeach esan a bheir buaidh
Air eagal beatha 's uamhann bàis,
'S a chòmhlaicheas le misnich crìdh'
A h-uile nì ata dha 'n dàn.

(Alexander the Great was no hero, nor was Caesar who subdued Rome, for although they conquered others, they remained slaves to their own desires.

It is not heroism to bludgeon people, nor is it fine repute to be frequently in fights; savage pride is not noble-mindedness, nor does merciless brutality equal bravery.

But the real hero is the man who conquers the fear of life and the terror of death, and who, with courage of heart, confronts everything that fate has for him.)

Hymnwriters themselves formed part of this model: Dugald Buchanan became an almost mythical figure, symbolising the spiritual warrior at his best. Although Buchanan was a catechist and preacher in the Rannoch area of Perthshire, he gained great fame throughout the Highlands.

The picture of the 'godly Gael' transmitted by Buchanan was not, of course, a homespun one, nor was it something derived from 'Celtic Christianity': the spiritual warrior is a thoroughly Biblical image which has exercised a potent influence across the centuries. It is found repeatedly in the praise of the saints (including Columba) in the early Middle Ages. It reappears in John Carswell's dedicatory portrait of the fifth Earl of Argyll, as he wields the sword of truth against error. Buchanan's spiritual warrior is also very much indebted to English models, mediated through the hymns of Isaac Watts (parts of which Buchanan incorporated into his own verse without any acknowledgement) and through Puritan writers, like Richard Baxter and John Bunyan, whose works (in Gaelic translation) made an immense impact on the Highlands.

The lessons of nature

In developing their themes and presenting their various messages, Buchanan's hymns make considerable use of the natural environment. In this too, they appear to conform to an age-old 'Celtic' pattern (see Chapter 5), but closer inspection reveals that Buchanan's interest in nature had been stimulated in large measure by the work of the influential poet, James Thomson (1700-48), a Lowlander who wrote a series of poems which were published in a single volume, *The Seasons*, in 1730. Buchanan's best known poem on a seasonal theme, 'An Geamhradh' ('The Winter'), uses winter as a metaphor for death, and takes its inspiration from the concluding section of Thomson's

poem on the same subject. For Buchanan, the seasons represent the
various stages of human life, and he urges the listener to make proper
preparation for death and the hereafter before *rigor mortis* sets in. The
natural world is also depicted in Buchanan's epic poem on the Day of
Judgement, in which the world is consumed by fire. The mountains,
which grudge their minerals to humanity, undergo a melt-down of
cataclysmic proportions (MacLean, *Spiritual Songs of Dugald Buchanan*,
p.19):

> *The surly mountains which never dispensed*
> *their resources willingly to any man*
> *are now generously pouring forth*
> *their molten treasure like a great river.*

As Buchanan comments darkly and rather gleefully in the next verse,
avaricious gold-diggers can now slake their thirst in the mighty
torrent. Not only is there a grim turning of the tables on sinners, but
the whole created order is also shown to be under the judgement of
Christ. It is by no means permanent or autonomous. Yet, despite the
sombre message and the borrowed themes, Buchanan's natural imagery
reflects close observation of the environment; the mountains, valleys,
rivers and vegetation of the region are vividly portrayed, and to this
degree his viewpoint is indigenous and appreciative - and 'Celtic'.
Nevertheless, the equation of such portraits with an innately 'Celtic'
view of the world is open to question, and their fashioning by a strictly
Calvinist poet, with an overwhelming sense of the impending
judgement of God, reminds us (once again) that whatever we may
choose to label as 'Celtic' in the religious context is not always allied
to a soft, sentimental theology.

The type of Protestantism which came into the Highlands through
the evangelical movement tended to deal with internals rather than
externals, by placing an increasingly great emphasis on personal
experience of the faith. In its initial stages, it was prepared to pay
attention to the natural environment as the handiwork of the Creator,
but interest in nature and the use of illustration from the natural world
diminished as evangelicalism took full effect. Nature became
background, rather than foreground. It became symbol rather than
substance, pointing beyond the fragility of humanity to an overarching
Providence. Thus the Revd John MacDonald of Ferintosh, who
visited St Kilda in the 1820s, described in prose and verse his impressions
of this massive, towering, wave-beaten set of islands. Their sheer
inaccessibility reinforced his sense of a divine call to proclaim the
Gospel to their inhabitants, but he also saw in them a parable of the
church of God, holding out bravely against the hammering of hostile
elements (Domhnullach, *Marbhrainn*, p.112):

On her the torrents are pounding,
and the waves surging roughly,
and occasionally they even threaten
to sweep her suddenly away.

But not one of these will overcome her,
they will never move her from her place;
she was strongly erected
on the certain, enduring rock of the ages.

The mountains and the natural scenery commonly form a more tranquil, sentimental backcloth to nineteenth- and twentieth-century accounts of the climactic point of Highland Presbyterianism, namely the open-air communion service. Donald Macphie provided, in 1917, the following picture of the setting of a communion service in his native Skye (Cheape, 'Communion Season' p.309):

> Does not the very moor, though from time to time gloomy to the eye, at other times, as in this season, bloom with heather and moss and plants? - yellow and green clumps shimmering more beautifully with the rays of the sun. Far off are the rugged, rocky pinnacles of the mountains, as if merged with the sky - a soft shadow like a purple dye on their face. Is it not possible that some measure of the significance of this spectacle - glorious, extensive, filled with the mystery of things that are hidden - will deeply affect a people on whom was bestowed in no small measure a sense of the sacred? It has often been noted by those who study the minds of their fellow creatures that there is an order of fellowship between the folk of the northern Highlands and of the islands and the creation of Nature before their eyes - namely the elements; the darkness lying in the hollows of the mountains; the shadows crossing the mountain-faces; the plaintive sound of the waves or howling of the ocean as it churns in the depth of the caverns. But the soul will also be responding to the tranquillity which falls on Nature in its own season as happens at this time.

This is a far cry from the sharply disturbing, didactic images in Dugald Buchanan's verse. In making a romantic link between faith and the natural environment, Highland Presbyterianism was by no means unique, as the location of the Keswick Convention, established by evangelical Anglicans in 1875 in the Wordsworthian environment of the Lake District, amply testifies.

Spiritual romanticism

In turning gradually from the pedagogic minutiae of the natural world to the intricacies of theology applied to the soul, Highland evangelicalism interacted more subtly with other aspects of human life, especially if these had a spiritual dimension. Thus it encouraged the retention of supernaturalism, provided that it could be accommodated within a Protestant frame. The motley band of local lay leaders known as 'the Men' is said to be the product of these supernatural forces. They were known for their depth of insight, unusual utterances and otherworldliness, which in some respects bore a curious, but largely accidental, resemblance to the qualities attributed to the Celtic saints of an earlier age (see Chapter 9). These features are said to reflect some degree of absorption of pre-evangelical practice, by a movement which is often seen as pitting itself relentlessly against the pagan practices of the Highlands. Mysticism, whatever its source, certainly appeared in a Protestant guise, and had an important role in the development of 'Highland spirituality'. Mysticism and supernaturalism were blended in key leaders of the movement: even some ministers were known to possess Second Sight, and to have seen beatific visions, while certain eminent women were reputed to know 'the Secret of the Lord' and to be close to God. Biographies of 'the Men' were written in the nineteenth century, and through these biographies 'the Men' came to represent the very best in Highland religious experience. It was then believed, or popularly accepted, that this was how 'Highland religion' may have functioned for the majority, and not only for the élite.

Entire communities were also visited by special dispensations of divine favour, pre-eminently through religious revivals. Revivals were relatively frequent in the Highlands, and occurred from the mid-seventeenth century, but became particularly common after 1800. They served to strengthen existing devotion, but more particularly to create godly communities, which, in their own way, helped to reinforce the idea that the Highlands were a place characterised by a special sense of the supernatural. Books on Highland revivals were written, itinerant preachers went to the Highlands to assist with the revival movements, and a great deal of publicity raised Highlanders to the status of people who enjoyed supernatural visitations. Particular areas of the Highlands and Islands, where evangelicalism had taken deep root, were portrayed as 'strongholds of the Gospel'. The revival-based evangelical faith of early eighteenth-century Ross-shire was immortalised in the Revd John Kennedy's *Days of the Fathers in Ross-shire* (1861; 1979 edn, p.26):

This extensive revival resulted from the blessing of the Lord on the stated preaching of the Gospel. It was preceded by much prayer. It began in the hearts and the closets of the people of the Lord. Its progress was attended by no unseemly excitement. There were no outcries or prostrations at public meetings in those days. It gave rise to no unwise multiplication of agents, means, and meetings. Deep impressions of their utter impotence under the power of sin, as well as of their utter inexcusableness under its guilt, with a distinct recognition of the necessity of regeneration and of the sovereignty of grace, distinguished the experience of the awakened.

Kennedy is here reacting against some of the alleged excesses of post-1800 revival movements in the Highlands, but it cannot be coincidental that the period to which he refers also witnessed, in the early 1760s, the publication of James Macpherson's 'Ossian'. As has been noted in Chapter 3, Macpherson's work imparted a spiritual tone to the Highlands, and Presbyterian ministers were not unaffected by it. Highland Presbyterianism came to have its own heroic age of great ministers and lay leaders, usually the first generation who, in each locality, laid the foundation of evangelicalism. Retrospectively, sublime spirituality was believed to have existed in the land of the mountains, and the faith in the Highlands was regularly portrayed as both primitive and pure. Spiritual romanticism flourished after 1800. Indeed, it is fair to claim that Highland Presbyterianism came to have its own distinctive version of the myth of naturalistic spirituality which undergirds 'Celtic Christianity', in which the 'Men' and great ministers of a bygone era replaced the Celtic saints. Its more liberal subscribers, such as Kenneth MacLeod (see Chapter 3), could produce highly romantic books like *The Road to the Isles*, full of 'mystery' and overflowing with supernaturalism. As created by evangelical Presbyterianism, however, the portrait of the 'godly Gael' flourished, and continues to flourish, not as a romantic ideal *per se*, but as a recognised image of the devout Protestant Highlander. It can still be used to berate modern laxities, or to define lost standards of Highland devotion.

While the deep spirituality and living faith of many individual Highlanders cannot be doubted, the creation of the 'godly Gael' as a broad-brush stereotype reflects the flowering, in a romantic milieu, of the aims of a religious movement which was originally concerned to convert the Highland people from their allegedly barbarous ways, and to confirm their transformation. Sometimes this movement could affirm the natural world as the work of the Creator (as in Dugald Buchanan's Gaelic hymns) and as a backcloth for worship, but more commonly after 1800 it rejected it as transient and earthly, and identified the Highland glens with 'vales of tears'. Spiritual romanticism tended, on balance, to turn its back on earthly concerns. Highland evangelicalism was often hard on 'the things of this world', because they were under a double condemnation - the condemnation of Scripture, and that of the earlier pre-1800 Highland lifestyle. Excessive drinking, immorality, superstition and cultural 'vanity' were among the primary targets; later evangelicalism refined the list to include dancing, secular (and sometimes sacred) music, cinema-going and other pastimes such as the reading of novels. Yet Highland evangelicalism also strengthened several key aspects of indigenous culture, most notably the Gaelic language.

The language of heaven

The manner in which Protestantism helped to reshape spiritual and cultural profiles in the Highlands can be illustrated clearly in changing attitudes to the Gaelic language. Two quotations, the one from the seventeenth century and the other from the nineteenth century, will make the point forcibly. The first is from the Education Act of 1616:

> Forsamekle as, the kingis Majestie haveing a speciall care and regaird that the trew religion be advanceit and establisheit in all the pairtis of this kingdome, and that all his Majesties subjectis, especiallie the youth, be exercised and trayned up in civilitie, godlines, knawledge and learning, that the vulgar Inglishche toung be universallie plantit, and the Irishe [i.e. Gaelic] language, whilk is one of the cheif and principall causis of the continewance of barbaritie and incivilitie amongis the inhabitantis of the Ilis and the Heylandis, may be abolisheit and removit...hes thocht it necessar that in everie parroche...a scoole salbe establisheit... (Donaldson, *Scottish Historical Documents*, pp.177-8).

The second is from a Free Church minister, the Revd John Kennedy of Dingwall, author of *The Days of the Fathers in Ross-shire*, speaking in 1875 at the Free Church debate on the Celtic Chair soon to be established at the University of Edinburgh (MacLeod, 'Highland-Lowland Divide', p.412):

> I like to see the language prized, in which I prefer to speak to God. As a Highland minister I feel thankful for all that would extend my acquaintance with the language in which I more frequently preach the gospel. And it is the duty of the Church, which licences so many to preach in Gaelic, to aid in securing to them the means of becoming acquainted with that, by the use of which alone they can perform the work to which they have been set apart.

The language equated with barbarity in 1616 had become, by 1875, the language by which an evangelical minister could have direct spiritual contact with the Almighty. As Kennedy was a native Highlander, it could easily be supposed that he was merely expressing his own internal prejudice to counteract an external prejudice, and there would be some truth in that. However, it is arguable that Kennedy's view of Gaelic, as a medium of spiritual communication, is but one of the strands in the portrayal of the new 'godly Gael' who spoke the language of heaven and communed closely with the Almighty.

Such a perspective is to be set not only in the context of the growing gulf between Highland Presbyterians and their Lowland counterparts in the late nineteenth century, but also in the frame of the even greater change which occurred in the perception of things Highland. This change in perception encouraged the view that the former savage had not only become noble, but, by the second half of the nineteenth century, had also become quintessentially spiritual, and his language was seen as a means of fostering and even preserving his distinctive spirituality. Although the Education Act of 1872 failed to mention Gaelic, and national education was slow to recognise the place of Gaelic in the curriculum, the Highland spokespersons of the churches were joining forces with some prominent folklore collectors in recognising the pre-eminent importance of Gaelic in religious life and definition, and were not afraid to impart a special religious worth to the language itself, while keeping well clear of aspects of secular culture which they defined as inimical to the Gospel.

New identities

The cultural consequences of the Protestant Reformation, and particularly those which flowed from evangelical activity after 1700, profoundly affected the Highlands and Islands of Scotland. The evangelical movement produced, as the Reformation had previously done, patterns of continuity and discontinuity. It forged (an ambiguous word!) a new identity, or set of identities, for the people whom it influenced, and often converted them into loyal members of the British Protestant state. The 'Celtic' label, if it was ever of any earthly significance before 1600 throughout the countries that we now call 'Celtic', was displaced by a sense of spiritual kindred based to a large extent on loyalties to churches and denominations.

The way in which Protestants view the 'Celtic Church' and the 'Celtic' past has much to do with the kind of identity - political, religious and social - which they adopt for themselves, and how they perceive the past relative to that identity. Although there is impressive evidence of continuities, some key aspects of the past were undoubtedly lost at the time of the Reformation; a major fissure was created within Christendom, and catholicity (in the eyes of some) was largely destroyed. It is possible to see the subsequent creation of 'Celtic Christianity' partly as an indicator, if not a consequence, of the unease which some Protestants have felt at having lost part of their 'Celtic', catholic past. It is no accident that, within the Protestant fold, 'Celtic Christianity' is often espoused most enthusiastically by ecumenically-minded people. Others will ally themselves with 'Celtic Christianity', not necessarily because they may be committed to the wider concept of a united church, but because they believe that the Protestant church, pre-eminently in its evangelical guise in the Celtic areas, has acted too harshly and too dismissively towards what it perceived as the 'vanities' of life, or has excluded some important aspect of worship or doctrine. Such people have a desire to restore and practise 'Celtic Christianity' in a form which redresses the balance in favour of their particular perspectives. 'Celtic' clergy can therefore be recommended as role-models, and claims for supporting parallels from the past can be advanced to strengthen a particular line of argument. In 1892, for instance, at a time of intense debate about the role of hymns and instrumental music in Highland church life, the Revd John George MacNeill argued as follows (*The Celtic Monthly*, November 1892, p.29):

> Columba was possessed of great musical ability...The ministry of the Columban church was a living, aggressive ministry of the Word, interwoven with psalm and song. The late eminent Dr. John MacDonald, Ferintosh, with his popular gift of poetry and song, was a genuine type of the early Celtic missionary. It never occurred to the early Gaelic clergy to eliminate hymns from public worshi p.This modern, short-sighted policy has divorced from religion one of its most winsome and powerful elements.

Most commentators who see such virtue in the churches of the early Middle Ages tend to forget that Christians in the Celtic regions in that period were as contentious and self-seeking as the rest, and that they too had a very clear concept of 'hell-deserving sinners' (see Chapter 5). On the other hand, conservative evangelical Protestants who may have an awareness of the 'Celtic Church' will not have any desire to restore a form of religion which panders to the 'vain things' - or even to hymns or instrumental music. Rather, they will regard their church as being a reincarnation of the 'Celtic Church' (see Chapter 6), and will be inclined to blame the Roman church for corrupting the purity of the faith as originally found in Britain and Ireland. The old illusions, with their many contradictions and illogicalities, die hard.

It is fascinating to note that the 'Celtic' country which retained its predominant Roman Catholicism - namely Ireland - was the first and (so far) the only region to wrest full independence from Britain, though several of those who sought independence (including Wolfe Tone and Charles Stuart Parnell) were Protestants. In nationalist movements beyond Ireland, political and religious identities with a 'Celtic' element have occasionally influenced one another across the years. In Wales, the process of evaluating identity in the twentieth century has sometimes brought the 'Age of the Saints' into direct comparison with modern cultural and nationalist revivalism, and the Protestant concept of 'revival' has been perceived as a link between past and present. A commentator in *Seren Cymru* in 1973 stated:

> In the midst of the national awakening and the contemporary ferment, [there is] the Welsh language - Welsh and road signs and the television and the courts and rural cottages and hunger strikes and protest campaigns. And there is no doubt that before long emphasis will be put on the relationship existing between Welsh and Christianity because the Welsh language has been bound up with the Faith from the time of Wales's birth as a nation in the age of the decline of the Roman Empire and the Age of the Saints - Dewi, Illtud, Dyfrig, Teilo, Padarn, the leaders of one of the greatest revivals Wales ever saw.

This claim demonstrates the new-found role of the Welsh saints in validating modern cultural revival, and no doubt also in removing the taint of rebellion from contemporary protest movements. It also bears eloquent testimony to the enduring usefulness of the saints in providing 'saintly' images for once 'barbarous' nations. The reference to 'one of the greatest revivals Wales ever saw' uses the term 'revival' in such a way as to make an emotive link between the saints and the potent religious revivalism of much later days. The past is repossessed for the benefit of the heirs of Calvinistic Methodism and wider Protestant nonconformity. The sixteenth-century claim that Wales had its own early, indigenous pre-Reformation form of Protestantism has probably helped to impart a Christian view of the past, and a special understanding of the relationship between faith and national identity, that has lasted much longer in Wales than in any other Celtic region. It seems likely, however, that Catholic and Protestant interaction at the intellectual level has been an even more potent factor. The modern perception of a strong religious bond between past and present in Wales was greatly stimulated by a leading Welsh nationalist who turned from Protestant Nonconformity to Roman Catholicism, namely the critic, poet, dramatist and prose-writer,

Saunders Lewis (1893-1985), whose writings have been enormously influential.

Scotland, and particularly the Scottish Highlands, have not had the equivalent of Saunders Lewis, and it is noticeable that a 'Celtic' past which is comfortable for, and can be commonly owned by, both Protestants and Catholics has not emerged. An appreciation of the Christian Middle Ages which is faithful to historical evidence, and also aware of spiritual achievements which all Christians, irrespective of denomination, can explore and celebrate without bias, is a highly desirable prospect.

Differences and difficulties of perception remain. Old stereotypes were certainly dismantled, at least partially, in the Highlands, but new - and exclusive - ones were created in the course of the years. The savage was replaced by the saint, but that saint was pre-eminently Protestant after 1600. The Protestant saint, like his early medieval precursor, was destined to fight the world, the flesh and the Devil, but to do so beyond the walls of a monastery - and he was (broadly) less inclined than his Welsh or Irish counterparts to sully his hands with politics. The line between the church and 'the world' was firmly drawn. The ideals of renunciation and mortification were proclaimed vigorously from Highland pulpits, and implemented strictly - even monastically - in the lives of devout believers. These ideals were based on the principles of the rediscovered New Testament and not on those of the 'Celtic Church'. The modern evangelical movement owed little or nothing to Columba. Any resemblance between the ideals of the legendary 'Celtic Church' and those of the Free Church owes more to (mis)perception - and to the reinvention of the ecclesiastical 'wheel' - than to pedigree.

Yet, as we have seen in Chapter 6, nineteenth-century Protestant bodies, in Scotland as in Wales, sometimes sought validation by appealing to their alleged links with the 'Celtic Church'. In reality, they were not in any way participants in a continuing 'Celtic' form of spirituality; they were participants in an age-old process of remaking the past to accommodate their own perspectives. In truth (a concept which the churches themselves did not always uphold at the historical level), they represented not a 'Celtic' consensus, but a broader British ideal of spiritual and political nationhood, based (in the case of Presbyterians) on seventeenth-century Puritanism, tempered by successive waves of evangelical revival. This form of the faith was indeed contextualised in a Gaelic cultural setting, and that setting influenced the shape and practices of the faith, but the very act of contextualisation does not necessarily imply full compliance with, or even sympathy for, preceding conventions. The immensely high esteem in which conservative Highland Presbyterians hold the

Westminster Confession (rather than the Rule of a Celtic saint) is a more than sufficent indicator of their real spiritual roots.

Devout Highlanders and Islanders of the present day - both Protestant and Catholic - who have a sense of their historical roots would be surprised to learn that they formed any part of, or were descended from, a wider 'Celtic Christianity' of the type currently in vogue, though this curious claim is made by some historians. They would be horrified by many aspects of the modern movement, and not least by the pagan-friendly tendencies of some of its branches and the ecumenism of others. In its place, however, they might have a reconstructed past of their own making which would serve to validate or challenge the present.

Protestant culture brokers

The coat of the 'Celtic Christian' has been created from more than one strand of perception, and it is by no means a uniform garment. The wearer is left to choose the dominant shades, depending on whether he or she favours Protestantism of the evangelical or liberal variety, Roman Catholicism, or a broad ecumenicity representing an interaction of different faiths or perspectives.

The term 'Celtic' is used nowadays as a convenient, but misleading, label for this spiritual coat (see Chapter 4). Much of it has been constructed from non-Gaelic materials, but fundamental parts of it are specifically Gaelic, and an important part in the weaving was played by Gaels themselves. These were not the 'Gaels on the crofts', but men who had moved into professional work, and had close links with intellectual coteries in the Lowlands, often in an ecclesiastical context. It goes without saying that those at the forefront of the post-1700 evangelical movement, like Dugald Buchanan and John Kennedy, were Gaelic-speaking, but James Macpherson, Alexander Carmichael, and Kenneth MacLeod were likewise Gaelic-speaking - and also Protestant. So too was Douglas Hyde, the son of a Church of Ireland clergyman, who made a major contribution to the concept of the 'spiritual Irishman'. Even the Iona Community, which was established by a non-Gaelic-speaker, has had, and continues to have, its Gaelic-speaking apologists, with Protestants prominent among them.

It is noticeable that in the Gaelic west the main 'Celtic' reconstructionists were themselves Gaels who stood on the fault-line between Lowland and Highland culture, between the 'natives' and the 'outsiders'. They were in effect 'culture brokers', and their most effective work was done at stages when the Highlands and Islands, and especially their Gaelic dimensions, required to be defended against the hostile non-Gaelic world, whether in the aftermath of 'Forty-five (as in the case of Macpherson, who produced his virtuous 'Ossian'), or as a response to the cumulative charge of ignorance (as in the case of Alexander Carmichael, who interpreted the Gaelic west through Renan's paradigm, and simultaneously acted as a bridge between Catholic and Protestant perceptions), or at a time when Lowland ways were seen to be bidding fair to remove the ancient landmarks of the Highland Presbyterian fathers and about to precipitate another Presbyterian secession at the end of the nineteenth century (as in the case of John Kennedy, who produced a romantic picture of evangelical idealism in eighteenth-century Ross-shire). Their overall goal was the creation of an image which would counteract the 'hard primitivist' view of Gaels as barbarians and savages. When Gaels needed a new, less frightening 'corporate identity', the 'soft primitivism' of 'spirituality' provided it, and does so still. Such 'spiritual primitivism' could be defined in Catholic or avowedly Protestant and Puritan terms, or in mixtures of these perspectives, depending on the needs of the hour. The 'spiritual primitivism' of the 'Celts', a myth forged in adversity, took on a life of its own, and retains its power into our own day. Its most effective creators and promoters at a popular level, certainly within Britain, were, and continue to be, Protestants.

It is difficult to deny the reality that provides at least a partial foundation for some of the factors which have been described in this book. There is some truth in each of the images or (to use a more modern concept) the 'windows' through which one can see the 'godly Gael' and ultimately the 'spiritual Celt'. By using only one 'window', and by reducing the view to a few special objects, bound together by a dominant ideology, it is possible to arrive at an exaggerated stereotype which can be Catholic or Presbyterian or 'Celtic' or whatever we want.

The assumption that others will conform to the preferred stereotype or spiritual 'brand' is evident in many of the wares of 'Celtic Christianity'. Little books, based on the recycling of *Carmina Gadelica* and carrying titles such as 'Praying with Highland Christians', ignore uncomfortable ecclesiastical facts and historical complexities, and misrepresent many Protestant Highlanders (to say nothing of many 'Celts') in the interests of finding a consoling and companionable, but ultimately misleading, view of Highland and 'Celtic' history. The total portrait is, of course, much greater and more complicated than any single part of the evidence can truly warrant. However, to concede its complexity would be to destroy the romantic 'Celtic' idyll, and also to privilege the 'Fringe' with determinative and even differentiating power which might be able to critique, and perhaps to criticise, the myths beloved by the dominant external power. Unfortunately, we also need to recognise that the 'spiritual Gael' who now exists in various guises in the minds of many, the typical 'Celtic

Christian' who is always conscious of the presence and power of God, had, and continues to have, his/her 'opposite type', not in barbarous Saxons or godless, worldly Lowlanders, but in the many Gaels and 'Celts' who have no interest whatsoever in spiritual matters.

Remaking the past

The distinctively Protestant versions of the 'Celtic Church' and 'Celtic Christianity', with their special slants towards particular sectors of the Protestant constituency in different regions of the British Isles, raise the fundamentally important issue at the heart of this book - the tension, if not the outright conflict, between a creative interaction with the past and fidelity to the record of the past as it has been preserved in surviving sources. This issue, which is by no means restricted to Protestants or to the post-Reformation period, needs to be faced by present-day reconstructionists of 'Celtic Christianity' and the 'Celtic Church' who are hard at work hammering out their own models of the past, and, having done so to their own satisfaction, would seek to offer their models confidently to others. We therefore turn finally to consider some of the hard questions that require to be asked in the light of previous patterns and contemporary concerns.

Chapter 13
CUTTING THE CELTIC KNOT: QUESTIONS THAT NEED TO BE ASKED

As has been demonstrated in Chapters 1-6 (and specifically in Chapter 3), the quest for 'Celtic Christianity' has a long history. As a 'Celtic' construct, it can be traced to Renan and Arnold in the nineteenth century, and to the romantic movement which was initiated by James Macpherson in the mid-eighteenth century. Its Protestant ecclesiastical version descends directly from the Reformation. Long before the Reformation, however, hagiographers who wrote the Lives of the saints produced some of our earliest Celtic sacred 'faction' (fiction with a basis in fact). They too were 'questing', and trying to construct the ideal model of the holy person according to current templates. It is fundamental to the quest that somewhere back in the past an ideal version of Christianity or the Christian church or the Christian saint is thought to have existed. The recovery and implementation of that ideal are believed to be of value in the present time. The notion of 'alternative Christianity' has been attractive throughout the centuries, particularly to those who are disillusioned with conventional Christianity. The contemporary 'Celtic' version of that notion is now to be found in Protestant, Catholic and New Age forms.

At the end of the twentieth century, the quest for 'Celtic Christianity' is espoused by a broad spectrum of writers, from the popular to the academic, from the sacred to the secular. Approaches vary accordingly. Yet it is very clear that the various exercises in recovering this ancient, but ever new, construct are underpinned by an experiential philosophy which places much more emphasis on the evidence of the senses than the evidence of reason; 'Celtic Christianity' is more of a 'feeling' than a demonstrable, rational fact. It therefore moves easily towards a form of vague, syncretistic spirituality which gives considerable place to the world of the 'spirit'. It shares boundaries with, and derives influences from, philosophies such as anthroposophy and theosophy (Chapter 4). It is able to absorb concerns and interests across the centuries, and interacts with present-day issues such as the environment and ecumenism.

In terms of theology, the range of views seems all-embracing, from the more evidently 'liberal' to the confessedly 'evangelical' and charismatic. Influences move across the theological spectrum, and it is superficially difficult to distinguish different forms of 'Celtic

Christianity'. In this chapter we draw together some of the common characteristics of the genre, and reflect on the issues that these raise for different groups of practitioners or users of this 'Celtic' faith.

Characteristics of contemporary writers

A particularly telling feature of the contemporary movement is that the great majority of its proponents are not from the Celtic areas of Britain and Ireland. Only a few are genuine Celts, who belong to these regions or have close connections with Celtic culture. In the present climate, which favours the vaguest possible application of the word 'Celtic', it is dangerous even to suggest that 'genuine Celts' could exist. Nobody wants to be excluded from anything on the grounds of culture or a criterion which may have ethnic overtones. If, however, we apply the simple linguistic test, and define a 'genuine Celt' as someone who has been brought up in a country in which a Celtic language is spoken, and/or who has learned that (or another) Celtic language to the point of fluency in both reading and writing, only a small minority of the popular writers on 'Celtic Christianity' will pass muster. Some writers may be broadly familiar with the circumstances of one or other of the Celtic languages, but few have learned a Celtic language to the point of fluency, and only a couple have learned it to the extent of being authoritative exponents of any aspect of the literature or culture relevant to the topic, especially those aspects which require access to source material in the early (pre-1100) forms of the languages. It would be expected that experts on French or German - or even English! - literature or culture (for example) would be familiar with the languages relevant to their studies. This rule apparently does not apply with the same force in the 'popular' field of 'Celtic Christianity'.

Knowledge of Celtic languages is not the only tool that is required to do justice to the field. In and of itself, it offers no guarantee whatsoever that the person concerned will produce work that is scholarly and reliable. To understand the wider context of the Celtic world, other languages (such as Latin) and disciplines (early medieval history, for example) are needed. Thus it is possible to find excellent historians who, while not fully conversant with Celtic languages, may be classicists who are able to contribute greatly to our understanding of the wider historical dimensions of real 'Celtic Christianity'. Some scholars may have more in the way of historical expertise, while others may have specialisms in languages and literatures.

Sharp, clear-minded thinking is essential in assessing the relevant cultures and periods, but 'popular' writers on 'Celtic Christianity' tend to neglect the application of mental rigour. Some writers are, nevertheless, trained historians and theologians, and it is perplexing to Celticists that even those scholars who have received rigorous academic training in such disciplines occasionally abandon close rational engagement with the sources when they explore the world of 'Celtic Christianity'. This is possibly because they have had no proper academic training in the analysis of genuinely Celtic material. Consequently, they rely on intuition and a very general familiarity with the wider Celtic heritage. Some may be subconsciously programmed to believe that 'Celtic things' do not wholly belong to the real world. This may explain why it becomes relatively easy for even 'good' minds to confuse 'Celtic things' with visionary experiences, 'prophecies' and the regression to childhood which seems to underpin the more autobiographical wing of 'Celtic Christianity'. The world of the 'Celts' is thought to be one of make-believe, and, in such a world, there is no perceived need for rigour. The approach can be as romantic and as creative as one cares to make it.

When a 'spiritual' frame is added to the 'Celtic' picture, the tendency to romanticise is probably increased. Yet the fact that a subject is 'spiritual' does not, of itself, provide an excuse for abandoning a rational, reasoned approach to understanding. 'Spirituality' is not some nebulous, self-inflating balloon which is divorced from the 'basket' of reality. It has an upward-seeking dimension, but it also has to do with the nitty-gritty world of humanity, which (for better or worse) has defined a considerable part of its course. Christian spirituality (whatever the precise parameters of 'spirituality'), even in its Celtic form, is profoundly down-to-earth, a point which should be more than self-evident to those who now wish to apply an 'incarnational' view to our understanding of the faith. Consequently, the human mind has to be applied to understanding the earthly - not to say, earthy - frames within which 'spirituality' is placed.

Unfortunately, it seems that the emphasis in much of the popular brand of 'Celtic Christianity' is not on applying the mind to understanding the historical contours of the subject, but rather on applying it to reconstructing the subject in such a way as to conform to the presuppositions of the thinker. The manner in which rational thinking is applied (or not applied) to 'Celtic Christianity' meshes with wider trends in society. The soft, soppy, re-interpretative method which is used seems to reflect much of the nature of postmodernity. Feeling and intuition and 'resonances' take precedence over reason, and hard facts are often at a discount.

The ease with which some modern academics engage in unearthly romanticism may reflect the extent to which experiential perspectives are now creeping into even the best academic minds. It seems that, for some writers at least, 'Celtic Christianity' is where one goes on one's mental holidays, to relax, away from the pressing demands of the

sources. Yet, to be fair to the Celts and their cultures, the mind of the
scholar has to be applied with the same rigour as one would expect in
the study of any other subject or discipline. To act otherwise does a
disservice to the Celts themselves, and no amount of romanticism can
disguise the weaknesses in this approach. To write from an essentially
non-Celtic external perspective which has not engaged in proper
interaction with genuine Celtic sources, and then to lay the consequent
interpretation at the door of the 'Celts', is less than complimentary to
the object which is allegedly being extolled.

It would be possible to rectify such deficiencies through close
consultation with Celtic scholars. It is, however, relatively rare for a
writer in the popular vein of 'Celtic Christianity' to seek advice from
Celtic scholars or academics. This underlines the external nature of
the overall exercise, and it also suggests that the writers regard their
own (usually English-language) culture as the one which holds the
proper academic power. Celtic scholars belong to the arcane, the
remote, the inaccessible, beyond the Pale and even the 'Fringe' itself.
Writers on 'Celtic Christianity' within the more academic wing of the
movement are more willing to consult collegial Celticists, but the
degree of interaction is not high. It is possible that exponents of 'Celtic
Christianity' are aware that Celticists might be unhappy with the
material presented to them for scrutiny, and Celtic scholars could well
be wary of involvement with non-specialists and fearful of taints from
external agendas. It is therefore easier for writers on 'Celtic Christianity'
to consult 'authorities' within their own cultural group; hence the
general tendency to quote from non-Celtic, Germanic writers on
theological matters. This opens the door to an influx of non-Celtic
concerns and ideologies.

The exponents of 'Celtic Christianity' tend to work within their
own circles, and frequently quote one another's books, with the result
that the extent of what may be termed 'secondary derivation' is very
high. A couple of the latest books appear to be based almost solely on
the works of recent popular writers in the field, who have themselves
written their books at a considerable distance from the primary
sources. The writers seldom make any obvious attempt to return to,
or base their work on, such sources. As a result of the shortage of
source material, from which most writers are debarred, the books
tend to cover much the same ground, and repeat many ideas and key
themes, as well as utilising the same range of evidence. A severe sense
of constriction soon becomes apparent, especially in those volumes
which pretend to exposition. What is usually enlarged is not the
source-base, or the depth of study, but the breadth of the application;
'Celtic Christianity' is applied to an ever-increasing range of options, and
seems (superficially at least) to have a limitless supply of lessons to teach.

The 'limitless' dimension of the applications is seen to be less impressive when one realises that what we have is a kind of merry-go-round, in which the same old (and new) hobby-horses go through 360 degrees with awesome regularity, attracting a fresh set of riders and a fresh coat of paint at each stop (see Chapter 3). The 'Celtic' merry-go-round is powered by various engines (see Chapter 2). One is the circuit of 'centres' and 'retreats' which attract a seemingly endless stream of enthusiasts. Another is the review column. The output of modern 'Celtic Christianity' is validated in reviews carried in denominational newspapers and journals. The reviewers are often even less informed about Celtic matters than the writers, but they do possess the authority of a masthead. Such reviewers, apparently unaware of their lack of appropriate knowledge, are responsible for affirming the writers as 'experts', and thus help to sell their wares to a wider, highly expectant public. Leaders of charismatic groups and influential preachers and teachers (with no obvious familiarity with real Celtic scholarship) also participate in this process of validation, offering their approval on the rearwords of less than authoritative volumes.

Facing facts

The quest for the popular brand of 'Celtic Christianity' is thus largely divorced from the quest for a proper, scholarly understanding of the forms and structures of the Christian faith in the early medieval period in Britain and Ireland; the challenges in recovering the evidence for this period are discussed in Chapters 7-10.

Taking the evidence overall, popular 'Celtic Christianity' forms a conceptual parallel universe which should not be mistaken for the real world of mainstream Celtic scholarship concerned with the forms of early Christianity in the British Isles. The difference between the two entities is so great that it is dangerous to use the term Celtic Christianity (without the inverted commas) to describe the latter; it is much better, though less concise, to employ a neutral descriptor, such as 'Christianity in the Celtic lands'. A major epistemological gulf separates the one from the other; the former is based on an experiential, subjective approach to knowledge; the latter is controlled by a rationalist perspective which seeks to elucidate the sources in their own terms.

The quest for a proper understanding of how Christianity was received and contextualised in the British Isles in the early Middle Ages is pursued by a number of outstandingly able scholars whose recent works are listed in the bibliography. There are points at which the academic quest and the more popular headlong 'chase' seem to meet; this happens because the popular writers do (occasionally) consult books written by Celtic scholars, and, in a broad sense, they may well be familiar with the drift of modern scholarship. Generally, however, the popular writers consult translations and treatises from a much earlier period of scholarship (often the late nineteenth or early twentieth century), and only gradually do they become aware of the existence of more recent scholarship. Some of the more academic writers in the field who have set out on the hunt for ideal 'Celts' do so as starry-eyed, romantic dreamers, but they gradually realise that the solid evidence will not sustain their delusions, and they become more sober (and may even recant) in the course of time.

Sadly, it is evident that many of the writers, in seeking the 'Celtic Way', have lost their own way in a number of fields, and are in the process of constructing what is 'another gospel' which does not represent the views of early Celtic Christians in these islands. Often it does not reflect the views of Christians in any island. What we need to find is not the 'Celtic way' but the 'critical way', in order to discover not some beguiling cave of mirrors, but a safe route through the maze of modernity's presuppositions and false reconstructions.

Finding the way

In cutting through the contorted Celtic knots which litter the 'Celtic way', some general principles of approach need to be set out.

The first of these relates to the use and misuse of sources. It is a basic working principle of historical analysis that, in order to arrive at an accurate view of the past, the earliest sources should be explored in their original forms. These furnish the primary evidence for the case which is to be constructed. Modern proponents of 'Celtic Christianity', on the whole, sit light to this important principle, since they approach the period(s) through translations which are outmoded and through secondary sources written by authors who (in many cases) are only vaguely familiar with the original source material. Those who wish to obtain an accurate overview of Christianity in the British Isles in the period before 1100 should begin their quest by finding a reliable, scholarly book which offers a broad sweep; the work of Kathleen Hughes is particularly useful in this respect, and offers an excellent starting-point in *The Modern Traveller to the Early Irish Church*, written jointly with Ann Hamlin. Those interested in the saints of Scotland will do well to consult the writings of Alan Macquarrie on Scottish saints. They should then begin their wider enquiry into the original sources, perhaps by reading Richard Sharpe's translation of Adomnán's *Life of Columba*, and the translations of early religious verse offered by Thomas Owen Clancy and Gilbert Márkus (*Iona: The Earliest Poetry of a Celtic Monastery*), while taking due note of the accompanying discussions. Columba and Iona provide natural bridges into the Irish affinities of saints active in Scotland.

Welsh readers should trace the corresponding types of volume for their own country. The bibliography of the present book classifies the different types of scholarly (and other) writing which are available.

The second general principle is the need to contextualise the source material, and to understand the distinctive features of particular phases of history. One of the most evident characteristics of popular 'Celtic Christianity' is its tendency to approach the subject in a synchronic manner, that is, in a manner which sees everything as if it belongs to a single period in which 'then' and 'now' seem to have much the same meaning. Thus, all evidence is given equal weight, whether that evidence belongs to the nineteenth century or the ninth; the massive changes in the spiritual and ecclesiastical complexion of the Celtic areas of the British Isles since c. 1100 (discussed in Chapters 11-12) are largely ignored. It is this approach to the subject which makes it possible for writers to pull the past into the present, and to extrapolate lessons from the tenth century which they think can be applied with equal validity to the twentieth.

The third general principle which requires to be recognised is the need to be aware of, and to maintain a critical distance from, the potent ideologies that have shaped 'Celtic Christianity'. As has been shown in Chapter 3, 'Celtic Christianity' owes much to constructs of 'Celts' which were elaborated in the nineteenth century. The process of reconstructing the 'Celts' has continued in the twentieth century. We need to be aware of how such constructs have shaped our thinking, and how they have furnished us with a set of clichés which all too readily spring to mind, even if we do not now know how the clichés were created.

Yet caution is also required, since it is all too easy to throw the Celtic baby out with the romantic Anglocentric bath-water. While a healthy degree of scepticism can do no harm, we need to be wary of over-reaction. The excesses of the less guarded devotees of 'Celtic Christianity' need to be exposed, but to dismiss genuine Celtic cultures, or certain aspects of these cultures, as a consequence is unwise. It is wise to pay attention to the revived dimensions of 'Celtic Christianity' (as in Ian Bradley's volume, *Celtic Christianity: Making Myths and Chasing Dreams*), but over-emphasis on this theme, and the failure to distinguish the actual historical reality from the 'revived version', may give the unfortunate impression that everything has been 'invented'. It is common nowadays to debunk 'tradition' as an 'invention', but it needs to be recognised that there are different kinds of 'tradition', some of which are eminently in need of debunking, and others which are well rooted in the historical cultures. As this book has sought to make clear, there *is* a rich and rewarding early Christian heritage within the Celtic areas of the British Isles. Its many dimensions

- saints, churches, theology, art, and literature, to name but a few - deserve to be understood *in their own terms*, and not reinvented. It is entirely proper, and potentially very fruitful, to explore the contextualisation of the Christian faith in the Celtic areas across the centuries, and equally useful to compare and contrast the process with what is found in other countries, but due care must be taken to ensure that external or personalised agendas are not dictating the contours of the study.

Although it is essential to distinguish between the real article and the reinvention, such distinctions are not always recognised, and the consequences for the discipline as a whole - and for the Celts - may be serious. Wholesale deconstruction of the Celts by certain writers, such as Malcolm Chapman and Simon James, who have become disillusioned with archaeological theories and are suspicious of reconstructionism of the kind represented by 'Celtic Christianity', has now reached the point of eliminating the Celts as a meaningful concept. While helpful in some respects, the observations of such writers with regard to properly Celtic matters are broadly misleading. They are part of a phoney war, sustained by misconceptions and vast generalisations which arise beyond language-based Celtic scholarship and often lack roots in a proper, internal knowledge of Celtic cultures.

'Celtic Christianity' and contemporary Christian expression

In Chapter 2 of this book, in an attempt to understand the current wide interest in the subject, we reflected on the general social and cultural context of the rebirth of 'Celtic Christianity'. We now sharpen the focus and consider specifically why it is that 'Celtic Christianity' appeals so strongly to modern Christians, and particularly those within evangelical circles. The reason for doing so is that contemporary leaders within the charismatic sector, such as Gerald Coates, are prepared to give their support to books on the subject, and observers who are in a position to know the wider evangelical scene in the British Isles are of the opinion that 'Celtic Christianity' will be a 'big thing' in the evangelical profile of the first decade of the new millennium.

It is a truism that all churches, including evangelical churches, are influenced by wider trends within society. Their complexions are shaped to a significant extent by their interaction with contemporary culture. They are not sealed units, immune from the world around them. There are, however, factors which apply specifically to their internal dynamism, and make them distinctive as churches. These factors derive from their foundational positions (constitutions and creeds), and have a bearing on their desire and also their ability to withstand (or absorb) the fashions and expectations of society.

Churches which have a strong credal position and stand by a regulative principle for their worship are less likely to play host to 'Celtic Christianity' or any form of Christianity which does not square with their foundational principles. Such churches may, of course, give some space to 'Celtic' things, perhaps by having a model of the 'Celtic Church' which they are prepared to regard as their ancestor, and which they 'dust off' from time to time, usually when they are feeling insecure. Churches which lack strict regulation, such as independent evangelical churches, house churches, or denominations or alignments of these, and also churches which are moving away from their older liturgies (such as the Church of England) may be more inclined to believe that 'Celtic Christianity' has 'something new to offer' in terms of worship styles, prayers or readings.

The key factor is perhaps the loss of authority within churches, and particularly the decay of Scriptural authority within evangelical Protestantism. In keeping with the principles of the Reformation, evangelical churches have usually given the highest priority to the exposition of Scripture and to the sermon as the key vehicle for such exposition. The unassailable position of Scripture is not, however, uniformly maintained in all evangelical churches at the end of the twentieth century. It is possible to attend services even in so-called 'evangelical' churches nowadays where there is no Scripture reading and only the briefest reference to Scripture. For a sermon, there may be no more than a collection of vague, spiritual thoughts. This is, in part, related to the erosion of rationality which we discussed earlier; it is also, it would seem, the result of a boredom factor, because contemporary people, on balance, are rather less willing to struggle with books (including the Bible) than their parents or grandparents. The context in which Christians study the Bible has also changed. Instead of listening to magisterial expositions of the Scriptures from teachers who had spent prime time in understanding the basic meaning and application of the texts, many evangelicals prefer group Bible studies, in which leaders (who are often busy people, with less time for study) direct the thoughts of the group. While such an approach undoubtedly liberates people's expression and allows a higher general level of involvement and honest enquiry than was possible even in the recent past, it also opens the door (potentially) to a much higher degree of subjectivism and (possibly) to wrong doctrine.

The nature of worship and mission within many churches is also changing. In order to reach 'the world' with the message of the Gospel - a laudable aim in itself, and one which should be foremost in the thinking of all contemporary churches - some churches and church leaders are prepared to move to forms of service which are radically different from those that are generally practised. The growing emphasis on informality opens the door still further to the ways of 'the world'. Certain charismatic churches now offer a form of 'worship' which is almost indistinguishable from secular 'rave culture'. At least one such church makes much of its 'Celtic' forms of worship. What precisely its leaders mean by the word 'Celtic' in such a context is perplexing; it appears to be a code for 'doing our own thing' - and doing it in terms of postmodern, secular society. Leaders of such churches are given to proclaiming the virtues of the 'Celts', particularly the manner in which the 'Celts' supposedly embraced secular and pagan culture. Sermons on 'Celtic' themes all but displace the proclamation of the gospel. Self-justification, rather than a desire to understand the processes of the past, seems to be the principal motivating factor. The secular world appears to be writing much of the churches' agenda.

In the face of such innovations, the place of order and traditional self-understanding within evangelicalism is being eroded, with little to replace it. This means that many churches, in an attempt to be relevant to the needs of the world around them, have lost their ancestral moorings. In many cases, they have little sense of historical perspective, and their identity (especially as denominations) is under serious threat. In a desperate attempt to find a place for themselves in the wider scheme of ecclesiastical development, some churches bypass generations of their own existence in order to find an 'earlier' identity.

The overall result of these processes is that evangelical Protestantism has lost the hard, protective shell of what is sometimes called 'classical evangelicalism'. It is thus very vulnerable to new fads and fashions. It is not so easy nowadays to debar doctrines which are potentially harmful, because fewer people possess the knowledge and authority with which to identify these doctrines or their deleterious effects. The drift towards tolerance and subjectivism allows a far higher degree of individual self-determinism in spiritual matters than was permitted fifty years ago. As a consequence of the 'openness' which came with the charismatic movement, many churches are in a mood for experimentation, as is evident in the various 'waves' which have swept through evangelical circles in the last twenty years.

'Celtic Christianity' is one of those fads which not only meets the need for experimentation and matches the moods of the moment, but also appears to offer a means of giving cohesion to such remnants of Christian belief as may yet be found among people at large, both within and beyond the churches. As the metanarrative (or 'grand story') of Scripture is displaced, 'Celtic Christianity' apparently provides an alternative model, or set of models, for gathering the surviving fragments of the 'grand story' into a meaningful pattern. It brings the scene of the action closer to home, and is thus believed to offer locally-based insights into the way in which Christians 'in these islands' acted within the society of their own time. The 'grand story' is, perhaps, thought to be more credible if the context in which it functions is within striking distance of those who have doubts about its validity. This produces a new hermeneutic and a whole new brand of religious 'faction', which has moved away from the biblical texts to non-biblical religious texts which are contextually nearer to the earthly territories of the churches. The inclusion of 'Celtic Christianity' in church services, in short, runs the risk of displacing the Scriptures in favour of a supposedly indigenous 'open canon' of non-scriptural poems and tales.

The broader quest for 'Celtic Christianity' is symptomatic of a wider, deeper search for spiritual meaning. Unfortunately, however, this postmodern quest is not being satisfied by the churches in their present form. Under such circumstances, the justifiable desire to be relevant to contemporary needs may tempt some culturally sensitive Christian leaders to incorporate aspects of 'Celtic Christianity' into their forms of worship, and thus to make the church more relevant to people's interests. It seems that well-meaning pastors and clergy are sometimes prepared to use poems and stories from 'Celtic Christianity', rather than (or in addition to) the Scriptures, as a way of providing a supposedly postmodern context for the Christian faith. But is this a wise route to take?

Issues which must be faced

If church leaders are thinking of bringing 'Celtic Christianity' into their services, there are several issues which they must face. At the outset, they would be wise to consider whether the form of Christianity practised in these islands before 1100 is a valid approach to take when meeting the challenges of the present time. Even if it were possible to replicate such a pattern, to what extent would it be likely to succeed as a transformational power in the land, given the changes which have occurred in society across the centuries? The analysis of 'Celtic Christianity' offered in this book (see Chapter 5) suggests strongly that the issues of the late twentieth century have already been incorporated into its profile, and it is therefore improbable that it will provide an adequate solution to the angsts of the age. It will offer more in the way of retrospective consolation than contemporary challenge. Modern 'Celtic Christianity', in fact, appears to be directed towards the religiously inclined and 'concerned' middle classes who have money to buy books and participate in 'retreats', and the time and the resources to go on pilgrimages and 'drop out' of the contemporary rat-race. It does not seem to have much to say to the practical challenges of planting churches in present-day housing estates, or to confronting contemporary drug culture and larger moral issues.

Further doubts are raised by the heterodox and selective nature of much of what comes under the label of 'Celtic Christianity'. This difficulty should be sufficiently clear from what has been said in this book. Whatever the flavour of Christianity in the Celtic areas of the British Isles before 1100, it cannot be claimed that it is accurately represented in modern 'Celtic Christianity', nor can it be asserted that *all* modern brands of 'Celtic Christianity' are theologically sound and orthodox. Some may be, but the writings which have done most to popularise the product are at pains to emasculate 'the faith once for all delivered to the saints'. There is no great emphasis on redemption or the cross as the place of atonement, rather than as symbol. The overall approach tends to be incarnational, but it is a type of incarnationalism which seems to diminish the role of divine intervention in converting and transforming humanity. The concepts which are less attractive to our own age, but which lie at the heart of early Christianity in the Celtic lands - a heavy emphasis on judgement, retribution, penance, self-denial and mortification (the 'doing to death' of the flesh and its desires), leading to (sometimes) severe asceticism, which may well be the *real* distinguishing features of this form of Christian devotion - have been removed, played down or nicely romanticised, and do not appear to have much practical significance in the outworking of 'Celtic Christianity'.

Given the mixed nature of 'Celtic Christianity', both churches and individuals need to reflect on whether it is something from which contemporary Christians can derive any wholesome spiritual benefit. At the very least, it must be approached with great discernment. Paganism and harmful teachings of various kinds can be mixed up in some (though not necessarily all) of the products. This alone should make Christians wary of giving it any significant place alongside the primary tenets of the Christian faith.

The individual's approach to 'Celtic Christianity' will be, by its very nature, different from that of the churches. It is easier for the individual to exercise discernment in what he or she chooses to read. Discerning readers can derive a certain amount of benefit from 'Celtic' prayers, and perhaps more specifically from the style and technique of these prayers. There is much that one can enjoy at the aesthetic level in the writings of David Adam, for example, as the present writer will gladly testify. However, the reader must understand that these are *the writings of David Adam*, and that, far from being Celtic in the strictly linguistic or cultural sense, they represent a romanticised vision of the past, influenced strongly by Anglicanism and written *in English*, but presented as 'Celtic'. David Adam does *not* at any time disguise his role as author, nor does he actively seek to mislead his readers - and that is true of most other writers also - but the use of the words 'Celtic' or 'ancient Celtic Christian tradition' on the package is sufficient to give the impression to the unwary (of whom there are many) that Adam is somehow the channel through which genuinely Celtic material of age-old significance is conveyed. The pose which is invented for such writers by their publishers and blurb-writers is that of intermediaries between 'ancient Celtic Christian tradition' and the present-day world.

Similarly, a church which wishes to employ 'Celtic' prayers must exercise some discrimination, since the consequences of mistakes will be all the greater. The fact that the church uses 'Celtic' material could be seen by the less wary members of the congregation as validation of the whole gamut of 'Celtic Christianity'. The minister or worship leader will therefore need to assess what material ought to be used, where it ought to be inserted, and how it can be guaranteed that the presence of this type of material will not be the first step on a slippery slope which sends some of his/her congregation headlong into the slough of serious compromise with harmful doctrines and philosophies.

Churches will also need to reflect on whether they can use 'Celtic Christianity' safely as a tool in evangelism. One of the ways in which Christians who have some critical awareness of the issues justify 'Celtic Christianity' is by claiming that it attracts the attention of the secular world to something which is, in a broad sense, Christian. This may be so, but one has to ask questions about how 'Christian' the material is. If it is not doctrinally wholesome, should it be used in evangelism? Is it right to use 'error' as a means of reaching people with the gospel of Jesus Christ? Or have eclecticism and syncretism now reached the point where 'error' is no longer seen to be a meaningful concept?

The unending quest

Modern 'Celtic Christianity' is a complex phenomenon. At the popular level, it is very much an amalgam of philosophies and ideas, bringing under one label a range of products, old and new. It is a mixed bag of orthodoxy, heterodoxy and wishful thinking. In this respect, it reflects the eclectic tendencies of our doctrinally barren, postmodern times. The faith of the 'real' Columba (as far as we can now tell) was rooted firmly in the New Testament, not in the New Age.

The focus of popular 'Celtic Christianity' is not always on Christian matters; there is seldom a strong emphasis on salvation, and grace is often at a discount. Secular agendas which displace Christian concerns usually lie just below the surface. 'Celtic Christianity' aimed at contemporary customers is, nevertheless, well packaged. It looks good, feels soothing, and is even attractive to the outside world, but it is not necessarily 'real' or true to its name. 'Celtic Christianity', in its populist guise, is focused pre-eminently on the needs of the spiritual consumer of the present day. All of us are vulnerable to its blandishments, since we are all 'questers' at heart.

The quest for some distinctive aspect or other of 'alternative Christianity' has been pursued across the centuries, and it is well attested at the end of the twentieth century. 'Celtic Christianity' has been part of that wider quest. It has its own specific agendas, and is able to respond to the needs of every generation. Today's agenda is different from yesterday's; this century's from that of last century; and no doubt the new century will put its own 'spin' on the theme. The differences, however, lie in the details and the emphases. Dissatisfaction or disillusionment with the present is a potent general factor in the contemporary quest, but perhaps the chief motivation in the remaking of the spiritual past - a motivation which transcends all the centuries, from Columba's time to our own - is loss: loss of key saints, loss of spiritual ideals, loss of innocence, loss of language, loss of connection with the flow of history, loss of identity and perhaps ultimately the loss of faith itself. To compensate for that loss, and to escape the chill winds of harsh reality, we search for a refuge in the warm shelter of retrospective spiritual romanticism. As we trek, we boldly go beyond the evidence to reconstruct imaginatively what we believe to have been the ideals which we now strive to achieve. We remake the past in our own image.

We are all potential volunteers or even victims. The romantic desire to return to Eden - or to Iona or Lindisfarne - is implanted deep within each of us, and we will gladly participate in a pilgrims' progress to 'magical, mystical islands' where the saints once lived.

CHAPTER 14
PILGRIMS' PROGRESS

It was an unforgettable September day in 1965. The skies were as clear as one ever sees them in the Inner Hebrides; feather-shaped wisps of cloud, driven by a light northerly breeze, occasionally stole the warmth of the sun. Standing on the wooden bridge-wing of the 'King George V' - David MacBrayne's splendid but increasingly elderly pleasure-steamer - as her razor-sharp bow cut through the Sound of Mull at an effortless eighteen knots, I could hear the squawk of seagulls, the hum of the turbines and the splash of the bow-wave; astern, I could see the steamer's elegant wake, fanning outwards from the propellers until the curdled surf gave way to gentle ripples which seemed to touch the shores of Morvern to starboard and those of Mull to port. On the decks was a rich assortment of humanity, with vacuum flasks and sandwiches, throwing desultory scraps to voracious seagulls whenever the magnetic magnificence of the landscape permitted the eyes to wander. Some were hanging on to the deck-rails, lost in the tourist's abandonment of the cares of life, while others were viewing the world through binoculars and Pentax lenses. Lismore lighthouse, tree-clad hillsides, precipitous slopes, Ardtornish Castle swishing past, Ardnamurchan Point to starboard, and Tobermory hard to port, nestling in its concentrated and superbly sheltered bay...the 'King George' carried us majestically on our course, with the pennant of David MacBrayne, the uncrowned king of West Highland shipping, barely holding its own at the peak of the main-mast. Once round the Cailleach headland, she began to roll, with the balance of the high-masted, narrow-beamed turbine-steamer; any feelings of sea-sickness were dispelled by the anticipation of landing on Staffa and ultimately setting foot on Iona. But would we be permitted to step ashore? The heavy swells of the past couple of weeks had made landing difficult at both points.

I too was among the tourists, having been invited by the master of the 'King George V', Captain Neil Campbell, to accompany him on the regular Saturday day-trip to Iona. The fare? It would suffice, said Captain Campbell, if I helped the crew to wash the dishes. Captain Campbell hailed from Tiree, my native island, and was one of a long line of sea captains produced by the island. Several Tiree men commanded MacBrayne steamers, and both their seamanship and their kindness have justifiably become part of the maritime folklore of the Hebrides. I had only recently moved to Oban, in order to continue my education at Oban High School, and the prospect of a trip on the 'King George', that masterpiece of Clyde engineering, was particularly appealing to someone with an innate love of West Highland steamers. But it was also an opportunity to visit Iona, an island which lay only a few miles to the south-east of Tiree, and could be seen on the horizon as the final low-lying eminence at the nose of the Ross of Mull.

Tiree had close contacts with Iona. In very recent times, Tiree crofters had crossed regularly to meet their Iona counterparts, and often to participate in their regattas. Tiree skiffs had a reputation for excellence, and the Iona men were skilled sailors too. Their rivalry was based on bonds of friendship and kinship, and the stories of the Iona regattas and the boats that won the race were told and retold in the cèilidh-houses of Tiree. The Salum men, in particular, related their Iona adventures with gusto.

Crofters crossed the water, but so too, in a much earlier era, did saints. The local community had legends about Columba, the principal holy man of the Inner Hebrides in the so-called Dark Ages, who was based at his monastery in Iona. It was said that he had a monastery in Tiree too, and that, on one of many occasions when he visited the island, he tied his coracle to a seaweed-covered rock in Gott Bay. Unfortunately (as we have seen in Chapter 10), the seaweed failed to hold the coracle, and she drifted out on the tide. Discovering the untimely departure of his ferry-boat, the infuriated saint cursed the rock, and from that time onwards it was called *Mallachdag*, 'The Little Cursed One'. It grew no more seaweed. The image of Columba, as a walking curse-dispenser who was prepared to condemn the rock rather than blame his own carelessness, stood in sharp contrast to what religious Hebrideans would normally regard as sanctity, and it also sat ill with the glowing (and growing) reputation which he and Iona otherwise enjoyed in the popular mind. The full Gaelic name of Iona, *I Chaluim Chille*, 'Iona of Calum of the Cell', was uttered with that awe and sense of respect which Gaelic-speakers have for place-names with a particular historical significance.

But who was Columba, and what was Iona like? My voyage on the 'King George' might help to answer these questions. Soon we were at Staffa, with its towering basalt pillars. Yes, we could land on the island, but, because of rock-falls, Fingal's Cave was off the itinerary. We clambered into the red ferry-boat which had come to meet us from Iona, and looked around briefly, before rejoining the ship and steaming southwards.

By mid-afternoon the 'King George V' was in the Sound of Iona, giving her turbines a temporary rest and rolling quietly as she tugged at her rusty anchor-chain. The 'red boats' which were used to ferry passengers from the steamer to the island were butting their way through the water, laden with inquisitive tourists. Having landed on the jetty, we walked through the village, passed the medieval nunnery, paused at St Oran's Chapel and Rèilig Orain ('Oran's Burial-ground'), and arrived at the restored cathedral, magnificent in its setting among the green fields. Across the narrow Sound of Iona, glittering in the sunshine, was white-shored Fionnphort, the ferry terminal on the Ross of Mull. The 'King George' looked particularly majestic in the middle of the sound.

Here, then, was the place hallowed by the arrival, in 563 A.D. or thereabouts, of Columba, the Irish abbot whose monastery was said by Dr Johnson to have been 'the luminary of the Caledonian regions'. Fourteen centuries had passed since then, and a huge celebration had been held in 1963 to mark the great arrival. But what remained of Columba? Not much, it would seem. The nearest we could get to the saint was to stand on Tòrr an Aba ('The Abbot's Hill') to the west of the restored Cathedral, a ridge which, on the evidence provided by his biographer, Adomnán, was reckoned to be the site of a cell which he used. Excavation in 1957 had revealed traces of a small building. Was this the great man's study? Archaeology could take us a little bit of the way, perhaps, but the imagination could do the rest: with Adomnán's assistance one could see Columba at work copying his manuscripts of the Psalter. It was possible to envisage the saint going around the work of the monastery. Responding to the beauty of the scenery, the warmth of the afternoon sunshine, and the waft of flowers and foliage, one could feel that some sort of 'experience' was soaking into the subconscious. Expectation was not disappointed. Looking back, I wonder if my impression would have been different if the weather had been foul, with a howling gale and driving rain in true Hebridean fashion.

In what seemed a remarkably short time, the day's batch of tourists was being shepherded down to the 'red boats', and back to the 'King George'. The bridge telegraph was ringing 'Stand by' in a matter of minutes, and the ship began to surge forward once again, cleaving the sound on the inward journey to Oban. Passengers made for the restaurant. I ate a hearty meal in the crew's quarters and duly paid my fare by washing the dishes with a sailor. By eight o' clock we were gliding into the tranquillity of Oban Bay, and the 'King George V' was soon berthed at the Railway Pier. Captain Campbell rang 'Finished with engines', went to his cabin, and exchanged his gold-braided cap and uniform for his suit. As he walked down the gangplank, I thanked him for his kindness, and for what had been a splendid day.

Columba's Isle had drawn another boat-load of tourists. In retrospect, I wonder what these tourists had expected to find, and whether their expectations had been fulfilled. Had they expected to see the beauty of one particular island, or to get closer to Columba, or to meet with a different dimension of living? Or were they trying to explore, and strengthen, their relationship with God, as each may have defined him? Or, by going on a modern package tour, were they, knowingly or unknowingly, satisfying the deep desire to go on a pilgrimage to a 'holy place'? Were they going to the 'Sacred Isle' for much the same reason as others go to the 'Holy Land'?

No doubt there were as many reasons as there were people on the 'King George V' on that fine September day. I certainly felt that something special had happened, but I was unable to describe it adequately, though I attempted to do so in a letter to my parents in Tiree. Gradually, the experience faded in a wave of homesickness, homework and hankerings of other kinds. Columba too seemed to lose the sparkle that he had achieved on that beautifully mystical day on *Tòrr an Aba*. Perhaps belief was, like beauty, in the eye (or should it be the heart?) of the beholder.

Columba lay forgotten in my mind, but he was to come to life again in the course of my academic studies in the universities of Glasgow and Cambridge. In the latter, where I enrolled in the Anglo-Saxon, Norse and Celtic Tripos in 1971, I had the privilege of studying the religious history of the British Isles in the so-called Dark Ages, under the guidance of two eminent teachers, Dr Peter Hunter Blair and Dr Kathleen Hughes. The former had a special interest in early Northumbria, while the latter was an authority on the church in early Irish society. Columba and Iona figured in the courses taught by both. From Hunter Blair I learned of Bishop Aidan's seventh-century mission from Iona to Northumbria, and I also studied the history of the mission which had come to Canterbury from Rome in 597 A.D., the year of Columba's death. That mission too had reached Northumbria, and its chief emissary, Paulinus, had conducted mass baptisms in the rivers. Kathleen Hughes demonstrated in her lectures that Columba was only one of a number of saints who had been active on Scotland's western seaboard. Compared with Columba, whose cult had been well managed through the ages, the others were minor figures, but they were nonetheless significant. There were also larger, but very shadowy, saints who belonged to mainland Britain and Ireland, and stalked the minds of historians: the 'problems' of Patrick and Ninian were part of the wider enigma of early missionary activity in the British Isles. Under Kathleen Hughes's formidable direction, I was challenged to interact with primary sources, and to provide arguments for or against the viewpoints expressed by scholars in their books.

By the time I left Cambridge I was equipped with an academic appreciation of the historical and cultural contexts of Columba, but also with a deep awareness of the pitfalls which awaited those who believed that a clear and unequivocal account of his life could be extracted easily from the existing records. In a sense, a new quest had begun - a quest to fit Columba and his fellows into an accurate, historical frame. My pilgrimage to Iona in 1965 subsequently became but a remote memory, but it was never entirely erased, and occasionally I still stand pensively (in my imagination) on *Tòrr an Aba*. In later years I returned to Iona on several occasions, but never with the sense of expectancy and momentary fulfilment which were associated with my first visit. What has lasted longer in my mind, in a much more tangible way, is the experience of sailing on the 'King George V', a magnificent specimen of Clyde ship-building. Even yet, I can feel her movement and I can hear the hum of her turbines...Some dreams are never destroyed. Nothing intervened in later life to banish the illusion. If I had been on the 'King George V' in a Force Eight gale, and had been as sick as ten dogs, I suspect that the memory of this beautiful ship would have been much less enticing. She could roll desperately, even in a flat calm, but she was so splendid on that particular day, so majestic in her black and red livery, with her rust-bespattered lower plates and her two lofty funnels blowing oily smoke and damp steam. She was to me then, and will ever remain, the greatest ship in the world.

It seems clear to me now that there was a difference between myself and the pilgrims who lined the decks of the 'King George'. For many of them, I presume, the trip to Iona was probably a once-in-a-lifetime experience. They were heading towards the Hebrides, and the magical Sacred Isle, for perhaps the first and last time. How they saw Iona on that day might have had a very real bearing on how they regarded saints like Columba for the rest of their lives. Most of them had no interest in the ship. For them, the image of Columba would have been paramount, and, in later life, nothing would have intervened to destroy its beauty. For me, as a West Highland steamer buff, the ship remained the 'dream image', but Columba gradually lost much of his romantic spell, though never his attractive significance as a powerful figure of history associated with an island that, on a clear day, seemed almost within easy sailing distance of Tiree. I myself was ultimately heading away from these islands, away from the Columba of boyhood dreams, and into a world where the mind and the intellect were prepared for rational enquiry.

In the course of my subsequent researches, initially into the history of the Baptist denomination to which I belonged, I discovered that religious bodies frequently produce romantic images of themselves, which they project into the past, or promote for a variety of reasons. Individuals, too, were inclined to the same practice. To 'see visions and dream dreams', in cultural, denominational or personal terms, is part of a greater spiritual quest. This book is a wider exploration of that theme.

Perhaps my boyhood adventure on the 'King George V' is something of a parable, a metaphor of the quest for 'Celtic Christianity'. Deep within each one of us, there is that profound desire for the pure and beautiful. For some that need is met by saints, and by pilgrimages to distant shrines, and encounters with 'Celtic' crosses with their huge wheel-heads standing bold against the sunset; for others it is satisfied by more earthly objects such as ships and cars from another era. Each acts as a 'dream trigger', setting off a range of associations, a sequence of pictures which (in Wordsworth's lines) 'flash upon that inward eye / which is the bliss of solitude'. The dream excludes the uncomfortable, the unacceptable, and the mundane, and invests life with another, more attractive, dimension of existence. A 'bypass mechanism' ensures that we see only what we want to see, and a mental 'search engine', which can take us effortlessly to the right spiritual websites, guarantees that we will create a pretty pastiche in which our quest will reach its self-directed goal.

The quest for 'Celtic Christianity' is, in its own way, 'real' for many, and doubtless provides much pleasure. It would be unkind to deny that. But, in its postmodern, romantic form, where is it heading? What is its destination? Is its destination an Arcadia in the west where everything is a fulfilment of 'visions and voyages'? Must it always be so? Is the incessant 'dreaming of dreams' - a pastime of which the 'Celts' have no monopoly - fair to those whose memory we cherish? Must we re-invent them for our own sakes? Must we live by the light of another Celtic Twilight? Must we always confuse the form of the faith with its substance?

There is surely a more honest, less deceptive quest which seeks to be true to the real Celtic past as reflected in the surviving sources at different stages. It may not be as beguiling as the self-constructed route which avoids the challenges and the difficulties of linguistic and historical reality, and it may even involve some serious thinking - but, at the journey's end, it may be much more rewarding. Then we may have a meaningful encounter with real Celtic Christians, and also with their God, who was the focus of their vision, and the motivation and consummation of their quest. Both their quest and their vision are summarised in a well-known hymn which is often sung for the beauty of its words and music. Rather than allowing ourselves to be distracted by the poetry, we may need to pay attention to what it really says:

Be Thou my Vision, O Lord of my heart;
Naught is all else to me, save that Thou art;
Thou my best thought by day and by night,
Waking or sleeping, Thy presence my light.

Be Thou my Wisdom, Thou my true Word;
I ever with Thee, Thou with me, Lord;
Thou my great Father, I Thy true son;
Thou in me dwelling, I with thee one.

With the High King of heaven, after victory won,
May I reach heaven's joys, O Bright heaven's Sun!
Heart of my own heart, whatever befall,
Still be my Vision, O Ruler of all.

(From Eleanor Hull, *Poem-Book of the Gael*, pp.119-20)

BIBLIOGRAPHY

A Reference works and background reading

1 Reference works

(a) Celtic

Connolly, S.J. (ed.), *The Oxford Companion to Irish History* (Oxford University Press, Oxford 1998)

Fletcher, Richard, *Who's Who in Roman Britain and Anglo-Saxon England* (Shepheard-Walwyn, London 1989)

Maier, Bernhard, *Dictionary of Celtic Religion and Culture* (Boydell and Brewer, Woodbridge 1997)

Stephens, Meic (ed.), *The New Companion to the Literature of Wales* (University of Wales Press, Cardiff 1998)

Thomson, Derick S., *The Companion to Gaelic Scotland* (Blackwell, Oxford 1983)

Welch, Robert (ed.), *The Oxford Companion to Irish Literature* (Oxford Univivesity Press, Oxford 1996)

Williams, Ann, *et al.*, *A Biographical Dictionary of Dark Age Britain: England, Scotland and Wales, c. 500-c.1050* (Seaby, London 1991)

(b) Theological, ecclesiastical and philosophical

Blackburn, Simon, *The Oxford Dictionary of Philosophy* (Oxford University Press, Oxford 1994)

Cross, F.L., and E.A. Livingstone (eds), *The Oxford Dictionary of the Christian Church* (Oxford University Press, third edn, Oxford 1998)

Ferguson, Sinclair B., and Wright, David F. (eds), *New Dictionary of Theology* (Inter-varsity Press, Leicester 1988)

McBrien, Richard P. (ed.), *The HarperCollins Encyclopedia of Catholicism* (HarperCollins, New York 1995)

Stevenson, J. (ed.), *Creeds, Councils and Controversies* (SPCK, London 1975)

2 History, literature and culture: theoretical studies

Bromwich, Rachel, *Matthew Arnold and Celtic Literature: A Retrospect 1665-1965*, 1964 O'Donnell Lecture (Clarendon Press, Oxford 1965)

Brown, Terence (ed.), *Celticism*, Studia Imagologica, Amsterdam Studies on Cultural Identity, 8 (Amsterdam and Atlanta, GA 1996)

Chapman, Malcolm, *The Celts: The Construction of a Myth* (St Martin's Press, New York 1992)

Chapman, Malcolm, *The Gaelic Vision in Scottish Culture* (Croom Helm, London 1978)

Cronin, Michael, *Translating Ireland: Translation, Languages, Cultures* (Cork University Press, Cork 1996)

deGategno, Paul J., *James Macpherson* (Twayne Publishers, Boston 1989)

Ferguson, William, *The Identity of the Scottish Nation: An Historic Quest* (Edinburgh University Press, Edinburgh 1998)

Franklin, Michael J., *Sir William Jones* (University of Wales Press, Cardiff 1995)

Hutton, Ronald, *The Pagan Religions of the Ancient British Isles: Their Nature and Legacy* (Blackwell, Oxford 1991)

James, Simon, *Atlantic Celts: Ancient People or Modern Invention?* (British Museum Press, London 1999)

Kidd, Colin, *British Identities before Nationalism: Ethnicity and Nationhood in the Atlantic World* (Cambridge University Press, Cambridge 1999)

Leerssen, Jeop, *Remembrance and Imagination: Patterns in the Historical and Literary Representation of Ireland in the Nineteenth Century* (Cork University Press, Cork 1996)

Morgan, Prys, 'From a Death to a View: The Hunt for the Welsh Past in the Romantic Period', in Eric Hobsbawm and Terence Ranger, *The Invention of Tradition* (Cambridge University Press, Cambridge 1983), pp.43-100

Piggott, Stuart, *Ancient Britons and the Antiquarian Imagination* (Thames and Hudson, London 1989)

Piggott, Stuart, *The Druids* (Thames and Hudson, London 1989)

Porter, R. (ed.), *Myths of the English* (Cambridge 1992)

Said, Edward W., *Culture and Imperialism* (Vintage, London 1994)

Said, Edward W., *Orientalism: Western Conceptions of the Orient* (Penguin, Harmondsworth 1995)

Smith, Iain Crichton, *Towards the Human: Selected Essays by Iain Crichton Smith* (MacDonald Publishers, Edinburgh 1986)

Stafford, Fiona, 'Primitivism and the "Primitive" Poet: A Cultural Context for Macpherson's Ossian', in Brown (ed.), *Celticism*, pp.79-96

Stafford, Fiona, *The Sublime Savage: A Study of James MacPherson and the Poems of Ossian* (Edinburgh University Press, Edinburgh 1988)

Womack, Peter, *Improvement and Romance: Constructing the Myth of the Highlands* (Macmillan, Basingstoke 1989)

3   Comparative religion and primal religions

Bediako, Kwame, *Christianity in Africa: The Renewal of a Non-Western Religion* (Edinburgh University Press, Edinburgh 1995)

Churchill, Ward, *Fantasies of the Master Race: Literature, Cinema and the Colonization of the American Indians*, ed. M. Annette Jaimes (Crimmon Courage Press, Monroe [Maine, USA] 1992)

Hinnells, John R. (ed.), *A New Handbook of Living Religions* (Penguin, Harmondsworth 1998)

Hinnells, John R. (ed.), *The Penguin Dictionary of Religions* (Penguin, Harmondsworth 1984)

MacLeod, Hugh, *Religion and the People of Western Europe 1789-1989* (Oxford University Press, Oxford 1997 edn)

Renault, Dennis, and Freke, Timothy, *Principles of Native American Spirituality* (Thorsons/Harper Collins, London 1996)

Riesbame, William E. (ed), *Atlas of the New West: Portrait of a Changing Region* (W.W. Norton & Co., New York 1997)

Taylor, John V., *The Primal Vision: Christian Presence amid African Religion* (SCM, London 1965 edn)

Wilson, James, *The Earth Shall Weep: A History of Native America* (Picador, London 1998)

4 Contemporary cultural and religious patterns in Britain

Anderson, Digby, and Peter Mullen (eds), *Faking It: The Sentimentalisation of Modern Society* (Social Affairs Unit, London 1998)

Barker, Eileen, *New Religious Movements: A Practical Introduction* (HMSO, London 1989)

Bebbington, David, *Evangelicalism in Modern Britain: A History from the 1730s to the 1980s* (Unwyn Hyman, London 1989)

Bruce, Steve, *Religion in Modern Britain* (Oxford University Press, Oxford 1995)

Burnett, David, *Dawning of the Pagan Moon: An Investigation into the Rise of Western Paganism* (Marc, Eastbourne 1991)

Drane, John, *Faith in a Changing Culture: Creating Churches for the Next Century* (Marshall Pickering, London 1997)

Ferguson, Ronald, *George MacLeod: Founder of the Iona Community* (Collins, London 1990)

Howard, Roland, *The Rise and Fall of the Nine O'Clock Service* (Mowbray, London 1996)

Walker, Andrew, *Restoring the Kingdom: The Radical Christianity of the House Church Movement* (Eagle, Guildford 1998 edn)

B Historical and literary studies of Christianity and its cultural contexts in Britain and Ireland before 1100

1 Historical analyses, collections, anthologies and literary criticism earlier than 1930

Arnold, Matthew, *The Study of Celtic Literature* (Smith, Elder, London 1900, popular edn)

Carmichael, Alexander, *et al.* (eds), *Carmina Gadelica*, 6 vols (Oliver and Boyd *et al.*, Edinburgh 1900-71)

Hull, Eleanor, *A Text Book of Irish Literature*, 2 vols (Gill, Dublin, and Nutt, London 1906)

Hull, Eleanor (ed.), *The Poem-Book of the the Gael* (Chatto and Windus, London 1912)

Hyde, Douglas, *Abhráin Diadha Chúige Connacht: The Religious Songs of Connacht* (Fisher Unwin, London, and Gill and Son, Dublin 1906)

Hyde, Douglas, *The Story of Early Gaelic Literature* (Fisher Unwin, London 1895)

MacDonald, Alexander, 'Celticism: Its Influence on English Literature', *Transactions of the Gaelic Society of Glasgow*, 1 (1887-91), pp.218-38

McLauchlan, Thomas, *The Early Scottish Church* (T. & T. Clark, Edinburgh 1865)

MacLean, Magnus, *The Literature of the Celts* (Blackie, London 1902)

MacLeod, Kenneth, *The Road to the Isles* (Robert Grant & Son, Edinburgh 1927)

MacNeill, Nigel, *The Literature of the Highlanders* (Aeneas MacKay, Stirling 1929)

Meyer, Kuno (ed.), *King and Hermit* (David Nutt, London 1901)

Meyer, Kuno, *Selections from Ancient Irish Poetry* (Constable, London 1911)

Renan, Ernest, *Poetry of the Celtic Races and other Essays*, transl. William G. Hutchison (Walter Scott Publishing Co., London [1896])

2 Modern anthologies, editions and literary studies

Bieler, Ludwig (ed.), *The Irish Penitentials*, Scriptores Latini Hiberniae, V (Dublin Institute for Advanced Studies, Dublin 1963)

Campbell, John L., 'Notes on Hamish Robertson's "Studies in Carmichael's *Carmina Gadelica*"', *Scottish Gaelic Studies*, 13, Pt i (Autumn 1978), pp.1-17

Carey, John (ed.), *King of Mysteries: Early Irish Religious Writings* (Four Courts, Dublin 1998)

Clancy, Thomas Owen (ed.), *The Triumph Tree: Scotland's Earliest Poetry AD 550-1350* (Canongate, Edinburgh 1998)

Clancy, Thomas Owen, and Márkus, Gilbert (eds), *Iona: The Earliest Poetry of a Celtic Monastery* (Edinburgh University Press, Edinburgh 1995)

Dooley, Ann, and Roe, Harry, *Tales of the Elders of Ireland: A new translation of Acallam na Senórach* (Oxford University Press, Oxford 1999)

Evans, D. Simon, *Medieval Religious Writings* (University of Wales Press, Cardiff 1986)

Ford, Patrick K., 'Blackbirds, Cuckoos and Infixed Pronouns: Another Context for Early Irish Nature Poetry', in Ronald Black, William Gillies, and Roibeard Ó Maolalaigh (eds), *Celtic Connections: Proceedings of the Tenth International Congress of Celtic Studies*, Vol. 1 (Tuckwell Press, East Linton 1999), pp.162-70

Greene, David, and O'Connor, Frank (eds), *A Golden Treasury of Irish Poetry A.D. 600 to 1200* (MacMillan, London 1967)

Haycock, Marged, *Blodeugerdd Barddas o Ganu Crefyddol Cynnar* (Cyhoeddiadau Barddas, Llandybie 1994)

Jackson, Kenneth, *A Celtic Miscellany* (Routledge and Kegan Paul 1951: revised edn, Penguin 1991)

Jackson, Kenneth, *Studies in Early Celtic Nature Poetry* (Cambridge Universtiy Press, Cambridge 1935; Llanerch 1995)

Mac Cana, Proinsias, 'The Influence of the Vikings on Celtic Literature', in Brian Ó Cuív (ed.), *The Impact of the Scandinavian Invasions on the Celtic-speaking Peoples c.800-1100 A.D.* (Dublin Insititute for Advanced Studies, Dublin 1975)

Mac Conmara, Mairtín (ed.), *An Léann Eaglasta in Éirinn 1200-1900* (An Clóchomhar Tta, Baile Átha Cliath 1988)

Mackey, J.P., 'Christian Past and Primal Present', *Études Celtiques*, 29 (1992), pp.285-97

McCone, Kim, *Pagan Past and Christian Present in Early Irish Literature* (An Sagart, Maynooth 1991)

McKenna, Catherine A., *The Medieval Welsh Religious Lyric* (Ford and Baillie, Belmont, Massachusetts 1991)

McKenna, Lambert (ed.), *Dán Dé: The Poems of Donnchadh Mór Ó Dálaigh and the Religious Poems in the Duanaire of the Yellow Book of Lecan* (Educational Company of Ireland, Dublin, n.d.)

Ó Corráin, Donnchadh, 'Early Irish Hermit Poetry?', in Ó Corráin *et al.* (eds), *Sages, Saints and Storytellers*, pp.251-67

Ó Corráin, Donnchadh, Breatnach, Liam, and McCone, Kim (eds), *Sages, Saints and Storytellers: Celtic Studies in Honour of Professor James Carney* (An Sagart, Maynooth 1989)

O'Dwyer, Peter, *Towards a History of Irish Spirituality* (Columba Press, Blackrock, Dublin 1995)

Robertson, Hamish, 'Studies in Carmichael's *Carmina Gadelica'*, *Scottish Gaelic Studies*, 22, Pt ii (Autumn 1976), pp.220-65

Sims-Williams, Patrick, 'The Invention of Celtic Nature Poetry', in Brown (ed.), *Celticism*, pp.97-124

Sims-Williams, Patrick, Review of McCone, *Pagan Past and Christian Present*, in *Éigse*, 29 (1996), pp.179-96

3 Celtic and other churches

(a) General

Dales, Douglas, *Light to the Isles: Missionary Theology in Celtic and Anglo-Saxon Britain* (Lutterworth, Cambridge 1997)

McNeill, John T., *The Celtic Churches: A History, A.D. 200 to 1200* (University of Chicago, Chicago 1974)

Wand, J.W.C., *A History of the Early Church to A.D. 500* (Methuen, London 1977 edn)

(b) Anglo-Saxon

Mayr-Harting, Henry, *The Coming of Christianity to Anglo-Saxon England* (Batsford, London 1972)

Ward, Benedicta, *High King of Heaven: Aspects of Early English Spirituality* (Mowbray, London 1999)

(c) Irish/Gaelic

Bieler, Ludwig, *Ireland: Harbinger of the Middle Ages* (Oxford University Press, London 1963)

Brown, Peter, *The Book of Kells* (Thames and Hudson, London 1980)

Gougaud, Louis, *Christianity in Celtic Lands* (Four Courts, Dublin 1992)

Hughes, Kathleen, *The Church in Early Irish Society* (Methuen, London 1966)

Hughes, Kathleen, *Early Christian Ireland: Introduction to the Sources* (Hodder and Stoughton, London 1972)

Hughes, Kathleen, and Hamlin, Ann, *The Modern Traveller to the Early Irish Church* (SPCK, London 1977; Four Courts, Dublin 1997)

Kenney, J.F., *Sources for the Early History of Ireland: Ecclesiastical* (Columbia University Press, New York 1929; Four Courts Press, Dublin 1993)

Mooney, C., *The Church in Gaelic Ireland: Thirteenth to Fifteenth Centuries* (Dublin 1969)

Richardson, Hilary, and Scarry, John, *An Introduction to Irish High Crosses* (The Mercier Press, Dublin 1990)

Walsh, John R, and Bradley, Thomas, *A History of the Irish Church 400-700 AD* (Columba Press, Blackrock 1991)

Whitelock, D. (ed.), *Ireland in Early Medieval Europe* (Cambridge University Press, Cambridge 1982)

(d) Welsh/Early British

Victory, Siân, *The Celtic Church in Wales* (SPCK, London 1977)

(e) Saints

Anderson, A.O., and Anderson, M.O. (eds), *Adomnán's Life of Columba*, revised by M.O. Anderson (Clarendon Press, Oxford 1991)

Attwater, Donald, *The Penguin Dictionary of Saints* (Penguin, Harmondsworth 1983)

Bieler, Ludwig, *The Patrician Texts in the Book of Armagh* (Dublin 1979)

Bourke, Cormac (ed.), *Studies in the Cult of Saint Columba* (Four Courts, Dublin 1997)

Broun, Dauvit, and Clancy, Thomas Owen (eds), *Spes Scotorum: Hope of Scots: Saint Columba, Iona and Scotland* (T. & T. Clark, Edinburgh 1999)

Chadwick, Norah K., *The Age of the Saints in the Early Celtic Church* (Oxford University Press, London 1961)

Delehye, Hippolyte, *The Legends of the Saints*, with a new introduction by Thomas O'Loughlin (Four Courts, Dublin 1998) de Paor, Máire, *Patrick the Pilgrim Apostle of Ireland: An Analysis of St Patrick's Confessio and Epistola* (Veritas, Dublin 1998)

Henken, Elissa R., 'The Saint as Folk Hero: Biographical Patterning in Welsh Hagiography', in Patrick K. Ford (ed.), *Celtic Folklore and Christianity* (University of California, Los Angeles 1983), pp.58-74

Herbert, Máire, *Iona, Kells and Derry: The History and Hagiography of the Monastic Familia of Columba* (Clarendon, Oxford 1988)

Hood, A.B.E. (ed.), *St Patrick: His Writings and Muirchu's Life* (Phillimore, London 1978)

Lacey, Brian, *Colum Cille and the Columban Tradition* (Four Courts, Dublin 1997)

Lacey, Brian (ed.), *The Life of Colum Cille by Manus O'Donnell* (Four Courts, Dublin 1998)

Macquarrie, Alan, *The Saints of Scotland: Essays in Scottish Church History AD 450-1093* (John Donald, Edinburgh 1997)

MacQueen, John, *St Nynia* (Polygon, Edinburgh 1990)

Márkus, Gilbert, *Adomnán's 'Law of the Innocents'* (Blackfriars Books, Glasgow 1997)

O'Loughlin, Thomas, *Saint Patrick: The Man and his Works* (SPCK, London 1999)

Sharpe, Richard (ed.), *Adomnán of Iona: Life of St Columba* (Penguin Classics, Harmondsworth 1995)

Walker, G.S.M. (ed.), *Sancti Columbani Opera*, Scriptores Latini Hiberniae, II (Dublin Institute for Advanced Studies, Dublin 1970)

Winterbottom, Michael (ed.), *Gildas: The Ruin of Britain and Other Documents* (Phillimore, London 1978)

4 Culture, society and religion

(a) Early Medieval

(i) General

Fletcher, Richard, *The Conversion of Europe: From Paganism to Christianity 371-1386 AD* (HarperCollins, London 1997)

(ii) Anglo-Saxon

Campbell, James (ed.), *The Anglo-Saxons* (Penguin, Harmondsworth 1991)

Colgrave, Bertram, and Mynors, R.A.B. (eds), *Bede's Ecclesiastical History of the English People* (Clarendon Press, Oxford 1969)

Hawkes, Jane, *The Golden Age of Northumbria* (Sandhill Press, Morpeth 1996)

Hunter Blair, Peter, *An Introduction to Anglo-Saxon England* (Cambridge University Press, Cambridge 1977)

Page, R.I., *Life in Anglo-Saxon England* (Batsford, London 1970)

(iii) Irish/Gaelic

Anderson, A.O. (ed.), *Early Sources of Scottish History 500 to 1286*, 2 vols (London, 1922; repr. Stamford 1990)

Byrne, Francis John, *Irish Kings and High Kings* (Batsford 1973)

Conlan, Patrick, *Franciscan Ireland* (Mercier Press, Cork 1978)

de Paor, Máire and Liam, *Early Christian Ireland* (Thames and Hudson, London 1978 edn)

Dillon, Myles (ed.), *Early Irish Society* (Mercier Press, Cork 1954)

Dumville, David N., *Councils and Synods of the Gaelic Early and Middle Ages* (Department of Anglo-Saxon, Norse and Celtic, Cambridge 1997)

Hughes, Kathleen, *Early Christian Ireland: Introduction to the Sources* (Hodder and Stoughton, London 1972)

Jackson, Kenneth H. (ed.), *The Gaelic Notes in the Book of Deer* (Cambridge University Press, Cambridge 1972)

Kelly, Fergus, *A Guide to Early Irish Law* (Dublin Institute for Advanced Studies, Dublin 1988)

Kelly, Fergus, *Early Irish Farming* (Dublin Institute for Advanced Studies, Dublin 1998)

McDonald, Andrew, *The Kingdom of the Isles: Scotland's Western Seaboard, c. 1100-c.1336* (Tuckwell Press, East Linton 1997)

Ó Cróinín, Dáibhí, *Early Medieval Ireland 400-1200* (Longman, London 1995)

Richter, Michael, *Medieval Ireland: The Enduring Tradition* (Macmillan, Basingstoke 1983)

Thomson, Derick S., *An Introduction to Gaelic Poetry* (2nd edn, Edinburgh University Press, Edinburgh 1990)

(iv) Welsh/Early British

Davies, Wendy, *Wales in the Early Middle Ages* (Leicester University Press, Leicester 1982)

Green, Miranda, *The Gods of Roman Britain* (Shire, Aylesbury 1983)

Thomas, Charles, *Celtic Britain* (Thames and Hudson, London 1986)

Thomas, Charles, *Christian Celts: Messages and Images* (Tempus, Stroud 1998)

Thomas, Charles, *Christianity in Roman Britain to AD 500* (Batsford, London 1981)

(b) Late Medieval and Modern

(i) Irish, Gaelic and Scottish

Ansdell, Douglas, *The People of the Great Faith* (Acair, Stornoway 1998)

Bannerman, John, 'The Lordship of the Isles', in J. Brown (ed.), *Scottish Society in the Fifteenth Century* (Arnold, London 1977), pp.209-40

Campbell, Murdoch, *Gleanings of Highland Harvest* (Christian Focus Publications, Tain 1989)

Cheape, Hugh, 'The Communion Season', *Records of the Scottish Church History Society*, 27 (1997), pp.305-16

Domhnullach, Iain, *Marbhrainn, a Rinneadh air Diadhairibh Urramach* (John Grant, Edinburgh 1890)

Donaldson, Gordon (ed.), *Scottish Historical Documents*, (Scottish Academic Press, Edinburgh 1974 edn)

Ford, Alan, 'James Ussher and the creation of an Irish protestant identity', in Brendan Bradshaw and Peter Roberts (eds), *British Consciousness and Identity: The making of Britain, 1533-1707* (Cambridge University Press, Cambridge 1998), pp.185-212

Ford, Alan, *The Protestant Reformation in Ireland 1590-1641* (Four Courts Press, Dublin 1997)

Hay, George Campbell, *Fuaran Slèibh* (MacLellan, Glasgow 1947)

Haykin, Michael A.G., 'Voluntarism in the Life and Ministry of William Fraser (1801-1883)', in William H. Brackney (ed.), *The Believers Church: A Voluntary Church* (Pandora Press, Kitchener, Ontario 1998), pp.25-50

Kennedy, John, *The Days of the Fathers in Ross-shire* (1861: repr. Christian Focus Publications, Inverness 1979)

Kirk, James, *Patterns of Reform: Continuity and Change in the Reformation Kirk* (T. & T. Clark, Edinburgh 1989)

Kirk, James (ed.), *The Church in the Highlands* (Scottish Church History Society, Edinburgh 1999)

MacArthur, E. Mairi, *Columba's Island: Iona from Past to Present* (Edinburgh University Press, Edinburgh 1998)

MacInnes, John, *The Evangelical Movement in the Highlands of Scotland* (Aberdeen University Press, Aberdeen 1951)

MacLean, Donald (ed.), *The Spiritual Songs of Dugald Buchanan* (John Grant, Edinburgh 1913)

Macleod, James Lachlan, 'The Influence of the Highland-Lowland Divide on the Free Presbyterian Disruption of 1893', *Records of the Scottish Church History Society*, 25 (1995), pp.400-425)

MacLeod, Finlay, *The Chapels in the Western Isles* (Acair, Stornoway 1997)

Macquarrie, Alan, and MacArthur, E. Mairi, *Iona through the Ages*, 2nd edition (Society of West Highland and Island Historical Research, Coll 1992)

Meek, Donald E. (ed.), *The Campbell Collection of Gaelic Proverbs and Proverbial Sayings* (The Gaelic Society of Inverness, Inverness 1978)

Meek, Donald E., *The Scottish Highlands: The Churches and Gaelic Culture* (WCC, Geneva 1996)

Robinson, Mary, *Signatures on Our Own Frequency* (Scottish Television, Glasgow, and Sabhal Mòr Ostaig, Skye 1997)

Watt, John, *The Church in Medieval Ireland* (University College Dublin Press, Dublin 1998)

Yeoman, Peter, *Pilgrimage in Medieval Scotland* (Batsford/ Historic Scotland, London 1999)

(ii) Welsh

Griffiths, Bruce, *Saunders Lewis* (University of Wales Press, Cardiff 1989)

Llywelyn, Dorian, *Sacred Place, Chosen People: Land and National Identity in Welsh Spirituality* (University of Wales Press, Cardiff 1999)

Williams, Glanmor, *The Welsh and their Religion: Historical Essays* (University of Wales Press, Cardiff 1991)

(iii) English

Chapman, Raymond, *Faith and Revolt: Studies in the Literary History of the Oxford Movement* (Weidenfeld and Nicolson, London 1970)

C Assessments of modern 'Celtic Christianity' and Celtic-related subjects

Bowman, Marion, 'Reinventing the Celts', *Religion*, 23 (1993), pp.147-56

Bowman, Marion, 'The Commodification of the Celt: New Age/Neo-Pagan Consumerism', *Folklore in Use*, 2 (1994), pp.143-52

Bowman, Marion, 'The Noble Savage and the Global Village: Cultural Evolution in New Age and Neo-Pagan Thought', *Journal of Contemporary Religion*, 10, No.2 (1995), pp.139-49

Bradley, Ian, *Celtic Christianity: Making Myths and Chasing Dreams* (Edinburgh University Press, Edinburgh 1999)

Bradshaw, Brendan, 'The Wild and Woolly West: Early Irish Christianity and Latin Orthodoxy', in *The Churches, Ireland and the Irish*, edited by W.J. Sheils and Diana Wood (Blackwell, Oxford 1989), pp.1-23

Culling, Elizabeth, *What is Celtic Christianity?* (Grove Booklets, Cambridge 1998 edn)

Márkus, Gilbert, 'The End of Celtic Christianity', *Epworth Review*, 24, No.3 (July 1997), pp.45-55

Márkus, Gilbert, 'What is Celtic Spirituality?', *Priests and People*, March 1997, pp.117-20

Meek, Donald E., 'Celtic Christianity: What is it, and when was it?', *The Scottish Bulletin of Evangelical Theology*, 9, No.1 (1991), pp.13-21

Meek, Donald E., 'Modern Celtic Christianity: The Contemporary Revival and its Roots', *The Scottish Bulletin of Evangelical Theology*, 10, No.1 (1992), pp.6-31

Meek, Donald E., 'Surveying the Saints: Reflections on Recent Writings on "Celtic Christianity"', *The Scottish Bulletin of Evangelical Theology*, 15, No.1 (Spring 1997), pp.50-60

Sims-Williams, Patrick, 'The Visionary Celt: The Construction of an Ethnic Preconception', *Cambridge Medieval Celtic Studies*, 11 (Summer 1986), pp.71-96

Sims-Williams, Patrick, 'Celtomania and Celtoscepticism', *Cambrian Medieval Celtic Studies*, 36 (Winter 1998), pp.1-35

D Volumes expounding or supporting 'Celtic Christianity'

1 Anthologies

Allchin, A.M., and de Waal, Esther, *Threshold of Light: Prayers and Praises from the Celtic Tradition* (DLT, London 1986)

Allchin, A.M., and de Waal, Esther, *Ar Drothwy Goleuni: Gweddi a Moliant o'r Traddodiad Celtaidd* (Cymdeithas Lyfrau Ceredigion, Aberystwyth 1992)

Bamford, Christopher, and Marsh, William Parker (eds), *Celtic Christianity: Ecology and Holiness* (Floris Books, Edinburgh 1986)

Bittleston, Adam (ed.), *The Sun Dances: Prayers and Blessings from the Gaelic* (The Christian Community Press, London 1960)

Davies, Oliver, and Bowie, Fiona (eds), *Celtic Christian Spirituality: An Anthology of Medieval and Modern Sources* (SPCK, London 1995)

de Waal, Esther (ed.), *The Celtic Vision: Prayers and Blessings from the Outer Hebrides* (DLT, London 1988)

McLean, G.R.D., with Foreword by Sally Magnusson, *Praying with Highland Christians* (Triangle/SPCK, London 1988)

2 Academic studies

Allchin, A.M., *God's Presence makes the World: The Celtic Vision through the Centuries in Wales* (DLT, London 1997)

Bitel, Lisa M., *Isle of the Saints: Monastic Settlement and Christian Community in Early Ireland* (Cornell University, 1990; Cork University Press, Cork 1993)

Duke, John A., *The Columban Church* (Oxford University Press, Oxford 1932; Oliver and Boyd, Edinburgh 1957)

Davies, Oliver, *Celtic Christianity in Early Medieval Wales: The Origins of the Welsh Spiritual Tradition* (University of Wales Press, Cardiff 1996)

Hardinge, Leslie, *The Celtic Church in Britain* (SPCK, London 1972)

Low, Mary, *Celtic Christianity and Nature: Early Irish and Hebridean Traditions* (Edinburgh University Press, Edinburgh 1996)

Mackey, James P., *An Introduction to Celtic Christianity* (T. & T. Clark, Edinburgh 1989)

Sheldrake, Philip, *Living Between Worlds: Place and Journey in Celtic Spirituality* (DLT, London 1995)

3 Writings on the saints

Adam, David, *Fire of the North: The Illustrated Life of St Cuthbert* (SPCK, London 1993)

Adam, David, *Flame in my Heart: St Aidan for Today* (Triangle/SPCK, London 1997)

Adam, David, *On Eagles' Wings: The Life and Spirit of St Chad* (Triangle/SPCK, London 1999)

Bradley, Ian, *Columba: Pilgrim and Penitent* (Wild Goose Publications, Glasgow 1996)

Ellis, Peter Berresford, *The Cornish Saints* (Tor Mark Press, Redruth 1998)

Fraser, Ian M., *Celebrating Saints: Augustine, Columba, Ninian* (Wild Goose Publications, Glasgow 1997)

Hume, Basil, *Footprints of the Northern Saints* (DLT, London 1996)

Kenny, Colum, *Molaise: Abbot of Leighlin and Hermit of Holy Island* (Morrigan, Killala 1998)

Leatham, Diana, *They Built on Rock: Stories of the Celtic Saints* (First edn. 1948; second edn, Hodder and Stoughton, London 1999)

Marsden, John, *Sea-road of the Saints: Celtic Holy Men in the Hebrides* (Floris Books, Edinburgh 1996)

Sellner, Edward C., *Wisdom of the Celtic Saints* (Ave Maria Press, Notre Dame 1993)

Toulson, Shirley, *Celtic Journeys in Scotland and the North of England* (Hutchinson, London, 1985; Fount, London 1995)

4   Popular explorations of 'Celtic Christianity'

(a) 'Historical' approach to the 'tradition'

Allen, Paul M., and Allen, Joan deRis, *Fingal's Cave, the Poems of Ossian, and Celtic Christianity* (Continuum, New York 1999)

Bradley, Ian, *The Celtic Way* (DLT, London 1993)

Cahill, Thomas, *How the Irish Saved Civilization* (Hodder and Stoughton, London 1995)

de Waal, Esther, *A World Made Whole: Rediscovering the Celtic Tradition* (Fount, London 1991)

de Waal, Esther, *The Celtic Way of Prayer: The Recovery of the Religious Imagination* (Hodder and Stoughton, London 1996)

Finney, John, *Recovering the Past: Celtic and Roman Mission* (DLT, London 1996)

Howard, Michael, *Angels and Goddesses: Celtic Christianity and Paganism in Ancient Britain* (Capall Bann, Chieveley 1994)

Joyce, Timothy, *Celtic Christianity: A Sacred Tradition, A Vision of Hope* (Orbis Books, New York 1998)

Ross, John, *The Orthodox Family: The Orthodox Family of Churches and the Restoration of the Celtic Orthodox Church* (Scottish Orthodox Mission, Fetterangus 1998)

Strachan, Gordon, *Jesus the Master Builder: Druid Mysteries and the Dawn of Christianity* (Floris Books, Edinburgh 1998)

Thomas, Patrick, *Candle in the Darkness: Celtic Spirituality from Wales* (Gomer Press, Llandysul 1993)

Toulson, Shirley, *The Celtic Alternative: A Reminder of the Christianity We Lost* (Rider, London 1987; reprinted 1990)

(b) Reflections, meditations, expositions, narratives etc.

Adam, David, *The Cry of the Deer: Meditations on the Hymn of St Patrick* (Triangle/SPCK, London 1987)

Adam, David, *The Eye of the Eagle: Meditations on the Hymn 'Be thou my vision'* (Triangle/SPCK, London 1990)

Burton, Linda, and Whitehead, Alex (eds), *Christ is the Morning Star: When Celtic Spirituality Meets Benedictine Rule* (Lindisfarne Books, Dublin 1999)

Clancy, Padraigín (ed.), *Celtic Threads: Exploring the Wisdom of Our Heritage* (Veritas, Dublin 1999)

Ellis, Roger, and Seaton, Chris, *New Celts: Following Jesus into Millennium 3* (Kingsway, Eastbourne 1998)

Fitz-Gibbon, Andy and Jane, *Prophetic Lifestyle and the Celtic Way* (Monarch, London 1997)

Maclean, Alistair, *Hebridean Altars: The Spirit of an Island Race* (Grant and Murray, Edinburgh 1937; Hodder and Stoughton 1999)

Mitton, Michael, *Restoring the Woven Cord: Strands of Celtic Christianity for the Church Today* (DLT, London 1995)

Newell, Philip, *Listening for the Heartbeat of God* (SPCK, London 1997)

Newell, Philip, *One Foot in Eden: A Celtic View of the Stages of Life* (SPCK, London 1998)

O Ríordáin, John J., *The Music of What Happens: Celtic Spirituality: A View from the Inside* (Columba Press, Blackrock 1996)

Sampson, Fay, *Visions and Voyages: The Story of our Celtic Heritage* (Triangle/SPCK, London 1998)

Simpson, Ray, *Exploring Celtic Spirituality: Historic Roots for our Future* (Hodder & Stoughton, London 1995)

Simpson, Ray, *Soul Friendship: Celtic Insights into Spiritual Mentoring* (Hodder & Stoughton, London 1999)

Van de Weyer, Robert, *A Celtic Resurrection: The Diary of a Split from the Church* (Fount, London 1996)

5 Creative writing based on 'Celtic' models and themes

Adam, David, *The Edge of Glory: Prayers in the Celtic Tradition* (Triangle/SPCK, London 1985)

Adam, David, *Times and Seasons: Modern Prayers in the Celtic Tradition* (Triangle/SPCK, London 1989)

O'Donohue, John, *Anam Chara: Spiritual Wisdom from the Celtic World* (Bantam Press, London 1997)

6 Study guides and resource books

King, Chris, *Our Celtic Heritage: Looking at our own Faith in the Light of Celtic Christianity* (St Andrew Press, Edinburgh 1997)

Wallace, Martin, *The Celtic Resource Book* (National Society/Church House Publishing, London 1998)

INDEX